Political Interventions

Pierre Bourdieu

Political Interventions

Social science and political action

Texts selected and introduced
by Franck Poupeau and Thierry Discepolo

Translated by David Fernbach

VERSO

London • New York

Liberté • Égalité • Fraternité
RÉPUBLIQUE FRANÇAISE

This book is supported by the French Ministry of Foreign Affairs as part of the
Burgess programme run by the cultural department of the French Embassy in London
(www.frenchbooknews.com).

Ouvrage publié avec le concours du Ministère français chargé
de la culture – Centre national du livre.

This work was published with the help of the French
Ministry of Culture – Centre national du livre.

1 3 5 7 9 10 8 6 4 2

Verso
UK: 6 Meard Street, London W1F 0EG
USA: 180 Varick Street, New York, NY 10014–4606
www.versobooks.com

Verso is the imprint of New Left Books

ISBN-13: 978-1-84467-190-8 (pbk)
ISBN-13: 978-1-84467-189-2 (hbk)

British Library Cataloguing in Publication Data
A catalogue record for this book is available from the British Library

Library of Congress Cataloging-in-Publication Data
A catalog record for this book is available from the Library of Congress

Typeset in Adobe Garamond by Hewer Text UK Ltd, Edinburgh
Printed in the USA by Maple Vail

Faced with the serfdom of the assembly line or the misery of shanty-towns, to say nothing of the torture and violence of concentration camps, Hegel's 'this is how it is' – permissible enough when gazing at mountains – becomes equivalent to a criminal complicity. Because nothing is less neutral, in the world of society, than the authoritative utterance of Being; the findings of science inevitably exert a political effect, which may not be that which the scholar intended.

Inaugural lecture at the Collège de France, 1982

If these interventions of science on the terrain of the most burning current topics had at any price to be justified, one could at least appeal to the critical functions they may exert in a time such as this, when political authorities evoke scientific competence and scientific guarantees in order to convert political problems into purely technical choices, and authorized commentators ever more frequently appeal to sources with a scientific appearance, such as opinion polls, which give the appearance of rational foundation to the ambition to speak in the name of 'public opinion'. In any case, it is not forbidden to hope that these limited contributions, subject to revision and often negative in their understanding of the present, may serve as an antidote to the scepticism and even irrationalism that the failure of grand prophesies has promoted.

'La science and l'actualité', 1986

Contents

CONTENTS

Editors' Note

This project of a collection of Pierre Bourdieu's political interventions originated in autumn 1999, based on a work of Frank Poupeau that was conceived for Latin American publication, 'Utopias sociologicamente fundadas', in Pierre Bourdieu, *El Campo politico* (La Paz: Plural Editores 2001).

While the thematic and chronological organization is our work, as also the choice of texts, these were approved in the main by Pierre Bourdieu, following the aim that we fixed for ourselves at the start: to bring up to date, simply by way of an organized alignment, the underpinnings of a work that was never cut off from the turmoil of social and political history.

Despite the international significance of Bourdieu's work, broadly commented on and discussed, we have privileged here, for reasons of clarity, the French dimensions of his interventions and the polemics that these sometimes aroused.

The majority of Pierre Bourdieu's texts have been reproduced under their original titles, simply with some stylistic corrections and some occasional cuts. The non-italicized quotations in our introductory material are Bourdieu's own, as well as the epigraphs on each historic period.

We are particularly grateful to Marie-Christine Rivière and Yvette Delsaut for their bibliography of the works of Pierre Bourdieu, without which this collection could not have been conceived: *Bibliographie des travaux de Pierre Bourdieu* (Paris: Pantin 2002).

We would also like to thank Jerôme Bourdieu, Michel Caïetti, Pierre Carles, Pascale Casanova, Patrick Champagne, Rosine Christin, Frédéric Cotton, Isabelle de Bary, Serge Halimi, Isabelle Kalinowski, Sébastien Mengin, Marc Panatella, Pierre Rimbert, Béatrice Vincent and Loïc Wacquant for their valuable assistance.

Finally, we thank all those who have authorized us to publish here texts that they jointly signed with Pierre Bourdieu – and our apologies to those we were unable to trace.

Introduction

A Specific Kind of Political Commitment

I run the risk of shocking those [researchers] who, opting for the cosy virtuousness of confinement within their ivory tower, see intervention outside the academic sphere as a dangerous failing of that famous 'axiological neutrality' which is wrongly identified with scientific objectivity. [. . .] But I am convinced that we must at all costs bring the achievements of science and scholarship into public debate, from which they are tragically absent.

Preface to *Firing Back*[1]

Pierre Bourdieu's public interventions in the wake of the strike wave of December 1995 were the object of often violent condemnation, especially on the part of those journalists and media intellectuals whose power he analyzed in his writings on television and the press. He was accused of 'belatedly' discovering political action, abusing his scientific renown, or returning to outdated intellectual models. What seems to have shocked most was the fact of a scholar intervening in this way, taking the arm of criticism into the political field: why should a mandarin like this descend 'onto the streets'?

The sociologist's interventions in the public sphere, however, date from his entry into intellectual life in the early 1960s, the time of the Algerian war. From this point on, a constant reflection on the 'social conditions of possibility' of his political commitment inspired him to distance himself both from pedagogic scientism and from the spontaneism of 'free intellectuals' that was so current at that time.

The present collection is not exhaustive, but it aims more than simply to gather together various 'political' or 'critical' texts that are often inaccessible or unpublished, extracted here from the archives of the Collège de France with the help of Marie-Christine Rivière. The object is above all to put these in context: the reader is invited to read work that has often been neutralized and made inaccessible by the conditions of its reception; a collection of analyses, interviews

[1] [*Firing Back* (London: Verso 2003), p. 12.]

and texts written for specific occasions, including drafts that in some cases appeared later in books in a more developed and 'scholarly' form. The object is to show, through the stages of Bourdieu's itinerary placed in its historical context, a certain articulation between scientific research and political intervention. This work of converting social impulses into critical interventions gives sociology that weight or utility without which, as Durkheim put it, 'it would not be worth an hour of trouble', as well as a vigilance that can help social science break with the banalization of political and social problems as everyday 'news', by placing them under a different light.

Apart from certain thematic continuities (such as education, opinion surveys, the independence of intellectuals, and journalism), we have preferred a chronological order, interspersing historical or biographical reminders, and extracts that link texts of a particular time with a look back by the author at their context of production.

By this route, we can trace the genesis of a specific style of political intervention: social science and activism, far from being opposed, are conceived as two sides of a single work, one of analysis, deciphering and critique of social reality, with a view to assisting its transformation. The trajectory illustrated by the texts that follow shows how sociology is itself enriched by such political commitment, and by reflection on its preconditions.

The time has come to go beyond the old alternative of utopianism and sociologism, and propose utopias that are sociologically based. This requires that specialists in the social sciences collectively manage to burst apart the censorship they believe they have to impose on themselves in the name of a mutilated idea of scientificity. [. . .] These sciences have paid for their access to scientific status (still contested, in any case) by a formidable renunciation: a self-censorship that amounts to a real self-mutilation, and sociologists – I start with myself, as I have often denounced the temptation to prophecy and social philosophy – have staunchly rejected, as deviations from scientific morality that threaten to discredit their authors, all attempts to propose an ideal and global representation of the social world.[2]

This venture of intervening in public debate implies a different way of 'talking politics', i.e. the construction of a different perspective on politics.

---

[2] 'Monopolisation politique et révolutions symboliques' (1990), in *Propos sur le champ politique* (Lyon: Presses Universitaires de Lyon 2000). [Ed.]

We live immersed in politics. We bathe in a constant if changing flow of everyday chatter about the prospects and merits of inter-changeable candidates. We have no need to read editorials in the daily or weekly papers, or those works of analysis by the same writers that flourish in the electoral season before piling up in the yellowing stocks of remainders – fodder for later historians of ideas, after their brief sojourn on the best-seller list. The 'ideas' that these authors offer us on every radio and TV channel are only so easily digestible because they are 'accepted ideas'. Everything can be said and repeated indefinitely, since in reality nothing is said at all. And our appointed debaters, who meet at the set hour to discuss the strategy of some politician or other, the image or silences of another, give the game away when they express the hope that their interviewer will disagree, 'so that there can be a discussion'. Political proposals, like the words in the air about sunshine and rain, are volatile in nature, and the game can only continue because they are constantly forgotten, so that their extraordinary monotony remains undiscovered.[3]

Bourdieu thus found himself in conflict not just with professional politicians (deputies, union officials, etc.), but also with the professionals of political analysis and semi-scholarly discourse on public affairs – those whom he called 'doxosophists': political journalists, media intellectuals and other essayists. If it is necessary to break with this discourse, as he maintained, it is not just because of its 'scientific mistakes', but rather because of the commonplaces and mystifications that it introduces into public debate. If the sociological critique of their social function seems to amount to a genuine 'attack on the norms of good manners', this is because it involves a transgression of the 'sacred frontier between culture and politics, pure thought and the triviality of the agora'.[4]

All this has indeed been present in recent critiques of the sociologist's political interventions: from 'scholars' who accused him of compromising science by playing the 'magus', to political and media protagonists who denied him the right to intervene precisely because he was not 'one of them'. At the end of the day, Bourdieu's interventions supposedly revealed the 'ill-intentioned intention' of his sociology, which for his part he defined as follows:

Sociology opposes the caution of academic good manners that encour-ages withdrawal towards the tried and tested; but it also opposes false boldness and shallow essayism, and the shameless arrogance of prophecy.

[3] 'Penser la politique', *Actes de la Recherche en Sciences Sociales* 71/72, March 1988, pp. 2–3. [Ed.]
[4] Ibid.

Beyond the alternative that traps those who would rather be wrong with Sartre than right with Aron, or vice versa, the alternative between a voluntarist humanism that is supposedly generous and a disenchanted indifference with pretensions to lucidity, sociology aims at submitting actuality, as far as is possible, to the ordinary demands of scientific knowledge.[5]

Sociological analysis does not just meet with 'resistance': the very nature of the object of politics presents a problem, to the extent that its 'facts' are not given, but pre-constructed by all those who define their interpretation so as to orient them as a function of their particular interests. The illusion of dealing with 'current problems' that are immediately accessible is the first obstacle to cross.

It is impossible to think of submitting the current situation to scientific analysis unless one has broken with the illusion of understanding everything right away, an illusion that defines the ordinary relationship to this immediately given of social experience. The break consists in making a question out of what appears beyond question, self-evident – in a way that arouses either ethical indignation, activist allegiance, or rational conviction. The social and mental distance between public debate and the scientific problematic is so great in this case that the inaugurating break is itself presented as proof of a position inspired by prejudice.[6]

This quest to 'politicize things by scientific work', and 'think about politics without thinking politically', was evident in Bourdieu's first works on Algeria. And as Abdelmalek Sayad has remarked, his entire sociology 'bears the mark of this initial apprenticeship'.[7]

[5] 'La science et l'actualité', *Actes de la Recherche en Sciences Sociales* 61, March 1986, pp. 2–3. [Ed.]
[6] Ibid.
[7] Abdelmalek Sayad, interview published in *MARS* 6, 1996. [Ed.]

1958–1962: Political commitment during a war of liberation

Algeria before independence was divided into three French departments with a European population of over one million, its administration being in the hands of the minister of the interior in Paris. The nine million 'Algerian citizens', whose average income was only one-twentieth that of the Europeans, voted in a separate electoral college, and only 15 per cent of Muslim children attended school. The war of independence, which began in November 1954, polarized French political and intellectual life for several years, triggering the fall of six prime ministers and eventually the collapse of the Fourth Republic. The Republican Front, which had brought Guy Mollet and the Socialists to power in 1956, followed a policy of heightened repression, in particular with the special powers legislation of March that year. This policy aroused various reactions among intellectuals. Even if, with Pierre Vidal-Nacquet, we need to emphasize the diversity of forms of commitment,[8] denunciation of repression and torture was the most widespread cause defended by the various committees of support for the Algerians. Journals such as France Observateur, L'Express, Témoignage Chrétien and Le Monde all waged at this time a battle for information. At this point in the struggle, Éditions de Minuit, headed by Jerôme Lindon, published La Question by Henri Alleg and Déserteur by Maurienne, leading to a number of prosecutions for incitement to disobedience and compromising state security.

Among the dominating figures of the intellectual scene, Albert Camus was torn between rejecting the positions of the Algérie française ultras on the one hand, and his reluctance to accept Algerian independence on the other, while Jean-Paul Sartre in 1956 took up a position in favour of the struggle against 'colonial tyranny'.[9] Sartre called for the immediate independence of Algeria and a struggle alongside the Algerian people, as well as denouncing torture, giving evidence at trials, taking part in demonstrations, signing the 'Manifesto of 121',[10] and lending his support to the 'Jeanson

---

[8] Pierre Vidal-Nacquet, 'Une fidelité têtue. La résistance française à la guerre d'Algérie', Vingtième siecle. Revue d'histoire 10, April–June 1986, p. 17. [Ed.]

[9] Jean-Paul Sartre, Situations V (Paris: Gallimard 1964), p. 42. [Ed.]

[10] 'The "Manifesto of 121" on the right to refuse orders in the Algerian war, signed by 121 intellectuals [. . .] did not just call for refusal or desertion but "respected" these as "justified" choices. It solemnly proclaimed that the cause of the Algerian people was that of all free men'; Pierre Vidal-Nacquet, Mémoires II (Paris: Seuil-La Découverte 1998) [Ed.]

network' of support for the FLN. The review *Les Temps Modernes* that Sartre edited became the organ of secular Third Worldism, and Frantz Fanon's book *The Wretched of the Earth*, to which Sartre wrote a preface, gave him the occasion to affirm his anti-colonialism and justify a violence seen as constituting, for the colonized, the 'means of recomposing their human nature'. Sartre's activism sought to counterbalance the lukewarm stance of the left parties and trade unions. In the camp of the liberal right, Raymond Aron, who condemned all illegal action but whose *Algerian Tragedy* (1957) was favourable to independence, found himself at loggerheads with *Le Figaro*, the paper he regularly wrote for, which was edited at the time by Pierre Brisson, a supporter of *Algérie française*.

1961–1963

The people will be what they are provoked to be: either a force of revolution lost to the revolution, or a revolutionary force.

I

Colonial War and
Revolutionary Consciousness

I undertook this research on temporal structures of emotional experience. [. . .] I used to think as a philosopher and it took a very long
time for me to accept that I had become an ethnologist. [. . .] I
wanted for example to establish the basis of the difference between
proletariat and sub-proletariat; and by analysing the economic and
social conditions in which economic calculation arose not just in the
field of economics, but also that of fertility etc., I tried to show that
the basis of this difference is located at the level of economic conditions
of possibility and rational foresight of which revolutionary aspirations
are also a dimension.

'Fieldwork in Philosophy', *Choses dites*, 1987

After a year teaching philosophy at a lycée *in Moulins (Allier), Pierre Bourdieu
arrived in Algeria in 1955 for his military service. He subsequently held a
position as philosophy assistant at the faculty of letters in Algiers, not leaving
until April 1960 when Raymond Aron offered him a teaching post at the
Sorbonne. During his years in Algeria, Bourdieu carried out ethnographic
investigations in Kabylia, under conditions described by his student and
colleague Abdelmalik Sayad as precarious and difficult. What Bourdieu
subsequently called 'the shock of Algeria'[1] aroused him to write his first book,*
The Algerians, *'in a logic of activism' – the American edition from Beacon
Press had the Algerian flag on its cover even before independence was proclaimed
– enlightened by a knowledge of Algerian reality which few French intellectuals
had at their command (see p.24).*

Bourdieu's first two political interventions appeared in Esprit *in 1961
(see p.7) and* Les Temps Modernes *in 1962 – two of the most influential
magazines of the time, though Bourdieu did not himself share the orientation*

---

[1] 'Tout est social', interview with P.-M. de Biasi, *Magazine Littéraire* 303, October 1992, pp. 104–11. [Ed.]

of either.² Written against an ethnographic background, the culmination of several months of fieldwork, these texts sought to break with an apolitical use of ethnology and make this an instrument of symbolic struggle. They analyze the de-structuring effects of the colonial situation, rejecting the principle of neutrality as a pretext of non-commitment.³

I wanted to be useful, by overcoming my feeling of guilt at being simply a participant observer in this disturbing war. My more or less happy integration into the intellectual field is perhaps at the root of my activities in Algeria. I could not rest content with reading the left-wing press and signing petitions, I had to do something as a scholar. [. . .] It was absolutely indispensable for me to be at the heart of events, in order to inform public opinion, whatever the danger that this might involve. To see, record, and take photographs.⁴

Rejecting both verbal radicalism and abstract humanist condemnation, which was how the Algerian revolution was made into an object of abstract debate at that time, Bourdieu's scholarly stance led him to analyze the conditions in which revolutionary consciousness develops. The moment of war is that which reveals the relationship of violence exercised by the colonial system: it is less an opposition between 'enemies' than an exposure of the revolt of a dominated society against this structure of domination. It is neither civil war nor war between nations, nor the struggle of one class against another, because what it takes as its target is the system of racial castes as such – with weapons that, for the first time, are more than simply symbolic. According to Bourdieu, this 'revelation' revolutionizes in turn the society that produces it, to the extent that it strips traditional forms of conduct of the natural character that seemed attached to them, and imposes on all an uprooting akin to immigrant experience.

And yet, does study of a colonial conflict by a science that is itself colonial not risk invalidating the scientific basis of any political intervention?

² 'Les sous-prolétaires algériens', *Les Temps Modernes*, December 1962, pp. 1030–51. In parallel with these texts, Bourdieu published other articles in more academic journals, such as 'Guerre et mutation sociale en Algérie', *Études méditerranéennes* 7, spring 1960, pp. 25–7, and 'La hantise du chômage chez l'ouvrier algérien. Prolétariat et système colonial', *Sociologie du Travail* 1, December 1962, pp. 313–31. [Ed.]
³ Cf. *Travail et travailleurs en Algérie* (with A. Darbel, J.-P. Rivet and C. Seibel) (Paris/The Hague: Mouton 1963); also *Déracinement* (with S. Abdelmalik) (Paris: Minuit 1964). [Ed.]
⁴ 'The Struggle for Symbolic Order', interview with A. Honneth, H. Kocyba and B. Schwibs, *Theory, Culture and Society* 3, 1986, p. 37. [Ed.]

We must recall, if only to put it to the test, the ideology according to which any research conducted in the colonial situation is supposedly affected by an essential impurity. In the words of Michel Leiris: 'It is still more evident than for other disciplines that in ethnography pure science is a myth, and we have to admit on top of this that the desire for pure scholarship weighs nothing in this case against the fact that, working in colonized countries, we ethnographers are not only metro-politans but metropolitan emissaries, since it is the state that defines our missions, so that we are less able than anyone else to wash our hands of the policy pursued by the state and its representatives towards those societies that we select for our study.'[5] With this kind of complicity, everything seems self-evident. We oppose 'pure' science to ideology engaged in the service of this or that power, this or that established order. And we add that the pure intention of doing pure science is necessarily doomed to failure. The postulate that serves as a basis for this demonstration is that the ethnographer, by virtue of his membership of the colonizing society, bears the weight of the original sin of colo-nialism. [. . .] But is this original complicity different in kind from that which ties the sociologist studying his own society to his class of origin? [. . .] Need we believe, as is often said, that the only 'pure' ethnography would be that done by indigenous people? What is the function of such ethical and epistemological privileges? These are all questions that no one is eager to raise, as they lead us away from the sure ground of undiscussed self-evidence.[6]

Setting out the colonialist implications of ethnology, in Bourdieu's view, should not lead to maintaining the impossibility of any social science: it implies an analysis of the gap, not made explicit, that separates the scholar and the dominated, in order to make visible what the latter, by their very situation, are unable to express. This reflective work on the research situation is not so much a moral imperative as a scientific necessity.

As soon as the choice is made to pose the problem in moral terms, we have to admit that, so long as the system lasts, even those actions that are most generous in terms of their formal intention prove in practice either perfectly vain or objectively bad, purely as a function of their context. And there is always the threat of being accused of profiting from injustice to do good. [. . .] Behind denunciation of

---

[5] Michel Leiris, 'L'éthnographe devant le colonialisme', *Les Temps Modernes*, August 1950, p. 359.
[6] 'Avant-propos' to *Travail et travailleurs en Algérie*, op. cit.

the compromises of ethnology there often hides the conviction that there is no pure science of an impure object, as if science and the researcher 'participated' in this object. Need we recall the lesson that Parmenides gave Socrates: in science there are not worthy and unworthy subjects.[7] [. . .] What can be demanded of the ethnologist, in all strictness, is that he should seek to restore to others the meaning of their behaviour, one of the many things that the colonial system has deprived them of.[8]

The ethnologist (or sociologist), according to Bourdieu, must be one of those 'mediations' furthering the acceptance of a 'rational politics' that can extend revolutionary activity into a genuine popular education (see p.14): the transposition of ethnographic methods to the study of French society (in particular the peasants of Béarn and the educational system) would transgress not only disciplinary boundaries but also the mental barriers that a society sets up against any view of itself. These writings on Algeria were thus something far more than a 'detour'; they made possible a change of perspective.

---

[7] This reference to Parmenides in the Socratic dialogue was used again by Bourdieu in 1975 in the opening text for the first number of *Actes de la Recherche en Sciences Sociales* (see **p.**93). [Ed.]
[8] 'Avant-propos' to *Travail et travailleurs en Algérie*, op. cit. [Ed.]

Revolution in the revolution*

The causes of and reasons for the war, the particular form it has taken and the consequences it has led to, all form a unity of meaning that must be grasped in the unity of an overall apprehension. If any one of these three aspects is dissociated from the whole in which it is inscribed, any understanding of this becomes impossible.

To deny that the revolutionary war is based in an objective situation would be to deny its very nature and even its existence. To claim that the war was imposed on the Algerian people by a handful of agitators using cunning and compulsion would be to deny that the struggle could possibly find its living forces and intentions in a deep popular sentiment, one inspired by the objective situation. Now the war exists and persists, and it will continue to do so. It exists and persists only as a function of the situation in which and from which it was born; but at the same time, it changes this situation by the very fact that it exists and persists. The indigenous society was turned upside down, to its very foundations, by the action of colonial policy and the clash of civilizations. Moreover, the whole colonial society was torn apart by a hidden or open tension between the dominant European society and the dominated Algerian society. The development of the colonial system has resulted in the distance (and correlative tension) separating the dominant and dominated societies steadily growing, and this is true for all areas of existence: economic, social and psychological. The almost stationary equilibrium in which the colonial society is held is the result of forces that are ever more sharply opposed, i.e. on the one hand the force that tends to increase inequalities and domination, 'founded objectively' – if one may say so – in social reality, the fact of pauperization and the breakdown of the original Algerian culture, and on the other hand the force constituted by revolt and resentment against growing inequalities and discrimination. In brief, carried along by its internal logic, the colonial system tends to develop all those consequences implicit in its very foundation, and to reveal its true image. Thus open aggression and repression by force are completely inscribed in the coherence of the system: if the colonial society is as little integrated as ever, war is an integral part of the colonial system, being its moment of self-confession.

The war brings into the full light of day the real basis of the colonial

---

* Published in *Esprit* 1, January 1961.

order, in other words the relation of force by which the dominant caste keeps the dominated caste in thrall. We can thus understand how peace presents the worst threat in the eyes of certain members of the dominant caste. Without the exercise of force, nothing could counterbalance the force directed against the very roots of this order, i.e. the revolt against a situation of inferiority.

The colonial system as such can only be destroyed by a radical challenge. [. . .] The 'hostile intent' of this war has something abstract about it. Two texts among others will serve as example: 'The Algerian revolution is not a holy war but an enterprise of liberation. It is not a work of hatred but a struggle against an oppressive system.' 'The Algerian war is not a war of Arabs against Europeans, nor one of Muslims against Christians. Nor is it a war of the Algerian people against the French people.' These phrases can be seen simply as propaganda. And yet they appear to express one of the essential characteristics of the war, i.e. the fact that it is directed less (in its hostile intent, we have to stress) against concrete enemies than against a system, the colonial system. The demand for dignity expresses the same intent in a different language; it is the first requirement of people for whom the reality of the colonial system and the division of colonial society into castes has been concretely experienced in the form of humiliation.

This is why the revolution against the colonial system and caste division cannot be equated simply with a class struggle inspired by economic demands, even if motivations of this kind are not absent, given that differences in economic position are one of the most flagrant signs of membership of one or other caste. No more can it be equated with an international or a civil war. If the struggle against the caste system takes the form of a war of national liberation, this is perhaps because the existence of an independent *nation* appears the only decisive means for achieving a radical change in the situation that can bring about the definitive collapse of the caste system.

Thus the war, by its very existence as well as by its form and duration, has transformed the situation out of which it was born. The social field in which everyday behaviour takes place has been radically modified, and by the same token the attitudes of individuals placed in this situation towards the situation itself. How should we describe and understand this rapid and total change, this revolution in the revolution?

The war of liberation presents the first radical challenge to the colonial system, and – something essential – the first challenge that is not, as in the past, simply *symbolic* and in a certain sense magical. Attachment to certain details of clothing (the veil or *chechia*, for example), to certain types of behaviour, certain beliefs and values, could be experienced as a way of expressing symbolically, i.e. by behaviour implicitly invested with the function of *signs*, the refusal to adhere to a Western civilization identified with the colonial order, the will to assert a radical and irreducible difference, to deny the negation of self, to defend a besieged personality. In the colonial situation, any renunciation of the indigenous civilization would objectively have signified a renunciation of self and an accepted allegiance to the other civilization, i.e. the colonial order. And this was indeed the sense that the upholders of the colonial order gave to what they called 'signs of development'. In the colonial situation, rejection could be expressed only in a symbolic manner. Thus the Algerians felt constantly under the gaze of the Europeans, and acted accordingly, as is shown by certain habitual formulas that express the concern not to give a basis or pretext for pejorative judgements: 'The French will see you', or 'Don't make yourself ridiculous.' This makes it possible to understand all the resistances that have accumulated through to today, whether consciously or otherwise, all the rejections that are apparently absurd and aberrant.

Thus the existence of people who say no to the established order, the existence of a rational and lasting organization able to confront and shake the colonial system – in a word, the existence of an effective negation established at the very heart of the system, and recognized, voluntarily or perforce, even by those who would bitterly deny it – is sufficient to render vain so much of the behaviour in which the dominated caste expressed its rejection of domination. The war, by its very existence, constitutes a language, and lends the people a voice that can say no. [. . .]

By virtue of its form and duration, the war has affected every aspect of reality, economy and demography as much as social structures, beliefs and religious practices or the system of values.

The Algerian people today are experiencing a genuine diaspora. Movements of population, whether enforced or voluntary, have grown to gigantic proportions. According to reliable estimates, the number of people displaced is somewhere in the region of two million, so that approximately one Algerian in four now lives away from their usual residence. Regrouping of population is only one aspect of these phenomena of internal migration, even if undoubtedly the most significant. The break with a familiar environment, a stable and habitual social universe in which traditional behaviour was experienced as natural, leads to abandonment of such behaviour once this is cut off from the original soil in which it took root. The transformation of the space of life demands a general transformation of behaviour. But the uprooting is usually so brutal and total, that disarray, disgust and hopelessness are far more common than the innovative behaviour that would be needed to adapt to radically new conditions. By a deliberate or thoughtless ignorance of social and human realities, the local authorities entrusted with organizing the resettlement villages often impose, without heed for the desires or aspirations of the population concerned, a totally foreign order, one which they are not made for and which is not made for them. In these immense conglomerations, alignments of buildings or *gourbis* arranged in a rigorous geometry, groups of diverse origin find themselves side by side, which tends to dissolve the old ties of community without allowing new solidarities based on common interest or participation in a common work to be born. All that these people generally share are their miseries and disenchantment. Removed from their land, the peasants condemned to idleness try to adapt as best they can; we thus see the appearance, as also in the towns, of a proliferation of small businesses with no clientele. A number of the resettlement villages, those seen as more 'successful', with wide streets, a well, bakery and coffee shop, have the desolate appearance of dead quarters. Those who live in them, even when they enjoy a level of comfort that they had not known before (which is indeed sometimes the case), are deeply discontent. Essentially, perhaps, because the most basic structures such as the rhythm of days or the organization of space have been broken. How can one express in a few lines, let alone feel, the thousand interwoven aspects of this fragmentation of the drama and art of life? The material poverty that often strikes observers is nothing compared with the moral misery of these people torn away from their familiar universe, their land, their houses, their customs and their beliefs – from everything that helped them to live – placing them in a situation in which they cannot even form the thought of inventing a new way of life to try and adapt to a world that remains totally foreign to them.

The internal migration also takes the form of an exodus to the cities, which appear to the country people as a refuge against misery and war. The shanty-towns grow larger and larger. Those who have been here longer receive relatives from the countryside. What is important from the sociological point of view is the process of 'urbanization' in which the whole of Algeria is caught up – or rather, if the neologism is permissible, a 'shanty-townization'. Resettled, emigrants, refugees from the cities, all are brutally thrown into an unknown universe, unable to assure them work, let alone those forms of security that could give stability and equilibrium to their existence. The man from a rural background, tightly bound by ties of community, closely steered by his elders and supported by the whole apparatus of tradition, gives way to one gregarious, isolated and disarmed, torn from the organic unities in and through which he existed, cut off from his group and his home territory, and often placed in a material situation in which his old ideals of honour and dignity are no more than a memory.

In brief, the war and its sequels have simply precipitated that movement of cultural disintegration that the contact of civilizations and colonial policy started off. Moreover, this movement now extends to a territory that up till now was relatively spared and sheltered from the colonizing enterprise, especially in the mountainous regions that are now particularly affected by the war, where small rural communities, withdrawn on themselves in stubborn fidelity to their past and tradition, were able to preserve the essential features of a civilization that can now be spoken of only in the past tense.

No one can fail to be aware that a deep abyss separates Algerian society today from its past, and that an irreversible movement has been accomplished. What counts is less the rupture itself, and more the sense of rupture. The result is a suspension and questioning of the values that previously gave a meaning to existence. The experience of a life that is permanently suspended and threatened makes traditions and beliefs that were held as sacred now appear vain. The most solemn prohibitions are broken. The revolutionary situation also shatters the old hierarchies associated with the outdated system of values, substituting for these new men whose authority rests most often on quite different foundations than those of birth, wealth, or moral and religious superiority. The old values of honour crumble before the cruelties of war. The ideal self-image and the values associated with it have been put to the most radical test.

Like an infernal machine, the war has flattened social realities to the ground; it is pulverizing and scattering traditional communities – village, clan or family. Thousands of men are in the *maquis*, in internment camps, in prison, or else refugees in Tunisia or Morocco. Others have left for the cities of Algeria or metropolitan France, leaving their families in the resettlement centre or village; others still are dead or missing. Whole regions have been almost emptied of people. In the deserted villages it is questionable whether even the memory of old traditions survives. The transmission of traditional civilization, which adherence to the new values tends to desacralize in the eyes of the young, is interrupted by separation. Only women and old men remain in the village with the children. The young, thrown into urban life, no longer learn from their elders the precepts, customs, legends and proverbs that form the soul of the community. This teaching gives way to the political education conferred by those able to read. The maintenance of tradition supposed continuous contact between successive generations, and a reverential respect towards the elders. The patriarchal family, a primordial community which – in the countryside far more than the town – had escaped disintegration and remained the cornerstone of the entire social edifice, is dispersed and often torn apart by the conflict between generations, expression of the conflict between old values and new.

The young people of the big cities escape traditional controls and the pressure of public opinion, based essentially on the order of the village community. On top of this, the absence of father or elder brother leaves them almost completely to their own devices. A number of young men, above all in the towns, find themselves today in the situation that the Kabyles call 'son of the widow', in other words that of a man without a past, without traditions, without a self-ideal. The authority of the father, if still very much alive, has greatly altered. The head of the family has ceased to be in every case the basis of all values and the governor of all things. War has overthrown the scale of values that gave the elders precedence and authority. Revolutionary values are the values of the young generation. Formed in the war, oriented to the future, and ignorant of a past in which the older generation, whatever they do, remain rooted, these adolescents are often inspired by a radicalism and negativism that divides them from their elders. The part they play in the revolutionary war is evidence of this.

To express the present state of things, older Algerians often say: 'We are in the fourteenth century . . .'. The fourteenth century is that of the end of the world, when everything that was the rule becomes the exception, and everything that was prohibited is now permitted, when for example children no longer respect their parents, women go to the market, and so on. Popular consciousness expresses in this way its experience of a world turned upside down, in which everything is inverted; it sees in the surrounding disorder and chaos the world of the end that heralds the end of the world. And we in Algeria are present at this end of the world. At the same time, this is experienced as proclaiming a new world.

Algerian society for the last 130 years has experienced as deep an upheaval as possible, and continues to do so today. There is not a single field of life that has been spared. The pillars of the traditional order have been shaken or destroyed, first by the colonial situation and now by the war. The urban bourgeoisie has been scattered and dispersed; the values that it embodied and preserved were carried away by the eruption of new ideologies and the appearance of new hierarchies, often issuing from the common people. The feudal magnates, often compromised by the support they granted – and still grant – the French administration, and thus associated in the eyes of the masses with the system of oppression, have lost in most cases both their material power and their spiritual authority. The mass of peasants, who opposed the innovations proposed by the West with a lively traditionalism and conservatism, have found themselves dragged into the maelstrom of violence that is abolishing the very vestiges of the past. Islam, by being dissociated from the magical and mythic practices and beliefs that anchored it to the land, and being used for a moment more or less deliberately as a revolutionary ideology able to mobilize the masses and engage them in struggle, has steadily changed its significance and function. In brief, the war, by its very nature, its particular form and its duration, has been accompanied by a radical revolution.

A society so thoroughly overturned will force the invention of revolutionary solutions, and mobilize the masses torn away from their traditional discipline and universe, thrown into a world of chaos and disenchantment, by offering them a new way of living, based no longer on undisputed submission to the rules of custom and the values handed down by ancestral tradition, but on active participation in a common task – before all else, that is, the building of a harmonious social order.

From revolutionary war to revolution[*]

The end of the war of national liberation places the Algerian people face to face with itself. The questions that everyone has raised up till now in an abstract and quasi-imaginary fashion (given how pressing the urgency of the immediate objectives) are today raised in a new context. How can the objectives of a revolution be substituted for those of a revolutionary war that were unanimously approved because imposed by a situation that was objectively and collectively experienced? How can this revision of goals that the emergence of a new situation demands be effected?

The most pernicious illusion is undoubtedly that which we can call the myth of the revolutionizing revolution, according to which the war somehow transformed Algerian society from top to bottom, as if by magic; resolving all problems, moreover, including those it raised by its own existence. There is no doubting the fact that the war, by its very form, its duration, and the significance it acquired in the minds of all Algerians, effected a genuine cultural mutation. Nor can we doubt that many cultural resistances are bound to disappear with the abolition of the colonial system and the establishment of a government of Algerians by Algerians. In this sense, to be sure, everything has changed. But is the old Adam dead for all that?

First of all, besides those for whom the revolution was an occasion to carry out a genuine revolution, and was experienced in this way, there are also those who went through the war without understanding it, those who, expelled from their homes, forced to abandon their traditional way of life for the shanty-towns of neighbouring cities or resettlement centres, could only submit and accept.

Undoubtedly the war and the revolutionary situation were responsible for an expansion of political awareness, in a large section of the population and especially those able to read, and more profoundly, for a real transformation in their vision of the world. As shown by studies carried out between 1958 and 1961, the revolutionary situation and the effort of political education promoted a uniformity of opinions. In fields as varied as the education of children or the future of Algeria, workers and shopkeepers, artisans and civil servants, townspeople and country folk, all tended to agree on essentials. Yet this unification of language should not be allowed to hide the diversity of attitudes. What is striking, indeed, is the distance between opinion and

---

[*] First published in François Perroux, ed., *L'Algérie de demain* (Paris: PUF 1962).

behaviour, between judgements made in the imaginary mode, the order of verbal conformity, on the one hand, and actual behaviour on the other. These divergences and unconscious contradictions express a profound disarray as well as an unexpressed attempt to reinvent new models of behaviour. As regards women's work, for example, the same individual will justify models taken from the West with arguments drawn from the logic of tradition, such as proverbs and sayings, and justify traditional precepts with reasons taken from Western logic. This kind of floating between two cultures must be the centre of any reflection on the problems of education in tomorrow's Algeria. The problem in fact is to help a whole people invent for themselves a system of models of behaviour, in other words a civilization, that is both innovative and coherent; and this requires discovering new educational techniques as well as giving teaching a new content.

The relative uniformity of opinions is evidence of the effectiveness of an effort of education and rational propaganda, but at the same time of its limits. It is no small thing to impose a common language. But we must take care not to forget that behaviour, attitudes and categories of thinking are very hard to change. Despite the force of conviction it may have when it is dispensed by recognized authorities, education that takes on the task of deeply transforming behaviour so as to adapt this to a new society and new objectives should not minimize the obstacles it has to remove – a long and painstaking work.

The action of political commissars, the influence of radio and the press, have spread a political education whose importance should not be underestimated. In summer 1960, at a resettlement centre in the Collo peninsular, I attended a discussion at which the comparative merits of the policies of Nehru, Tito and Castro were compared. In a general sense, one is struck by the breadth of political culture and the subtlety of judgements; the behaviour of the Algerian masses following the ceasefire is objective evidence of a profound political maturity. None the less, given the manner in which this has been transmitted, it is only natural that this formation often remains superficial, and is not accompanied by a genuine revolution in conduct.

Undoubtedly the war and the suffering it has inflicted have amounted to a political education in itself. Through the trials they have experienced, the Algerian people have become aware of their real situation. But we should not ignore the fact that affective political awareness is in advance of rational awareness. This is particularly true for women, who experienced the war more passively and passionately than actively and rationally. Among them, political sensibility often has no common measure with political awareness and culture. The same goes for young people who have grown up during the war, and indeed for many Algerians to different degrees.

In particular, it is only at the cost of a distortion of reality inspired by the concern to apply classical explanatory models that the peasantry can be seen as the only revolutionary class. The peasantry is indeed a *force of revolution*, but not a revolutionary force in the strict sense. The Algerian peasants undoubtedly played a key role in the struggle, as both actors and victims. They are well aware of this. Undoubtedly they have everything to win and nothing to lose. They were the foremost victims of colonialism, and undoubtedly have a very acute memory of the expropriations and despoliations of which they were victim. 'You see over there, between the two trees, that's my land. The French took it after the revolt of 1875 and gave it to so-and-so who betrayed us.' And these old men have pinned in the folds of their burnous the act of application of Napoleon III's Senatus Consult that stripped them of their property, even if they are unable to read it. The essential thing perhaps is that the peasant world in Algeria experienced particularly deep overthrow, as a result of major land laws, confiscations, and more recently war and resettlement. The effect is that there is no risk of the peasant masses playing the role of a brake on the revolution, as has happened elsewhere.

For all these reasons, the rural masses form an explosive force, but a force that is available for the most contradictory actions. Unable to define their own goals other than in an emotional and negative manner, they await their destiny being revealed to them. Inspired by a deep sense of revolt, instilled with energies that are less rational than passionate, they are the easiest prey for demagogy; they can also, on condition that one knows how to lead them and steer the force that they bear, continue to play in the revolution the role of flying wing that they did in the revolutionary war.

The same is true of the urban sub-proletariat – unemployed, casual labourers, hawkers, petty employees, porters, commissionaires, caretakers, those who sell single packets of cigarettes or a bunch of bananas. Habituation to prolonged unemployment and the most casual and poorly paid work, along with the lack of any regular employment, prevent the development of a coherent organization either now or in future of a system of expectations towards which all activity and existence can be oriented. For want of possessing this minimum grasp on the present that is the precondition for a deliberate and rational effort to grasp the future, all these people are prey to incoherent resentment, rather than inspired by a genuine revolutionary consciousness; the lack of work, or its instability, go together with the absence of perspective on hopes and opinions, the absence of a system of rational projects and forecasts of which the will to revolution is an aspect. Enclosed in a condition marked by insecurity and incoherence, their own vision is generally itself uncertain and incoherent. They experience, feel and resent the wretchedness of their condition rather than having an objective conception of it, something that would presuppose a certain distance as well as instruments of thought that are inseparable from education. It is natural too that this experience, lived as a trial, is expressed in the language of affect. The most frequent kind of expression is what can be called 'affective quasi-systemization', i.e. a vision of the colonial world as dominated by an all-powerful and malign will. 'The French don't want to give me work', said an unemployed man from Saïda. 'All these gentlemen around here have no work. They all have certificates: one is a builder, the other a driver, they all have a trade. Why don't they have the right to work? We lack everything. The French have all that's needed to live well. But they won't give us anything, not work or anything.' And another, a café owner in Algiers: 'It seems as if we're struggling against fate. A friend said to me, "Wherever I knock I am preceded by God, with a sack of cement on his back and a trowel in his hand; I open a door, and he seals tight the next one along."' Everyday life is experienced as the result of a kind of systematic plan dreamed up by a malign will. The colonial system is perceived as a spiteful and hidden god, embodied according to occasion and circumstance by 'the Europeans', 'the Spanish', 'France', 'the administration', 'the government', 'them', 'that lot'. It's the impersonal 'they' that people refer to when they say: 'They want such and such.'

With steady work and a regular wage, with the appearance of real perspectives of social advance, an open and rational awareness of temporality can develop. At that point, the contradictions between over-ambitious expectations and available possibilities, between opinions offered on an imaginary level and real attitudes, disappear. Actions, judgements and aspirations arrange themselves as a function of a plan of life. It is then, and then only, that the revolutionary attitude takes the place of escape into dreams, fatalist resignation, or a raging resentment.

This is why we have to doubt the thesis which claims that in the colonized countries the proletariat is not a real revolutionary force, because – as opposed to the mass of peasants – it does have everything to lose, in terms of its role as an irreplaceable cog in the colonial machine. It is true that, in a country ravaged by unemployment, those workers assured of a steady job and regular income are in many respects a privileged category. First of all, they are in a position to realize in a fairly coherent fashion their aspirations to a modern way of life: stable employment and an assured wage are the condition for access and adaptation to modern housing, and by the same token, an existence endowed with a certain basic comfort. Then, because their working life puts them in touch with industrial society, they have been able to adopt and integrate techniques, forms of behaviour and ideas – a whole attitude, in fact – towards the world. Since all the aspects of this vision of the world, the centre of which is a certain attitude towards the future, form a coherent whole, the adoption of a 'rational conduct of life' is inseparable from the formation of a rational revolutionary consciousness.

Despite the economic dualism that characterizes colonial society, an important section of the Algerian population, especially in the towns, shares at least to a certain degree the benefits offered by the modern sector: education for their children, regular employment. Should this be seen as a poisoned chalice of colonialism? Should we consider attachment to these 'privileges' (which are claimed as rights by reference to the Europeans) and the existence of needs created by the effect of demonstration, as forming actual obstacles to the realization of a revolutionary politics? Quite the opposite, in fact; only those individuals equipped with a coherent system of aspirations and demands, able to locate themselves in the logic of rational calculation and prediction, can understand and deliberately accept the inevitable sacrifices and renunciations. Only those individuals accustomed to submitting to rational necessities will be able to unmask the pretensions of demagogy and insist on a rational policy on the part of those responsible for the fate of their country. The success of such a policy also presupposes that, by an effort of education, it is possible to appease or quash the magical impatience of the urban sub-proletariat and de-ruralized peasants who expect from independence everything that the colonial system had denied them.

To say that the peasants and the urban sub-proletariat are inspired by an emotional radicalism, and can be led in the most opposing directions, does not mean that they will subscribe to any kind of politics. The danger can be imagined of a fall into a contrary radicalism, a kind of technical hyper-rationalization that is ignorant of social realities. It follows from this that the first problem, whatever is done, is that of the political formation of the masses, or more precisely, of the dialogue between mass and elite.

One of the contradictions of the situation derives from the fact that the revolt of the masses has its root in the destruction of social structures and traditional culture. Recent colonial policy and war have only finished off, with a kind of blind and methodical bitterness, what colonization had already started, destroying or altering the economic foundations of the traditional society, its social structures, systems of representation and values. A policy of revolutionary rationalization can only tend to accentuate the questioning of traditional culture; in this respect, the most catastrophic heritage of colonization may have a positive function, in that by having been manipulated to so great an extent, the masses offer less resistance to the efforts of rational reconstruction of a new social order. Here again, however, the reality has a double face: if it is true that the transformation demanded by an education aiming to introduce new techniques, new models of behaviour and new values, will be slight in comparison with those brought about by colonial policy and war; if it is true that Algeria is in a sense greatly favoured because the questioning of the traditional order has been so profound, because the new models and values that need to be introduced will not be totally new for those who have to adopt them, it remains that disintegration and disarray supply a favourable soil for ideologies of passion, and possibly retrograde ones. To sum up, it is up to the leaders and elites, in the face of this ambiguous reality, to turn to good what could equally turn to bad.

How can this emotional radicalism, born from experience and severe test, be brought into line with the revolutionary radicalism born from reflection and systematic consideration of reality? How can the gap be bridged between aspirations marked by ambiguity and incoherence of sentiment, and revolutionary rationalization? How can dialogue be established between the masses inclined to summary identification or passionate commitment, and a leadership that would prefer to give only second place to denouncing the legacy of colonialism, focusing its criticism and action on the internal contradictions of Algerian society; that cannot evoke the survivals of imperialism and awaken old resentments without running the danger of triggering uncontrollable explosions; that refuses to turn against colonialism, a scapegoat already sacrificed, the revolt of the masses frustrated by the miracles of independence; that would choose rigorous analysis of the situation and realistic confrontation of reality against mystifying escape into nationalist mystique?

The most urgent problem is that of intermediaries. The success of a rational politics supposes that this is understood and accepted by the greatest possible number. When the attempt is made to achieve profound transformations, one cannot rely only on the basic discipline of the time of struggle; it is necessary to convince and persuade, i.e. to engage in dialogue and education. The attitude of the masses towards the elite is extremely demanding, but at the same time dismissive: 'If my son doesn't get the same education as you,' said a worker to a student, 'your education doesn't count for me.' And the people will be what they are provoked to be, either a force of revolution lost to the revolution, or a revolutionary force.

A retrospective on the Algerian experience*

At the request of Tassadit Yacine, and for the ears of the young scholars who are here today, I would like to explain the socio-historical context in which my work on Algeria developed. The procedure of studying the characteristic intellectual problematic of an era, in order to situate one's own work in its genuine context, is a very important moment in the quest for *reflexivity*, one of the imperative conditions for the practice of the social sciences. It is also the condition for a better and fairer understanding of the work of one's forerunners. Every scholar, in every age, takes as their point of departure what was the point of arrival of their predecessors, but without always seeing the path that they had to tread.

In the late 1950s and early '60s, everything relating to the study of North Africa was dominated by a tradition of Orientalism. Social science of that time was hierarchized, with sociology proper being reserved to the study of Europeans and Americans, ethnology to so-called primitive peoples, and Orientalism to peoples of non-European languages and religions. It is unnecessary to say here how arbitrary and absurd this classification was. In this context, my own work, dealing with Kabyl society, fitted somewhere between Orientalism and ethnology . . .

As far as Orientalism is concerned, the view at this time was that knowledge of the Arabic language was both a necessary and a sufficient condition for understanding society. The Marçais family offered the example in Algeria of Arabizing scholars, lacking any specific formation, but who reigned over the Algiers faculty, distributing research topics and representing what was called colonial ethnology. The faculty there had a quasi-autonomy intellectually in relation to the faculties of metropolitan France, its hierarchies, modes of local recruitment and reproduction all being to a certain degree independent. There were Arabizing or Berberizing linguists who did a bit of sociology, civil administrators, soldiers, geographers and historians – some of whom, like Marcel Émerit, saved something of the honour of science. Émerit was actually hung in effigy by *pied-noir* students, for the crime of establishing that the rate of educational enrolment in Algeria had been far higher before 1830 than after, a fact that seriously upset the colonial university establishment.

* Intervention at a colloquium organized by Tassadit Yacine at the Institut du Monde Arabe on 21 May 1997, published under the title 'Entre amis' in *Awal* 21, 2000.

There were independent historians, such as André Nouschi, who helped me a great deal, as well as Émile Dermenghem, who supplied a tremendous introduction to the secrets of bibliography. The essential point however is that with very few exceptions, which I shall come on to name, the link with the scientific mainstream (previously very strong, with such people as Doutté, Montagne, Maunier, etc., and more recently Thérése Rivière and Germaine Tillon) had been broken. This was not just the case for those outside the university, e.g. the White Fathers who did extremely useful linguistic and indirectly ethnographic work – Père Dallet, in particular –, the Jesuits, military and civilian administrators, but also for academics at the Algiers faculty, such as Philippe Marçais (future OAS deputy) or Bousquet (author of a book on the Berbers in the 'Que Sais-Je?' series and admirer of Pareto, Yacono, etc.). Hence the importance of the work of people like Jacques Berque, which, though I later discovered its limitations, was an extraordinary guide for the young ethnologist/sociologist that I was at that time. I am thinking of course of his great book *Les Structures sociales du Haut-Atlas*, the notes being full of extremely suggestive indications about North African societies, the role of customary law, relations between Berber and Islamic traditions, etc., as well as his article in *Annales* titled 'Cinquante ans de sociologie nord-africaine'; it was he who, with the advice of Émile Dermenghem, enabled me to find my bearings in the immense bibliography, very scattered and uneven, devoted to North African societies.

At this point in time, a number of Algerian intellectuals did ethnology in the form of fiction – what were called 'ethnographic novels'. This is a feature to be found in several colonized countries, the transition from literature to ethnography. We may naturally think here of Moloud Feraoun, a schoolteacher who described the customs and traditions of the Kabyl mountains, and who read and annotated my first texts on Kabylia; also Malek Ouary or Moloud Mammeri. This last, who I later got to know well, taught me a great deal on the *imusnawen* (plural of *amusnaw*), custodians of an incomparable wisdom and poetic art.

The impulse that led to my choice to study Algerian society was civic rather than political. I think in fact that the French of that time, whether they were for or against Algerian independence, all had in common a very poor knowledge of the country, and equally poor reasons for being for or against. It was very important therefore to supply the elements for an adequate judgement and understanding, not only for the French but also for educated Algerians, who for historical reasons were also often ignorant about their own society. (Among the grievous effects of colonization can be mentioned the complicity of certain left-wing French intellectuals towards Algerian intellectuals, a complicity that led them to close their eyes to the ignorance in

which these latter often stood about their own society. I am thinking particularly of Sartre and Fanon . . . This complicity had very serious effects when
these intellectuals came to power after independence and showed their incompetence.) I thus presented a first critical balance-sheet of everything I had
gained from my lectures and observations in the book *Sociologie de l'Algérie*
in the 'Que Sais-Je' series,[9] using such theoretical instruments as were available
to me at the time, i.e. those supplied by the culturalist tradition, but recon-
sidered in a critical sense (for example with a distinction between the colonial
situation as a relation of domination, and 'accculturation').

I steadily became involved in a more ambitious project of economic ethno-
sociology. (The opposition between sociology and ethnology is one that I
have always rejected.) To understand the logic of the transition from precapitalist to capitalist economy, which, though accomplished in Algeria under
external constraint, was of a kind that could shed light, as I saw it, on the
origins of capitalism and the debate between Weber, Sombart and various
others, a subject I was passionate about, it was necessary to take into account
on the one hand the specific logic of the precapitalist economy (with the
problem of relationship to time, to calculation, to forecasting, etc., the
problem of honour and symbolic capital, the specific problem of non-
commodity exchange, and so on), and on the other hand the logic of changes
in the economy and economic attitudes (as I did in *Travail et travailleurs
en Algérie* and *Le Déracinement*), as well as that of the household economy
(a study that I never published, though some of its conclusions were summed
up in *Algérie 60*).[10]

I also had in mind other problems that were more political. The political
question that preoccupied the revolutionary intellectuals of that time was that
of the choice between Chinese and Soviet models of development. In other
words, the question to answer was whether the peasantry or the proletariat
was the revolutionary class. I sought to translate these almost metaphysical
questions into scientific terms. With this object, I organized my study according
to INSEE[11] guidelines, with sampling, a statistical questionnaire designed to
assess the faculty of calculating, anticipating, saving, controlling births, etc.
These parameters were correlated in the same study with the capacity to undertake coherent revolutionary projects. It is here that I observed how the sub-
proletariat swung between a great desire for change and a fatalistic resignation
to the world as it is. This contradiction on the part of the sub-proletariat
struck me as extremely important, as it led me to a rather reserved stance
towards the revolutionary dreams of the leaders of the time. Unfortunately

[9] *The Algerians* (Boston: Beacon 1960).
[10] *Algeria 1960* (Cambridge: CUP 1979).
[11] [Institut National de la Statistique et des Études.]

this was subsequently verified. Algeria as I saw it – and this was far from the 'revolutionary' image given by activist literature and writings of struggle – was made up of a vast sub-proletarianized peasantry, an immense and ambivalent sub-proletariat, a proletariat that was basically established in France, a petty bourgeoisie that was quite out of touch with the realities of Algerian society, and an intelligentsia whose particular characteristic was a poor knowledge of its own society and a failure to understand anything of its ambiguities and complexities. For the Algerian peasants, like their Chinese counterparts, were far from how they were imagined by the intellectuals of the time. They were revolutionary, but at the same time they wanted to maintain traditional structures, as these gave a certain protection against the unknown. I was also very aware of the potential conflicts that would arise from the country's linguistic division, in particular that the opposition between Arabic and French speakers, only temporarily obscured by the unifying logic of anti-colonial struggle, was certain to find expression.

To be sure, this gave my scientific work a politically committed turn, but in no way would I go back on this orientation. A seemingly abstract analysis can make a contribution to solving political problems, even in their most burning form. Because I took up my position on a terrain that was not really occupied, neither by ethnology nor sociology (so that French ethnologists acted as if I did not exist), I was able to enter the traditional object of these disciplines from a new angle.

But the transformation of the relationship to the object of ethnology and sociology that I gained from my comparative reading of Kabylia and Béarn also had effects that I hold important for knowledge of the knowledge relationship, for the science of social science that is undoubtedly the major condition for the progress of this science. Convinced that it was necessary to take a distance in order to approach, to put oneself in the frame in order to exclude oneself, to objectivize oneself in order to de-subjectivize knowledge, I deliberately took as the first object of anthropological knowledge this anthropological knowledge itself, and the difference that inevitably separates it from practical knowledge. This led me paradoxically to 'de-exoticize' the exotic, to rediscover in our common practices, once adequately analyzed, the counterpart of the strangest behaviours, rather like rituals, to recognize the practical logic of strategy in what has been so often described in the theoreticist language of the model, and so on. And I could quickly add that, as soon as we abandon the intellectualist vision that artificially places the scientific truth of our practices at a distance, we are forced to discover in ourselves the same principles of the 'savage mind' that we impute to primitive peoples. I have in mind for example the cognitive-practical principles of the masculine view of the world. It is possible and legitimate to speak of others only at the price of a double historicization, of both the object and the subject of knowledge. This means that the scientist must put himself in the frame in order to exclude the frame, he has to work to know himself to be in a position to know the other; all progress in knowledge of the object is a progress in knowledge of the subject of knowledge and vice versa.

All this means that the ethno-sociologist is a kind of organic intellectual of humanity, and as a collective agent, can contribute to de-naturalizing and de-fatalizing human existence by placing his skill at the service of a universalism rooted in the comprehension of different particularisms. I believe that specialists in Arab and Berber civilizations are not the worst placed to fulfil this mission of *Aufklärung*, inasmuch as they are confronted with an object that is itself confronted today by the most radical questioning. I need only cite Mahmoud Darwish, the great Palestinian poet, who declared in a language that could have been that of Kafka on the Jews of his time: 'I do not believe there is any other people in the world who have been so required each day to prove their identity as are the Arabs. No one says to the Greeks: "You're not Greek", or to the French: "You're not French".'[12] Nothing seems more legitimate to me, both scientifically and politically, nor more fruitful, than to return to the particularity of the Arabs – or, more precisely, of the Palestinians, Kabyls or Kurds – not to fetishize it in any form of essentialism, of positive or negative racism, but rather to find in it the basis for a radical questioning of the particularity of a condition that raises in its most universal form the question of human universality.

---

[12] Mahmoud Darwish, *La Palestine comme métaphore* (Arles: Actes Sud 1997).

My feelings about Sartre[*]

On the 'total intellectual'

'Sartre and me' is the topic I've been asked to write about: my *personal* feelings towards Sartre! (Cf. the special tribute issue of *Libération*.)[13]

My initial response was to say no. (Out of habit?) With a certain bad conscience, to be sure. These are nice people, and I'm fond of them.

Infinitely close, and infinitely distant. It was Jeanson,[14] then working underground, who took my first texts for publication in *Les Temps Modernes* – extracts from the book on Algeria that I was in the process of writing. (I gave *Esprit*, for some unknown reason, a more political article titled 'Revolution in the Revolution'.) François Pouillon, whom I would see at Lévi-Strauss's laboratory, took a fragment of my study on bachelorhood in Béarn, which was likewise published in *Temps Modernes* under the title 'Relations Between the Sexes in Peasant Society'. And there was far more than that: shared affinities, or rather shared rejections, which sometimes inspired common projects.

But I still don't really know what to say. I never met Sartre. Not that I wouldn't have wanted to, when I was a student. But for what reason, and to tell him what? I didn't have the cheek of some of the 1968 leaders, who made their youth an authoritative argument. And then, at the time when I could and should have met him, at least on those demos that were captured in a thousand photos, with Foucault at the megaphone, etc., I didn't want to be part of that, for anything in the world. (Habit again?)

Part of what? Sartre, the bourgeois, the top of the class (or, what comes to the same thing, the quintessential *normalien*, who wrote a 'review' of his own doctoral thesis), the Frenchman (in the 1950s) and 'philosopher' (in the sense that this word has in the corridors of the Ecole Normale) . . . Just what I liked!

I don't want to repeat here the sociological analysis of the Sartrean 'project' that I wrote on Sartre's death for the *Times Literary Supplement*. The most

[*] Published in *French Cultural Studies* 4, 1993, pp. 209–11.

[13] 'Sartre, 'l'invention de l'intellectuel total', *Libération*, 21 March 1983. See also 'Comment libérer les intellectuels libres', in *Questions de sociologie* (Paris: Minuit 1980), and 'Impersonal Confessions', postscript to *Pascalian Meditations* (Cambridge: Polity 2000).

[14] Francis Jeanson led a network of French Communist activists, the 'Réseau Jeanson', in illegal support work for the Algerian FLN, their main activity being to provide funds and false papers for Algerian agents operating in the metropolis.

I can do is record my emotional reactions, which are certainly not unrelated to what sociological analysis seeks to grasp, but which simply display an incompatibility of habitus in the mode of what is generally called 'intellectual antipathy'. I have in mind a rather dreadful text in which Canguilhem related the opposition between two philosophies that marked his epoch (if I remember correctly, between a rationalist philosophy anchored in the history of sciences and epistemology, and an irrationalist philosophy, or in any case one very concerned to assert its distance from scientism and positivism) to the attitudes of the one camp (particularly Cavaillès)[15] and the other to the German occupation. A reaction of bad feeling, undoubtedly excessive, and having much to do with differences of habitus.

But how can an emotion be condemned? I am certainly among the least well placed to do so. After having shared for a moment – in an ambiguous and rather divided way – the vision of the world of the 'French École Normale philosopher of the 1950s', which reached a culmination – one could almost say a paroxysm – with Sartre, and particularly the contempt with which he considered the human sciences – psychology and psycho-analysis, not to speak of sociology, which he precisely did not consider at all –, I could say that I constructed myself, as soon as I emerged from the educational system, against everything that the Sartrean undertaking represented for me.

Close study of the workers of Algeria, as well as its non-workers, unem-ployed, sub-proletarians, landless peasants, etc., meant breaking with the capitalized discourse on the Workers, or the Proletariat and the Party, that would resurface a little later with Althusser and his *normaliens*, as well as with the intellectual ritual of petitions – even if politically necessary and sometimes admirable from a human point of view (I'm thinking of the '121').[16] To do sociology (not even anthropology . . . or those mixed forms of philosophy and 'science' that yield so much prestige), and 'hard' sociology at that, based on statistics and quantification, means rejecting any attempt at establishing the human sciences as science of a special kind, or restoring (a genuine restoration) the methodological separatism defended by the *Geisteswissenschaften* movement and the 'hermeneutic' tradition: here I have in mind Habermas, or Ricoeur talking about psychoanalysis, and all those who still indefatigably pursue today, as Sartre did yesterday, the quest for an idiosyncratic understanding of the human, in this way claiming for them-selves all the guaranteed prestige of a knowledge that is supposedly superior because it flatters the 'spiritual point d'honneur' that slumbers within every

---

[3] Jean Cavaillès, philosopher and mathematician born in 1903, was arrested for Resistance activities in 1942 and later shot.
[4] See **p. xvii, note 10.** [Ed.]

intellectual, as well as claiming the privilege of defining or founding the tasks that they allocate to the workhorses of positive science. I could pursue this theme a good while further. What I like least about Sartre is everything that made him not only the 'total intellectual' but the very ideal of an intellectual, and in particular his unmatched contribution to the ideology of the free intellectual, which brought him the eternal recognition of all intellectuals.

But I don't rank myself with those who celebrate the death of Sartre and the end of intellectuals, or – rather more subtly, perhaps from a concern to save the position that Sartre created in the obscure hope of occupying it themselves – invent an opposition between Sartre and Aron that never in fact existed, in order to praise the latter for his reason and lucidity. First of all because, as I see it, the resemblances between Sartre and Aron are far greater than their differences, starting with what I find deeply sympathetic about both of them, despite everything: what I would call a certain naivety or even innocence. If I can't give personal testimony in the case of Sartre, I knew and loved Raymond Aron well enough to be able to attest that the disenchanted analyst of the contemporary world hid (badly) a sensitive or even sentimental man, and an intellectual with a naive belief in the powers of the intellect.

Both were pure products of a triumphant educational institution, which granted its 'elite' unconditional recognition, for example making a competitive recruitment examination (the philosophy *agrégation*) into an instance of intellectual consecration (look for example how Simone de Beauvoir wrote about all this in her memoirs). These infant prodigies, all twenty years of age, had conferred on them the privileges and obligations of genius. In a France that had economically and politically declined, but was still as triumphant as ever intellectually, they could devote themselves in all innocence to the mission assigned them by the university and by a whole tradition convinced by power of habit of its universality: a kind of universal magistrature of the intelligence. Armed with their intelligence alone – they scarcely encumbered themselves with any positive knowledge – they could confront the most immense intellectual tasks, such as philosophically founding the science of society or history, or summarily laying down the ultimate truth about political regimes or the future of humanity. But this limitless assurance was matched on the other hand by an unconditional recognition of the obligations that their dignity brought with it.

No one believed more than Sartre in the mission of the intellectual, and no one did more than he did to give this self-interested myth the force of social belief. Yet this myth, and Sartre himself, who in the splendid innocence of his generosity was both its producer and its product, creator and creature,

27

has to be defended at all cost, against everything and everyone, and above all against a sociologically reductive interpretation of the sociological description of the intellectual world. Even if it is far too great for the greatest of intellectuals, the myth of the intellectual and his or her universal mission is one of those ruses of historical reason that have given even those intellectuals most sensitive to the seductions and privileges of universality an interest in contributing, in the name of motivations that may have nothing universal about them, to the progress of true universality.

1964–1970

Those whom education has liberated more than others are inclined to believe in the liberating effect of education. Alienated by their own education, they put their faith in the liberating school at the service of the conservative school, which owes to the myth of the liberating school part of its power of conservation.

2

Education and Domination

The School . . . this privileged instrument of the bourgeois sociodicy which confers on the privileged the supreme privilege of not seeing themselves as privileged, manages the more easily to convince the disinherited that they owe their scholastic and social destiny to their lack of gifts or merits, because in matters of culture absolute dispossession excludes awareness of being dispossessed.

Reproduction in Education (with Jean-Claude Passeron), 1970[1]

After holding a professorship in sociology at the faculty of letters in Lille (1961–4), Pierre Bourdieu returned to Paris as director of research at the École Pratique des Hautes Études. He was also appointed general secretary of the Centre de Sociologie Européenne (CSE), founded by Raymond Aron in 1960 with the help of a grant from the Ford Foundation. In the course of these years, a group of scholars came together, including Luc Boltanski, François Bonvin, Robert Castel, Jean-Claude Chamboredon, Patrick Champagne, Yvette Delsaut, Claude Grignon, Gérard Lagneau, Madeleine Lemaire, Rémi Lenoir, Francine Muel-Dreyfus, Jean-Claude Passeron, Louis Pinto, Monique de Saint-Martin and Dominique Schnapper. Studies were launched on the educational system, the intellectuals, and the cultural practices involved in museums and photography, and Bourdieu jointly authored several investigations and collective works.[2]

1964 saw the foundation of the series 'Le Sens Commun', published by Éditions de Minuit, a response to the need to acquire a relatively autonomous publication structure with an editorial policy that was both scientifically ambitious (the publication of major works in the French critical tradition and the translation of corresponding foreign-language works, to strengthen the series of major studies that members of this collective of sociologists were themselves producing), and

[1] *Reproduction in Education* (Cambridge: Polity 1977).
[2] *Photography: A Middle-Brow Art* (with Luc Boltanski, Robert Castel and Jean-Claude Chamboredon) (Cambridge: Polity 1990); *The Love of Art* (with A. Darbel and Dominique Schnapper) (Cambridge: Polity 1990); *Le Partage des bénéfices* (in collaboration with the statisticians and economists of the INSEE) (Paris: Minuit 1966); *Le Métier de sociologue* (with Jean-Claude Chamboredon and Jean-Claude Passeron) (Paris: Minuit 1968). [Ed.]

concerned to escape the confines of scholarship and reach a broader public, marked by certain political expectations, that was associated with the Minuit label. It was in this connection that Bourdieu published the same year, together with Jean-Claude Passeron, Les Héritiers,[3] a book in which Raymond Aron subsequently saw one of the seeds of May 1968. During the événements*, Aron gave an address at the Centre de Sociologie Européenne as a rallying point for the Comité pour la Défense et la Renovation de l'Université Française; a year later, Bourdieu founded a team of scholars with its own programmes: the Centre de Sociologie de l'Éducation et de la Culture (CSEC).*

This Centre then took part, in its own way, in the events of May 1968. One of its major interventions at this time was an 'Appeal for the organization of a general assembly of education and research' (see p.41); the idea of such a general assembly (taken up again thirty years later in 1996 and 2000) (see pp.280 and 361) signalled a form of collective demand that should not be confused with a 'discussion among beneficiaries of the system', and was not intended to reinforce the exclusion of those who, eliminated from the system, were deprived of the means to contest it.

A leaflet calling for the organization of a general assembly, launched during the events of May 1968, inaugurated a series of thematic dossiers that were collectively edited by various members of the CSE, on the procedures of teacher recruitment, overcoming the effects of class heritage by changing the contents of education, criticism of the degree qualification as sole criterion of competence, transformation or suppression of the traditional exams, continuous assessment, recourse to new pedagogic techniques, transformation of the career structure and a new division of powers in higher education, the suppression of the agrégation,[4] *etc. (see p.41)*

In the following years, Pierre Bourdieu returned on many occasions to the crisis of the 'university order' that erupted in 1968, and analyzed what the limits of this were: the reform of the most visibly authoritarian aspects of the educational system had not dismantled the authoritarian structure of the 'pedagogic relationship' and its power to legitimize inequalities;[5] the spontaneist style of speech of the 'May leaders' should not obscure what the political positions championed at this time by the students and junior lecturers owed to their objective interests in the academic world.[6]

In the same way that the studies collected in Rapport pédagogique et communication[7] *showed 'the determining role of linguistic inheritance in educational*

---

[3] [The Inheritors, (Chicago: University of Chicago Press 1979).]
[4] [The agrégation is a competitive examination designed to recruit lycée teachers.]
[5] Cf. *Reproduction in Education*. [Ed.]
[6] *Homo Academicus* (Cambridge: Polity 1988). [Ed.]
[7] *Rapport pédagogique et communication* (with J.-C. Passseron, Monique de Saint-Martin et al.) (Paris: Mouton 1965). [Ed.]

success', The Inheritors starts from the statistical link between social origin and education achievement to show how the teaching system favours those who are best endowed with cultural capital by their class origin. The apparent neutrality of the school enables this to transform social differences into educational differences by passing off properties acquired in the family milieu as 'natural gifts'. In a society where obtaining social privileges depends ever more closely on the possession of educational titles, this ideology of 'gift', by which those who 'inherit' become those who 'merit', fills an essential function in legitimizing the social order.

Reproduction in Education was sharply attacked on its publication in 1970, particularly by the educational historian Antoine Prost in the magazine Esprit, *who denounced its 'fatalistic view' of school and society. It did not find a better reception in the milieus of the left, and especially that of the Communist party, as Bourdieu explained in an interview printed below (p.49). This was also the time that the CSE, and later CSEC, initiated its investigations into the* grandes écoles, *which culminated in 1989 in* The State Nobility, *the prologue to which insisted on the political role of the educational institution and thus of the sociology of education:*

Thus the sociology of education is a chapter, and not a minor one at that, in the sociology of knowledge and the sociology of power, not to mention the sociology of philosophies of power. Far from being the kind of applied, and hence inferior, science (only suitable for educationalists) that has ordinarily been the view of it, the sociology of education lies at the foundation of a general anthropology of power and legitimacy. It leads us, in fact, to an understanding of the 'mechanisms' responsible for the reproduction of social structures and for the reproduction of the mental structures that, because they are genetically and structurally linked to these objective structures, favour the misrecognition of their truth and thus the recognition of their legitimacy. Given that [. . .] the structure of social space as observed in advanced societies is the product of two fundamental principles of differentiation – economic capital and cultural capital – the educational institution, which plays a critical role in the reproduction of the distribution of cultural capital and thus in the reproduction of the structure of social space, has become a central stake in the struggle for the monopoly on dominant positions.[8]

---

[8] *The State Nobility* (Cambridge: Polity 1996), p. 5. [Ed.]

Jacobin ideology*

Why is the educational system so rarely subjected to radical criticism? I want to show that verbal radicalism or terrorism most commonly hides a surreptitious complicity with the logic of the system, the values that underpin it and the functions it objectively fulfils. It is only too easy to denounce the system's inadequacies, sticking simply to those that it owes to the economic and political conditions of its operation.

To denounce and combat all attempts to transform an archaic system, in the name of an escalation of demands, is undeniably useful, but it is also undeniably reassuring. First of all, there is the self-justification of verbal revolutionism derived from reasserting demands on the conditions of operation of the system, which dispenses one from examining its actual operation, analysing its logic and discovering its real function. This is why I am convinced that the Jacobin ideology on which the traditional criticism of the teaching system is based, as well as certain traditional criticisms of government reforms of this system, actually justify the system under the guise of challenging it, as well as justifying the pedagogic conservatism of a number of those who demand these reforms, even within the university.

The majority of criticisms, in fact, implicitly accept that the educational system does fulfil the functions that it ideally proposes to fulfil, in other words offering equal opportunities of access to higher education and the social advantages this education provides. By this very fact, they are complicit with the system that they denounce. One might object that programmes and manifestos compete in their denunciations of the inequalities that higher education involves; in fact, no meeting like the present one takes place without recalling that the children of workers make up only 6 per cent of students; but once this is said the matter ends there, with no further reflection on what such figures mean. We are absolved from asking what is the real function of an educational system that actually operates to eliminate from school, over the years, children from the popular classes – and to a lesser extent even from the middle classes; we are absolved from asking what *characteristics of its operation* make possible this objective result, i.e. the differential elimination of children by their social origin. It is true that a reflection of this kind is in no way reassuring for those who undertake it, above all

* Communication to the 'Semaine de la Pensée Marxiste', 9–15 March 1966, published in *Démocratie et liberté* (Paris: Éditions Sociales 1966), pp. 167–73.

when, whether student or teacher, they are themselves privileged by the system. Jacobin ideology comes into its own here, as it permits a challenge to the system that still essentially accepts it. In point of fact, faith in the school as an institution of liberty and equality obstructs the discovery of the school as conservative and actually unjust despite – and even because of – its formal equality.

A perfect expression of this egalitarian myth can be found in the letter from a certain professor published in *Le Monde* on 28 July 1964, referring to competitions:

> The suppression of competitions and their replacement by assessment of course work would favour mediocre students from the bourgeoisie rather than those of humble origins. Our forefathers, well acquainted as they were with the dangers of kinship, recommendation and fortune, made the Revolution in order to establish competitions that guarantee places solely on merit; competition or examinations marked in strict anonymity is the very touchstone of democracy in matters of recruitment. True democracy consists in permitting all young people to present themselves for every competition for which they are suited, not by suppressing competitions so as to permit mediocre children from well-placed families to slip into positions in which they will not serve society or the nation well.

This text seems to me a perfect revelation of the self-mystification effected by Jacobin ideology. Denunciation of an imaginary danger, which may well have been real in a previous era, serves to conceal a present danger, the very danger that is supposedly denounced, i.e. that competitions favour just as much the children of the better-off classes – indeed more successfully, since the appearance of equity is preserved.

It is true, indeed, that competitions are open to all; it is just as true that – as if by chance – students are more successful in these if they come from a milieu that is more favoured economically and culturally. In the same way, museums are open to all, they are even free on Sundays, and yet the proportion of workers who visit them is extremely small, more or less on a par with the proportion of children of workers enrolled in higher education. In other words, individuals from disfavoured classes have the formal possibility of visiting museums or passing the competitive entry examinations, but they do not have the real opportunity to make use of this formal possibility. Since it is a known scientific fact that opening these competitions to all poses no threat to privilege, one might conclude that Jacobin ideology indulges in self-mystification when it tries to persuade itself that by defending competitive examinations it defends a conquest of the Revolution. Like the defence of competition, any action that tends to strengthen formal equality among pupils and students in the face of the teaching system is *irreproachable*. But perhaps this is the true and only function of such equality. Those maintaining it are protected in this way from reproach, and avoid having to examine and challenge the actual operation of a system that fulfils its function of conserving and legitimizing inequalities all the better in that formal equality is more completely realized.

It is necessary then to raise the real questions that all these ideologies systematically elude. What is the responsibility of the school? I deliberately mean 'the school' as a system, not those agents involved in its operation. What is the responsibility of the school in its historical French form in the perpetuation of social inequalities? Inequalities both vis-à-vis the school and inequalities transmitted by the school? As soon as this question is properly raised, the scientific response is beyond doubt. The values that the school conveys, that it requires of both teachers and taught, its characteristic peda-gogic methods (or, for certain kinds of teaching, the absence of pedagogic method), the criteria of recruitment and judgement it deploys, the content of the culture it transmits – all these contribute to favouring the most favoured and disfavouring the most disfavoured. As a result, the formal equity that governs the entire educational system is actually unjust, and, in any society that proclaims democratic ideals, it protects privileges all the better than would their open and obvious transmission.

This can be very quickly demonstrated. In fact, in order to favour the most favoured and disfavour the most disfavoured, all that is necessary and sufficient is for the school to ignore in the content and teaching it transmits, in the methods and techniques of transmission and the criteria of judgement it deploys, the cultural inequalities that divide children from different social classes. In other words, by treating all students, however much they differ, as equal in rights and duties, the educational system actually gives its sanction to the initial inequality in relation to culture. All sociological research shows that a close relationship exists between social origin and the aptitudes that the school measures: children succeed that much better at school if they come from a milieu that is more favoured economically and especially cultur-ally. This means that educational democracy presupposes economic and social democracy, and also a school that is genuinely democratic in its methods, its values and its spirit. Given that the cultural inheritance children receive from their family milieu is quite unequal, inequalities towards culture will perpetuate themselves so long as the school does not give the disinherited the real means for acquiring what others have inherited. The educational system in its present form tends to grant an additional privilege to children from the most favoured milieus, because the implicit values it presupposes and conveys, the traditions it perpetuates and even the content and form of the culture it transmits and demands, have an affinity of style with the values and traditions of culture of the favoured classes.

This is also true at the level of the contents of culture. For example, the teaching of literature assumes a whole experience of knowledge and pre-knowledge already acquired, which is only the case with children from the cultivated classes. One could show in the same way how the devaluation of scientific and technical culture has an affinity with the values of the dominant classes; or again that the language in which the transmission of culture is effected differs greatly in its vocabulary and syntax from the language used by children of the middle class and popular classes in their everyday lives. Finally we could show how the values implicitly involved in teaching are simply those of the cultivated class. To take a single example, the belief – so widespread among teachers and students alike – in the existence of natural gifts. This ideology of 'gifts' is to my mind the cornerstone of the whole system. In fact, it permits aptitudes socially acquired to exist and be treated as natural and personal aptitudes, and – by the same token – absolves teachers from giving those who have not received these aptitudes from their family milieu the means of acquiring these. In a paradox that is quite surprising, the school devalues as scholarly the aptitudes that have been acquired at school, thanks to a scholarly effort, by those who have not inherited them from their milieu. Similarly, the school in its higher reaches devalues as elementary the only techniques and methods of transmission which can compensate for the handicapping of the most disfavoured, and to which primary education in the *belle époque* owed its success as an instrument of upward mobility. Besides permitting the cultivated elite to feel justified in their way of being, the ideology of natural gifts contributes to shutting members of the popular classes into the fate that society assigns them, by leading them to view as lack of natural aptitude something that is simply an effect of an inferior condition.

To take this argument to its conclusion: are the values applied by teachers themselves socially neutral? As products of a system devoted to transmitting a culture that is aristocratic in both content and spirit, teachers are inclined to espouse these values with all the more ardour, the more completely they recognize in them their own culture and the symbol of their social success. Moreover, we need to go back to the statistics of access to higher education, which everyone repeats but no one reflects on. If we know that the faculties and the *grandes écoles* from which professors are recruited are still today very aristocratic in their operation, all the more so as one goes up the educational hierarchy, we might conclude that the same is true of the teaching corps, and again all the more so in the higher reaches of teaching. How could teachers not deploy the values of their milieu of origin in their manner of teaching and way of judging, even and above all unknowingly? It would no doubt be abusive and summary to describe relations between the upper classes and teachers as some kind of conspiracy. What is rather involved, though, is something more serious, a *complicity* that is unconscious, and often hidden beneath generous professions of faith, a complicity based on an affinity of lifestyle and values. This is clearly the way that the educational system is able to serve the perpetuation of privileges without the privileged having to manipulate it.

Besides, the school consecrates inequalities, in other words sanctions and legitimizes them. It transforms inequalities of fact into inequalities of merit. The son of the top manager who succeeds his father has none of the obvious appearances of an heir. Yet he owes a large part of his success at the École Nationale d'Administration or the École Polytechnique to aptitudes that he acquired in his milieu (unlike those eliminated from the educational system), and that the school treats as natural gifts even though they are actually a social inheritance.

The school also has a function of mystification. On the one hand, it persuades those whom it eliminates that their social destiny – very closely linked to their educational destiny, i.e. their occupation, their income, their social rank – is due to their lack of natural gifts, and in this way contributes to preventing them from discovering that their individual destiny is a particular case of a collective one, as statistics of access to higher education reveal. We sometimes see how the exceptional success of a few individuals who escape their collective fate gives a semblance of legitimacy to educational selection, and in this way contributes to accrediting the myth of the liberating school even among those who have experienced elimination from it, making them believe that success is simply a matter of work and gifts. We see less often how those whom the school has liberated are more inclined than anyone else to believe in the liberating school, and in this way the actual conservatism of the school shows its hold over them. Alienated by their liberation, they have to pay for their educational success by faith in the liberating school, this success only redoubling their faith in the school, which is responsible for at least a part of it. They put their faith in the liberating school in the service of the conservative school, which owes to the myth of the liberating school a part of its power of conservation.

The educational system thus contributes to legitimizing economic and social inequalities by giving a social order based on the transmission of economic and – still more so – cultural capital the appearance of an order based on educational merit and individual gifts. Knowing on the one hand that, in societies that tend ever more towards formal rationalization, positions in the economic and social hierarchy are – in every field and sector of activity – increasingly bound up with the qualifications obtained (parallel paths such as access through rank or internal competition being increasingly closed), and on the other hand how educational success is very closely dependent on social origin, we can see by simple deduction how the educational system tends to perpetuate the social order in its present form. When we speak of the liberating effect of the school, then, it is necessary to make clear whether we are speaking of the school as it presently is, or the school as it should be. In the present state of affairs, the school makes a very major contribution to the rigidity of social structure. Everything seems to indicate that inequalities in relation to schooling, the privileged instrument of social mobility and cultural progress, are more pronounced in our society than are economic inequalities, and if the awareness of cultural dispossession is less acute than that of economic dispossession, this is because in the field of culture awareness of deprivation decreases inversely with the increase of deprivation itself; the school itself contributes towards persuading people that the distribution of degrees of culture corresponds to the distribution of degrees of merit. For this reason, an awareness of the actual function of the education system seems the condition for the real transformation of this system, if only to the extent that the mystified representations of the system and the system's actual operation contribute to ensuring its fulfilment of its function. The school must therefore be understood as a conservative school, in order to genuinely raise the question of knowing the conditions under which the school can liberate.

I see May 1968 as having two faces. On the one hand, like any situation of crisis in which social censorship is relaxed, the face of the resentment of the lower ranks of intellectuals who, in the university, the newspapers, the radio and television, settled accounts and expressed loud and clear their repressed violence and social fears. On the other hand, the face of social innocence, the inspired youth who, among other things by their refusal to accept established formalities, questioned everything that was accepted as self-evident, and produced in this way an extraordinary social experiment whose results social science has still not finished analysing. What has remained of this great shake-up in the symbolic order? In the political field as such, almost nothing: the logic of apparatuses and parties, which libertarian criticism did not spare, is better placed to express the virtuous rationalization of corporate interests than the anti-institutional mood that remains for me the truth of that springtime of laughter.*

---

* 'Son opinion aujourd'hui', published together with those of Raymond Aron and Jacques Attali in *Lire*, May 1983.

CALS Main Library

Customer ID: **********2931

Items that you checked out

Title:
 Acts of resistance : against the tyranny of
 the market / Pierre Bourdieu ; translated
 from the Frenc
ID: 37653007304648
Due: Tuesday, August 15, 2017

Title:
 Political interventions : social science and
 political action / Pierre Bourdieu ; edited
 and introdu
ID: 37653014167467
Due: Tuesday, August 15, 2017

Total items: 2
Account balance: $0.00
7/18/2017 4:52 PM
Checked out: 4
Overdue: 0
Hold requests: 1
Ready for pickup: 0

Thank you!

Appeal for the organization of a general assembly of teaching and research*

At a moment when the students by their courage have won the first battle, a group of teachers and researchers, meeting in Paris on 12 May, have deemed it useful to call all parties interested in a democratic transformation of the French university to define the major lines of a programme, and to offer certain facts and orientations without delay for everyone to discuss. The object is less to reassert demands that are or will be asserted in any case (right of students to take part in the management and control of teaching, transformation of the nature of the pedagogic relationship, right to non-university expression and activity in the faculties, etc.), than to state the *gaps* that any programme defined within the institution by the beneficiaries of the system is very likely to present.

It seems to us that the participation of teachers and researchers in a movement that they have followed rather than initiated can no longer be based – without risk – on worthy sentiments, whether these are the 'affection' of 'teachers' for their students or legitimate indignation against police repression. Our view is rather that only an objective analysis of the operation of the university and its functions, social as well as technical, can provide the basis for *a programme of demands that is explicit and coherent enough to resist those attempts at technocratic or conservative recuperation* that are already steadily growing. And that it is necessary therefore to recall two fundamental facts that the very conditions in which the movement arose risk making us forget.

In the first place, the main victims of the present operation and organization of the system are, simply by definition, outside the system and eliminated from it; those groups whose voices are not heard in university discussion, discussion between beneficiaries of the system, are the very ones who have the most direct interest in a genuine transformation of the system – even if, in the present state of things, their exclusion prevents them from formulating their demand for a system able to integrate them.

Secondly, any questioning of the educational institution that does not bear fundamentally on this function of eliminating the popular classes, and thus the socially conservative function of the entire school system, is a vain pretence. Moreover, despite their apparent radicalism, all partial and superficial challenges have the effect of shifting the point of application of criticism,

* Archives of the Collège de France.

and contributing in this way to the preservation of the 'university order' as a mechanism for perpetuating the 'social order'. This is why it is necessary to denounce attempts to reduce the present crisis to a generational conflict, as if membership of a particular age group, or even the condition of student, could magically wipe away the differences between social classes.

The initial proposals listed below do not claim to constitute a complete programme for transforming the university, but are simply designed to illustrate some main lines of a policy for higher education. The important thing is to be armed against the danger of a technocratic use of the situation created: if the crisis of the university is simply an 'unease' bound up with anxieties about future employment or the frustrations imposed by a conservative pedagogic relationship, it is easy to present as solution to all these ills a technocratic planning of the development of education simply as a function of the needs of the labour market, or fictitious concessions on the participation of students in university life. The changes that the student movement has introduced de facto in the faculties – and that may contribute to the constitution of a *critical* attitude able to spread beyond the pedagogic relationship – can only hope to have a lasting effect on university life, and social life in general, if relations between university and society undergo a radical transformation. By declaring the university 'open to workers', even if this is just a symbolic and illusory gesture, the students have at least shown that they are open to a problem that can only be resolved by action on those mechanisms that block the access of certain classes to higher education.

I. In a concern to promote *democratization*, i.e. to put in a place a policy designed to neutralize as completely as possible the effect of those social mechanisms that maintain inequality in general, and its perpetuation in relation to school and culture in particular, it is important to maintain that:

1) The real scope of a transformation of the educational system is measured by the degree to which *the recruitment of both teachers and taught* is transformed. This implies that the problem of higher education cannot be separated without mystification from the problems raised by the organization of other orders of teaching. By restricting discussion and action to higher education, where the dice are already cast (and have long been so), any genuine transformation of education, including that of higher education, is ruled out.

2) The real scope of a transformation of the educational system is measured by its ability *to counteract the specifically educational measures of*

elimination and relegation as a deferred elimination: democratization of entry into secondary education remains fictitious, in other words, owing to the inequality of establishments, and by children from different social classes being placed in different streams. A technocratic orientation, let alone one of selection, could only perfect and sanction the operation of a system that at all levels (from CEG to IUT)[9] sets up snares or sidings for the popular classes.

3) The real scope of a transformation of the educational system is measured by the degree to which it succeeds in *minimizing the effects of class inheritance* by redefining the contents transmitted (i.e. programmes), transmission techniques, and the ways of monitoring the effect of transmission.

4) The real scope of a transformation of relations between the educational system and the social system is measured by the degree to which it succeeds in *removing from educational certificates their function of an exclusive criterion of competence*, at the same time as ensuring a professional use of skills: today in fact degrees are one of the main mechanisms opposing the application of the principle 'equal pay for equal work', making work or workers appear unequal simply because they are divided by educational certificates. This phenomenon is observable in every sector of activity, but especially so in education, which takes advantage at every level of the lesser cost of teachers who are deprived, by subtle differences between certificates, of rights logically attaching to the function that they actually perform (in *lycées*, for example, qualified teaching assistants, or, in higher education, lecturers, assistant lecturers, course leaders).

II. As regards inscribing in the educational system the social demands of democratization and the scientific demands of teaching and research, the first and most urgent matter to be dealt with is that of the mechanisms governing the operation of the traditional university:

1) Any attempt to change pedagogy, programmes, work organization and techniques of transmission that is not accompanied by a transformation (or even the *suppression*, wherever possible) of the *traditional examination* necessarily remains a fiction.[10] In any case where examination cannot be replaced by continuous assessment (and it can be for most of the time in higher education, where teachers judge their own

9 [Cours d'Enseignement Général and Institut Universitaire de Technologie.]
10 Cf. 'L'examen d'une illusion' (with J.-C. Passeron) in *Revue Française de Sociologie*, 1968, vol. 9, pp. 227–53. [English translation in *Reproduction in Education*, op. cit.] [Ed.]

students, if the means of supervision are sufficient), it should be the object of a clearly defined contract between teachers and taught: a list of topics should be established by discussion, with the teachers committing themselves to ask only what they have taught and in conformity with a clearly defined model; they would then be legitimately authorized to ask questions on everything they have taught, i.e. everything that explicitly defines the level of competence attested by the qualification; the collective of teachers and taught in a particular discipline should rationally determine, if it has been formed as a genuine unit of teaching and research, the kinds of tests, i.e. by reference to the objectives of formation and the different publics; teachers charged with monitoring results should be scientifically trained in techniques (not just those of examination) enabling them to monitor the knowledge acquired and the work submitted by reference to explicit criteria. As every mark awarded is a judgement, it goes without saying that the examiner must be in a position to justify it if called to do so.

2) The profession of teacher (whether in primary school or in a faculty) should no longer be defined simply according to traditional criteria of competence but rather by ability to transmit to all, with the use of *new pedagogical techniques*, what some students, i.e. those from privileged backgrounds, have acquired from their family milieu.[11]

3) The transformation of the functioning of higher education establishments and in particular *the structure of careers and the distribution of power within teaching and research units* is the precondition for any genuine transformation of pedagogic and scientific practices: the redivision of assignments and responsibilities should be the exclusive responsibility of a body recognized by the totality of members of each teaching and research unit. (This implies taking equally into account pedagogic ability and scientific work, and consequently suppression of exclusive and automatic reference to a thesis or any other qualification [*grande école, agrégation*], even and especially that of seniority.) In the short term, the first action needed is to remove those obstacles to any redefinition of pedagogy and scientific life that are *agrégation* and the doctoral thesis, being individual productions subject to archaic criteria. In sum, the point is to seek every way of removing the obstacles to the realization of a better adjustment between competence and function, by breaking the institutional barriers opposed to the circulation of teachers and taught between different orders and domains of teaching and research.

---

11 Cf. 'Pour une pédagogie rationelle' (1964). [English translation in *The Inheritors*.] [Ed.]

44

III. The technical development of a programme for the systematic transformation of the university in accordance with these principles can only be the work of *all those with a stake in it*, i.e. genuine representatives of every group participating in the function of all orders of teaching, from elementary to higher, and most especially, of those social classes currently excluded by the teaching system and their corresponding organizations.

The undersigned call all parties mentioned above to undertake without delay the organization of a general assembly of teaching and research, and prepare this by discussions between teachers and students, as well as by drawing up notebooks of charges and complaints.

[THERE FOLLOWS A LIST OF NAMES]

Dossier no. 1 du
Centre de sociologie européenne,
6 rue de Tournon, Paris VIe
MED 39–00

SOME INDICATORS FOR A POLICY OF DEMOCRATIZATION*

Any project of technocratic inspiration is marked by the fact that it tends to let the social mechanisms that eliminate disfavoured classes remain in place: *there is no technical choice that is socially neutral,* and in the field of education and culture, laissez-faire is a seemingly *irreproachable* way of favouring those already most favoured.

Any democratic transformation thus presupposes that from primary school on, institutionalized mechanisms are established that can counteract social mechanisms. Knowledge of the latter automatisms makes it possible to define the following principles.

1. Since inequality between children from different milieus fundamentally arises from differences between popular and scholarly language, the languages spoken in different milieus being removed from the latter to a varying degree, teaching must give a *very major* place to *exercises in verbalization,* right from the first years of primary school. Apprenticeship in a complex language is in fact the way in which a general ability to manipulate complex logical structures can be developed.

2. This inequality between children from different milieus also arises from differences in cultural practice, so that *every means must be deployed, right from primary school, to give all children the experiences that children from the favoured classes receive from their family* – or else a substitute for these experiences. This presupposes that teachers are provided with the institutional and material means (and particularly, in secondary education, teachers of history, literature and art education) to offer all children contact with cultural works and other aspects of modern society (organized visits to museums and monuments; geographic and historical trips; organized theatre outings; slide projection, listening to records, etc.).

3. As entry to secondary education is one of the main occasions for eliminating disfavoured classes, a systematic effort must be made to counteract the effect of the mechanisms determining this elimination. [. . .]

---

* Archives of the Collège de France.

– Action of information on establishments (and especially quality hierarchies of establishments, with the educational effects these imply) and on streaming (likewise): this action must bear as a matter of priority on *instituteurs*, who at present have actual responsibility for the orientation of the popular classes, also of course on their families.

– Far greater funding for secondary education grants to disfavoured families.

4. Since inequality between establishments of secondary education is one of the fundamental factors leading to inequality of access to higher education, a systematic effort must be made to reduce differences in quality between these establishments.

The object here is to endow every establishment with a similar proportion of teachers in different fields (whether by bonuses or the like, or quite different procedures), similar cultural equipment, etc. And similarly to set up all the institutional mechanisms needed to counteract the obstacles that habits and the lack of economic resources present to the access of children from the popular classes to quality establishments.

5. As boarding schools in the present state of affairs have a distorting action rather than a positive one, a policy of transforming them is needed. The object would be to create a body of teaching assistants, properly paid and assured of a genuine career, as well as suitably trained, who would give supplementary evening classes rather than be mere guardians, as well as tutorial sessions (with no more than twenty students per supervisor).

6. Extra classes for catching-up and compensation must be established, both in the course of the school year and during vacations, and special facilities provided for children from disfavoured classes so that they can benefit from these: these classes (or directed work) would be designed to help children compensate for their particular weaknesses in one or other subject, at the same time as affording collective preparation for graduation to the next stage of education.

7. A complete recasting of secondary teaching must be undertaken, with the object of giving a preponderant place to the teaching of French (conceived in a very different spirit from that of the humanist tradition) as instrument of expression and also logical instrument for the teaching of both logic and mathematics. The establishment of a common basic curriculum up to sixth-form level would serve to delay as far as possible the choice between 'humanities' and 'science', and enable everyone to acquire both cultures.

8. The traditional teaching of humanities must make way for a genuine teaching of culture that would give every student a historical and ethnological knowledge of Hebrew, Greek and Roman cultures. [. . .]
All archaic pedagogic practices must be abolished: this means as well as the myth of the utility of Latin and Greek, the myth of the utility of grammatical analysis, which is unsuited to the logic of the French language. Reform of spelling would serve to reduce the disadvantage of the most disfavoured (studies have shown that, among children in secondary education, spelling is mastered better by those further up the social hierarchy). A systematic reflection on academic language and on all those subjects known as 'culture' should be undertaken (humanities, French literature, philosophy, etc.)

[. . .]

by assuring, in the faculties themselves, an intensive preparation for this examination in the form of evening classes.
The teaching designed to prepare for this examination (the programmes for which should be redefined as a function of the requirements of teaching) could gradually become a genuine popular evening-class education, by way of an action of methodical information.

15. Everything should be done to bridge the gap between the marginal institutions of ongoing education or cultural distribution (houses of culture, cultural events, etc.) and the institution of the school. The anti-school ideology of the majority of those in charge of these organizations can only be combated if recruitment is profoundly changed and teachers are closely associated with these enterprises at every level. [. . .]

16. Awarding students a grant without any kind of weighting would be a demagogic measure unless it formed part of a systematic and varied policy of support for education (cf. family allowances).

A look back at the reception of
The Inheritors *and* Reproduction in Education*

It seems from this remove that *The Inheritors*, the first book in which I presented the results of my work on education, was a kind of thunderclap in the political sky. The book was very successful. It was read by a whole generation, and had the effect of a revelation even without saying anything very extraordinary: the facts were well enough known by the research community. For a long while already, investigations into the differential elimination of children by their milieu of origin had been available.[12] What was striking, I believe, was that as distinct from works in English, this book drew conclusions, or rather laid bare the mechanisms, at the root of empirical observations. We were not content just to say that the educational system eliminated children from disfavoured classes, but tried to explain why this was the case, and especially what was the responsibility – or rather the contribution, as the word 'responsibility' is already normative – that the educational system, and thus teachers, made to the reproduction of social divisions.

Readers of sociology books spontaneously tend to read in a normative perspective. Their second error is to invest their own interests; contrary to what one might believe, people have a great deal of interest invested in the educational system – teachers in particular. Paradoxically, those with undoubtedly the greatest interests at stake are those whom I call the 'miraculously saved', i.e. those who got where they are through the educational system, parvenus of culture such as the children of *instituteurs*. I said more or less this at the Semaine de la Pensée Marxiste, a week of intellectual discussion that the Communist party, still very powerful at the time, organized every year. Beside me on the platform were Juquin, son of a railway worker, and Cogniot – both university *agrégés*, parvenus of culture, who had invited me but were paralysed with fear by what I was going to say. And evidently I lived up to their expectations, as my principle has always been to say what is hardest for my audience to swallow – the very opposite of demagogy. Instead of making a grand speech, I said that 'those whom the school has

* Extracts from an interview conducted in Tokyo in October 1989 by T. Horio, H. Kato and J.-F. Sabouret, published in *Sekaï*, May 1990, pp. 114–34.
[12] A whole series of studies on these phenomena were launched in the course of the 1950s and '60s: in Britain the Early Living, Crowther, Newson, Robbins and Plowden reports, in the US the Coleman report. In France, various inquiries by the Institut National des Études Démographiques, in particular on the orientation of children in primary school, were undertaken by Alain Girard. [Ed.]

liberated put their faith in the liberating school in the service of the conservative school' . . . (see p. 38) There wasn't a great deal of applause, despite an audience of three to four thousand. The feeling was that I had not been very eloquent, very different from Juquin, who made the kind of grand speech that is customary in such situations, in other words the very opposite of analytical.

This is not just a petty anecdote. It demonstrates one of the most violent reactions there was to what I had published, and it came from rank-and-file members of the Communist party, i.e. the 'miraculously saved', who had two reasons to be angry with me: first of all for saying what they were unconsciously aware of but had repressed; but above all, as intellectuals, analysts and political cadres, for saying what they should have said. This is where they stuck to the Langevin-Wallon report.[13] It was the alpha and omega, the Bible. And no one would budge from it.

If I relate certain things that might seem to belong to ancient history, it is [. . .] because I am trying to convey a certain manner of viewing political discussion on education or any other matter – whether in France or in Japan. With people who take up a position, whether leftist or conservative, on the question of education, it is always necessary to ask what interests they have in the educational system, to what degree their capital is bound up with mobility through this institution, and so on. I believe that, in the intellectual world in the broad sense, relationship to the educational system is one of the major explanatory principles for practices and opinions.

To return to my analysis. At the time I refer to, the ideological foundation in the teaching corps was that of the liberating school: there was a periodical with that name, *L'École Libératrice*, and the Syndicat National des Instituteurs was permeated with it. Pierre Vilar, for example, a very important Marxist historian, publicly reproached me for having written what I did in *The Inheritors*. For those whom I call the 'miraculously saved', there is something scandalous about displaying the social determinants of educational success. Among other reasons, because this removes all their merit. A good number of these people became ultra-conservative during and after the student movement. They moved from the classical left, the Communist party in particular, to the classical right, sometimes even to the far right. The student movement was a real trauma for them, destroying their idea of themselves. Against them, the student movement

---

[13] The commission on problems of teaching, set up after the Liberation, was chaired first by Paul Langevin and then by Henri Wallon, both professors at the Collège de France. It had a number of Communist members, and championed the organization of education according to the 'principle of justice' and meritocracy. [Ed.]

developed the idea that students were a class, and described the relationship between students and professors as a class struggle. Professors who came from the popular or middle classes, all good pupils who had succeeded by their 'merit', found themselves overtaken on the left by students who appeared to them as failures of bourgeois origin. The students also had a mystified representation of their condition. They were unwilling to see the differences that divided them. For example, the national student union undertook an inquiry that ignored the variable of parental occupation. The big problem was the 'economic independence' of students, and responses were analyzed as a function of residence (with parents or elsewhere). Here again, a sociologist can upset many received ideas, demonstrating that there are social differences among students and shattering the idea of students as a class.

Later on there was my book *Reproduction in Education*. And the word 'reproduction' had a catastrophic effect. On the one hand it contributed to the success of a certain 'paradigm', especially in the United States, according to which the educational system contributes to reproducing the social structure, but at the same time it blocked a proper reading of the book. Literary history well shows how very often what is common to the intellectual life of an era is not the actual content of books but rather their titles. In the 1880s, for example, everything was 'saturnine': poems, poets, etc. It was the same in the 1970s with 'reproduction'. The word was topical, but people didn't read the book, just said (sociologists above all): 'Bourdieu says that the educational system reproduces classes.' And as they read it in a normative perspective, the implication was: 'He says that's a good thing, so he's conservative.' (I think that Alain Touraine read *Reproduction in Education* in this sense, and still today he ascribes to me a mechanistic and pessimistic view, which doesn't take the effervescence of the social world into account.) The same was true of Antoine Prost. Others read it the other way round: 'Bourdieu says that the school reproduces, and that's bad.' In this case, two things came into play: the title, but also the epigraph. I amused myself by quoting a poem by Robert Desnos, 'Jonathan's Pelican', the pelican that lays an egg, from which comes another pelican, and so on, as long as no one makes an omelette. Then people said: 'Bourdieu says that we need a revolution.'

A whole series of people were disturbed by the publication of this book. Those most upset, of course, were my sociological colleagues, especially those who saw themselves on the left, people who were supposed to be doing sociology of education and were members of the Communist party or close to it, such as M. Snyders (just to give one name), or Mme Isambert, or a progressive Catholic such as M. Prost, who had started working on the history of education after reading *The Inheritors* – which did not prevent him from being unjust, quite the opposite. They set up a kind of 'cordon sanitaire'. And they attacked from all directions, saying all kinds of things.

Prost's article is interesting in this respect, in that he both reproaches me for my despair about the republican *instituteur*, and claims an affinity with Ivan Ilitch. He resorts to a strategy that is used very often in politics to shake off a message from the left that genuinely raises real and disturbing difficulties and problems: a position is radicalized to the point of absurdity – the school conserves, so it must be suppressed. This is an idiotic idea, unrealistic and unrealizable. It is not even utopianism, simply a form of stupid nihilism. Prost was certainly aware despite himself that *Reproduction in Education* was a progressive book – and this was precisely why he found it disturbing. So he neutralized the unease that the book provoked in him by seemingly going still further, though in reality he remained behind . . . This is a well-known phenomenon, ultra-leftism often being a form of conservatism. At the same time, there were many attacks from the direction of the Communist party, in various magazines. I did not read them, but some of my students working on the history of the Communist party have told me that I was the French intellectual most attacked by the party – a fact that at first sight seemed quite astonishing.

This is what I call the 'cordon sanitaire', this whole work to cancel the effects of the message. It is a very well-known phenomenon, as the sociology of prophecy shows. I do not mean that the message of *Reproduction in Education* was prophetic in any strict sense, but like prophecy, it put forward a truth that overturned mental structures and changed people's view of the world. Previously, the educational system appeared as a place where people went in order to learn universal and progressive things. Then came a message that overturned received ideas and showed how the educational system had conservative effects. This message had to be neutralized. The phenomenon has been studied in many societies: the caste of priests appear and say that nothing has happened.

Twenty years later, the whole world agrees in recognizing the fact of reproduction through education as self-evident. This is heard on television, and yet the defence system (in the Freudian sense) is still in place. Among recent forms of defence mechanism, there is that which amounts to saying: 'That's the way it is, you can't do anything about it.' Today this is said on a massive scale. Everyone agrees that in France the educational system serves social reproduction. But they act as if this were a fact of nature. You can't change the law of gravity! The paradox I have to recall is that it's precisely the law of gravity that enables us to fly: this is what I always said, from *The Inheritors* onwards, particularly in the conclusion on 'rational pedagogy', which some people saw as reformist. It is by knowing the laws of reproduction that we can have a chance, however small, of minimizing the reproductive effect of the educational institution.

1971–1980

When social positions are identified with 'names', scientific criticism must sometimes take the form of an ad hominem critique. Social science denotes individuals only in so far as they are the personification of positions: it does not aim to impose a new form of terrorism, but to make all forms of terrorism more difficult.

3

Against the Science of Political Dispossession

Speech is always a reprise of the speech of others, or rather of their silence.

Homo Academicus, 1984

At Arras in 1971, Pierre Bourdieu gave a lecture with the title 'Public Opinion Does Not Exist', printed two years later in Les Temps Modernes.[1] *This text was innovating in many ways: the critique it made of opinion polls and their use was directed both at researchers conducting these and at policies that made them an authoritative argument.*[2] *Taking 'don't knows' into account in such polls raises the problem of the competence needed to speak of politics, and the dispossession experienced by those who leave it to mandated delegates to represent their political speech (see pp.61 and 64). The first to be surprised by this critique were political scientists, who initially accepted its principle as a methodological basis, before reacting, as one of them did ten years later, to its political foundations: 'In the attack made against opinion polls in the name of democracy, I am firmly on the defensive side. This no doubt has to do with my conception of democracy, which is incurably liberal . . . This is a conception that rests on my faith in universal suffrage . . . The basis of criticism made against opinion polls could equally be used against universal suffrage . . . In both cases, the "silent majority" are challenged in the name of minorities who alone know "what it means to speak".'*[3]

For Bourdieu, to criticize the uses that political scientists made of 'public opinion' also meant defending the autonomy of sociology at a time when researchers often found themselves subject to political and administrative demands, increasingly dominated by a pole of applied research whose chief representative in the 1970s was Jean Stoetzel. A professor at Paris I (where he taught social psychology), he was also director of the Centre d'Études Sociologiques and the Institut Français

---

[1] 'L'opinion publique n'existe pas', in *Les Temps Modernes* 318, January 1973, translated in *Sociology in Question* (London: Sage 1993). [Ed.]

[2] These critiques are repeated from different angles in *Distinction* (Cambridge: Polity 1979) and *Language and Symbolic Power* (Cambridge: Polity 1991). [Ed.]

[3] Alain Lancelot, *Opinion publique*, (Paris 1982); for more details on this polemic, see Pierre Bourdieu, 'Le sondage: une science sans savants', in *Choses dites* (Paris: Minuit 1987), pp. 217–24. [Ed.]

d'Opinion Publique (IFOP), developing the technique of opinion polls that was imported from the United States; he controlled access to both the Centre National de la Recherche Scientifique (CNRS) and the Revue Française de Sociologie, *one of the four major journals in the social sciences at this time.*[4]

As for the political foundations of this critique, Bourdieu formulated the terms of these in a lecture given before the Association Française des Sciences Politiques in November 1973, in which he took up a distinction that Durkheim had made between suffrage resulting from the mere addition of individual votes and suffrage expressing 'something collective'. The question was to understand that 'the essential principle of dispossession, and the most concealed, resides in the aggregation of opinions'. Attention has to be focused on the relationship between opinion and the mode of existence of the social group – which explains the importance of new forms of political demonstration (sit-ins, boycotts, etc.) in which the groups mobilized resist being dispossessed of speech. It is for these reasons that, from this period on, Bourdieu saw the necessity of an alliance between researchers and activists: by unveiling the hidden wellsprings of domination, scientific analysis was capable of becoming an instrument of emancipation in the service of the social movement.

Liberal philosophy identifies political action with solitary action, even silent and secret action, its paradigm being the vote 'acquired' by a party in the secret of the polling booth. In this way, by reducing group to series, the mobilized opinion of an organized or solidaristic collective is reduced to a statistical aggregation of individually expressed opinions. We can consider Milton Friedman's utopia, which proposes, as a way of taking account of the different points of view that families have in relation to schooling, distributing vouchers that would enable people to buy educational services supplied by competitive businesses. [. . .] Political action is thus reduced to a kind of economic action. The logic of the market or of the vote, in other words the aggregation of individual strategies, imposes itself each time that groups are reduced to the state of aggregates – or, if you prefer, demobilized. When, in effect, a group is reduced to impotence (or to individual strategies of subversion, sabotage, wastefulness, go-slows, isolated protest, absenteeism, etc.), because it lacks power over itself, the common problem of each of its members remains in a state of unease and cannot be expressed as a political problem. [. . .] The political question is to know how to dominate the instruments that had to be applied in order to overcome the anarchy

---

[4] Cf. *Science of Society and Reflexivity*, 2004; Also Johan Heilbron, 'Pionnier par Défaut? . . .', *Revue Française de Sociologie*, 1991, xxxii-3, pp. 365–80; Loïc Blondiaux, 'Comment rompre avec Durkheim . . .', *Revue Française de Sociologie*, 1991, xxxii-3, pp. 411–42. [Ed.]

of individual strategies and produce a concerted action. How the group can control the opinion expressed by its representative, who speaks in the name of the group and on its account, but also in its place. [. . .] The atomistic and aggregative mode of production dear to liberal opinion is favourable to the dominant, who have an interest in laissez-faire and can happily content themselves with individual strategies (of reproduction) because the social order, the structure, plays in their favour. For the dominated, on the contrary, individual strategies, grumbling, go-slows, etc. and all other forms of the daily class struggle are not very effective. The only effective strategies here are collective ones, which presuppose strategies of construction of collective opinion and its expression.[5]

The intellectual legitimacy that opinion polling, a 'science without scientists', lends the mechanisms of domination, formed the basis of Bourdieu's critique of 'doxosophists', those professionals of opinion manufacture who produce an ideology that conforms to the interests of the dominant (see p. 60). In his view, therefore, political criticism must be accompanied by a sociology of intellectuals, used as a symbolic weapon against the pseudo-scholarly justifications of the social order (see p. 64). An undertaking which inevitably meets with resistance, as evidenced by the constancy of the arguments advanced (particularly on the theme of determinism) in the polemic between Bourdieu and certain Marxist intellectuals (in La Nouvelle Critique*) and left Christians (in* Esprit*) (see p. 79).*

---

[5] 'Formes d'action politique et mode d'existence des groupes' (1973), in *Propos sur le champ politique*, op. cit. [Ed.]

The doxosophists*

I say, then, that to form an opinion (*doxazein*) is to speak (*legein*), and opinion (*doxa*) is a word spoken (*logon eirèmenon*).

Plato, *Thaetetus*, 190a

The whole of 'political science' has never been anything but a certain way of presenting the ruling class and its political personnel with its spontaneous science of politics, endowed with the external appearance of science. The references to canonic authors, Montesquieu, Pareto or Toqueville, the quasi-juridical use of the most recent history, that learned from a religious reading of the daily papers only of use for conceiving each event in the logic of the one before – the ostentatious neutrality of tone, style and statement, the supposedly technical vocabulary, are all signs designed to make politics part of the order of decent objects of conversation, and suggest a detachment which is both academic and worldly on the part of the enlightened commentator, or else to display, in a kind of parade of objectivity, the effort of the impartial observer to keep an equal distance from all extremes and all extremisms, which are both indecent and pointless.

'Political science' as it is taught at the Institut d'Études Politiques should not have survived the appearance of modern techniques of sociological investigation. But that is to leave out of account a subordination to commission that, combined with positivist submission to the raw material, is supposed to exclude all questions and questioning that are contrary to political good manners, reducing simply to the anticipated registration of votes a science of public opinion that is thus in perfect conformity with the public opinion of science.

This 'political-sciencing' is one of the most effective techniques of depoliticization. [. . .] It is a weapon of struggle between forces of depoliticization and forces of politicization, forces of subversion of the existing order and of adherence to this order: whether this is the unconscious adherence that defines doxa or the deliberate adherence characteristic of orthodoxy, right opinion or belief – in this case, that of the political right.

---

* Published in *Minuit* 1, 1972, pp. 26–45; extract from the conclusion.

Public opinion*

What began to be known as 'public opinion' in eighteenth-century France was the public expression of the personal opinions of a limited though significant fraction of the population who, with the weight of their economic capital, and above all their cultural capital, claimed to exercise power and sought to influence political authorities by writings and especially the press. During the nineteenth century, the democratic vision that saw the 'will of the people' as the sole source of political legitimacy transmuted the publicly vaunted opinions of 'social elites' into opinions of the people; the representative political system led members of the 'social elite', constituted as elected representatives, to consider themselves the natural spokesmen of 'the people', and to see the opinions they championed not as the narrow and limited expression of class interests or those of a particular group, but rather the universal revelation of the general interest and common good.

It is only very recently, however, in connection with the appearance of new techniques invented by the social sciences, such as opinion polls, closed questionnaires, automatic and rapid processing of results by computer, that the notion of public opinion has in some sense found its full realization, even if the existence of its objective reference remains always uncertain. This technology, one must admit, has everything needed to give the notion of public opinion a foundation that is both 'democratic', since everyone is questioned, and 'scientific', since the opinions of all are methodically gathered and counted. Used first of all in politics, in the electoral arena, with a view to ascertaining the voting intentions of electors before the polls, it has been able to supply data that are both spectacular in their predictive power and scientifically unquestionable, their precision and reliability being verified by the election itself. These pre-election polls, in fact, do not really ascertain 'opinions' in the proper sense of the term, but rather behavioural intentions, and moreover in a field, that of politics, in which the investigative situation reproduces in a fairly precise manner the situation created by the electoral consultation. It is quite a different matter when, at the request of political authorities, and more recently of major press organs, polling companies conduct surveys aiming to determine 'public opinion', understood as majority opinion on problems that are extremely varied and sometimes highly complex

* Co-authored with Patrick Champagne, and published in Youri Afanassiev and Marc Ferro, eds, *50 idées qui ébranlèrent le monde* (Paris: Payot 1989)

– such as questions of foreign or economic policy – on which most of the individuals questioned have no established judgement and do not even consider the question until it is presented to them. Though 'don't knows' form a distinct minority, owing particularly to the technique of pre-coded and closed questions, those that explicitly declare themselves as such, and their non-random distribution by sex, level of education and social category, are a sufficient reminder that the probability of having an opinion is very unevenly distributed. Failure to take this fact seriously means that the opinion poll institutes, far from confining themselves to collecting pre-existing opinions, in fact completely produce, in many cases, a 'public opinion' that is actually a pure *artefact*, obtained by recording and statistically aggregating reactions of approval or rejection of opinions already formulated, often in uncertain or ambiguous terms, which their inquiries present to representative samples of the population of voting age. *Publication* of these results by 'journals of opinion' – very often those who commissioned the production – is thus in many cases a political 'coup' endowed in all appearance with the legitimacy of science and democracy, through which a public or private pressure group, with the economic resources to cover the costs of such an inquiry, can give its particular opinion the semblance of universality that is associated with the idea of 'public opinion'.

The widespread practice of opinion polls has profoundly changed the operation of the political game: politicians now have to reckon with this new agency, largely controlled by political scientists, which is supposed to say – better than the 'representatives of the people' – 'what the people want and think'. Opinion poll institutes now intervene at every level of political life; they conduct confidential soundings for the political parties in order to determine, in a logic of marketing, those themes in the coming election campaign that will be particularly weighty, or even those candidates who are easiest to promote. They are also at the heart of the majority of broadcasts that the mainstream media devote to politics, tending to transform television viewers into arbiters of the 'qualities' of political figures; the national press constantly commission polls on current political subjects and publish their results. To the extent that an increasing number of apparently scientific mechanisms claim to measure the influence that the communications policies of the main political leaders can exert on 'public opinion', we see a redefinition of what is called 'politics'. Political action increasingly appears as the art of using a set of techniques developed by specialists in 'political communication' to 'shift public opinion' – i.e. the more or less artificial distributions produced by opinion poll companies on the basis of the individual and private responses that they 'collect' in an artificial situation from a population who remain for the great majority only poorly informed of the subtleties of the political game. In every case, therefore, an opinion survey produces the same effects, i.e. to make appear as resolved, by the combined forces of imposition of the problematic and aggregation of isolated responses, one of the major problems of political action, which is that of *constituting* as such both individual opinion and what can be particularly presented as a collective opinion by way of delegation.

Intellectuals and social struggle[*]

MICHEL SIMON: I believe this discussion is first of all an occasion for us to mark the importance of Pierre Bourdieu's research. The first result of this – just to speak of the most well-known part of his findings – is to have helped not simply to measure better the exclusion of the mass of the people from access to cultural goods, but to understand better the procedures, often very subtle, by which this exclusion is effected. This is a new step in the critique of the illusions of formal equality, and a very important one.

From this point of view, study of education assumes all the more importance in that, taking account of the ongoing development in the social division of labour (increase in the wage-earning classes and decline of small proprietors), the school occupies a still more determining place in the reproduction of class structures than it did in the relatively recent past. To show the specific role of cultural factors in the origin of inequalities, and their internalization by children and families of the popular classes in such a way that they blame themselves for their fate, their lack of ability, etc., amounts to a very fertile innovation – which in no way means denying, as Bourdieu has indeed recently stressed, the weight of economic factors. I particularly have in mind his article 'Avenir de classe et causalité du probable', published in the *Revue Française de Sociologie* in 1974.

The second point is a corollary of the first, and especially touches us as intellectuals (and teachers): this is the often unconscious role that the various bodies of specialists in the production and transmission of cultural goods play in these processes of exclusion; here again, the case of the school is typical, though not exclusive. And this leads on to a third problem: that of the position of intellectuals in the field of class struggle, and that of their alliance with the working class. I will not elaborate here on the analysis which, to my mind, is the basis for the necessity and possibility of this alliance: this would mean summarizing everything that we believe we have established about class relations in the conditions of state monopoly capitalism. But a detailed analysis is required, and one that is in no way complacent.

[*] A discussion published under the title 'Les intellectuels dans le champ de la lutte des classes' in *La Nouvelle Critique* 87, 1975, pp. 20–6. ('As an interrogation of the paths trodden by the sociologist today, this discussion between Pierre Bourdieu, Antoine Casanova and Michel Simon is not simply a "confrontation". It is rather, for each participant, the occasion to assert, and still more to refine, his positions on a question that is essential today: the alliance between intellectuals and the working class.')

Without the assistance of a sociology of the different sectors of the intel-ligentsia, that can explain the effects produced on this knowledge itself, its distribution etc., the position and conditions of the different agents involved, it would be extremely hard to establish this alliance with any clarity. But it is essential for Communists, who – to paraphrase Lenin – must look at every question from the standpoint of the oppressed masses. This means the quite irreplaceable character of that work, those procedures, modes of ques-tioning and pathways that are specific to sociology, especially in a field where analysis also involves self-analysis.

PIERRE BOURDIEU: My intention was to make more fully explicit certain subtle mechanisms that have been known in principle for a very long time. For example, we can say that there is an effect of domination that is exercised by the mediation of culture, but so long as we have not analyzed these mechanisms, and the part played in their operation by agents who in appear-ance are completely disinterested, we are always prey to their resurgence. 'Bodies', whether these are bodies of priests or bodies of professors, all have their specific interests. And what interests me most is the elaboration of this notion of interest.

I think in fact that the majority of misunderstandings in the represen-tation that intellectuals have and give of themselves rests on the fact that we have an impoverished and economistic definition of interest. The majority of things that we call 'disinterested' – in the sense that we say of a mathematician that his research is 'disinterested' – are in actual fact interested, but in terms of a fuller definition of interest. I have tried to grasp the specific logic of such professional bodies, to see how they give rise to stakes and interests that clearly are less reducible to material interests in the crude sense of the term in those spheres that are more autonomous, where so-called 'disinterested' strategies can actually be the most inter-esting, where interest can only be satisfied on condition of being disinterested (for example pure art, art for art's sake). I have tried to analyze the processes by which specific interests are generated, interests that are often censured and euphemistic forms of interest in the primary sense of the term, for example of economic interest.

In order to take full account of these processes that are understood in their general configuration, we have to advance to almost idiographic analyses of the specific logic of each particular field: for example, in the university system, we cannot stick to the level of humanities, but must study a particular discipline and characterize its position in the structure of disciplines. It is only on condition of grasping these logics in all their subtlety that we can see the infinite complexity of the mediations by which these mechanisms are accomplished, which we previously thought to have grasped already by denoting them in a global fashion.

MICHEL SIMON: It should be said, in a general sense, that bringing to light what was previously not perceived often has a fundamental importance. To take the case of education, it is at one and the same time a highly segregating filter and an instance of the imposition of the norms of the dominant class (even if it is not just or totally this). And it is so both by its explicit contents and by the implicit procedures that range from the occupation of space to the employment of time and the individualization of performance, these being all the more unperceived by the agents involved in so far as they have themselves been formed in similar conditions. This is obvious enough for example with the colonialist contents of certain history books, but there are many other aspects besides this.

This means that study of the educational system was perhaps a necessary step for you, and that at root the real object of your investigation is the problem of what is meant by the domination of the dominant class and its means of domination – a theme that is a common concern for many of us.

PIERRE BOURDIEU: Indeed. One of the things that interests me at the present time is the often hidden relationship between systems of classification, whether educational or other – for example, all the forms of taxonomy with a social function, those used to class art objects, those used to class students at school, such as classification by discipline – and the structure of social classes; in other words, I'm interested in relations between classes and classification, in which the educational system functions as a system of classification as well as a system of production of classifications, which in the final analysis are always referable to social classes, but in a more or less concealed fashion.

To give one example, I discovered a quite astonishing document: the files that a professor in a preparatory class for a *grande école* kept on his students, in which he wrote down their marks, his appreciation of them, and their social origin. By a simple graph I was able to show the relationship that came into being between social class origin, the system of classification, i.e. the adjectives used to denote the performance of the student in question, and their marks. We have here a kind of 'ideological machine'. An ideological machine in the strict sense, with the entry of people marked by their social origin (even though they were over-selected), a professor who had himself been classed by the system of classification that he went on to apply, in a way that was all the more insidious in that he had never consciously formulated it (we have all marked essays, and put comments such as 'heavy', 'plodding', 'clumsy', 'vulgar', etc. when we are unsure what to say). This professor applied a grid that was neutral in appearance, so much so that when he wrote 'subtle', he didn't really think he was judging a *grande bourgeoise*, and when he wrote 'servile', he was quite unaware that he had in mind a cleaning woman's daughter.

In other words, the system of euphemistic classification has the function of establishing a connection between class and marks, but precisely by denying such a connection – by denegating it, in the psychoanalytic sense. We thus see how it is possible, in perfectly good faith, to continue perfectly operating an ideology that one verbally condemns, because this ideology presents itself not in the form of a discourse to be approved or disapproved, but rather that of quite unconscious mechanisms. These classifications internalized in a euphemistic form enable professors to think in a class language without bad faith.

Basically, all I have done is take seriously Durkheim's idea, in a Marxian transposition, that logical classes are social classes: the entire system of adjectives used to judge a work of art, a literary essay, a person, etc., has a social connotation. I have thus tried to give a 'sociological' critique of the judgement of taste. The majority of such judgements that we bring to bear use this socially marked system of classification, with greater or lesser degrees of euphemism (the closer one gets to specialized fields, philosophy for example, the greater the degree of euphemism). Thanks to the obscuring effect of the system (forbidden words are inserted into a network of relationships, so they are no longer visible), the language of such relatively autonomous bodies as philosophy, religion, etc. can speak in the most decent fashion of the most indecent things, without anyone thinking badly of it.

Whereas mythology is the collective product of an entire group, of the same order as language (although even in the most primitive societies there is always the beginning of a division of religious labour), ideology is the product of a field of specialized producers. In order to understand ideological production, it is not sufficient to relate the product to a social requirement; it has also to be related to the social conditions in which the producers have developed this product. This leads to introducing into the explanation of the properties of this production the specific interests of the producers (as explicitly in the work of Weber, which helped me a great deal here, in the case of religion). I think that analysis of ideologies presupposes analysis of the interests that their producers have in producing them. And this is why I became interested in the various fields of religion, art and intellectual production, trying to discover, via homologies of structure, properties that remain unseen as long as one works directly on the intellectual field, precisely because we are ourselves part of this, and a certain number of objectifications of interests are not always easy to carry out. [. . .]

MICHEL SIMON: As regards the class situation of intellectuals, empirical study is irreplaceable. Certainly, as far as we are concerned, we locate this study within an overall theory (itself empirically based) of the capitalist social formation at its present stage. But it is precisely here that things have to be pinned down more closely, and by doing this we rediscover questions that are at the source of your own research, particularly on the present functions of higher education, the system of the *grandes écoles*. [. . .] A fraction of the graduates of the *grandes écoles* move into the genuinely dominant class, i.e. the financial oligarchy, and are integrated into it: there are phenomena here of renewal (or rather, violent struggle), even of osmosis, which we still do not understand well. But this does not attenuate the fact that at the other pole, an antagonism is asserted between the truly dominant class and its 'retinue' of trained assistants, on the one hand, and on the other the immense majority of intellectuals, including graduates of the *grandes écoles*. [. . .]

PIERRE BOURDIEU: Struggles within a relatively autonomous field (the church, the school, etc.) may, thanks to this homology, take the appearance of external struggles; the basic strategy, which has long been described, consists in universalizing particular interests: those dominated in a field such as this (the lower clergy, for example), by virtue of this homology, have an interest in asserting their unity of interest with those occupying the dominated position in the ultimate field which is that of class struggle. In the same way, those dominant in the university field, for example, can count on the unconditional support of members of the ruling fractions of the dominant class, as in the defence of Latin and Greek, or of traditional spelling.

It is on the basis of these homologies, which always give rise to terrible misunderstandings, that a heap of confused alliances are made. I think that the alliance between intellectuals and proletariat is at permanent risk of owing something of its properties to this mechanism. The sociology of intellectuals is certainly the weakest point in the whole of sociology, and for good reason: in this case the intellectuals are both judge and object. [. . .]

ANTOINE CASANOVA: One final question: that of the relationship between the most rigorous possible scientific work and political and social struggles, a relationship that exists in both directions. The scientific approach excludes both false neutrality and confined obedience to any immediate political instruction.

PIERRE BOURDIEU: Yes, I would like to make a strong distinction between a critique that is 'decisionist', arbitrary, and the kind of critique implicit in the very logic of research because it is the condition for the construction of its object, because research forces the accepted self-evidence to be turned upside down. Positivism is a political theory to the extent that it registers the data that it itself constructs.

In the same way, a current that is making a big noise in sociology in the United States at this time, so-called 'ethno-methodology', has the object, among other things, of describing the naive experience of the social world, the experience of the social world that goes without saying. This can be very interesting, on condition that one knows what one is doing and does not present this science of the lived experience of the social world as the science of the social world as such. Criticism is part of scientific practice. Pre-constructed objects, i.e. things that offer themselves ready-made to science, 'social cases' (delinquency, criminality, prisons, etc.) are often poor objects of sociology if they are taken as given. It is only by being scientific, in other words by revealing the hidden (as Bachelard said, 'the only science is of what is hidden') that sociology has a critical effect.

Giving voice to the voiceless*

Is it true that in France today the message of politics does not get across, or only poorly?

Paradoxically, we find in the field of politics and public affairs a division analogous to that observable in matters of art and literature; it's just that it is better concealed. People accept without thinking – in politics as elsewhere – the division between the competent and the incompetent, amateurs and professionals: politicians of course, but also journalists and a wider category of intellectuals, who have a de facto monopoly on the production of political discourse, on political problems. I believe it is necessary to raise and constantly keep raising the problem of the legitimacy of the delegation and dispossession that this presupposes and brings about.

So the language of politics is elitist, a language of initiates?

Just as there is a world of art, so there is a world of politics, with its own specific logic and history, i.e. relatively autonomous; and by the same token with its own problems, its own language and its specific interests. This is what I call a field, in other words a kind of space of play. To enter into the game, you have to know the rules, dispose of a certain language and a certain culture. Above all, you have to feel that you have a right to play. This sense of a right to speak, however, is in fact very unevenly distributed. As shown by the analysis of 'don't knows' to the questions asked by opinion polls (or again by the social composition of party apparatuses), it is more common among men than women, among the more educated than the less educated, among the urban than the rural population, and so on.

Isn't what you say about politicians also true of intellectuals, or certain categories of intellectuals – for instance, at the present time, those known as the 'nouveaux philosophes'?

All intellectuals share this monopoly of speech. But it is possible for them to use it to try (I deliberately say 'try') to give voice to the voiceless – and

---

* Interview with Pierre Viansson-Ponté, published under the titles 'Le droit à la parole' and 'La culture pour qui et pourquoi?' in *Le Monde* on 11 and 12 October 1977.

there are certain sociologists who make this their business. This opens them somewhat to the suspicion of vulgarity in the eyes of other intellectuals.

As far as the '*nouveaux philosophes*' are concerned, I think they have found a way of saving the face of the old-style intellectual that suits today's fashion. In point of fact, intellectuals today are faced with a challenge that is certainly unprecedented: the ruling fraction, in order to legitimize itself, appeals to its competence, even its science: it prides itself on its 'intelligence'. It's not just the university that has its 'mandarins': the technocrat, like the Chinese mandarin, owes his authority to competitive examinations, and to the competence these are supposed to guarantee. This gives rise to an aspect that is both triumphalist and a little puerile: he governs, deaf and blind, with his eyes fixed on economics textbooks – sometimes even those he has written himself. His whole political philosophy is contained in his representation of economic information: information that lay people have to possess in order to comprehend, and thus accept, the economic decisions of the professionals. These are the adversaries with whom old-style intellectuals, and philosophers above all, have to dispute the monopoly of production and representation of the social world.

In sum, the intellectual in the old sense of someone who knew, who had culture, who held the keys of knowledge or at least was assumed to do so, is in the process of being replaced by a practical intellectual, closer to life, who has to develop a new kind of dominant philosophy?

Yes, the old intellectuals also have to take into account this new variety of intellectual – experts, service intellectuals, masters of action rather than of thought, who claim to possess a 'political science', the science of politics. In place of the entrenched opposition between 'artist' (or 'intellectual') and 'bourgeois', today we have a continuum which ranges from corporate presidents – statistics show that these have ever more in the way of formal qualifications – and top civil servants through to the so-called 'free intellectuals', by way of experts, researchers in the public or private sector, who depend on public or private contracts for their material existence. This is how what are called pure intellectuals find themselves relegated to the grand moral prophecy that is characteristic of the age of the mass media. They give a representation of the great moral figure of the intellectual that is often derisory – and always rather exasperating.

Mandarin or prophet, are there no other options? Sociologists are often ascribed a pessimistic reputation. Do you think there is nothing for them to do but accept what is?

It would be easy for me to reply that knowledge of sociological regularities (what right-wing political figures hasten to call 'sociological inertia' to justify their inaction or impotence) is the condition of success for any action that aims to transform these. To know the probability of a phenomenon is to increase the chances of success of an action that aims to prevent it.

But this is not enough. Many social 'mechanisms' owe a large part of their effectiveness to the fact that they are misunderstood. This is the case for example with those 'mechanisms' that tend to eliminate from the school system children from the most economically and culturally deprived families. We observe, however, that these families believe (with some nuances) that personal gifts and merit, rather than environment, are solely responsible for educational success, and all the more so, the more culturally deprived they are, and thus more directly victims of these environmental effects.

We see right away how a science that reveals and unmasks can have a major impact by itself. On condition, to be sure, that its effects are known by those who have the greatest interest in knowing them. But what is called pessimism on my part – which is simply a sense of realities – shows its strength here: distribution of the findings of science obeys the law of any cultural transmission, and knowledge of the effects of cultural dispossession is all the more unlikely among those who are culturally most dispossessed.

Does this recognition of laws not have political effects?

Yes, of course. Economic and social hierarchies owe a large part of their legitimacy, in other words the recognition that is granted them both consciously and above all unconsciously, to the fact that they appear based on educational inequalities alone, i.e. on inequalities of gift and merit.

In other words, a revealing discourse does have a specifically political effectiveness?

I believe that, for a series of historical reasons, we tend to underestimate the effectiveness of that symbolic power which is a dimension of any kind of power. All political minds are haunted by economism, and this leads to a kind of fatalism, dispossessing groups of the legitimate ambition of taking control of themselves as groups. I believe that politics would be completely different, and political action would have a completely different effectiveness, if everyone were convinced that it was up to them to take their political affairs in hand, that no one was more competent than they were to manage their own interests. This would need a competition in the political field that forced politicians to authorize and promote forms of organization and expression (enterprise committees, district assemblies, community assemblies rather than municipal councils), enabling citizens, all citizens, to genuinely contribute to the production of political discourse and action.

Everything should be done to enable everyone to feel that political matters are their business, to recognize themselves in this field, as we say, to find their own problems, all their problems, in it: not just power over firms, but also social relations within the firm; not just motorways, but also traffic accidents, and so on. For example, when people speak of class struggle, they *never* think of the class struggle in everyday life, the contempt, arrogance and crushing ostentation (about children and their successes, or holidays and cars), the wounding indifference and injury, etc. Social misery and resentment – the saddest of social passions – arise from these everyday struggles, in which the issue at stake is dignity, self-esteem. If life is to be changed, this must also include those little things that people's lives are made up of, and which are presently abandoned to private initiative or the preaching of moralists.

It almost seems as if you are between two stools here: on the one hand you denounce economism, on the other you are well aware that economic realities govern people's lives.

Well of course, economism at least has the virtue of a warning against 'funny money', those who pay in words. And there is a conservative use of symbolic strategies. Governments – and our own in particular – are very adept at paying in funny money. But it is possible to conceive a demystifying and liberating use of symbolic power. There is a whole aspect of social reality that economism, and the conviction that the only serious measures are those bearing on economic realities, make people forget. All my work leads me to believe that we underestimate the power, the actual political power, for changing social life by changing the representation of the social world; by giving imagination a bit of power.

In other words, a science of cultural and symbolic capital is designed to provide resources for combating economism and the abusive uses of the symbolic.

Yes. Economism leads to partial revolutions, or failed ones. Stalinism, which still looms on the horizon of so much discourse on the social world, is also a kind of scientific utopianism, based on a pathological faith in the powers of social science, or, more precisely, of a social science that is still at its initial stage and reduced to its simplest expression, to the state of slogans and instructions. One of the lessons of social science is that of the limits of any action oriented by social theory alone. Scientism always bears the potentiality of terrorism. Social science has learned its limitations by its very progress.

You believe then that there is at present a complete separation between political parties – all parties – and the masses?

To put it simply, i.e. by simplifying a lot, we could say that in the present state of the political division of labour, those who are most deprived, economically and culturally, can only turn to parties for the formulation of their demands; which means that the parties tend to be responsible for both supply and demand.

To close the subject of politics, before turning to culture, do you think that future development will go in the direction of a simplification of discourse, a better communication, or that the misunderstanding and difficulties that you note risk getting worse?

Sad to say, I do not see many signs of a change in the style of political life. Any system of language functions both as a means of expression and a means of censorship. Paradoxically, though language is what enables people to say what they have to say, it also prevents saying and thinking a whole series of things that other styles might permit. Televised debate, for example, which could be an instrument of democracy – it appeals directly to 'the people', and displays things that certain might prefer to keep hidden – can be constantly censored by the fact that a certain kind of freedom of language or dress is not acceptable. There is a collar-and-tie style which means that certain people cannot speak or cannot be spoken about. I read in a very 'highbrow' daily paper: 'Marchais will be excellent when he no longer makes errors in French.' Giving power to imagination can also mean painting the dictionary red.

Is this what you have called 'linguistic fetishism'?

We are familiar with the language of apparatuses and apparatchiks, mechanical and stereotyped language, which is a form of censorship because it deprives what it expresses of reality. Being *outspoken* – an excellent expression – should be reintroduced into politics.

Is the political philosophy of politicians betrayed in their language?

Yes. It is present in their relationship to language, in their hyper-correctness or verbal pomp; it is present in their words, and thus in their brains. In politics as elsewhere, there are no innocent words. By speaking constantly of 'summits' and 'meetings at the highest level', we end up believing and making believe that politics, political solutions, political agreements, only exist at these high levels frequented by sovereign spirits. What would happen if these 'summits' launched an appeal for ordinary people to seek and find a good agreement?

The fact that this idea immediately seems utopian is already interesting. Changing life also means the small step of changing ways of talking about and conceiving life. I believe in fact that social classes, social hierarchies, always have a double existence, in reality and in the mind. And it is likely that if they ceased existing in reality, they would still return to life, because people would continue to project them onto reality, into reality, as long as they haunted their brains. [. . .]

Without at all wanting to authorize a sociologism that describes what exists as inevitable or necessary – in the double sense –, sociological knowledge does not lead either to utopianism.

What statistical observation registers is the resultant of a heap of individual strategies, which, even if they are not lived as such, are all strategies of investment: choice of school and holiday where the student can improve language skills, etc. All these individual choices, aggregated and summed up, end up expressed in the statistical regularities attached to each social class.

In fact, sociologists are often viewed as clandestine conductors of social reality, as slightly demonic architects who promote or prevent developments.

That is a terrible overestimation of the power of sociologists, but the image does have a sociological foundation. In fact, the legitimate representation of the social world is an issue at stake in social struggles, and to try to impose a vision of the social world means asserting a claim to exert a form of power over this world. In this sense, sociology could be a way of doing politics by other means. This power, that of intellectuals and party leaders for example, is particularly visible in situations that are confused and undecidable, such as crisis situations (those which, as the history of religions shows, call for prophetic discourse): in such cases, prediction is a self-fulfilling prophecy, a discourse on the future which contributes to bringing about what it proclaims. Predictions are always instruments of power; to predict the future of others is to give oneself power over them. We need only think of the effect on the fate of peasants of the discourse of social planners who prophesied their disappearance, i.e. predicting and advocating at the same time their probable future. Convincing a group of its decline means contributing to accelerating that decline. Those who say what is going to happen contribute to bringing about what they say. Politics almost always speaks a language of approximation, a language that helps bring about what it states, to make what it pronounces exist. As a result, even when he tries to speak in a language of fact, even when he simply tries to state what is, the sociologist can appear to be helping to bring this into existence, by disguising as a statement of fact what is in reality a desire or a wish.

For example, when you speak of culture, it is tempting to ask you to propose a new definition of culture.

All I can say is what culture does, or what one does with culture. Culture is at every moment the stake in a struggle. This is understandable, since through the idea of culture or human excellence (the cultured man is in every society the accomplished man), what is at issue is human dignity. This means that, in a society divided into classes, those people deprived of culture are and feel attacked in their dignity, in their humanity, in their being. Those who possess culture, or believe that they do (the belief is essential here) almost always forget all the suffering, all the humiliation, inflicted in the name of culture. Culture is hierarchized, and itself hierarchizes: like a piece of furniture or clothing, which immediately indicates the point in the social or cultural hierarchy at which its owner is situated. It is not just in the field of politics that culture and the respect it inspires reduce those deprived of it to silence. But in order to see the full issue at stake in the struggles around culture, we should remember all the illusions that result from the fact that culture is embodied, that it shares the body of its bearer, and thus appears the most natural and personal of properties, and thus the most legitimate.

You have shown how this is quite particularly true for language.

Indeed. Hence the silence of those whose only choice is between borrowed language or outspokenness, and the self-assurance of those who can always count on what is called their sense of ease or their 'natural distinction'.

We have almost arrived back at our starting point, which was political discourse. Is the key to politics first of all a question of language?

Yes. I believe that in speaking of linguistics, one should always remember that this is also a question of politics, and conversely, in speaking of politics, that this is also a question of language. Political competence, inasmuch as there can be a universal definition of it, undoubtedly consists in the ability to speak in universal terms about particular problems – how to survive dismissal or redundancy, an injustice or an accident at work, not as an individual accident, a personal mishap, but as something collective, common to a class. This universalization is possible only by way of language, by access to a general discourse on the social world. This is why politics is in part bound up with language. And here again, if you like, we can introduce a bit of utopia to attenuate the sadness of sociological discourse, and convince ourselves that it is not too naive to believe that it can be useful to fight over words, over their honesty and proper sense, to be outspoken and to speak out. Besides, it is worthwhile to fight to make known the universal right to speech, a speech capable of ensuring the return of the social repressed. The political activist is not just – that's a fine example of political, i.e. performative, language – I mean he should not just be someone who sticks up posters or carries out instructions, but someone who has his own word to say and says it, expresses himself and demands expression, is in control of what he says, what he does and what is said to him.

Esprit *magazine and Pierre Bourdieu's sociology*

A monthly magazine midway between culture and politics, and specializing in 'social debates', Esprit published one of Bourdieu's first interventions in the 1960s (see p. 7).

Bourdieu subsequently subjected the magazine to a sociological analysis, and in Actes de la Recherche en Sciences Sociales *attributed it a key role in the production of the dominant ideology (see pp. 97–116).*

Esprit *also published some of the most virulent criticisms of Bourdieu, especially on the publication of* Reproduction in Education *in 1970 (see p. 32), then of* Distinction *in 1979. Bourdieu responded to the latter article in the text that follows here: this reaction to the criticism of a philosopher, Philippe Raynaud, offers an example of a polemical argument put forward particularly in relation to academic oppositions such as freedom and determinism.*

Several years later, Esprit *was among the publications that reacted most strongly to Bourdieu's position in support of the strikes of December 1995, and the subsequent publication of the collection* Raisons d'Agir *(see p. 271).*

Blessed are the poor in spirit*

Once again *Esprit* wants to teach me a lesson. For this is indeed a lesson, a lesson in morals, of course, but again one of those dreadful lessons in the *agrégation* or *terminale* classes, in which, preaching to the converted, it is easy to win approval by casting to outer darkness, by way of a few theoretical anathemas, the human sciences and their claim to 'reduce' the irreducible, explain the inexplicable, the 'subject', the 'person'. The principle of this lesson is the famous *esprit de sérieux*, the major index of adherence to the subject being taught, and proclaimed all the more strongly whenever the required seriousness and information are uncertain. With a little cheek and a great deal of conviction, even simple errors of fact can be overlooked. Like this one: 'We know that – except for the Communists, who can easily place the analyses of *Reproduction in Education* in their eschatology [. . .] the main effect of this book has been to contribute to discouraging teachers. It is likely, moreover, that the most intelligent reading of it will be a *conservative* one.'[6] The truth is that, in reply to protests that had already been received from its readers in response to an article in which the PCF's petty authorities classified *Reproduction in Education* as 'a petty-bourgeois translation of Marxism',[7] *La Nouvelle Critique* wrote (and I am not inventing this): 'In the same way, moreover, as the Synod of Bishops [. . .] these ideologists [the authors of *Reproduction in Education*], by their analyses, drive teachers, parents and students into apocalyptic mirages, behaviour of withdrawal and escape, a *demobilizing* despair. [. . .] To put it simply, in our own theoretical and practical perspective we were led to emphasize, in their most recent theses, a reinforcement of the nihilist and *demobilizing* tendency.' And further on, though again I have to cite it in full:

'As with Hobbes (or Pascal!), institutions are based on force, and any authority is usurpation. How can we not see [. . .] the logical consequences of this problematic, both erroneous and *demobilizing*: it would be contrary to the interest of the dominated classes to set themselves such objectives as

* Published under the title 'Où sont les terroristes?' in *Esprit* 11–12, November-December 1980, pp. 253–8.
6 *Esprit* has never lacked a certain consistency: Antoine Prost, cited by our author (Philippe Raynaud, 'Le sociologue contre le droit', *Esprit* 3, March 1980), already invoked the same argument in an article in which he counterposed the 'inspired' spontaneism of Ivan Illitch to the fatalism of *La Reproduction* (Antoine Prost, 'Une sociologie stérile: *La Reproduction*', op. cit.).
7 A. Gudj and F. Hincker, 'Le malaise des enseignants. Faut-il brûler d'école?', in *La Nouvelle Critique*, January 1972, p. 18.

"compulsory schooling" (p. 57), the "democratization of teaching" (p. 59) or the defence of secularism (p. 62), etc.'[8]

We need to analyze the logic of this *rhetoric of suspicion*, which both these texts share: the 'moreover' in the phrase 'in the same way, moreover, as the Synod of Bishops'; the term 'ideologists'; the 'would be contrary' – a distancing and insinuating conditional. We also need to examine the processes by which the criticism of an institution (or apparatus), an intellectual criticism conducted in a position of political strength and intellectual weakness, is reduced to the logic of a *trial*: I am thinking for example of the anathemas ('ideologists'), the amalgam (the reference to Hobbes and Pascal), and above all the caricature summary ('institutions are based on . . .') and the pure and simple falsification, which border on slander or police informing, while concealing themselves under the appearance of seriousness (with page references): *Reproduction in Education*, hear me well, Comrades (it is clearly intellectual comrades that are aimed at here), is not what you might believe, you who, thanks to the stubborn work of Communist sociologists, have held faithfully to the Langevin-Wallon plan [see p. 50, n.13]. It attacks the very foundations of the Party programme for education: secularism (cf. the 'Synod of Bishops'), democratization, and the conquest of conquests, compulsory school attendance. We have to deal with it!

Gaudium et spes![9] Communists and Christians come together in condemning the sociological fatalism that makes 'bourgeois ideology the winner all along the line'.[10] But those in charge of the Semaines de la Pensée Marxiste and the Centre Catholique des Intellectuels Français should not rejoice too hastily: for *La Nouvelle Critique*, this demobilizing pessimism is a pale imitation of the Synod; for *Esprit*, it betrays the survival of Stalinism. To relegate something undesirable to the side of what one detests is after all good tactics (even if there is something rather Stalinist in the amalgam associated with such ostracism). But the question remains as to what these enemies actually betray, in agreeing to relegate to the enemy the enemy who is relegated to them. If they certainly agree in expelling this enemy of the enemy who is even so not a friend, this undesirable absolute, it is because they have in common, beyond conflicts over particular issues at stake, the interests that they have in the game itself, in the very existence of this game, which imposes on them, beyond 'political differences', the same sacred horror of anything that threatens the game itself, and the vital issues associated with it.

---

[8] 'L'École: un débat', *La Nouvelle Critique*, April 1972, p. 78. (I am indebted to Jeannine Verdès-Leroux for these references.)
[9] ['Joy and hope!']
[10] As note 8.

In the one case it is the interests of the apparatus intellectual that are defended, at the price of a permanent double game, by those who put the authority of their status as qualified intellectual in the service of a political apparatus, and seek to draw from this an (intellectual?) authority among intellectuals: we have already noted, in the text cited above, how the (cultivated) reference to Hobbes, and the (treacherous) one to Pascal, serve to authorize a defence of the educational system and professorial authority that are threatened by sociological objectivization. In the other case it is the institution of philosophy that is defended, or institutionalized philosophy (with its canonic authors, which form the specific capital of the philosophy professor), i.e. the institutional authority that those participating in the institution appeal to. And they do so above all, of course, in defence of this institution. The entire institution is needed, in fact – I mean the 'establishment', as the English say, the established intellectual order and the right-minded,[11] – all these admirable[12] defenders of every good cause – the individual, art, culture, intelligence, i.e. every 'individual' who loves to see themselves as intelligent, creative, cultivated, starting of course with intellectuals and artists, who are all this by definition – all this is needed, to proceed to condemn a long analysis of Kant's *Critique of Judgement* without invoking anything but the anticipated complicity of every believer, i.e. every reader attracted by this work.[13] Magistral discourse, as we well know, expresses itself as something self-evident.

One may perhaps begin to grasp here that what I believe to be a struggle against intellectual terrorism can be experienced as terrorist by those who participate so naively in such intellectual terrorism.

The *esprit de sérieux*, let alone the proclaimed respect for the 'Other' that is so characteristic of *Esprit*, are deployed here again to conceal errors of reading that one cannot even be sure are deliberate. I have in mind the idea, which I have explicitly denied time and time again, that I have something

---

[11] To speak, against the evidence of the facts, of 'the very generally favourable reception that critics reserved' for *Distinction*, when almost every article devoted to this work was actually unfavourable, if not openly hostile or even slanderous (I have in mind for example the article in *Le Nouvel Observateur* that spoke of 'new look Zhdanovism') and conclude that '*Distinction* is a book by intellectuals for intellectuals', 'a satisfying book for the intelligentsia', is to give oneself the air of a sniper, a free and courageous intellectual, who takes the risk of resisting the currents of fashion and conformism (right-wing intellectuals have always played this game). But with the caution of a true professor, our hero in the struggle against 'intellectual Stalinism' (what he actually writes is: 'This is perhaps no more than an avatar of intellectual Stalinism') surrounds himself with every possible guarantee (Hegel, Marx, the Collège de Philosophie, etc.) and guarantor (I immediately note, glancing through the references, Boudon, Lefort, Castoriadis, Besançon and repeatedly Prost). Let him be assured, he fights the good fight.

[12] I cite here 'Let us remember here the admirable responses of . . .' (Philipe Raynaud, 'Le sociologue contre le droit', op. cit., p. 92, note 21).

[13] 'One cannot read without a certain surprise the pages that Pierre Bourdieu devotes to the *Critique of Judgement*' (ibid., p. 83). As for me, I must say, this divine surprise is no surprise at all.

to do with the equation Marx + Bachelard.[14] This would be no more than a simple and unimportant mistake, resulting as it does from the need to reduce the unknown to the known (which in the present state of formation and information of 'philosophers' means reducing it to very little . . .), were it not that we find again here the intention of cataloguing by the imposition of defamatory stigmas (as in the other case: 'Hobbes + Pascal') and contaminating amalgam (with 'Althusser's theory of ideology', which, to my mind at least, is the very opposite of what I am trying to do). How can one not be astonished to discover, in such a vehement (and courageous . . .) denouncer of 'intellectual Stalinism', one of the most characteristic strategies of the intellectual apparatchik, that of the ideologically suspect?[15]

No doubt some people will wax indignant and violently reject the intention or pretension to describe the struggle of classifications, and the function ascribed in this struggle to culture and those who claim to represent this. What could be more odious, more typically 'Stalinist' in fact, than the very intention to catalogue the cataloguers, classify the classifiers, categorize the producers of all categorical categorems conveyed by newspapers, magazines and books?[16]

Despite being convinced that our professional reader has not read my book (I mean the book I actually wrote, about which he says nothing), it would not occur to me to react in the very widespread and typically terrorist way of accusing him for speaking of it without having read it, and with every appearance of seriousness. But at the risk of appearing a terrorist or even a Stalinist, I believe I can explain why he was *unable* to read it: challenged, like so many others, in his 'person' as a man of culture, he could not without demeaning himself deal with or attack either the empirical facts (which he dismisses right away in the name of the postulated independence of the theoretical schema in relation to the data), or the theoretical construction itself – more exactly, the order of reasons that gives coherence to the facts –, which would have consisted in granting a work in the 'human sciences' a treatment reserved to works of philosophy. Having in this way purely and simply disqualified the work in question by depriving it of everything that

[14] 'If one had to define Pierre Bourdieu's starting point in French thought, one could say that he has attempted an original synthesis of sociology, Marxism understood as critique of domination and theory of ideologies, and Bachelardian epistemology as this was understood by the philosophical generation of the years 1955–65' (ibid.). A typically professorial view of research as the quest for originality.

[15] On this strategy, see for example 'Le lecture de Marx, ou Quelques remarques critiques à propos de "Quelques remarques critiques à propos de *Lire le Capital*"', *Actes de la Recherche en Sciences Sociales* 5/6, November 1975, esp. p. 75, the equation 'Structuralism = Hegel + Feuerbach'.

[16] Nothing moreover is more normal, more banal, more appropriate in a word, nothing that less merits legitimate anti-Stalinist indignation, than this phrase that everyone has recently been able to read, signed by an arbiter of intellectual elegance [Pierre Nora] in a (very) Parisian weekly: 'In any case, there is no such thing as French philosophy.'

makes up its form and substance, it can be treated as a kind of political essay (a concentrate of 'fellow traveller' ideology), simply separated from the last fashionable pamphlet by a difference of talent. By situating oneself openly on the terrain of politics, where all blows (and all ignorance) are by definition permitted, it is possible to tilt at windmills, i.e. a 'concentrate' of accepted ideas, a hundred times rejected or refuted, which drift around everywhere about my work: it is 'static', 'pessimistic' or 'Stalinist', 'the sociologist sees himself as God the Father' (he has the 'certainty of having refuted in advance all possible objections'), etc. To the point where one ends up wondering what there can be about this detestable book to make so many normally intelligent people say such stupid things.

There is no way to refute a system of defence mechanisms (in the Freudian sense), especially a collective one. All that is possible is to try to analyze its functioning, without any hope of convincing or converting. With this in mind, there is just one point in my argument that I will repeat here, one that is at the very heart of the debate, and where the blindness to which the logic of unfavourable prejudice leads is particularly clear, when this is combined – as is often the case – with the most complete ignorance of the real logic of research operations:[17] I refer to the fact that scientific discourse, despite being put forward purely in terms of stating *what is*, is read here – and this is a very common error – as if it were one of those discourses of everyday existence that only ever speak of the social world in a normative sense – one might better say 'performative' – concealing the desire or pious wish beneath the appearance of a factual statement. Where I thought I had stuck to stating the fact that men (and still more so women) from the economically and culturally most disfavoured classes leave their political choices to the party of their choice, and the Communist party in particular, so that the despotism of apparatuses and apparatchiks, far from being a historical futility, is at least for a good part based on the resignation of the 'people' to whom they appeal, I supposedly condemned the dominated to resign themselves completely to their appointed representatives, ignoring the 'highest quality of the people' and preaching the unconditional submission of both proletariat and intellectuals to the Communist party. All this, of course, under the hypocritically terrorist guise of science:

Why should we be surprised that the path of emancipation, for the dominated, lies in a total and unreserved alienation of their identity to the Party? We see how Pierre Bourdieu's work, despite its distinctive

---

[17] Thus an elementary acquaintance with statistical reasoning would enable us to save a great many dissertations on sociology and freedom.

origins, finds its place in a constant current of French culture, one that Jean-Paul Sartre in his time illustrated so wonderfully in *The Communists and Peace*. Like Sartre at this point, Bourdieu seems to see no other alternative to the political non-existence of the actual proletariat than its unreserved submission to the Party, in a 'dialectical' reversal to which the theoretician alone has the key. [. . .] For Bourdieu there is no problem of pedagogy, as it is precisely the people's ignorance that becomes their highest quality. Perhaps this enables us to understand better Bourdieu's insistence on the cultural dispossession of the dominated, the continuity with which, in defiance of those symbolic or 'scholarly' forms that popular cultures formerly still produced, he presents their current state of decline in social life as a sign that the dominated – pole of vulgarity – embody a state of nature against the refinements of distinguished culture: in such a setting, even the vulgarity of Georges Marchais would find its raison d'être.[18]

He's overdoing it, as the 'people' would say. And he should have spared himself the final sentence, which in the language of 'scholarly' rhetoric is known as a *drop in register*. Is there any need to say that I never sought to *celebrate* popular manners (though I have indeed *defended* them against the racism of class that breaks through at every point in the text just cited), and simply tried to understand their *logic* (as I equally did for bourgeois manners)?

Even the risk of facing the thunderbolts of anti-terrorist terrorism will not prevent me from thinking and saying that those who are accustomed to speaking the language of the norm – and no one will challenge the fact that *Esprit* is the site of that subjective perfection that is the very principle of any imposition of norms – are not the best placed to triumphantly profess this misinterpretation and use the occasion to present themselves as guardians of ethical purism. But so gross a mistake would certainly not have been possible if there were not such a burning hurry to shake off the critique of this tyranny exercised by culture and in its name, even on the terrain of politics, a tyranny that all 'cultured people' take part in. It was necessary at all costs to convince the reader (and convince oneself as well) that this enunciation (which is *eo ipso* a denunciation) of tyranny ended up in an exhortation to annihilate oneself in submission to the tyranny of the Party, in that typically religious logic that has often led intellectuals into the Party.

The same stroke also makes it possible to settle some accounts in the field of politics in the strictest sense. It is impossible to read without a certain surprise, as our author likes to say, a phrase that we can only regret did not

---

[18] Philippe Raynaud, 'Le sociologue contre le droit', op. cit., p. 92.

surface until the very end, after so much high philosophy: 'How is it possible, for example, that in the course of a recent session of the ISER (a body close to the Socialist party), we could see the majority of the Socialist leaders present partake of the *sacrament* (my emphasis) in their admiration for such a concentrate of "fellow-travelling" ideology?'

Here we have it then! Open your eyes, Christian Socialists and Socialist Christians: Bourdieu is to the vulgar Marxists what Chevènement, as a distinguished variant of vulgar Communism, is to Marchais![19] But the issue of relations between Rocard, Mitterrand and Chevènement was on the agenda right from the start. And admitting this would save us the lesson (rather overwhelming) about Leibniz, Hegel, Marx and other authorized authorities, who have no bearing on the matter at all.

---

[19] 'To sum up, this book, completely constructed on the opposition between "distinction" and vulgarity, finds its centre of gravity perhaps – and the reasons for its success – in the fact that it represents today the distinguished form of vulgar Marxism' (ibid., p. 93).

4

Dominant Ideology and Scientific Autonomy

The Birth of Actes de la Recherche en Sciences Sociales

If there is any truth at all, it is that truth is a stake in struggles
'A class as object', 1977

While the 1970s saw the flourishing of French-style leftism, civil servants in the high administration continued their work of 'modernizing' national capitalism. These transformations led to an increase in the grip of political power over the intellectual world. Ever since the 1950s, there had developed between intellectuals deprived of temporal power and men of power whose authority was increasingly based on specialized competence, a population of 'administrative researchers' and 'scientific administrators' attached to research institutions that responded to the orders of the administration.[1]

The journal Actes de la Recherche en Sciences Sociales, *which appeared in 1975, sought to contribute to strengthening the autonomy of sociology by endowing it with an independent means of distribution, subject only to the requirements of the procedures of verification and scientific criticism. Its editorial policy, marked by a desire to break with academic formalism and the normalizing standardization of research, deliberately juxtaposed 'finished' articles with notes, interim reports, statistical documents, photographs, facsimiles and comic strips (see p. 95). This policy for sociology was not designed just to 'deconstruct' the sacred texts of the academic world, but also to 'destroy the pretences and prevarications forged by a religious view of humanity, which is not a monopoly of the revealed religions'. By effecting a 'reversal of the hierarchy of research subjects' established by a science with such little independence of political demands as sociology, where scientific censorship is very often only concealed political censorship,* Actes de la Recherche *sought to overturn the opposition between 'the priest of high academic orthodoxy' and 'the distinguished heresy of snipers firing blanks'.*[2] *The variety of methods employed thus related to a variety of themes that had*

---

[1] Cf. 'Le production de l'idéologie dominante' (with Luc Boltanski), *Actes de la Recherche en Sciences Sociales*, 1976, no. 2/3, pp. 5–6. Other articles were also devoted to this transformation, in particular that of Michael Pollak, 'La planification des sciences sociales', ibid., pp. 105–21. [Ed.]
[2] 'Scientific method and the social hierarchy of objects,' p. 95 below.

87

previously been considered scarcely worth studying: haute couture, cars, comic strips, technical education, social workers, Marxist rhetoric, etc.

The original project of Actes *was summed up in one particular text, 'La production de l'idéologie dominante', which opened with an 'Encyclopaedia of Accepted Ideas', drawn up on the basis of a body of canonical texts in the dominant social philosophy (books, interviews, articles by powerful intellectuals and others):*

> First of all, the writings of the forerunners, often professionals in the culture industry, who provide the 'active members' of the dominant class with the fundamental themes that they incessantly reproduce, accompanying them with their specific concerns; secondly, the products (i.e., reports of commissions) of a collective work of elaboration tending to wipe out individual differences for the benefit of commonplaces that have the unanimous agreement of the dominant fraction of the dominant class; and finally, the productions of the simple reproducers, educational exposition of knowledge directly acquired in the schools of power or planning commissions.[3]

Beyond the seeming diversity of their various positions, the 'producers of the dominant ideology' form a relatively homogeneous group, since the majority of them have participated in one way or another in the elaboration of the national plan, the teaching of the Institut d'Études Politiques and the ENA, being themselves products of the same grandes écoles *(Polytechnique, Institut d'Études Politiques, ENA, etc.).*

> The selection of themes formulated in the most concise and least euphemistic fashion made it possible to demonstrate the 'commonplaces' of an ideology able to leave its presuppositions implicit under the cover of the 'norms of good conduct' of a language of power invested in 'neutral places' – places of intersection between the intellectual field and the field of power, the points at which speech becomes power, in commissions where the enlightened director meets the enlightening intellectual [. . .] and the Institutes of Political Science where the new ideological *koinè*, pedagogically neutralized and routinized, is imposed and inculcated, and thus converted into patterns of thinking and political action.[4]

---

[3] 'La production de l'idéologie dominante', op. cit., pp. 10–11. [Ed.]
[4] Ibid., p. 5.

These apparatus intellectuals, just like the doxosophists, endanger the autonomy of scientific knowledge by deriving from the world of politics an intellectual legitimacy that the scholarly world would not grant them, and importing political logics and purposes into the field of research. If such institutions as the Commission du Plan have developed a technocratic ideology of consultation, the production of the dominant ideology has a history going back to the 1930s and the convergence between an economic-administrative pole (particularly represented by the Polytechniciens *of X Crise) and an intellectual pole grouping the 'non-conformists' of that decade, who included the 'young right', Ordre Nouveau and Action Française, as well as the Uriage cadre school and the group of activists around* Esprit.[5]

The practical application of these patterns of thought and action found its most complete conditions in the Institut d'Études Politiques: the accumulation of functions of its teaching body and the over-representation of 'men of action' (high officials and economic decision-makers) in relation to academics expressed the ambiguity of an institution at the intersection of the political and intellectual spheres.

---

[5] Formed during the crisis of the 1930s, these discussion groups developed an anti-parliamentary 'economic humanism' that sought to be 'neither right nor left' and combined rejection of both capitalism and collectivism in a condemnation of the power of money and the power of the masses. They promoted a 'civilization project' based on an asceticism of commitment and respect for a hierarchical order based on competence. [Ed.]

Declaration of Intent,
Actes de la Recherche en
Sciences Sociales 1, January 1975

We shall present here, side by side, texts differing very greatly in their style and function: 'finished' texts, on the one hand, as they are called by academic journals, but also short notes, accounts of oral presentations, work in progress such as interim research projects and reports, in which theoretical intentions, empirical procedures of verification, and the data on which these are based, are all that much more visible. The desire to provide access to the workshop, which has different rules from those of method, and to present archives of a work still under way, implies a rejection of the most clearly ritual formalisms: justified typography, standard rhetoric, articles and issues of similar length, and more generally, everything that leads to the standardization and 'normalization' of the products of scholarship. Recognizing no other imperative than those imposed by the rigour of demonstration, and secondarily by the aim of visibility, will mean freedom from the censorships, artificial devices and perversions generated by a concern to conform to the established customs and good manners of the university field: a rhetoric of caution or false prediction, with the apparatus and panoply of celebratory discussion that is never more than self-celebration, the ostentatious display of signs of belonging to the most selective and select groups in the intellectual universe.

This renunciation of established form will also make it possible for us to seek a mode of expression genuinely adapted to the demands of a science that, taking for its object social forms and formalisms, should reproduce in the exposition of its results the operation of demystification that enabled it to reach these. Here we come up against the undoubted reason for the specificity of social science: obtained in the face of social mechanisms of dissimulation, its findings can only inform practice, whether individual or collective, if their distribution succeeds in escaping at least partially the laws governing the circulation of any discourse on social reality. To transmit, in this case, is to supply – in every case that this is possible – the means of remaking, in practice and not just in words, the operations that made it possible to obtain the truth of these practices. Having to provide instruments of perception and facts that can only be grasped by the means of these instruments, social science has not only to demonstrate but also to display, to present recordings of everyday existence, photographs, transcripts of speech, facsimiles of documents, statistics, etc., and to make visible, sometimes by a simple graphic effect, what is generally hidden. Genuine access to the knowledge of objects that are very commonly invested with all the attributes of the sacred can only be gained by supplying the weapons for sacrilege: unless one believes in the intrinsic force of the true idea, it is only possible to break the charm of belief by opposing symbolic violence to symbolic violence, and putting the weapons of polemic, if need be, at the service of the truths obtained by the polemic of scientific reason.

The discourse of science appears disenchanting only to those who have an enchanted view of the social world. It differs both from a utopianism that takes its desires for reality, and from a sociologism complacent in the killjoy evocation of fetishized laws. Social science is happy to destroy the pretences and prevarications forged by a religious vision of humanity, of which the revealed religions have no monopoly.

Scientific method and the social hierarchy of objects*

When Parmenides asked Socrates, trying to embarrass him, whether he accepted that there were 'forms' of things 'that might seem rather ridiculous, such as a hair, mud, dirt, or any other object of no importance or value', Socrates admitted that he could not decide to accept these, for fear of falling into 'an abyss of foolishness'. Parmenides replied that Socrates was young and new in philosophy, and still cared for men's opinions; one day philosophy would take hold of him and make him see the vanity of such disdain in which logic plays no part (*Parmenides*, 130d).

The philosophy of philosophy professors has hardly retained Parmenides' lesson, and there are few traditions where so marked a distinction is made between noble and ignoble objects, or ignoble and noble ways of treating them – noble here meaning highly 'theoretical' ways that are consequently emptied of reality, neutralized and euphemized. But even scientific disciplines suffer the effects of such hierarchical arrangements, which shy away from less prestigious objects, kinds, methods and theories at one time or other. And it is possible to show how certain scientific revolutions were the product of importing, into fields that were socially devalued, mechanisms current in the more prestigious domains.[6]

The hierarchy of objects – legitimate, legitimizable and unworthy – is one of the mediations through which the censorship specific to a particular field imposes itself, and in the case of a field whose independence in relation to the demands of the dominant class is poorly established, it can itself be the mask for a purely political censorship. The dominant definition of things that can be properly spoken about and things unworthy of interest is one of the ideological mechanisms responsible for things just as good to speak about not being spoken about, and subjects no less deserving of interest not interesting anyone or being possible to deal with only in a shame-faced or dissolute fashion. This is the reason why 1,472 books have been written on Alexander the Great, though if we are to believe the author of the 1,473rd, only two were really needed; indeed this author,[7] despite his iconoclasm, is hardly well placed to inquire whether a book on Alexander is necessary or

* Published in *Actes de la Recherche en Sciences Sociales* 1, 1975. pp. 4–6.
[6] J. Ben David and R. Collins, 'Social Factors in the Origins of a New Science: The Case of Psychology', *American Sociological Review*, August 1966, 31 (4), pp. 451–65.
[7] R. L. Fox, *Alexander the Great* (London: Allen Lane 1973).

not, and whether the redundancy observed in the most frequently visited fields is not the price for the silence that surrounds other objects.[8] The hierarchy of domains and objects orients *intellectual investments* by the mediation of the structure of (average) prospects of material and symbolic profit that it helps to define. The writer always participates in the importance and value that is commonly attributed to the object, and there is very little chance that he will not take into account in choosing his intellectual interests, either consciously or unconsciously, the fact that the most important works (from a scientific point of view) on the most 'insignificant' objects have little chance of having as much value, in the eyes of all those who have internalized the prevailing system of classification, as the most unimportant and anodyne works (from the same scientific standpoint) on the most 'important' objects.[9] This is why those who tackle objects that are devalued on grounds of their 'futility' or 'unworthiness', such as journalism, fashion, or comic strips, often expect to find in a different field, even the one that they study, the gratifications that the scientific field refuses them in advance, something that does not help incline them to a scientific approach.

We should start by analysing the form taken in different fields and at different times by the division into noble and vulgar, serious and futile, interesting and trivial – a division that is accepted as quite self-evident. This would undoubtedly lead to discovering that the field of possible research objects always tends to be organized around two independent dimensions – the degree of legitimacy, and the degree of prestige within the limits of legitimate definition. The opposition between the prestigious and the obscure that can pertain to domains, genres, objects and manners (more or less 'theoretical' or 'empirical' according to the prevailing taxonomies) is the product of applying dominant criteria that determine the degrees of excellence within the universe of legitimate practices: the opposition between orthodox objects (or domains, etc.) and those objects claiming attention that might be labelled avant-garde or heretical, depending on whether we situate ourselves on the side of the defenders of established hierarchy or that of those seeking to impose a new definition of legitimate objects, expresses the polarization established in any field between institutions or agents who occupy opposed

---

[8] It is hardly necessary to state here that this accumulation is highly functional, from the standpoint of the functioning and perpetuation of the present system, as it constitutes right away a genuine defence against external criticism, which can only be exercised in objective alliance with a specialist – something quite improbable.

[9] Scientific language puts words from ordinary language in apostrophes, to mark a break with common usage. This break may be that of an objectifying distancing (whether objects are 'insignificant' or 'important' depends on whether they are considered as such at a particular point in time), or else a tacit or explicit redefinition determined by the insertion in a conceptual system of ordinary words thus constituted as 'entirely relative to theoretical science'. Cf. Gaston Bachelard, *Le Matérialisme rationnel* (Paris: PUF 1953), p. 216.

positions in the structure of distribution of the specific capital. This evidently amounts to saying that the terms of such oppositions are relative to the *structure* of the field under consideration, even if the functioning of each field tends to have the effect that these cannot be perceived as such and appear to all those who have internalized those systems of classification that reproduce the field's objective structures as intrinsically, substantially and genuinely important, interesting, vulgar, fashionable, obscure or prestigious. All that is needed to mark this space is to indicate a few points by examples taken from social science: on the one hand, the grand theoretical synthesis, with no other point of support in reality than the sacralizing reference to canonical texts – or at least the most important and noble objects of the sublunary world, i.e. preferentially 'planetary' ones, established by ancient tradition; on the other hand, village monographs, doubly tiny, both by their object – minuscule and socially inferior – and by their method, which is vulgarly empirical; and as against both of these, semiological analysis of photo-novels, illustrated weeklies, comic strips or fashion, the application of a correct method just heretical enough to attract the prestige of avant-gardism to objects condemned by the guardians of orthodoxy but predisposed by the attention they receive on the borders of the intellectual and artistic fields – fascinated by every form of kitsch – to be the object of strategies of rehabilitation that are all the more profitable, the more risk they involve.[10] The ritual conflict between the high orthodoxy of the academic priesthood and the distinguished heresy of the blank-shooting snipers is among the mechanisms contributing to maintain the hierarchy of objects, and by the same token, the hierarchy of those groups that draw from this their material and symbolic profits.

Experience shows how those objects that the dominant representation treats as inferior or minor often attract those who are least prepared to deal with them. Recognition of this unworthiness still dominates those who adventure onto the forbidden terrain, when they believe it necessary to display the indignation of the puritanical voyeur who has to condemn to be able to consume, or a concern for rehabilitation that presupposes intimate submission to the hierarchy of legitimacies or even a clever combination of distance and participation, disdain and valorization, which permits one to play with fire in the fashion of the slumming aristocrat. Knowledge of the object has as its absolute condition, here as elsewhere, knowledge of the different

---

[10] In the same way that the hierarchy of domains maintains a close relationship with social origin (but a complex one, since mediated by educational success), it is likely that orientation towards one point or other in the space of research objects expresses both position in the field and the trajectory leading to it. (Cf. P. Bourdieu, L. Boltanski and P. Maldidier, 'La défense du corps', *Information sur les Sciences Sociales*, 1971, no. 10–4.)

forms of naive relationship to the object (including that which the researcher may maintain with it in everyday practice), meaning in this case knowledge of the position of the object studied in the objective hierarchy of degrees of legitimacy that condemns all forms of naive experience. The only way to escape the naive relationship of absolutization or counter-absolutization is to grasp as such the objective structure that commands these mechanisms. Science does not take sides in the struggle to maintain or undermine the dominant system of classification, it takes this as object. It does not say that the dominant hierarchy that treats conceptual painting as art and comic strips as an inferior mode of expression is necessary (except in a sociological sense); nor does it say that it is arbitrary, as do those who take a position of relativism in order to overthrow or change it, and who, at the end of the day, simply add a final degree to the scale of cultural practices considered legitimate. In short, it does not oppose one value judgement to another, but *takes note* of the fact that reference to a hierarchy of values is objectively inscribed in practices, and in particular in the struggle of which this hierarchy is the issue, as expressed in opposing value judgements.

Those fields with an inferior rank in the hierarchy of legitimacies offer the polemic of scientific reason a privileged occasion to exercise itself in complete freedom, and tackle *by proxy*, on the basis of the homology established between fields of unequal legitimacy, the fetishized social mechanisms that also function under censorship and masks of authority in the protected universe of high legitimacy. Thus the appearance of parody that all acts of celebration assume when, abandoning their usual objects, pre-Socratic philosophers or symbolist poetry, they address themselves to objects so poorly placed in the prevailing hierarchy as comic strips, betrays the truth of all learned accumulations. And the same effect of de-sacralization that science necessarily produces to establish itself, and reproduces to communicate itself, is more readily obtained if one forces oneself to consider the too prestigious and familiar world of painting and literature via an analysis of the symbolic alchemy by which the universe of haute couture produces faith in the irreplaceable value of its products.

Declaration of intent, Actes de la Recherche en Sciences Sociales 5/6, November 1975

The common feature of the works presented here is that they go beyond the critique normally assigned to social science. Guilty of lèse-majesté, they take as their object philosophy, the dominant discipline that traditionally assigns sciences their limits, classifies and arranges them, and under the guise of freedom makes its own contribution to establishing order – not just in science. This was a necessary decision: if philosophy, whose writ used to run far and wide, is to survive today, it has to proclaim its own death, and seek to dissolve this itself by diluting itself into social science.

In a world where social positions are so often identified with 'names', scientific criticism must sometimes take an ad hominem form. As Marx taught, social science only 'deals with individuals in so far as they are the personification' of generic positions or dispositions – in which those who describe them may themselves participate. It does not aim to impose a new form of terrorism, but to make all forms of terrorism that much more difficult.

Intelligence is the key virtue of the modern leader (or guide). As a creative adaptation to change, it makes it possible to confront with efficiency, dynamism, openness and realism the problems of complexity and ever-growing scale that are posed by the modern world.

It is the brain of a social body with an ever increasing need for this organ in a world where extra brains have replaced extra soul. It is scientific, and scientifically legitimate: it speaks the imposing language of entropy, information, computing, microprocessing and linear programming; its preferred metaphors are borrowed from biology and physics. Its eugenic propensity appeals freely to genetics. Its realism is inspired by lessons from the history of political regimes, by Keynesian economics and the ethology of Lorenz.

The new elite possesses the most natural authority: that of knowledge, which is not transmitted by heredity. Its legitimacy needs no legitimization: it rests on the inequality of gifts, in an equality of opportunities that separates those with greater aptitude from those with less – the excluded, the left-behind, the handicapped (in brains), those who cannot keep up the pace.

Intelligence makes it possible to foresee and predict the revolts of the excluded, of which May 1968 is the most famous example. It imposes a policy of assistance and re-education that alone can draw the excluded away from anxiety or revolt, by leading them to find happiness in accepting the inescapable. It distinguishes the new leaders, turned towards the future and able to confront the shock of the future, because they have understood the lessons of the past, from all those backward-lookers, whether right or left, who reject the modern world and refuse to recognize the inescapable character of development.

Encyclopaedia of accepted ideas and commonplaces used in neutral spaces*

'We have to know all the fashionable books, all fashionable subjects: on the blocked society, on all blocked societies – post-industrial and pre-industrial – as well as unblocked societies, consumer societies and leisure societies.'

Institute d'Études Politiques student

America 'The USA offers [. . .] a sociological model some ten or fifteen years ahead of us, and thirty or forty years ahead of the Eastern bloc countries.'

– M. Poniatowski

'Economically, one American is worth three Frenchmen.'

– L. Armand

'The Americans, who precede us in the present development.'

Cf. Backward, Evolution

Backward 'Backward in relation to the United States and Russia, we can only note the increase in this backwardness despite the progress we realize, as we are moving more slowly. To change gear, we need a change of dimension.'

– L. Armand
Cf. Competition, Growth

Blocked (opp. Open, Unblocked) 'Everyone now accepts that French society is a "blocked society", even if the term is not yet common usage.'

– M. Crozier

Centralization (opp. Decentralization)
(1) Ex. 'The suffocating Napoleonic centralization.'

– M. Crozier

---

* This text, which appeared in *Actes de la Recherche en Sciences Sociales* 2/3, 1976, is an evident spoof on Flaubert's *Dictionary of Accepted Ideas*. The adjacent text 'Intelligence is the key virtue . . .' is in the same genre. See 'Declaration of intent, *Actes de la Recherche en Sciences Sociales* 5/6, November 1975', p 97, above.

(2) 'We have to try and naturalize the citizen by seeking the means to raise individual aspirations to the level of major decisions. Deconcentration, decentralization of government and business, economic regionalism – these are all efforts in the right direction.'

– V. Giscard d'Estaing
Cf. Blocked, Divisions

Classes (absence of) 'It is striking to see society moving towards a structure without classes.'

– M. Poniatowski

'Besides, the equalization of conditions of life tends to be brought about by dress and habitat. In this way, divisions between classes are in the process of dissolving.'

– L. Armand

Communism 'Socialism, in the accepted sense of the term – it would be better to say collectivism or communism – is the negation of time, the aspiration to unchangeability, nostalgia for those primitive societies that continue just as they are for thousands of years, and where the slow progress of ideas and forms is reminiscent of the immobilty of the gods.'

– C. Harmel

Cf. 1. Backward, Blocked, Ideologies
Cf. 2. Trade unionism

Competition 'International competition must bring in its wake a growing industrial concentration'.

– ENA examination, 1966.

Cf. America, Evolution, Growth

Complexity 'The government of a country has assumed in thirty years a complexity that did not previously exist. Efficiency requires technical knowledge of problems, mechanisms, methods of administration, that is mastered only by a long apprenticeship.'

– M. Poniatowski

Cf., Elites, Intelligence, Leaders

Gifts 'People are born men or women, as only children or in families of ten. Similarly, there are children with a gift for study and others with a gift for manual work.'

– V. Giscard d'Estaing

'A scientific society is built on education: innate inequalities in educational aptitude now generate social inequalities as strong as the hereditary inequalities of landed property.'

– J. Fourastié

Cf. Brains, Exclusion, Genetics, Handicap, Intelligence

Happiness 'The cultural advance of our society will follow from economic growth. Does this mean that in such conditions happiness will be better assured? If this could only be defined, there would be no more need for philosophy.'

– V. Giscard d'Estaing

(neo-) Liberalism 'The most scientific form of modern economic thought is that of liberalism. [. . .] It contains very original ideas such as the theory of continuous growth and the theory of the quest for equilibrium at a certain economic level. It is thus a very advanced and new theory. Hence, in my opinion, the need to give it a new name: neoliberalism.'

– V. Gisard d'Estaing

Cf. Change, Growth, Overtaking

Rearguard 'Some people, gripped by anxiety, show reactions of defence and blind rejection, and desperately wage a rearguard action. Others, on the contrary, fall into the opposite excess and insist on the immediate adoption of radical measures going ahead of, and most commonly even alongside, the future that awaits us. For example, the "pasionarias" of the Women's Liberation Movement or the nihilist and leftist professionals of destruction.'

– M. Poniatowski

Soil (pej.) 'Attachment to one's native soil is a respectable sentiment, but it is a considerable brake on moving house.'
'Abandoned zones should not become antiquated lands where traditional activities are steadily declining, with embittered populations condemned to a permanent state assistance that is always insufficient.'

Cf. Abandoned, Excluded, Farmers, Left behind.

Traditional 'This problem is becoming particularly urgent for us in France, to the extent that our way of acting and our form of organization now seem increasingly ineffective in the modern world. No matter what we think, we all feel a certain collapse of our traditional style.'

– M. Crozier

Cf. Changes

Unblocked 'We were aware that each producer could produce far more than he does, if he made the effort, if certain difficulties were removed, if certain obstacles were unblocked. This is perhaps the key idea in French planning.'

– J. Fourastié

'At the heart of the republican synthesis lay a particularly complicated society that could be called blocked. [. . .] French society in the early 1960s is a mixture of old and new features. The changes taking place are the most extensive since the Revolution: society is becoming unblocked.'

– S. Hoffmann

USSR 'The most blocked society that there is.'

– M. Poniatowski

The royal science and the fatalism of probability*

A condemned past

The prevailing discourse on the social world owes its practical coherence to the fact that it is produced on the basis of a small number of generating patterns that themselves derive from the opposition between the (outdated) past and the future – or, in vaguer and seemingly more conceptual terms, between the traditional and the modern.[11] Like the oppositions of myth, the fundamental oppositions in this practical system – open/closed, blocked/unblocked, small/large, closed/open, local/universal, etc. are at the same time both formal relationships, which can function in the most varying contexts and be applied to the most diverse objects, and personally experienced contrasts, opposing experiences such as the opposition between the small village and the big town, the grocery and the drugstore, the market and the supermarket, the pre-War and the post-War, France and America, and so on. Whatever the particular field to which it is applied, the pattern produces two opposing and hierarchized terms, and at the same stroke the relationship that unites them, in other words the process of *evolution* (or else involution) leading from one to the other (for example the small, the large, and growth).

Each of these fundamental oppositions more or less directly evokes all the others. This is the way for example that the opposition between 'past' and 'future' leads on to the opposition between 'small' and 'large', in the double meaning of 'planetary' and 'complex'; or again to the opposition between 'local' – i.e. 'provincial' or 'national' (and nationalist) – and 'cosmopolitan', which, seen from another angle, is identified with the opposition between the 'immobile' and the 'mobile'. From a different angle again, the underlying opposition evokes the opposition between acquired rights, inheritance, 'privileges', on the one hand, and on the other, 'dynamism' and 'mobility', 'mutation' and 'change'. By systematically inverting the table of values of an earlier traditionalism, the past is never appealed to in a positive light; it is simply a 'brake' to be 'unblocked', a 'factor of backwardness' to be neutralized. Those who hold more than any

---

* See Declaration of intent, *Actes de la Recherche en Sciences Sociales* 5/6, November 1975, p.97, above.
[11] As seen by the usages of everyday conversation or political struggle, this opposition, depending on its ideological mood, can lead equally to deploring what has been lost or to exalting progress. In either case, the problematics it produces are intrinsically dangerous.

other to this 'outdated' past which has to be abolished are 'peasants' (and to a lesser degree 'artisans'), whose attachment to their 'native soil' forms an obstacle to the 'mobility' required by technological progress. By way of the opposition between 'closed' and 'open', the 'parish-pump mind' and the cosmopolitan mind, it is possible to rediscover the opposition between 'blocked' and 'unblocked', 'compartmentalized' and 'un-compartmentalized', in other words, all the antitheses implied in the opposition between France and America. [. . .] To the extent that these brakes and resistances are identified with the defence of 'established rights' and 'privileges' (Poujadism), a resolutely progressive appearance is given to the 'function of elimination' that planning is supposed to accomplish.

But the most directly political effect of the key opposition is shown when, applying the new system of classification to the opposition between right and left, it is maintained that this opposition fundamental to the space of politics is itself 'outdated', and by the same token, so is politics itself. From the standpoint of a taxonomy that lumps together in the 'backward-looking' camp peasants and trade unionists, the bureaucracies of the state and political parties, 'Poujadism' and 'Communism', there is no more decisive evidence of a 'backward-looking mentality' (especially among intellectuals) than the fact of refusing to relegate to the past the most radically outdated opposition between right and left, and everything that might in any way resemble classes and class struggle. It is in the name of this postulate, completely implicit, that a public-opinion survey, quite unconsciously and without any explicit intention of imposing its own problematic, can ask a question such as this: 'For a long time in France two main political tendencies have been distinguished, left and right. Do you believe that this distinction still has any meaning, or is it outdated?' (SOFRES, February 1970). The only explicit assertion here ('two main political tendencies . . .') conceals a series of implicit propositions: first, that two main tendencies can still be distinguished today – otherwise the question of their meaning would be redundant; second, that this distinction previously had a meaning – the assertion implied in 'still' and 'outdated'; and third, that this distinction is already outdated or in the course of being so – since respondents are asked if it still has any meaning. Thus the very fact of constructing the question in terms of an opposition *previously this was true / is it true today?*, and in this way introducing the idea of development and with it the idea that the opposition between right and left might be outdated, serves to produce a false alternative between 1) 'still has a meaning' (for certain people), in other words is not yet outdated but will become so in time (and thus is already in the past for those who know which way things are going), and 2) 'is already outdated'. A question that is ostensibly objective (cf. the symmetry of aims) conceals a political thesis (the distinction may be outdated), which itself contains a subtly worldly-wise political warning: are you so outdated (whether on the right or left) that you don't yet realize that the opposition between right and left is outdated?

All this is implied by the sole fact of treating these opposite terms as moments in a necessary development. 'Marxism' is 'archaic', just as is 'fascism' and 'parliamentarism'. The relationship between the 'closed' and the 'open', the 'small' and the 'large', the 'immobile' and the 'mobile', the national and the multinational, France and the United States, is that of the outdated past and the inevitable – and thus desirable – future. Those who, in the present, are 'isolated', 'closed', 'hermetic', 'sclerosed', 'rigid' or 'blocked' are condemned in advance, and deservedly so: the 'conservatism' of 'traditional elites' (mayor, priest, local dignitary), the 'tendency to Caesarism', 'Poujadism', 'small businesses', 'resistance to institutional competition, which creates risks and destroys monopolies', 'Malthusianism', 'privileges', 'resistance to change', 'attachment to established rights and status', 'obscurantism', 'ill-adapted and outdated parliamentarism', 'Marxism' and its 'backward-looking politicians'. The transformation is calculated with the rigour of Darwinian selection: the 'fear of the future' that dominates the 'backward-looking' (i.e. the 'weakest citizens', those who, like the 'peasants', are 'worried', dare not confront the 'future shock', seek (social) 'security' and protection, and cannot 'assume their own time') is well founded: the future is one of 'technical progress', 'openness', 'mobility', 'competence', 'competition' and 'communication'.

The symbolic effectiveness of the dominant discourse is due on the one hand to the fact that its soft logic and its characteristically partial and biased adjustment to reality endow it with the power to impose itself on all those who lack a competing system of classification – and even, in more than one case, on those who, capable of opposing it with an established body of doctrine, apply without realizing it the patterns of thought that underlie it. It would not be hard to find manifest applications of the dominant patterns well beyond the limits that political divisions assign them, and political polemic takes great delight in these gaps between expressions of habitus and the conscious and controlled expressions of specifically political competence. If this is the case, it is because the institutional careers that the established political units offer, groups conscious of themselves, defined by the *boundaries* they give themselves, i.e. by a strict delimitation of membership and exclusion, introduce discontinuities into the continuity of habitus: minds seemingly structured can thus find themselves cast from one side of the boundary to the other. As a system of distinctive intervals, political classification tends to generate discontinuity out of continuity (in the same way as language produces distinctive phonemes out of a continuum of sound), and maximize these intervals and distances by forcing political groups to use at every moment the political space it defines. The opinions and practices generated by habitus (for example on terrains that are not politically constituted) can thus enter into contradiction with those implied by a determined position in political space, and that political competence can at the same time be producing.

A political rhetoric

The history of regimes, institutions, events and ideas does not operate like *historical culture*, a simple accumulation of symbolic goods that is an end in itself, but rather as a method of political perception and action, a set of operational schemas that makes it possible to generate, outside any reference to original situations, discourses and actions that are charged with a whole historical experience. This is the way that a purely rhetorical pattern like that which consists – according to the explicit teaching of 'Sciences-Po' – in opposing two extreme positions (*dirigisme* and liberalism, parliamentarism and fascism, etc.), in order to transcend them by 'raising the debate', in fact operates as a matrix of discourses and actions that are universally conformist (conforming to certain well-understood class interests), because it reproduces the double exclusion of the conservative rearguard and the progressive vanguard that synchronically defines enlightened conservatism: the positions that it generates only to dispose of them (and thus impose its own third way) represent the historic past of the dominant class, the paths it has already explored and its past defeats, i.e. the essentially Radical-Socialist parliamentarism that culminated in the Popular Front, and Vichyism that led to the collapse of 1945 and the 'Communist threat'. This rhetoric includes a politics because it includes a history. [. . .]

The end of ideologies and the end of history

The most important lesson from history, however, is the discovery that nothing more can be expected from it, that the universe of possible political regimes (modes of domination) has come to an end. In the discourses of conversion and reconversion designed for backward fractions of the class, the triadic scheme is applied to the great impasses of the past – historic 'temptations' of the dominant class such as parliamentarism or Pétainism, liberalism or *dirigisme*, which still divide the dominant class as they have always done – in order to impose the necessity of opening a third way. First in line of these past impasses is parliamentarism, which brought both extremisms into being, followed by fascism, as a permanent temptation of the reactionary fraction of the dominant class, in which a fraction of intellectuals was able to recognize, at least for a moment, its dream of a dictatorship of competence. History converted the most radical alternatives of the past into dilemmas of despair.[12] Fascism and Communism were mortally reconciled in Stalinism. If the most opposite roads have converged, the time of politics is over. The theory of convergence (of capitalist and Communist regimes) teaches that there is no longer any place in history for the dream of this radical break with immanent tendencies that is called revolution. All quiet on the Eastern front. History has exhausted the universe of possible political solutions. In this finished political space, with its roads all explored and leading nowhere – like fascism, the now impossible continuation of liberal democracy by other means, or like Communism, only leading at best to the same end, i.e. economic growth, and at an incomparably higher cost – the time of 'ideologies' is over, and outside enlightened reformism there is nothing left but utopian dreams.

In order to produce this effect of absolute closure of the universe of possibilities, which condemns Billancourt[13] to the reasonable expectations offered by the newly dominant, it is sufficient to effect an identification of extremes that transforms alternatives into dilemmas. Liberalism is the centre of a line whose extremes meet: 'fascist totalitarianism' and 'Communist totalitarianism' come together, defining from both sides the space of liberalism. Because they can be either opposed to one another or merged in the same rejection, the two 'authoritarianisms' – 'fascist' and 'Soviet' – can either function as opposite poles of a political space with liberalism at its centre, the point of equilibrium, or else meet together as one of the two extremes in a new triad. This is how the 'consultative' or 'steered' economy of 'indicative planning' is opposed on the one hand to 'authoritarian planning' ('fascist' or 'Soviet') and on the other hand to 'liberal anarchy'; in the same way as 'rationalized parliamentarism' is opposed on the one hand to 'Caesarism' ('fascist' or 'Soviet') and on the other to the 'ineffective parliamentarism' of the Fourth Republic. Once all the outmoded alternatives are disposed of, there remains only the self-evidence of the forced choice, that of economic growth and liberal planning.[14]

---

[12] The new dominant discourse brings together people with the common feature of returning from all sides: from fascism if they come from the right, from Communism if they come from the left.

[13] [Boulogne-Billancourt in the Paris suburbs, site of the large state-owned Renault works, was a centre of industrial struggle in the 1960s and '70s.]

[14] The closure of the field of possibilities and the 'realist' opposition inevitably generated by the theory of convergence when this is associated with the mystique of growth prohibits conceiving revolutionary demands other than on the model of *jacquerie*: the desperate desire for levelling and equalization in poverty inspired by resentment. (Cf. for example, P. Massé, 'L'universe d'Edmond Maillecottin', *Le Monde*, 3 July 1968.)

The royal science

The fatalism that the ideology of the 'end of ideologies' contains, and the correlative exclusion of all possible alternative developments, are the hidden condition for a scientistic use of statistical prediction and economic analysis. Once the universe of the conceivable is defined, economic science (and, above all since May 1968, also social science, on the part of the technocrats of happiness) *is* politics, in so far as, beneath the semblance of stating what is, it pronounces what has to be. Conceived and applied by people who, having ruled out any radical change axiomatically, have been converted to the idea that in matters of politics – as in a previous age in matters of religion – 'good judgement is all that is needed for good action'; that their science is politics and their politics scientific, the national plan is a genuine politics, even if, as we could say, depoliticized, neutralized, and promoted to the state of simple technique. It subsequently represents the form of performative language par excellence. If there is such a thing as political science, or – what comes to the same thing – a scientific politics, the only future is the future of science, the property of the most competent, who are justified in their monopoly of politics by their monopoly of science. Econometric modelling, reproductive projection, enables a necessary future to be extracted from the past, once we take as constant the parameters on which the reproduction of the established order depends – i.e. the set of orderly relations that constitute the social structure. Hence the absolute sociologism of prospective discourse: any utopia is ruled out by definition, there remains only the choice of the necessary, which is imposed by sheer evidence alone on rulers competent and lucid enough to accede to a total vision, above the private interests and partial perspectives in which the hoi polloi are enclosed. This kind of politics is the royal science that any contemporary *Politics* speaks of: its job is to impose the self-evidence of its choices on those who, incapable of recognizing their necessity, simply suffer their effects, proving the 'inevitable' constraints these imply either in the 'political apathy' that is falsely deplored, or in a revolt that is really deplorable. This is why enlightened conservatism sees itself as inseparable from an immense work of education, a kind of economic and political *Aufklärung* from which will emerge the new man capable of choosing freely the sovereign good that his sovereigns have chosen for him. [. . .]

Neither science nor fantasy, the dominant discourse is a politics, that is to say, a discourse of power, which though untrue is capable of making itself true – one way among others for it to be verified – by bringing about what it proclaims, partly by the very fact of proclaiming it. The effectiveness of the national plan is not one of right, even if we are reminded of its true nature by the fact that oppositions which in appearance are simply formal, such as closed and open, local and cosmopolitan, actually conceal politics, i.e. legislative and administrative measures (financial ones in particular) such as the suppression of customs barriers and other forms of protection that ensure the survival of social groups to be liquidated. In the manner of Weberian regulation, the plan only works if the interest in obeying it prevails over the interest in disobeying it.[15]

The purpose of the dominant discourse on the social world is not simply to legitimize domination but also to steer action designed to perpetuate it, giving moral and morale, direction and directive, to those who direct and who put it into effect. This is why it can only have its effectiveness and impose itself as a realistic policy, i.e. a project for action endowed with reasonable prospects of success, to the extent that it proposes a *vision* that is at the same time *biased*, because partial and interested, and *realistic*, i.e. capable of imposing its own necessity on all those who place themselves at the point of view from where it is taken – like a perspective view. The fundamental structures of this vision, such as the cardinal oppositions between closed and open, local and multinational, denote in a very realistic manner the centre of conflict opposing the 'technocratic' vanguard to social groups with a local basis: to do away with the parliamentarism of local dignitaries whose exclusive attention to corporate and/or local interests condemns them to a blindness towards national (read: multinational) problems means also doing away with those groups – peasants, artisans, small shopkeepers – whose interests they defend and in whose name they oppose national (read: multi-national) directives; it means bringing about the unification of the economic and symbolic market by the disappearance of local markets endowed with a relatively autonomous logic of their own. [. . .]

Political power in the proper sense of the term does not lie in simple adaptation to structural tendencies, nor in the arbitrary imposition of directly self-interested measures, but rather in a rational exploitation of structural tendencies (brought to light by statistics), aiming to reinforce by deliberate intervention the probability of the one possible future among others that best conforms with the interests of the dominant. This is how information – as hymned by the ideology of the modern 'boss' – plays a determining role by making it possible to anticipate probable futures, assessing their 'claim to exist' as Leibniz put it, and evaluating precisely

---

[15] This is the foundation, which is in no way mysterious, of the power that the new dominant discourse grants to information, as explained very well by Fourastié, with his usual innocence: 'To convince people to do something, but convince them by presenting them with the situation, by giving them an awareness of reality, rather than by any kind of regulation. It is not a question of forcing people to act, but rather of informing them of certain realities and leading them to decide that it is in their interest, it lies in their nature, to act in certain directions and by certain methods.' (J. Fourastié, *Planification économique en France*, op. cit., pp. 32 and 40.)

the chances of success and costs of action required to make the favoured choice exist.

One of the functions of 'neutral spaces' is to promote what is commonly called exchange of views, i.e. reciprocal information on the vision of the future held by those agents who have respectively most information and most power over the future. There would be no science of tendencies without the prescient representation of these tendencies given by those with the power to inflect them, i.e. without the mutual prescience of intentions ensured both by the orchestration of habitus and the consultation promoted by organized or informal meetings. The banker who pioneers a new form of credit only succeeds as well as he does because besides his knowledge of tendencies (this tool known as the 'needs of the clientele') he has a certain information on policy, which – itself based on the knowledge of tendencies – contributes to determining those tendencies that have to be reckoned with (or, if you prefer, to producing the 'need' for credit that he exploits). This can equally be put the other way round: an economic policy can only succeed on the basis of a dual knowledge of this kind: the planning commissions and committees of wise men (to which should be added boards of directors and fashionable clubs) are an occasion not simply to accumulate information about new tendencies but also to confront the different representations of tendencies and the actions suited to modifying them. It is impossible to overestimate the role played in this circulation of information by the homogeneity of habitus associated with a shared educational (and, by implication, social) origin: as products of the same conditions and conditionings, endowed with the same patterns of thought, perception and appreciation, the directors of banks (who almost all stem from the Inspection des Finances), nationalized companies and a large number of private companies, all think and desire the same as is thought and desired by those in charge of political decisions, who directly or indirectly produce the conditions of success for their decisions, and vice versa.

The underlying basis for efficient action on the part of the dominant lies in their capacity to foresee and exploit tendencies in order to satisfy their interests. It would be possible to show how a number of the most profitable 'innovations' (in banking, for example) have amounted to drawing economic and social advantage from the *venture* of producing institutions adapted to the already existing future presented by American society, taken as an *advanced* form (in the double sense of anticipation and ideal) of French society. Finding in the statistics of the US economy an anticipated image of the French economy, and in US economic institutions the orientations and instruments of an appropriate policy framework (for the state, banks, industry, etc.), means accepting, at least implicitly, the political project that consists in making one particular possible future into a necessary destiny by acting as if this future were the only one possible, and using the symbolic effect of prophecy to make it happen that much more quickly and completely.

The fatalism of probability that lies at the root of the ideological use of statistics has the effect of making people forget that knowledge of the most probable is precisely what makes possible, by way of a particular political intent, the realization of the less probable: the science of those tendencies inherent in the structure is the condition for the success of political actions designed to work with the structure so as to bring about less probable possibilities. The majority of political figures have been agents of social laws of which they are ignorant: as instruments of the structure invoked by the structure, they would undoubtedly not have acted differently had they understood these laws, since they wanted nothing other than what lay implicit in the structure. A politics designed to transform these structures and neutralize the effect of tendential laws would have to make use of a knowledge of the probable in order to improve the prospects of the possible: knowledge of the tendential laws of the social world is the condition for any realistic (in the sense of non-utopian) action designed to prevent the accomplishment of these laws. If a science of the probable exists, the chances of the possible are thereby increased (a fact that sufficiently condemns anti-scientific fideism, a common expression of the confused sense of guilt of the intellectual). Any politics that ignores the probable that it seeks to prevent is exposed to the risk of collaborating to bring it about despite itself; whereas a science that reveals the probable has at least the virtue of disclosing the function of laissez-faire.

Realized ideology

As instruments of knowledge of the social world that are by this very fact instruments of power, these political theories in the practical state are congruent with the political action that they command and express. If they can assume the appearance of scientific discourse, it is because they impose themselves as prescriptive descriptions on all who either consciously or otherwise accept the censored axiomatics that serves as their foundation (that is, everything that is implied in the will to perpetuate domination), and this is sufficient to have them put into practice and thus ensure them a form of verification, by de facto ruling out other possible outcomes. In this way they show an affinity with the mythical-ritual systems that owe their absolute self-evidence, for those who accept in practice their underlying axioms, to the fact that they structure the vision of the social world according to the very structures of this world (with the result that it is immaterial whether they contribute to producing it or are simply its reflection). These political theories in a practical state, instruments for the rational preservation of structures that are themselves the product of the structures to be preserved, owe their practical systematization and adjustment to reality to the fact that the patterns that generated them are themselves the historical product of the social structures that they tend to reproduce, and are located within the limits of the closed universe of political solutions that are acceptable and practicable for the dominant class in a determined state of relationship of class forces.

Speaking of the 'dominant ideology' does not in itself mean escaping idealism: ideology makes itself a material thing in order to achieve its ends; and analysis must follow the metamorphoses that transform the dominant discourse into an active mechanism. The dominant discourse is simply the accompaniment of a politics, a prophecy that contributes to its own realization because those producing it have an interest in its truth and the means to make it true. The dominant representations continuously objectify themselves in things, and the social world contains the realized ideology on every hand, in the form of institutions, objects and mechanisms (not to speak of the habitus of agents). Each new choice that the dominant politics succeeds in imposing contributes to restricting the universe of the possible, or more exactly, increasing the weight of constraints that a politics oriented towards the possibilities that are rejected at each moment must reckon with. This is to say that any political action must come up against the structure of the social world in so far as it is itself, at least partly, the product of previous political actions: historical heritage is also capital. The objectivized trace of past political actions faces the revolutionary intention with the need to choose between the destruction, disqualification or reconversion of a large part of the capital accumulated, or else simply a change in the methods of management of this capital and the functions assigned to it. The 'realists', whose disenchanting good sense finds its formal expression in the economic theory of externalities or the organicist theory of systems, always have social rationality on their side, and sometimes also social science, when, implicitly playing on the double sense of the word 'law', this reduces the possible to the probable (i.e., sociologism). The progressive objectification of representations and political actions oriented towards the reproduction of the established order is analogous to a process of *ageing*, and indissociably from this, of disenchantment, which tends to strengthen the antagonism between the two political modalities of apprehending reality, utopianism and sociologism (as a form of realism), by continuously reducing the share of utopianism that realism – or, rather, realistic utopianism – authorizes.

And if we actually spoke about Afghanistan, instead of saying what people should think about Afghanistan as a function of that said by those only concerned about what should be said?[*]

Between the discourse of those service intellectuals who put their supposed professional competence in the service of a 'line', and – already knowing the result – massage the facts until the sum comes out right (something that is all the easier, the more complex the reality under consideration, the more ambiguous and refractory to familiar models), between this and the silence of specialists who speak only for their peers, and find the limits imposed by the rules of academic good manners a reason or an excuse to abstain, there is room for a kind of analysis that seeks to speak about the object in question, and that, without going beyond the (very real) due limits of knowledge, tries to provide at least the elements of a critical vision.

This is what we have tried to demonstrate here, by questioning Pierre and Micheline Centlivres, Swiss ethnologists from the University of Neuchâtel, who spent several years in Kabul and northern Afghanistan, and are the authors of major works on the country: its economic and social structures, inter-ethnic relations, popular art and the condition of women.

[*] Presentation of an interview with Pierre and Micheline Centlivres, *Actes de Recherche en Sciences Sociales* 34, September 1980, p. 3. The Centlivres's books include *Un Bazar d'Asie centrale. Forme et organisation du bazar de Tâshqurghân, Afghanistan*, (Wiesbaden: L. Reichert 1972) and *Popular Art in Afghanistan*, (Graz: Akadem. Druck-v. Verlagsanst 1976).

The culture of the rich*

Politics is also the constitutive principle of 'general culture', and especially of that literary culture required in the oral examination of the entrance competition for the École Normale d'Administration: the political taxonomies that prevail in Sciences-Po provide the basis for the selection of authors adopted and the principles of classification that are applied to them. For instance, the preparatory course for the ENA at the Centre de Formation Professionelle et Perfectionnement (from where the following list is taken) distinguishes among twentieth-century writers the 'traditionalists' (Saint-Exupéry, G. Bernanos, H. de Montherlant), the 'neo-monarchists' and 'neo-fascists' (C. Maurras, M. Barrès, R. Brasillach), those 'writers committed to the search for a new humanism' (S. Weil, E. Mounier: 'personalism and the twentieth-century revolution', the 'heroic humanism of Camus and Malraux', etc.). But this disparate culture, which does not flinch from referring to Sartre, Marcuse and Marx, is not just an instrument for the internalization of 'virile' values – those of the 'leader' – a cult maintained by the ENA: the 'great physical lyricism of sport' (Montherlant), the 'taste of the people' and 'fraternity' (Péguy), 'stoicism (Saint-Exupéry), the quest for the 'fusion of those two deep passions [. . .], the human order and God' (Teilhard de Chardin). Its other function is to supply the future high officials who are inculcated with all this the weapons they need to attack the adversary on his own ground, that of 'left-wing thought resolutely hostile to capitalism', or even Marxist culture (in the way that Chirac reminded Marchais in a media debate of the 'fundamental principles of Leninism').

---

* See 'Declaration of intent, *Actes de la Recherche en Sciences Sociales* 5/6, November 1975,' p. 97, above.

The anatomy of taste*

'Certain people believe that luxury is the opposite of poverty. No, it is the opposite of vulgarity'

Coco Chanel

Scientific discourse on art and the social uses of the work of art is condemned to appear both vulgar and terroristic: vulgar, because it transgresses the sacred boundary that distinguishes the pure reign of art and culture from the inferior domain of politics, a distinction that lies at the very root of the effects of symbolic domination exercised by culture and in its name; and terroristic, because it claims to reduce to 'uniform' classifications everything that is 'free' and 'illuminated', 'multiple' and 'different', enclosing an experience that is par excellence that of 'play' and 'jouissance' in the prosaic propositions of a 'positive' (and thus 'positivist') knowledge, 'totalizing' (and thus 'totalitarian'), in the favoured expression of those disturbed by this knowledge on their luxury cruises in a boat named desire.

This discourse, whose only object is to bring to light certain of the most common patterns of thought, does not really reveal anything that is not already known by all – but only in a partial and biased manner, self-interested and polemical, in flashes of class contempt and hatred, before the shades of ordinary unconsciousness soon close on it again. 'Conforama is the Guy Lux of furniture':[16] class prejudice lies at the root of the self-interested lucidity of all the statements of this ilk that the everyday class struggle generates. Only the mental work needed to construct the field of struggles within which partial points of view and antagonistic strategies are defined, makes it possible to accede to a knowledge

---

* Declaration of intent, *Actes de la Recherche en Sciences Sociales* 5, October 1976.
[16] M. Righini, 'L'entrée dans les meubles', *Le Nouvel Observateur*, 17 May 1976.

that is distinguished from the blind clairvoyance of participants without identifying itself with the sovereign gaze of the impartial observer.[17] This objectification is not complete unless it objectifies the site of objectification, that unseen point of view, the blind point of all theories, the intellectual field and its conflicts of interest, in which an interest in truth is sometimes generated by a necessary accident; as well as the subtle contributions that it brings to the maintenance of the symbolic order, even by the subversive intent – purely symbolic – that the division of labour of domination most commonly assigns to it.[18]

[17] This is why we have refrained from illustrating with extracts from interviews or documents certain expressions of petty-bourgeois or popular taste, fearing that in the eyes of some people, simple objectification might become what it often is, i.e. the pillorying of a taste that can only be 'bad', given the position of those whose taste it is.

[18] Is it not significant that intellectuals and artists, 'individuals' who like to be treated as 'personalities' and oppose a violent resistance to any questioning of the sources of their cultural capital, or to any objectification of their material or symbolic advantages, arrogate to themselves a universal right of objectification, and only accept statistics when these are applied to the 'masses'? (One might look in vain for any other basis for the ritual distinction between a sociology of the reception of works of culture, which is acceptable, and a sociology of 'creation', seen as profaning and vulgar.)

1970–1980: political commitment and ideological shift

Whilst working-class mobilization retreated from the front of the political stage, now occupied by the engagement of intellectuals in social and political struggles, Michel Foucault established in February 1971 the Groupe d'Information sur les Prisons (GIP), a space for discussion of the 'political oppression' exercised through the various institutions of incarceration. An investigation into the conditions of life of inmates focused on the functioning of the prison system: demonstrations were organized, often marked by violent polemic, as on the occasion of the prison riots in late 1971.

The context of these activities, which broke with the traditional forms of trade-union and party-based protest and action, was that of a 'counter-cultural leftism'[19] marked by the formation of a large number of collectives in various sectors of social space: the Mouvement de Libération des Femmes (MLF), the Front Homosexuel d'Action Révolutionnaire (FHAR), Front de Libération des Jeunes and other autonomous movements found in the themes of marginality, dissidence and illegality slogans that summed up their contestational and anti-institutional mood.

According to Foucault, the Sartrean model of the universal intellectual (who sought to be present on all fronts of thought) was in the course of being supplanted by the figure of the 'scientific expert' who spoke in the name of a local truth. This 'specific intellectual' required the establishment of a new link between theory and practice, in order to establish the cross-fertilization of knowledge that would make the school and the university sites of exchange between magistrates, doctors and social workers. The most prominent authors at the experimental university of Vincennes, Gilles Deleuze, Félix Guattari and Jean-François Lyotard, embodied this avant-garde style and made a major contribution to the production of these anti-repressive themes.[20] 1973

---

[19] Cf. Gérard Mauger, 'Gauchisme, contre-culture et néo-libéralisme. Pour une histoire de la generation 68', in *L'Identité politique* (Paris: PUF 1994), pp. 206–26. [Ed.]

[20] For an analysis of this ideological conjuncture and the 'anti-repressive' themes, cf. Louis Pinto, *Les Philosophes entre le lycée et l'avant-garde. Les métamorphoses de la philosophie aujourd'hui* (Paris: L'Harmattan 1987), pp. 109–19; for a history of the University of Vincennes, cf. Charles Soulié, 'Le destin d'une institution d'avant-garde: histoire du département de philosophie de Paris VIII', in *Histoire de l'Éducation*, January 1988, no. 77, pp. 47–69. [Ed.]

saw the launch of the daily *Libération*, with Sartre as its first director, and the self-proclaimed objective of 'giving speech to the people'. Yet political life remained monopolized by the Common Programme of the left and the perspective of an electoral victory. Subsequently, the weight of economic crisis and unemployment re-centred social challenge around classical objectives: wages and employment.

In parallel with these developments, the same years saw a major shift in the ideological conjuncture: the economic difficulties of the Eastern countries, the repression in Czechoslovakia and Poland and the reception of Solzhenitsyn's *Gulag Archipelago*, all contributed to the relative retreat of Marxism in the reference points of the intellectual and political left that came to power in May 1981: the revelation of the crimes committed in Cambodia under the regime of Pol Pot, and in China during the Cultural Revolution, contributed to de-legitimizing Maoist and Third Worldist commitment.

Revolutionary enthusiasm was thus followed by (re)conversion and repudiation, as illustrated by the trajectory of the '*nouveaux philosophes*'. A group of young writers close to *Le Nouvel Observateur*, who included André Glucksmann and Bernard-Henri Lévy, moved in the space of a few years from a more or less clearly asserted leftism to dramatic questioning of the nature of totalitarianism. The echo that this reversal immediately found in the media contributed to the discredit that subsequently afflicted any social and political challenge – a tendency that continued to strengthen in the wake of the political disillusion generated after 1981 by the governments of the left.

In this context, and beyond the theoretical differences that separated Michel Foucault and Pierre Bourdieu, their commitment alongside the CFDT[21] signalled a desire to put their scholarly prestige at the service of progressive causes, basing themselves on the sentiment of political upheaval provoked by the advent of the left to power in May 1981. The favourable response to the government's first measures, which Foucault wrote were 'inscribed in a left-wing logic', in no way implied unconditional support: the mobilization for Poland in December 1981 was the most striking example of this mode of 'restive cooperation'.

---

[21] [Confédération Française Democratique du Travail, the second largest trade-union federation, with Christian origins, but fully secular since 1964, and in the 1970s influenced by ideas of self-management.]

1981–1986

The power of conceiving society and changing it cannot be delegated, above all not to a state that arrogates itself the right to effect the happiness of the citizens without their own involvement, or even despite them. This power of transformation, more or less revolutionary, cannot be delegated to apparatchiks of any kind, who are always ready to become apparatchiks of the state.

5
Lay People and Professionals in Politics

At the start of the 1980s, the texts that P:.rre Bourdieu published on the field of politics analyzed the separation between professionals and lay people in politics, which reinforced the logic of party apparatuses. The support he gave to the 'clown vote' – the candidacy of the comedian Coluche in the presidential election of 1981 – was part of the critique of this closure on itself of the world of politics.

Silence on the conditions that face citizens with the alternative between the resignation of abstention and the dispossession of delegation – and all the more sharply if they are economically and culturally deprived – is to 'political science' what silence on the economic and cultural preconditions of 'rational' economic behaviour is to the science of economics. To avoid *naturalizing* the social mechanisms that produce and reproduce the break between 'politically active' and 'politically passive' agents,[1] and establishing as eternal laws certain historical regularities that are valid within the bounds of a determined state of the structure of distribution of capital, cultural capital in particular, any analysis of political struggle has to base itself on the economic and social determinants of the division of political labour.[2]

As it happened, it was an international event that revealed the results of this political closure most acutely. In Poland on the night of 12–13 December 1981, the forces of General Jaruzelski, supported by the USSR, intervened against the trade union Solidarnosc, arresting several of its leaders. In response to a journalist's question as to whether the French government intended to take any action, the foreign minister, Claude Cheysson, stated: 'Absolutely not. It should be clearly understood that we are not going to do anything. We are keeping informed of the situation.'[3] In the face of this lack of reaction on the part of the French

---

[1] Max Weber, *Wirtschaft und Gesellschaft*, vol. 2 (Berlin/Cologne: Kiepenheuer & Wirsch 1956), p. 1067.

[2] 'La représentation politique. Eléments pour une théorie du champ politique', in *Actes de Recherche en Sciences Sociales*, 1981, no. 36/37, pp. 3–24. [Ed.]

[3] Cited by Jean-François Sirinelli, *Intellectuels et passions françaises. Manifestes et pétitions au XXe siècle* (Paris: Fayard 1990), p. 298. [Ed.]

government to the proclamation of martial law, Pierre Bourdieu – who had just been promoted to the chair of sociology at the Collège de France – proposed to other public figures, including Michel Foucault, that they should sign an appeal to exert pressure on the Socialist government.

The object was to assert the necessary autonomy of intellectuals vis-à-vis political power, even if this was Socialist and sought to embody, as the minister of culture Jack Lang had prophesied in the media, 'a transition from darkness to light'. The sharpness of Lang's response is evidence of the fact that an appeal by personalities of the left criticizing the action of the government amounted in his eyes to heresy: 'What clowns, what dishonesty!' he declared in Les Nouvelles Littéraires, *before denouncing, in* Le Matin, *'the typically structuralist inconsistency' of this group of intellectuals.[4] Jack Lang subsequently organized a demonstration of support for the Polish people at the Paris Opéra, on 22 December, and coordinated a counter-petition published in* Le Monde *on the 23rd, which denounced the repression while supporting the action of the French government.*

The first appeal that Pierre Bourdieu signed, and the interview he gave the following day on the occasion of a second common appeal by the CFDT and the group of intellectuals, are reproduced below (see pp.126–30); looking back on this intervention in 1985, he recalled the context, which enabled him to analyze his motivations and specify the relations that intellectuals maintained with the Communist and Socialist parties, and with the trade unions (see p.131).

This commitment to Poland also went together, at the time when the sociologist published Ce que parler veut dire,[5] *with a reflection on the basis of the authority of 'speakers' and delegates. In order to 'disclose the wellsprings of power', he maintained, it was necessary to demonstrate the 'magic of words', which – far from being mere instruments of communication – possessed the symbolic effectiveness of constituting social reality (see p.133). A work that philosophy should equally help to clarify, as Bourdieu explained in a comment in the* Libération *books section, announcing the appearance of an essay in analytical philosophy:*

Appealing to the authority of the conception of philosophy held by analytic philosophy, I simply want to mention the subversive import, and not just at the theoretical level, that an application of the therapeutic analysis of language could have on the world of society. [. . .] What precisely is the University, the Church or the State? What does the existence of each of these entities involve? Can one say that a church or a state exists in the same sense as a stone, an animal or an idea?

[4] Cited by Didier Éribon, in *Michel Foucault* (Paris: Flammarion 1991), p. 318. [Ed.]
[5] Paris: Fayard 1982. [Ed.]

The inclination to reification of concepts and the propensity to abusive generalization are inscribed in the words with which we speak of the social world. And all the more forcefully so to the extent that there are all kinds of people with a vital interest in slipping in an existential statement – the nation exists, France exists, etc. – under a predicative statement – the nation is unanimous, public opinion is indignant.

The panoply of virtues that this way of philosophizing offers is readily understandable: by proposing to do justice to language [. . .] by a work of criticism that aims in its very act to offload concepts, it makes an important contribution, on condition that it is generalized to all domains of existence, such as the critique of the magical, theological and fetishistic thinking that still so commonly haunts the world of society.[6]

---

[6] 'Zaslawski contre la magie des mots. Sur Analyze de l'être. Essai de philosophie analytique de Denis Zaslawski, Paris 1982', Libération, 7 December 1982. [Ed.]

Notice to the people
COLUCHE THE CANDIDATE

I call on the lazy, the dirty, drug addicts, alcoholics, queers, women, parasites, the young, the old, jailbirds, dykes, apprentices, Blacks, pedestrians, Arabs, French, the hairy, the mad, transvestites, former Communists, convinced abstentionists, all those who politicians leave out of the count, to vote for me, put their name on the voters' list and spread the news.

ALL TOGETHER TO KICK THEM IN THE BUTT WITH COLUCHE

THE ONLY CANDIDATE WITH NO REASON TO LIE

Poster for Michel Colluci, known as Coluche, as candidate in the presidential election of 1981.

Politics belongs to them*

[As for] the use that certain politicians make of the accusation of irresponsibility which they launch against lay people who try and meddle in politics: scarcely accepting this intrusion into the sacred circle of politicians, the accusation calls them to order in the same way as clerics remind the laity of their lack of legitimacy. At the time of the Reformation, for example, one of the problems that arose was that women wanted to say mass and give extreme unction. The clergy defended what Max Weber called their 'monopoly of the legitimate manipulation of the goods of salvation', and denounced an illegal practice of religion. When a simple citizen is told that he is politically irresponsible, he is accused of illegally practising politics. One of the virtues of these irresponsible people – of whom I am one – is that they bring to light a tactic presupposition of the political order, precisely that lay people are excluded from it. Coluche's candidacy was one of these irresponsible acts. I would like to recall that Coluche was not an actual candidate, but called himself a candidate for candidacy in order to remind people that anyone could be a candidate. The whole media-political field was mobilized, across all political differences, to condemn the downright barbarity of questioning the fundamental presupposition that only politicians are allowed to talk politics. Only politicians have the necessary competence (a very important word, both technical and legal) to talk politics. It is their business to speak of politics. Politics belongs to them. That tacit presupposition is inscribed in the very existence of the political field.

* Extract from a lecture given on 11 February 1999, published under the title 'Le champ politique' in *Propos sur le champ politique* (Lyon: Presses Universitaire de Lyon 2000), pp. 55–6.

Missed opportunities:
after 1936 and 1956, 1981?*

Several intellectuals express their indignation in the wake of Claude Cheysson's statements

The French government must not be allowed, like Moscow or Washington, to claim that the establishment of a military dictatorship in Poland is a domestic matter that will leave the Polish people able to decide their own fate. That is an immoral and lying assertion. Poland has just woken up under martial law, with thousands interned, trade unions banned, tanks in the street and the death penalty threatened for all disobedience.

This is certainly not a situation that the Polish people wanted! It is a lie to present the Polish army and the party to which this is so closely tied as an instrument of national sovereignty.

The Polish Communist Party which controls the army has always been the instrument of subjecting Poland to the Soviet Union. You could say that the Chilean army was also a national army.

By claiming against all truth and morality that the situation in Poland is simply a matter for the Poles, the French Socialist leaders show that they attach more importance to their domestic allies than to the help due a nation in danger.

Their good relationship with the French Communist Party would thus seem to be more important to them than the crushing of a workers' movement under the military jackboot. In 1936, a Socialist government was confronted with a military putsch in Spain, and in 1956, a Socialist government was confronted with the repression in Hungary. In 1981, the Socialist government is confronted with the coup in Warsaw. We do not want its attitude today to be the same as its predecessors. We remind it of its promise to put obligations of international morality above realpolitik.

FIRST SIGNATORIES:
Pierre Bourdieu, professor at the Collège de France; Patrice Chereau, theatre director; Marguerite Duras, writer; Costas Gravas, film-maker; Bernard Kouchner, Médecins du monde; Michel Foucault, professor at the Collège de France; Claude Mauriac, writer; Yves Montand, actor; Claude Sautet, film-maker; Jorge Semprun, writer; Simone Signoret, actress.

* *Libération*, Tuesday 15 December 1981.

Rediscovering the left's libertarian tradition*

You took the initiative last Monday, along with ten other intellectuals and several hundred other signatories, in launching an appeal in support of Poland, which severely criticized the French government. These criticisms seemed particularly strong in that they were addressed to a Socialist administration.

Faced with events such as those in Warsaw, there is no room for beating about the bush. Speaking out and action are needed. But how? The only possible action for an ordinary French citizen is via the French government. In this sense, our text dealt with Poland and only with Poland. It seemed particularly intolerable to us that a Socialist government, which rightly claimed to give its actions a moral dimension, did not utter a clear and immediate symbolic condemnation of the coup de force. It acted as if the only choice was between declaring war and doing nothing. This is very convenient when the intention is to do nothing, or to justify oneself in doing nothing. But if you only look around, there is a whole arsenal of economic and symbolic weapons. The government has started finding some of these, under pressure of public opinion, which still needs to bear on it so that it really does act.

But to return to this point: what is abnormal about addressing oneself to the government? On such questions of foreign policy, it alone has the ability to speak and act effectively in our name; we have delegated to it our powers in this matter. As intellectuals, we have the privilege of being able to exercise with particular effectiveness a right that every citizen has. (Even if the publication of our appeal met with a certain resistance . . .). One might have expected the President of the Republic to come and explain a month later, in a fireside chat, what he thinks of Poland and what he was able to say at secret 'summit' meetings! Twenty years of the Fifth Republic have atrophied basic democratic reflexes. A government can be recalled to order, and has to be in this case.

There was your 'ethical' reaction to the repression in Poland, but the initiative of some of the first signatories of this text, to propose a joint appeal with the CFDT, went rather further. To what extent do you believe that the Polish crisis justifies the declaration of a kind of state of emergency for the intellectual movement?

* An interview with René Pierre and Didier Éribon, published in *Libération*, 23 December 1981.

The regime under which we find ourselves is that those who govern hold all powers. This strikes me as an unhealthy situation, in any case. But it is especially so when those who hold power feel themselves invested, supported and justified by the popular forces, so that it is hard to see how these can express themselves. The only effective countervailing power that I see is the criticism of intellectuals and the action of trade unions. I believe that intellectuals are quite right, like any other citizens, to exercise a critical vigilance – which does not mean to say a negative one – at all times. It was not so long ago that the silence of intellectuals was deplored. Now, when they do speak, it is seen as a scandal. This means in all logic that no other right is granted intellectuals, and by extension all other citizens, but to speak in support of the government. On this point, our appeal had a revelatory function ('a trap for fools', Sartre would have said). It provoked certain stupid and ridiculous statements, that were both indecent – I'm thinking of the attacks against Yves Montand and 'left intellectuals' in general – and disturbing – such as the tones, worthy of Kanapa,[7] that our minister of culture used to oppose the 'perfect loyalty' of the Communist ministers to the typically 'structuralist' inconsistency of the intellectuals.

But why the connection with the CFDT? There are evident reasons. This organization immediately reacted, before any other body, in the way that all trade-union organizations should have done in the face of the military clampdown on a trade-union movement. This normal action only appeared unusual because of the abnormal failure of the organs of expression of the workers' movement. It was not us who selected the CFDT as our only partner in dialogue.

But why did such a connection between intellectuals and trade unions seem necessary to you?

In the first place, for its symbolic value, to the extent that it evoked what was one of the original aspects of the Solidarity movement. And by this very fact it could contribute to the defence of Solidarity. But there was also a certain convergence in our analysis of the Polish situation. Solidarity is a major and non-militarized workers' movement that was crushed by military force, and also a movement directed against state socialism. The power of conceiving society and changing it cannot be delegated, above all not to a state that arrogates itself the right to effect the happiness of its citizens without their involvement, or even despite them. This power of transformation, more or less revolutionary, cannot be delegated to apparatchiks of

---

[7] Jean Kanapa, a journalist on *Humanité*, was the embodiment of Stalinist sectarianism. [Ed.]

any kind, who are always ready to become apparatchiks of the state. That is something that the Polish movement brought home: the bankruptcy of a system in which movement is supposed to take place from above.

Does this mean that you think a permanent alliance should be formed between the intellectuals and the CFDT?

Each side has to decide for itself on this point. As far as I am concerned, I think that the appeal we launched together was a particular event, and that if such an initiative were needed again, it would have to be discussed afresh in the circumstances of the time. That said, it seems to me that, as things now stand, the CFDT has 'expressed' or 'recuperated', depending on your point of view, the whole anti-institutional current that was one of the major components of the French left. There was May '68 and the critique of the education system; there has been ecology and the questioning of a whole way of life; there has been the feminist movement; and there has also been, which is not the least important, the critique of apparatuses, of centralism, of hierarchical relations and authority relationships at work, at school, in the family and so on. And the CFDT for its part, by virtue of the position it occupies in the field of competition between the different trade-union federations, and particularly in relation to the CGT – also because of the particular qualities of its activists, who are particularly sensitive to symbolism and the symbolic forms of domination – understood and expressed all this best. But that would require a very long analysis.

The encounter between intellectuals and the CFDT might also be explained by the fact that both sides are sensitive to the fact that anti-constitutional currents have felt poorly expressed since the election of 10 May [1981]. Programmes and promises are handed down, as if everything that did not go through the mill of apparatuses, congresses, programmes and platforms did not exist. People forget that, for sociological reasons that I cannot go into here, French society has been the site, over the last twenty years, of a prodigious work of political invention, and that there are places, in this intellectual world and elsewhere, that this work is continuing. We certainly can't say that imagination is in power.

Can intellectuals have a social and political expression that is specific to them? And isn't this link with the social movement very problematic?

It is hard in fact to make intellectual criticism really effective. The question is to give social force to intellectual criticism, and intellectual force to social criticism; ruling out from the start the posture of 'fellow-traveller' who swallows whatever is offered, and the Leninist dream of the intellectual giving discipline to the working-class apparatus. Certainly the situation of the free intellectual – the 'irresponsible' intellectual if you prefer – is the condition for any free political analysis, and particularly a free analysis of the world of politics. My intention at any rate is to defend this position without any kind of complex against all those with 'responsibility' who place the interests of organizations before the interest in the truth, against all who speak with the voice of the Communist party. In a more general way, the main obstacle to establishing new relationships between intellectuals and the workers' movement arises from a convergence between the *ouvriérisme* of certain cadres of working-class origin in the left organizations and the anti-intellectualism of certain intellectuals who use the apparatuses of the left to strengthen their position as intellectuals. Here again, the analysis needs protracted development and precision.

To come back to the action in support of Poland, I think that the link between intellectuals and the broad trade-union movement is undoubtedly the best means to give this action its full effectiveness, and make it exert pressure on the government. Since Zola, intellectuals have not invented any new means of action; they suffer from the ineffectiveness of petitions, and the star system to which these condemn them. I would add that the logic of petitions – which always presupposes an initiative, and therefore an initial origin – tends to divide a milieu that is destined to individual competition by the very logic of its operation. That is why for a long time I have put forward the utopian idea of establishing a group of intellectuals who would sign texts collectively, with these being written by whoever is the most competent on the question at issue, and read out by an actor. In this sense, the Montand-Foucault broadcast on Europe 1, which aroused such a strong reaction on the part of our leaders – and also among the public, which is the most important thing – strikes me as exemplary.

Is your present action a weapon against the French Communist Party?

I will at least say that the PCF, which claims to be concerned for domestic peace in Poland (as well as within the French government), has undoubtedly underestimated the power it can wield, as the eldest daughter of the (Communist) church, in favour of such domestic peace. It is enough to note the echo that the remarkable statements by Berlinguer have had, to measure the seriousness of the PCF's complicity.

Poland is certainly not Chile, if only because every situation is always different; there is no principle of identity, or an identity of intellectuals.

Intellectuals and established powers[*]

A retrospective on our support for Solidarity

When I called Michel Foucault on Monday, 14 December 1981, to propose that we should write a joint appeal on Poland and make contact with the CFDT, I evidently had in mind the idea of establishing an analogous connection to that which had been made in Poland between intellectuals and the workers of Solidarity.

Now, if this connection did come into existence, and had a very great symbolic effect, its subsequent development was certainly not all that I had hoped. This is why I believe I owe it to the truth, and to the memory of Michel Foucault, who did not mince words, to say what I expected, in the hope that this might be useful on a future occasion.

As I saw it, the object in this initiative was to break with the old tailist model of the party intellectual, in an action of international solidarity with a movement that was itself characterized by the fact that intellectuals were not reduced to the role of fellow-travellers that they have generally been assigned. The assertion of the existence of intellectuals as a group, no more and no less justified in their existence than other groups, but able to impose their views by using their particular weapons, appeared particularly necessary to me at a point when the newly prevailing political order in France was one that had traditionally covered itself with intellectual justifications. Is it not significant that there was never so much said about the silence of the intellectuals as at the very time when they really did speak out, about Poland, arousing the fury of organic intellectuals?

Intellectuals *and* the CFDT. Intellectuals *of* the CFDT.[8] The whole issue at stake lies in this difference. In order for there to be a connection, two sides are needed. Intellectuals have no need to justify their existence in the eyes of their partners by offering their services, even what might seem the noblest of these in their eyes, such as theoretical services. They have to be what they are, to produce and impose their vision of the social world, which is not necessarily better or worse than any other, and give their ideas all the strength they are capable of. They are not representatives of universality, still

[*] Published in *Michel Foucault, une histoire de la vérité* (Paris: Syros 1985).
[8] The same distinction would be valid *a fortiori* elsewhere.

less a 'universal class', but it does happen that, for historical reasons, they are often *interested in universality*.

I will not develop here the reasons that make me think that it is urgent today to create an international of artists and scientists able to propose or impose reflections and recommendations on the political and economic powers that be. I will just say – and I believe Michel Foucault would have agreed – that the only possible basis for a power that is specifically intellectual, and intellectually legitimate, lies in the most complete autonomy in relation to all existing powers.

Revealing the wellsprings of power[*]

What struck me in your book Ce que parler veut dire *is that the question of power and domination actually runs through it from one end to the other.*

Any kind of discourse, whatever it may be, is the product of an encounter between a *linguistic habitus*, i.e. a competence that is inextricably both technical and social (both the ability to speak and the ability to speak in a certain socially marked fashion), and a *market*, i.e. a system of price formation that contributes to give linguistic production an orientation in advance. This is true at the level of the basic dyad, in the dialogues of everyday existence, but also, and in a more evident way, in confrontation with an *audience*, with discourses uttered on official occasions or with philosophical writing, as I tried to show in relation to Heidegger. Now, all these relationships of communication are also – except by special convention – relations of power, and the linguistic market also has its monopolies, whether these are languages that are sacred or reserved for a caste, or secret languages, with the languages of science somewhere in between.

More deeply, this book gives the impression of drawing in outline a general theory of power and even politics, particularly by way of the notion of 'symbolic power'.

Symbolic power is a power (economic, political, cultural or other) that is in a position to have itself recognized, to obtain recognition; and at the same time have itself misrecognized in its truth as power and arbitrary violence. The specific effectiveness of this power is exercised not in the order of physical force but rather that of meaning and knowledge. The noble, for example, as the Latin *nobilis* makes clear, is a man who is 'known' or 'recognized'. That said, as soon as we escape from the physicalism of power relations and reintroduce relations of knowledge, the logic of necessary alternatives means that we have every chance of falling into the tradition of the philosophy of the subject, of consciousness, and conceiving these acts of recognition as free acts of submission and complicity. But meaning and knowledge in no way imply consciousness, and we have to look in a quite opposite direction, that indicated by the late Heidegger and by Merleau-Ponty: social agents,

[*] Interview with Didier Éribon, published in *Libération*, 19 October 1982.

133

and the dominated themselves, are bound into the social world (even the most repugnant and revolting social world) by a relationship of complicity that makes certain aspects of this world lie always beyond or behind the possibility of critical questioning. It is by the mediation of this obscure relationship of quasi-corporal adherence that the effects of symbolic power are exercised. Political submission is inscribed in the postures and movements of the body, and the automatisms of the brain. The vocabulary of domination is full of bodily metaphors: 'bowing', 'lying down', 'showing flexibility', 'bending', 'getting into bed with', etc. Sexual metaphors also, of course. Words only express the political gymnastics of domination as well as they do because they are, along with the body itself, the support of deeply buried assemblages in which a social order is inscribed in the long term.

So you think that language should be at the centre of any analysis of politics?

Here again, we have to guard against the alternatives of ordinary usage. Either we speak of language as if its only function were to communicate; or we set out to find in words the principle of the power that in certain cases is exercised through language (I have in mind here, for example, orders and slogans). Words actually exert a power that is typically magical: they make people see, make them believe, make them act. But just as with magic, we have to ask where the origin of this action lies, or more exactly, what are the social conditions that make possible this magical effect of words. The power of words is only experienced by those who are disposed to hear them and listen to them – in other words, to believe them. In Béarn dialect, the word for obey is *crede*, which also means believe. It is the whole of early education, in the broad sense, that deposits in each person the wellsprings that words (a papal bull, a party slogan, a psychoanalytic suggestion, an expert witness in a divorce case, etc.) can trigger at a later date. The origin of the power of words lies in the complicity that is established, by way of words, between a social body incarnated in a biological body, that of authorized representatives, and biological bodies that are socially fashioned to recognize their orders – but also their exhortations, insinuations and injunctions, these being the 'subjects addressed', the believers, the faithful.

But there are specific effects of language, and a specific effectiveness?

It is surprising in fact how those people who never stop speaking of language and speech, or even of the 'illocutionary force' of speech, have never raised the question of the representative speaker. If political work is essentially work with words, this is because words contribute to making the social world.

One need only think of the countless circumlocutions, periphrases and euphemisms that were invented, throughout the Algerian war, out of a concern to avoid granting the recognition implicit in the fact of calling things by their name instead of euphemistically denying them. In politics, nothing is more realist than quarrels over words. To put one word in place of another is to change one's vision of the social world, and by that very token, contribute to transforming it. To speak of the working class, to make the working class speak (by speaking for it), to represent it, is to give a different existence to a group that the euphemisms of ordinary unconscious-ness symbolically deny (the 'humble', 'ordinary people', the 'man in the street', the 'average Frenchman' – or, for certain sociologists, the 'modest categories'). The paradox of Marxism is that it has not included in its theory of classes the theoretical effect that the Marxist theory of classes has produced, and that has contributed to making it possible for something such as classes to continue to exist today.

As far as the social world is concerned, the neo-Kantian theory that confers on language and more generally on representations a specifically symbolic effect in the construction of reality is perfectly well founded. Groups (and especially social classes) are always from one point of view artefacts; they are a product of the logic of representation that enables a biological individual, or a small number of biological individuals – general secretary or central committee, pope and bishops, etc. – to speak in the name of a whole group, to make the group speak and act 'as one man', to make believe – and first of all make the group that they represent believe – that the group exists. As a group made man, the representative embodies a fictitious individual, the particular kind of mystic body that a group is; he removes the members of the group from the state of a mere aggregate of separate individuals, enabling them to act and speak through him with one sole voice. In exchange, he receives the right to act and speak in the name of the group, to take himself for the group that he embodies (France, the people, etc.), and to identify himself with the function to which he gives himself body and soul, thus giving a biological body to a constituted one. The logic of politics is that of magic, or if you like, that of fetishism.

Do you see your work as a radical questioning of politics?

Sociology has an affinity with comedy, in that it reveals the wellsprings of authority. Through disguise (Toinette as doctor), parody (the cod-Latin of Diafoirus) or caricature, Molière unmasks the hidden machinery that makes possible the production of the symbolic effects of imposition and intimida-tion, the tricks and dodges that make up the powerful and important of all ages – the ermine, the toga, the mortarboard, the Latin, the scholarly titles – everything that Pascal was the first to analyse.

After all, what is a pope, a president or a general secretary, if not someone who takes himself for pope or general secretary – or more exactly, takes himself for the church, the state, the party or the nation? The only thing distinguishing him from a stage character or a megalomaniac is that he is generally taken seriously, and his right to this kind of 'legitimate imposture', as Austin puts it, is generally recognized. Believe me, the world seen in this way – i.e. as it is – is pretty comical. But as has often been said, comedy goes side by side with tragedy. It is rather like Pascal staged by Molière.

All racism is essentialism*

Though there are many demonstrations of racism and xenophobia, there is a discrimination that does not have a name, though it is rampant: racism on the grounds of belonging to a social class.

I would like to say first of all that we must bear in mind that there is not just one racism, but several: there are as many racisms as there are groups that need to justify existing as they do – which is the invariant function of all racisms.

It strikes me as very important to bring analysis to bear on those forms of racism that are undoubtedly the most subtle, the most open to mis-recognition, and thus the most rarely denounced, perhaps because those who usually denounce racism themselves have some of the properties that incline people towards these forms of racism. I have in mind racism of the intelligence.

Racism of the intelligence is a racism of the dominant class that is distinguished by a number of properties from what is customarily denoted as racism, i.e. petty-bourgeois racism that is the main focus of the classical critiques of racism, starting with the most vigorous of these, such as that of Sartre.

This racism is specific to a dominant class whose reproduction depends, in part, on the transmission of cultural capital, an inherited capital that has the property of being an *embodied capital* and thus apparently natural and innate. Racism of the intelligence is racism through which the dominant aim is to produce a 'theodicy of their specific privilege', as Weber put it, i.e. a justification of the social order that they dominate. It is this that makes the dominant feel themselves to be of a *superior species*.

All racism is essentialism, and racism of the intelligence is the form of sociodicy characteristic of a dominant class whose power rests in part on the possession of titles that, like educational titles, are supposed to be guarantees of intelligence and have in many societies replaced earlier titles such as titles of property or nobility, even for access to positions of economic power.

* Published under the title 'Classe contre classe' in *Différence* 24–25, July 1983, p. 44, along with statements by the journalist Clara Cardiani, the writer Françoise Mallet-Joris and the priest Pierre Pihan (Mouvement Contre le Racisme et pour l'Amitié entre les Peuples).

On Michel Foucault*

The commitment of a 'specific intellectual'

On the death of Roland Barthes, Michel Foucault said: 'I've lost a friend and a colleague.' Today I can say the same. That is my only authorization to speak of him and his work.

I would like to try and say something that is certainly very far from obvious: constancy and coherence, theoretical and practical rigour. The constancy of an intellectual project, and of a way of living the intellectual life. Starting with the desire to break – which explains and excuses some of his famous apothegms on the death of man – to break with the totalizing ambition of what he called the 'universal intellectual', often identified with the project of philosophy; but to do so in the sense of escaping the alternative between saying nothing about everything or else everything about nothing.

In order to invent what he called the 'specific intellectual', it was in fact necessary to abandon 'the right to speak as a master of truth and justice', to abandon the status of 'moral and political conscience', of a spokesman and mandatory. And indeed, Michel Foucault never stopped maintaining that in questions of thought no delegation is possible. Without however succumbing to the illusory cult of thinking in the first person.

He knew better than anyone that games of truth are games of power, and that power and privilege lie at the very root of efforts to discover the truth about powers and privileges.

Michel Foucault sought to substitute for the absolutism of the universal intellectual, specific works drawing on actual sources – and we are in his debt for having exhumed whole regions of historical documentation that had been ignored by historians – but he did so without abandoning the broadest ambitions of thought. In the same sense, if he deliberately rejected the grand airs of the great moral conscience – a favourite object of laughter for him – he always stubbornly rejected the division between intellectual investment and political commitment that is so common and so convenient.

His political acts, which he conducted with passion and rigour, sometimes with a kind of rational fury, owed nothing to the sentiment of possessing ultimate truths and values, in the style of the Pharisees of politics and others.

---

* This text, published under the title 'Le plaisir du savoir' in *Le Monde* on 27 June 1984, was written in homage to 'the philosopher and professor at the Collège de France Michel Foucault, who died in Paris on 15 June at the age of fifty-seven'.

For him, the critical vision was applicable first of all to his own practice, and in this respect he was the purest representative of a new kind of intellectual who has no need to mystify himself as to the motives and themes of intellectual acts, nor to foster illusions about their effect, in order to practise them in full knowledge of their cause.

Nothing is more dangerous than to reduce a philosophy, especially one so subtle, complex and perverse, to a textbook formula. I will say right away that Foucault's work was a long exploration of the transgression of crossing social boundaries, which is an inseparable function of both knowledge and power. Hence undoubtedly his interest, right from the start with *Madness and Civilization*, in the social genesis of the division between the normal and the pathological that is materialized in the asylum.

This study of one of the most decisive social boundaries, that which underlies the state of reason, was at the same time a transgression of the boundary that divides off what remained unthought by Marx (Foucault liked to say that the best way to consider past thinkers was to make use of them, or even supersede them, and in this way kill two birds with one stone). While it would be easy to note many typically Marxist assertions in *Madness and Civilization* or *The Birth of the Clinic*, Foucault observed that psychiatric hospitalization, psychological normalization of individuals and penal institutions undoubtedly have a limited importance if only their economic function is considered. This does not however prevent them from playing an essential role in the machinery of power.

This led on to the analyses in *Discipline and Punish* on the omnipresence of power: relations of force exist also in relations of reproduction, in families, small groups, sexual relations and institutions. And above all perhaps in brains themselves. We come back here to transgression in the strictly philosophical sense, as an effort to think the unthought, the unthinkable, the taboo, i.e. that which limits thought and prohibits its going further.

To explore the unthought means first of all giving a history of the categories of thought, and of the knowledge that they permit and prohibit at one and the same stroke. This critical intention, in the Kantian sense, was realized in a social history that has little in common with the ordinary history of historians – but who will not think here of those exemplary exceptions provided by the works of Dumézil, one of Foucault's models, or by Duby on the *Three Orders*? This intention was evident in *Words and Things*, it was at work in *The Birth of the Clinic*, a social history of the clinical vision, of the medical will to see, and in *The History of Sexuality*. Close here to Bachelard and Canguilhem, who was one of his absolute models, as well as to Cassirer in his *Structure and Function* or *The Individual and the Cosmos*; by focusing on truth in the nascent state, i.e. fertile error,

Foucault transgressed the limit of their unthought by working to produce a materialist history of ideal structures.

Above all, however, it was by pressing to the limit an interest in error, by studying as a priority those sciences where the boundary between error and truth is most fragile, those most contaminated by ideology, such as clinical medicine or psychopathology, that Foucault sought to unveil the unthought of science, the unconscious of the sciences of thought.

Just as the history of knowledge refers constantly to error and defeat – for example in *The Birth of the Clinic*, error in bodily observations made in the absence of a genuine tissue analysis – so the hermeneutics of the subject that the history of sexuality proposes is a history of error and violence, which is never so visible, paradoxically, as in those disciplines – in both senses of the term – that the enlightened understanding of liberal reformism invented in order to control human behaviour: psychology, clinical medicine, the life sciences.

This discipline, a combination of knowledge and power, is realized first and foremost in language. And transgression here must find its weapons outside the tradition and world of canonic masters, on the side of the heretics. Nietzsche, of course, but also Sade, Artaud, Bataille, Roussel, Blanchot and Deleuze. According to Nietzsche, the key to sociology is philology. The social critique of reason leads to a social critique of language as the major limit of human thought. The taboo on words, of course, but above all perhaps the necessary transgression of the forbidden, the duty of freedom, the extorted confession, all recall that power lies in knowledge, but that knowledge lies in power; knowledge, and self-knowledge included, is exposed to the effects of power. Morality is haunted by politics.

I would have liked to express better this thought so stubbornly set on winning self-control, i.e. the control of its history, the history of the categories of thought, the history of wishing and desires. And also this concern with rigour, this rejection of opportunism, in both knowledge and practice, in the techniques of life as well as in political choices, which make Foucault an irreplaceable figure.

1984–1990

*Of someone who brazenly lies,
the Kabyles say: 'He gives you East
for West.' The apparatchiks of the
left have given us right for left.*

6

Education and Education Policy

From one government report to another

Elected to the Collège de France in 1982, Pierre Bourdieu continued his sociology of intellectuals with Homo Academicus, *which proposed an explanation of the determinant factors in political commitment among scholars caught in the academic game. Against the double bind formed by the challenge to university hierarchies in the name of 'democratization' and the defence of these hierarchies in the name of the quality of teaching, 'a pair of forces that act to maintain the status quo in all essentials', Bourdieu maintained the necessity of revisiting the place of scientific work in the university, something that the reforms of this time did not permit envisaging (see p.147).*

Drafted in the collective context of the Collège de France, and at the request of President Mitterrand, the report titled 'Propositions pour un Enseignement de l'Avenir' *provided Bourdieu with the opportunity to put into practice a commitment that was bound up with his position as a 'celebrated heretic' (see p.156).*

What pedagogic circles seem to have retained from these proposals is above all the critique of 'indifference to differences'; and yet the authors of the report did not link the diversification of forms of excellence so much to the abolition of all selection, as to the attenuation of educational verdicts that weighed on students as so many self-fulfilling prophecies. As Bourdieu explained in the columns of La Quinzaine Littéraire *(see p.160), this report sought to question the 'hierarchy of principles of hierarchization' and champion the validity of scientific and artistic experiment, the development of critical mechanisms, the establishment of a 'common minimum', the periodic revision of the curriculum, the right to education at every age, as well as the use of modern techniques of distributing information and an opening to interventions from outside. Finally, to go beyond the antinomy between statism and liberalism, the report proposed making establishments autonomous by the diversification of sources of finance, with the object of substituting for concealed and unequal competition a spirit of open and controlled emulation, via a redefinition of the role of the state.*

Bourdieu was subsequently very critical of the use made of this report (a personal supplement to the 'Lettre du président de la République aux Français' in the 1988 election campaign), and did not agree to chair the commission on the educational curriculum that was set up the following year by Lionel Jospin, minister of national education in Michel Rocard's government, during Mitterrand's second term as president.[1] *These seven 'principles for a discussion of the contents of education', commonly known as the 'Bourdieu-Gros report', proposed a restructuring of disciplinary divisions and of the conditions of their transmission (see p.173).*

How could 'the most critical sociology, that which presupposes and implies the most radical self-criticism',[2] *lend itself to such a reforming action? Did the works of Bourdieu and his collaborators not show how the school (and pedagogic activity in particular) imposed a 'cultural arbitrariness' favourable to the dominant classes? Far from claiming to overturn everything, the main object of this report was to investigate the share of inequalities that the teaching system could correct, leaving aside that which the system was in no position to tackle.*

The report of the Collège de France does not utter the word 'reproduction', nor even 'democratization'. It nowhere says that the educational system will equalize opportunities, that it will give culture to all. Nowhere . . . and that is very important. For the educational system is organized in such a way that it cannot in practice be made democratic; the best that can be done is to avoid strengthening inequality, rather than reinforcing by its particular effect, which is essentially symbolic, those pre-existing differences between the children entrusted to it. There are a whole series of proposals in this direction. The most important, from this point of view, is a warning against the fatal effect by which the educational institution transforms pre-existing social inequalities into natural inequality. If I were minister, the first recommendation I would make to teachers is: never make a value judgement on your students, you have no right to use words such as 'idiot' and 'stupid', you have no right to write in the margin 'this reasoning is imbecile', no right to put 'zero', and so on. In other words, you must avoid all value judgements that bear on the individual. You can say 'this exercise is not well done' or 'this solution is wrong', but you may not say 'you are hopeless in maths' or 'you're not cut out for maths'. Maths teachers should know and understand that they have a diabolic power of naming that is exercised on the very identity of adolescents, on their self-image, and that they can inflict terrible traumas, all the more so as their verdicts are often echoed and reinforced by angry and upset parents. Finally, I

---

[1] Michel Rocard had championed since the 1970s a 'modernized' and 'realistic' socialism, which claimed to be inspired by Pierre Mendès-France but very rapidly inspired a neoliberal current within the French left. He twice failed to win the Socialist presidential candidacy, in 1981 and 1988, and eventually owed his political rise to his appointment as prime minister in Mitterrand's second term. [Ed.]

[2] 'Sur l'objectification participante. Réponse à quelques objections', *Actes de la Recherche en Sciences Sociales* 23, September 1978, p. 68. [Ed.]

think that what is most progressive in this report is what it does not say, the fact that it does not promise the impossible, it does not demand that the educational system do things that it cannot do.[3]

His involvement in official reports of this kind, however, did not prevent Pierre Bourdieu from remaining attentive to the social movements that shook the teaching system and French society. The 1980s in fact saw the emergence of untypical forms of protest: actions by nurses in 1986 and the teachers' strike against the redistribution of powers in primary schools in 1987. At the time of the student mobilizations against the Devaquet project,[4] for instance, Bourdieu gave an interview that provided the opportunity to criticize the policy of both left and right-wing governments, and the lack of any political project for a school left prey to the liberal ideology of competition (see p.167). This attention to ongoing conflicts is found in his letter to the school students of Les Mureaux (see p.181), who had contacted him at the time of the lycée mobilizations of September–November 1990, in the course of which the media and political recuperation of certain incidents facilitated the stigmatizing of 'wreckers' who were promptly identified with 'youths from an immigrant background'.

These perspectives on politics – as government adviser and involved in social movements – pervaded his analysis of the structure and function of the 'field of power' presented in 1989 in The State Nobility, *the culmination of the studies Bourdieu had begun on the* grandes écoles *in the late 1960s: the struggles among the dominant for the preservation or transformation of educational institutions charged with the 'reproduction of the field of power' actually expressed a struggle for control of the state; but they 'add to the field of power a bit of that universal – reason, disinterestedness, civic-mindedness, etc. – that, originating as it does in previous struggles, is always a symbolically effective weapon in the struggles of the moment'.[5] All the same, this 'advance towards the universal' did not fill the gap between, on the one hand, the state bureaucracy (its legitimacy lying in its possession of educational titles) and political professionals (who govern with 'their eyes fixed on opinion polls'), and on the other, those who 'protest outside the established frameworks' – to whom Bourdieu devoted subsequent interviews and analyses in* The Weight of the World, *which proposed the inauguration of 'a different way of doing politics'.[6]*

---

[3] Interview conducted in Tokyo in October 1989, op. cit. [Ed.]

[4] From the name of the junior minister for research and higher education in the Chirac government, who proposed a university reform that particularly included raising enrolment costs. This unpopular measure triggered a student protest movement that was sufficiently strong as to lead to the withdrawal of the projected measure. [Ed.]

[5] *The State Nobility* (Cambridge: Polity 1996), p. 389. [Ed.]

[6] Pierre Bourdieu et al., *The Weight of the World* (Cambridge: Polity 1999), p. 627. The authors of this collective work were Alain Accardo, Gabrielle Balazs, Stéphane Beaud, François Bonvin, Emmanuel Bourdieu, Philippe Bourgois, Sylvain Broccolichi, Patrick Champagne, Rosine Christin, Jean-Pierre Faguer, Sandrine Garcia, Rémy Lenoir, Frédérique Matonti, Francine Muel-Dreyfus, Michel Pialoux, Louis Pinto, Denis Podalydès, Abdelmalek Sayad, Charles Soulié, Bernard Urlacher, Loïc Wacquant and Anne-Marie Waser. [Ed.]

The naked emperors of the university*

Pierre Bourdieu in this week's Le Nouvel Observateur, *that's something surprising. People say that you don't much like journalists.*

People say all kinds of things . . . In fact, I analyze the effects produced in the intellectual world by the introduction of outside criteria that are imposed by journalists, such as the fact of 'looking good' on television. Or belonging to a network of 'friends'. I actually see it as indispensable to recognize the mechanisms by which intellectuals are manipulated and dispossessed of the power to assess their own production.

I could show precisely how the softening of the division between intellectuals and journalists, and the confusion that results from this, damages both sides alike, journalists as much as intellectuals. I believe it is necessary to defend everything that can contribute to increasing the autonomy of the intellectual world. For a whole series of reasons that I explain in *Homo Academicus*, this autonomy is increasingly threatened by political and journalistic power. This has the result, in more than one case, that intellectuals have no other option left but to retire from the game.

We have seen in the debate on the 'silence of the intellectuals' how people's propensity to engage in this debate was undoubtedly that much greater if they had a greater need for journalistic consecration, and that they were then that much less able to play the role that I see as being that of the intellectual – one of its basic dimensions being irreverence towards all forms of power.

Following your analyses of the university, are you then proposing an analysis of journalism today?

I think that in the world of politics, the press contributes to defining what is politically conceivable and even determining who are legitimate actors in the political game – among other ways, by whom it invites onto programmes such as 'Le Club de la Presse'. In the same way, in the intellectual world, they claim to define the real actors and their respective rank. Just think of all the effects exercised by TV and radio broadcasts through their various awards, summing up the literary year or decade, etc. It is increasingly common for them to even impose questions and issues by

* Interview with Didier Éribon, published in Le Nouvel Observateur, 2–8 November 1984.

way of surveys and interviews, which are so many forms of *commission*, with nothing in exchange but a kind of advertising. In both cases they have a highly conservative effect.

The 'Clubs de la Presse', and similar 'Heures de Vérité', only ever give the word to authorized spokespeople – Marchais and Lustiger, Chirac and Ceyrac, etc. And in the same way, the ordinary or extraordinary verdicts of the cultural pages of the dailies and weeklies are devoted to individuals who are already consecrated. Or people who owe their consecration to the power of consecration that they wield as journalists or journalist-academics. Don't ask me to give examples. This situation threatens any kind of genuine research, artistic as well as scientific, for example by distracting even the most insensitive academics, by the seductions of immediate success, from their patient work and the long obscurity that major work presupposes.

Why then agree to give an interview? Why go onto the enemy's ground?

To defend there the values of autonomy and the criteria specific to the most autonomous regions of the scholarly world, among people who are poorly informed rather than badly intentioned.

You speak of autonomy and present your work as scientific. But it has triggered furies and passions that have little to do with science.

All science arouses resistance, especially in its early stages. You remember how Freud listed the big blows that science had struck to human narcissism: Copernicus, Darwin, and psychoanalysis itself. To study the sociology of intellectuals is, I believe, a new attack on their collective narcissism, and perhaps even more unpardonable. If all these people, and myself first among them, have chosen to do what they do, it is always to some degree to be able to conceive themselves as 'subjects', pure subjects 'with neither attachments nor roots', as Mannheim put it.

Sartre embodied this ideal of the especially intelligent intellectual, master and possessor of all the principles of his own intelligibility. But the sociology of intellectuals reminds us that we do all have attachments and roots, passions and interests, positions and thus points of view . . . and mis-view. This reminder of the specific libido found at the root of intellectual action seems to have something insufferable about it for a large number of intellectuals . . .

It is also said that the sociologist tries to put himself above the whole world. That you see yourself as God – 'Bourdieu-le-père'.

Certainly the very project of sociology, and particularly what is called the 'sociology of knowledge', is never devoid of the personal ambition to pose as absolute subject, able to take other people as object and to understand better than them the truth about what they are and what they do. The essential thing about my work in *Homo Academicus* was precisely to try to discover, in order to destroy it, everything that my analysis might owe to that kind of professional bias.

Other people before you have drawn attention to the fact that intellectuals have passions and interests, that they have a social situation . . .

There are different ways of doing this. The reduction of an opponent's reasons to causes, i.e. most commonly to interests of an inferior kind, is the daily bread of intellectual life. It goes together with a constant cataloguing, the everyday Zhdanovism practised so eagerly by the qualified detractors of Zhdanovism, all those who never stop proclaiming that so-and-so is 'Stalinist', 'the last Marxist', or a 'mandarin'. And so on.

What separates my work from behaviour of this kind is that I describe the whole game in which not only are specific interests generated – in no way reducible to the class interest denounced by the Marxist heavy artillery, with big cannon-balls but always aimed too high – but also partial insights about other people's interests. I need only cite by way of example a perfect pair of perspectives that are each blind about their own standpoint: Raymond Aron on left intellectuals in *L'Opium des intellectuels*, and Simone de Beauvoir, in *La Pensée de droite aujourd'hui*, on those of the right.

My book shows how the field of play and the positions historically constructed within this space govern the intellectual and political positions that are adopted. People may cry 'sociologism', but this relationship (a statistical one, to be sure) between objective and subjective positions is a fact. I should even admit that I am constantly surprised and sometimes shocked by the rather indecent naivety with which intellectuals, those specialists in discussion, reveal their social motivations. I can't help seeing this as a professional defect.

By giving your book the title Homo Academicus, *did you intend to put a label on those who generally produce books?*

Yes, quite so. Perhaps you've read the short story by David Garnett, 'A Man in the Zoo', which tells the story of a young man who quarrels with his girlfriend in the course of a visit to a zoo. He writes to the director in despair, a kind of suicide note, offering him a mammal that is missing from the zoo's collection: himself. He is put in a cage along with a chimpanzee, with a label that says – I quote from memory: 'Homo sapiens. This specimen is the gift of John Cromantie, Esquire. Visitors are requested not to tease the man with personal remarks.'

At bottom, this is rather like what I did, and rather like what I would have wanted to write on the label. Thanks to me, and with me, 'Homo classifier' has fallen into his own classifications. I find this somewhat comic, and I believe that my book should raise a good laugh. As well as other things.

It's rather like Molière's dog-Latin?

Yes, because I also wanted to emphasize in the title this kind of eternity of academic life, where so many historical invariants reappear, rather like the Sorbonne's condemnation of the writings of heretics . . .

In your inaugural lecture at the Collège de France, you said that you wanted to conduct 'a sociology of the categories of professorial understanding'. Is this book the realization of that programme?

Quite so. Except that, for reasons of ethics, I refrained from pushing too far the evidence of relationships between positions occupied in the university and the content or form of publications. I could have given far more analyses of the kind that I offered on the subject of the Barthes-Picard debate,[7] apropos conflicts between the old and new history, or the dispute about the *nouveaux philosophes* . . . I believe however that all the elements and instruments are there, so that interested parties, as people say, can make the analyses themselves.

Because you think they have an interest in doing so?

From my point of view, which is that of a strictly scientific advance, I am sure this is so. I would even say that there is a great ethical advantage to be drawn from this kind of socioanalysis: it offers a way of assuming one's social destiny, which does not mean accepting it with resignation. But I don't believe very many will take this opportunity . . . I think on the contrary they will use it instead to produce individual or collective instruments of defence.

[7] 1965 saw a lively polemic between Raymond Picard, professor at the Sorbonne and a typical representative of classical literary erudition, and Roland Barthes, champion of the 'new criticism' inspired by the social sciences, under the name of semiology. [Ed.]

They might well accuse you of terrorism.

I know. But I maintain that, for those who can stomach it, the sociological treatment has many scientific virtues, and political ones as well: it gives a better knowledge of what one is doing and saying. And it gives protection from self-destructive confessions. I have in mind a certain philosopher who recently wrote about a book on education: 'This book is important for philosophers, not because it gives them a gratifying image of their discipline, but – far more essentially – because it recognizes the full importance of teaching philosophy in France.' Interested parties can at least find in my book the means to protect themselves from statements that so cruelly reveal social motivations as this does, that say in the second part of a sentence precisely what they deny in the first.

Why do you always target philosophers?

I see them as the most stubborn defenders of intellectual narcissism. Those people who constantly talk about radical doubt, critical activity, deconstruction, etc., always fail – as Wittgenstein already remarked – to put in doubt the belief that leads them to take this position about doubt, this kind of professional *point d'honneur* of philosophy, this prejudice of an absence of prejudice, which is how they maintain their distinction from common sense, from public opinion, from the pedestrian positivism of scientists . . .

I have in mind all those professional prejudices that are never put in question, for example the intrinsic superiority of philosophical language over ordinary language. To offer an example here, I can appeal to the authority of a philosopher with credentials, John Austin, who provides good elements for a sociological analysis of what he calls the 'scholastic view' of the world. In short, the sociological critique only radicalizes the philosophical critique of prejudices by offering the means to also grasp the presuppositions inscribed in institutionalized philosophy. Hence to realize more completely many of philosophy's traditional ambitions.

Finally, to sum up all you have just said, your book could appear a kind of disguised autobiography.

It would be more of an anti-autobiography, to the extent that an autobiography is often a way of constructing a mausoleum, or even a cenotaph. In one sense, at least, you are right. My book is also an enterprise of self-recognition. If I can say something that is rather banal, but not well-known: the most intimate truth of what we are, the unthought and unthinkable, is inscribed in the objectivity of the positions that we have occupied, in the present and the past, and in the whole history of these positions.

The truth of the Sorbonne professor lies on the one hand in the history of the Sorbonne, leading to the present position of the Sorbonne in the space of university positions. The same goes for the professor at the École des Hautes Études or the Collège de France. Sartre sought the truth about Flaubert, Flaubert as writer and through this Sartre himself, in a kind of social genealogy, in family origins or at least imaginary experience. I believe that the truth about Flaubert, or Sartre, or any intellectual whatsoever, lies at least as much in what I call the intellectual field, i.e. in the set of relations of competition or even conflict that both unite him and oppose him to other academics and other intellectuals. I know, for example, that to understand what Barthes (or Picard) was doing, what he wrote on criticism (or the criticism that he wrote), you need to know the historically constituted position from which he was writing: École des Hautes Études or Sorbonne, social science or humanities, hastily digested Saussure or Lanson in disguise, etc.

Listening to you, and especially reading you, gives the impression that your only interest is a theoretical one. Nothing about politics, no programme, no project, no advice . . . You're clearly not after a position as minister of education.

Let me reply to one joke with another: do you think a minister of education is indispensable? Or rather, don't you believe that at least as far as higher education and research is concerned, laissez-faire, in other words autonomy and self-management, would be the best of possible policies? But for this to be more than a joke, I would have to present a long argument.

Indeed, given that your books, especially The Inheritors *and* Reproduction in Education, *have often been used to justify or condemn certain particular policies, it seems to me you can hardly remain silent.*

That is a real problem, which we mentioned at the start of this interview. What do you want me to do? A feature article in *Le Monde*? A press conference? A petition?

The only scientists that politicians like are dead ones. My books have been used to justify measures that have no connection with them at all, and in any case, as if they had been produced by an author from the past, whom no one would think of asking for advice. The problem is that in France there is no status for competent discourse on social affairs. I had envisaged together with Michel Foucault preparing a *White Book* that would bring together a number of specialists in a rigorous critique of a certain number of political measures, particularly in the field of culture and education . . .

In any case, I believe that the scientific community, by way of the Collège de France, will soon give its opinion on the future of scientific research and science teaching. Unusually, an established body of recognized scientists has been given a mandate by the government to deal with its own affairs. This is certainly no trivial matter, rather a political act of first magnitude.

You have often been accused of pessimism and fatalism. Do you really believe that there is no possible state policy that can assist research and teaching?

It is true that my analysis does not suggest an optimistic response. Especially in so far as it demonstrates these infernal pairs of complicit adversaries, which compel the teaching system and those who govern it to a perpetual motion swinging between what are called right and left, which actually are two different forms of preserving existing advantages, two forms of individual or collective defence against the sanctions of the educational and scientific marketplace.

Challenging university hierarchies (which is concealed beneath the slogan of democratization) and the defence of these hierarchies (which appeals to the quality of teaching) form a pair of forces that between them maintain the status quo on all essentials, i.e. the production and transmission of knowledge. What would be needed is a process leading to a distribution of material and symbolic profits that is rather less independent than it is today of the pedagogic and scientific contributions of different actors. This strikes me as both necessary and very hard to imagine. Besides, it is a very general problem, of which the university simply offers a limiting case.

But you don't propose any solution.

No. One thing though is certain: to stop this swing back and forth, we need more than reforms undertaken without investigation or analysis, like all the successive reforms of the last twenty years, based on an almost complete ignorance of the real issues and mechanisms – yesterday a superficially egalitarian demagogy, today the cult of effort and the bravos of the Société des Agrégés.

In a more general sense, it is impossible to act on worlds so finely differentiated as these by formal and universalist reforms, incapable of dealing methodically with the singularity of cases that are always particular, and most commonly inspired by representations – platforms, programmes, or reports of commissions – that say more about the specific interests of their authors than they do about the reality of the teaching system.

If I understand rightly, you don't offer political measures but you criticize politics as such.

What is at issue here, and what ordinary discussion on politics never tackles, is the very idea of what political action can be and can do – what used to be called 'government'. Politicians should meditate on the distinction made by the Stoics between those things that depend on us and those that do not. The main root of error, as we well know, lies in ignoring this boundary.

All that politics can do is control fields of forces quietly and insensibly, something that is clearly in contradiction with the spectacular and exhibitionist character of reforms. It can draw from the field of forces, and the struggles that take place in this, those forces able to shift the field in the desired direction. We are closer here to Fourier and his art of utilizing the passions than we are to Marx. We have to learn to conduct a politics of little well-placed pushes, which can release mechanisms that are blocked today by a system in which sanctions and profits are distributed in a random manner.

In any case, the present situation cannot last indefinitely, as I think it has been realized that when rats are subjected to a treatment like that inflicted today on teachers and researchers, distributing electric shocks and grains of wheat haphazardly, they go mad.

You seem to have a very pragmatic view of politics. Do you think it necessary to do away with general visions of the world and grand ideologies?

Not at all. It's not a question of proclaiming once more the end of ideologies. But the experience of the left, as we may call it, has made it broadly clear – and this is a positive advance – that the main oppositions between right and left are not where the left located them. What has become clear today was concealed from the eyes of politicians by the logic of competition between parties, and within the same party between currents and tendencies.

The resulting disarray may favour an indifference to politics that is very dangerous, but it may also offer an opportunity to seek more freely the genuine roots of cleavage, on condition that the space thus created is not filled by ideological fixes such as computing, which is supposed to solve all problems from individual isolation to foreign trade. On condition, too, that the discovery of economic constraints and the weak margin of freedom that these leave for political choice do not just strengthen the tendencies to economism.

Economism is often combined with technicism – in Lenin's case it was electricity, today it is electronics – to make up for the lack of genuine political invention based on a deeper knowledge of the social world. Politicians have learned something of economics, but they are still almost hopeless in sociology.

But who is going to come up with this invention?

Not politicians alone, certainly. What they need to do is recognize the limits of political action. This would already presuppose a genuine personal conversion on their part, and a complete redefinition of the social image of their role. They would have to stop thinking in the logic of rules and regulations for everyone, good for all and for always, and practise instead a kind of rational casuistic, combining attention to the individual case with knowledge of the general laws of operation of the various worlds involved, and of the most particular forces and interests of people on which the success of such an undertaking depends. Without this, the best intention in the world risks leading to results completely opposed to the goals pursued. All this would presuppose a great deal of intelligence, modesty, knowledge of realities, attention to details and to 'little people' . . . A real revolution, indeed!

Do you mean a revolution in mentality? That's the rarest thing with those who make revolutions . . .

Yes, as there is more political invention in an institution like 'SOS Grands-mères' than in the two years' work of a Plan commission or twenty reports by Mr X or Y, let alone congresses of apparatchiks. We have to look out for everyday political invention of this kind – encourage it, orchestrate it, generalize it with mechanisms that are more those of the gardener than the social engineer.

Proposals for the future of education*

On 13 February 1984, François Mitterrand asked the professors of the Collège de France to 'reflect on what they would see as the basic principles of teaching in the future, integrating the widest possible literary and artistic culture with the knowledge and methods of the most recent sciences'. The President subsequently responded to the Collège that there were three principles in its report that he would take up: unity within pluralism, openness in and through autonomy, and periodic revision of the subjects taught, as well as three proposals: the creation of an open university 'making use of the techniques of teaching at a distance and making a broad contribution to the permanent education of adults', setting under way the project of 'an educational and cultural television channel', and the idea of an ongoing assessment of educational establishments.

---

* Report on the reform of teaching commissioned from the professors of the Collège de France.

Proposals for the Future of Education

Presented at the request of the President of the Republic by the Professors of the Collège de France

Contents

Presentation of themes

Principles

1. The unity of science and plurality of cultures.
A harmonious education must be able to reconcile the universalism intrinsic to scientific thought with the relativism taught by the human sciences, paying attention to the plurality of ways of life, forms of wisdom and cultural sensibilities.

2. The diversification of forms of excellence.
Education should do everything to combat the monistic view of 'intelligence' that leads to a hierarchy of accomplishments ranked in relation to a single one, and should diversify socially recognized forms of cultural excellence.

3. Multiplication of opportunities.
It is important to attenuate as far as possible the consequences of pedagogic judgements, and prevent success from simply consecrating some people for life and failure from condemning them, by multiplying the routes and paths of transition, and attenuating any irreversible ruptures.

4. Unity in and through pluralism.
Education should transcend the opposition between liberalism and *étatisme* by creating the conditions for genuine emulation between autonomous and diversified institutions, while protecting the most disfavoured individuals and institutions against educational segregation that can lead to an unchecked competition.

5. Periodic revision of the subjects taught.
The contents of education should be subject to a periodic revision with the aim of modernizing the subjects taught and removing

outdated or subsidiary knowledge, as well as introducing new advances as rapidly as possible, though without giving in to modernism at any price.

6. Unification of knowledge transmitted.
All educational establishments should propose a range of knowledge considered necessary at each level, the unifying principle of this being historical unity.

7. Uninterrupted and alternating education.
Education should be continued throughout life, and everything should be done to reduce the break between the end of education and entry into working life.

8. The use of modern educational techniques.
The state's action of stimulation, orientation and assistance should be exercised by way of an intensive and methodical use of modern techniques of cultural diffusion, in particular television and distance learning, making it possible to offer everyone everywhere an exemplary teaching.

9. Openness in and through autonomy.
Educational establishments should associate outside figures with their discussions and activities, coordinate their action with that of other institutions of cultural diffusion and become the focus for a new associative life and a site for the practical exercise of genuine civic instruction; in parallel, it is necessary to reinforce the autonomy of the teaching body by revalorizing the function of professors and strengthening the competence of lecturers.

APPLICATION OF PRINCIPLES

Twenty years before the Collège de France report

But it is not sufficient to take as one's goal the true democratizing of education. In the absence of a rational pedagogy doing everything required to neutralize the effect of the social factors of cultural inequality, methodically and continuously, from kindergarten to university, the political project of giving everyone equal educational opportunity cannot overcome real inequalities, even when it deploys every institutional and economic means. Conversely, a truly rational pedagogy, that is, one based on a sociology of cultural inequalities, would, no doubt, help to reduce inequalities in education and culture, but it would not be able to become a reality unless all the conditions for a true democratization of the recruitment of teachers and pupils were fulfilled, the first of which would be the setting up of a rational pedagogy.[8]

---

[8] *The Inheritors* (Chicago: University of Chicago Press 1979), p. 76.

The Collège de France report.
Pierre Bourdieu explains*

In 'Leçon sur la leçon', your inaugural lecture at the Collège de France, you said: 'The greatest service that could be rendered to sociology would perhaps be not to ask anything of it.' Now, three years later, here you are drawing up a report at the request of the President of the Republic.

You know, there is never a reply to a request that does not imply a redefinition of the request . . . it is unsure whether this report replies to the question that was asked . . . That said, however, the fact of asking an institution like the Collège to reply to a question about the operation of the educational system is already a very important political act. It was the Collège that was approached, and not Messrs X or Y. This is a kind of irreversible gain, in the sense of recognizing an autonomy of the intellectual field that has constantly increased – from Voltaire to Sartre, via Zola, Gide, etc.

Besides, even if I did play a certain role in drafting the report, it is not just my text. It expresses a collective view, and that of a collective authorized by its position in its specific world, by the request made to it and by its own recognition of this position. I believe this is one of the preconditions for its effectiveness. It is a normative text, which says 'this must be done' – something I never say in my books. It is possible, drawing on the English philosophers of language, to say that only groups are permitted to say 'this must be done'. On the other hand, however, it reminds us that no group really has the right to say 'this must be done'. That is something rare, and perhaps makes this 'must' rather stronger than is generally the case.

If I can redefine my question: does this not mean that the author of Reproduction in Education *has (to quote again from your lecture) 'encountered, realized in his object, his own social science of the past' – often, indeed, at loggerheads with what might have been expected? Hasn't the 'liberating effect of knowledge' and establishment of the facts often led to a normative effect in a perverse fashion? I have in mind all those reformers supposedly 'inspired' by your books . . .*

This is a key question, which I hardly know how to start answering. It bears on the very status of sociological discourse. How many times have I recalled

* Interview with Jean-Pierre Salgas, published in *La Quinzaine Littéraire* 445, August 1985.

that true ideas have no intrinsic force? . . . The uses of sociological discourse can themselves be analyzed sociologically: thus sociology also to a certain extent offers an understanding of its own reception. What people retain from a complex discourse are those aspects that agree with their own interests, and there is no question but that certain professors have made use of this at moments of crisis to abdicate their pedagogic work. Scientific analysis can be alienating, it can be liberating: knowledge also makes it possible to act on the mechanisms analyzed in knowledge of their cause. It frees one from utopianism, but it does not impose sociologism. I realize this is not a sufficient reply. The very fact of registering something implies a ratification. To register a marriage means transforming a relationship into marriage. I believe that sociological writing, in its social reception, sometimes operates in the mind of its readers like an act of registration that consecrates the thing that is registered.

Did some of these various reformers appeal to your authority?

Very few of them. That being said, my analyses certainly were used in specifically ideological ways. Social strategies are never completely unconscious: many of those who appeal to me are well aware that I would have said the opposite . . .

What distinguishes this report is that it does not pretend something can be done that in fact cannot be done. Action is restricted to the space in which it is performed. For example, we do not say that the educational system can resolve the problem of 'democratization'. That word is never uttered. Those who make out that they are democratizing, when they lack the means to do so, really mean something quite different: 'democratization' is an ambiguous slogan that makes it possible to present the interests of certain categories of teachers in the equalizing of careers within the educational system as equivalent to the interests of the dominated in the social world.

Furthermore, we do not say what cannot be done. In *Reproduction in Education*, we did not say that the school produced or reproduced inequalities. We simply said that one aspect was that it 'contributed' to reproducing these. It is this aspect that can possibly be controlled.

You are referring to points II and III of the report . . .

Yes, I believe that the two major contributions that the educational system makes to reproduction are the verdict effect, the effect of a destiny that traps those it judges in an essence, a nature ('this is what you are and not something else'), and the hierarchy effect, which consists in making out that there is a linear hierarchy of skills, that all these are only degraded forms of a perfect competence – that of ENA or Polytechnique graduates. Everyone else is just a failure by comparison . . .

To understand the verdict effect, I always mention an analogy with Kafka's *The Trial*. You can read this as a metaphor of the educational system. It is a world that you enter in order to know what you are, and with all the more anxious expectation, the less you are expected there. It says to you, in an insidious or brutal fashion: 'You are just a . . .' – generally followed by an insult that, in cases such as this, is sanctioned by an institution beyond discussion and recognized by all.

You can imagine the effects that these verdicts have on children, verdicts without appeal and most often reinforced by parents (in different forms according to social class). These traumas of identity are undoubtedly one of the main pathogenic factors in our society, even if they are doomed to pass unnoticed, above all to the eyes of teachers. One might well wonder, in fact, whether one of the charms of this undervalued profession does not lie in the possibility if offers of dispensing verdicts, i.e. playing God-the-Father, even to a class of thirty.

I am struck by the fact that the word 'philosophy' is not mentioned in these 'Propositions pour l'Enseignement de l'Avenir' – *except by mistake. In the first chapter, you attribute to the natural and human sciences 'critical mechanisms' that are generally attached to them, whereas a whole chapter (VI) is devoted to history. I deliberately link these together because both have been issues of very powerful contention in recent years. Is it not also necessary to link this 'omission' with the fact that at its most conceptual level, the debate on education that is currently under way can be seen as a conflict between Bourdieu's 'habitus' and the Cartesian or Kantian cogito, independent of any social determination, that is posited by your opponents?*

This is a deliberate omission. Where are the critical virtues of philosophy? This image of philosophy as criticism is often belied by the facts. You need only think of Kantianism as the official theory of the Third Republic, or more recently, the reception given to Heidegger in France – or, still closer to us, such things as the Collège de Philosophie, established in the wake of a political change . . . This is an argument of fact, and whatever its validity, there was indeed a time at which the friends of wisdom were judged by their wisdom. So why give history a fundamental place? This is not necessarily history as defined by historians. It is rather history as instrument for the actual genealogy of concepts, modes of thought, mental structures; and in this respect, everything is still to be done. To reintroduce the historical stand-

EDUCATION AND EDUCATION POLICY

point would be to free education from the dogma that gives results without problems, the solution that has won out without remembering the alternative, whether we are talking about mathematics, physics or art . . . That would mean giving each person the means to reappropriate the structures of their own thought.

This is a point at which scientific and political imperatives come together, since liberation from dogma would also mean liberation from fatalism: verdicts often owe their dogmatic brutality to the fact that they are pronounced in the name of knowledge and mental structures, with a rigidity that results from their canonization by apprenticeship and the *agrégation*.

History conceived in this way could realize one of the proclaimed ambitions of philosophy, that of radical questioning. Besides, there are philosophers with a 'philosophical' label who already do this kind of work . . . There is clearly no teaching that does not imply something like a philosophy. In this case, this is in the new role ascribed to the history of sciences and ideas, etc.

In the opening pages of the report, you present it as 'a coherent set of directive principles'. You insist elsewhere on the 'different or even antagonistic interests' that the educational system serves. I would maintain that apart from certain broad lines – of which history is one – the reader often gets the impression that juxtaposition substitutes for coherence. As if what is recommended is to do a bit of one thing and a bit of another . . .

That is your pessimism coming out . . . The text says that at the present time the fight is over false problems: elite/mass, public/private, integrating national culture/open universal culture, humanities/sciences, etc. The function of debates over false problems, or problems that are insoluble in practice, is often to distract attention from the real problems. It is clear that one can reach immobilism, preservation, either by way of conflict, or by consensus on the grounds of conflict and thus non-conflict.

The report shifts and destroys certain fictitious problems. To take an example: exams have the effect of a verdict. It is possible to reason with the logic of all or nothing, which is a good way of justifying the status quo. One can say that exams should be suppressed. But one can also say that, given the present state of human arrangements, a motive is needed, specific mechanisms for determining the propensity to invest. Competition is one of these. One can on the other hand work to weaken the verdict effects of competition: by creating new and different terrains of competition, with the result that someone who fails at the high jump might excel at putting the shot; or – and this is not exclusive – by replacing individual with collective competition . . . This is how the 'Proposals' are meant to operate. It is not a question of doing a bit of both. It is rather to do more of one thing within the limits of the other. For example, the most competition possible within the limits of protecting the interests of the most deprived, which moreover means reinventing the role of the state. People act as if the only response to the alternative of liberalism and *étatisme* was in terms of all or nothing, once and for all. In fact, the introduction of a bit more competition can – in a particular situation – be a means, even the only means, of actually neutralizing the undesirable effects of *étatisme*. On the other hand, the intervention of the state is needed in order to neutralize the unsupportable effects of unchecked competition – which, incidentally, is already established even if concealed.

Another paradox is that only a central instance can effectively combat centralization. And this raises another problem: how, in a system where everything is decided by people who, for the most part, are born in a radius of a kilometre or so around the VIIth arrondissement in Paris, one can find the social force needed for a central action of decentralization.

'Doing more of one thing within the limits of the other', you say. A related question is how we should understand the notion that you introduce in chapter IV, of a 'minimum common culture . . . the core of basic and obligatory knowledge and know-how that all citizens should possess'. We are never sure whether this is actually a maximum not directly linked with the social destiny of the individual in question, or rather a kind of little pre-professional luggage, as conceived for example by the former minister Haby, for a school directly oriented to the world of production . . .

There is no ambiguity here. I can even tell you that the choice of expression was deliberate. What must be borne in mind is that those who are deprived of this minimum are unaware that they can and should claim it, in the same way that they might claim the minimum wage. Cultural alienation tends to exclude awareness of this alienation. The more deprived one is, the less conscious one is of one's deprivation, which is not the case in the economic field. Under these conditions, to establish the idea of a minimum in no way means confining people to a certain basic and rudimentary knowledge, but rather means telling them that they should claim the minimum that enables them to continue learning. In other words the maximum.

Take the example of computing. This can be a minimum, something that is learned in order to be a good technician. It can also provide the opportunity to acquire certain minimum mechanisms of thought that are actually very complex. The difficulty is that this whole basic – not elementary – culture has to be defined, along with the pedagogic techniques for transmitting it as early as possible.

You give the example of computing in a more general context, that of science and technology, where it is easy to distinguish the 'hard' core of social use that is made of it. But what about classical literary culture? Reading your books on Reproduction *and* Distinction, *on the other hand, gives the impression that these all serve a social purpose. To take Proust, for example – and I deliberately take this example of a novelist who seems to function rather as your sociological 'ego ideal' – does he have a place in this minimum common culture?*

You get back here to the effect of ratification. It is a fact that cultural goods are subject to social uses of distinction that have nothing to do with their intrinsic value. Am I for or against Proust? How can one not want there to be countless people able to do what Proust did, or at least read what he wrote? Those who attack me on this point, or use against me the 'defence' of philosophy, are people whose intellectual pride is more bound up with the social use of intellectual things than with these things themselves. I believe that one of the most recalcitrant obstacles to the distribution of a sociology of culture, which is inevitably a sociology of intellectuals, is the resistance of intellectuals themselves, which evidently varies with the position they occupy in the intellectual hierarchy. Those quickest to defend philosophy against me – not that I attack it – are those with the greatest need to be known and recognized as 'philosophers' in the social sense of the term.

You can then find yourself defending – not so much as a sociologist, but rather as author of the Collège de France report – certain contents along with those who, according to your theory of habitus, make an opposition between particular knowledge and the face-to-face of the thinking subject. It is Milner who I have in mind.

The Collège de France 'Proposals' do not talk in terms of hierarchies (though it is a mystification to deny their existence) except to say that there should be a large number of these, which is the only way of weakening the effects bound up with the existing monopoly. 'Equalization' should not be sought in 'levelling' (the criticism from the right is quite correct in seeing that the root of this is resentment), but in the multiplication and diversification of grounds on which differences can be asserted, and in the weakening of the hierarchies between the various principles of hierarchization.

I spoke just now of resentment, and this raises another question. What does a social group have to be, in order to say what is said in the report? It has to be made up of people who have sufficient labels and guarantees to be free of labels and guarantees. As I argued in *Homo Academicus*, people always defend their last little difference, that which makes for their *value*. The professors of humanities at the Collège d'Enseignement Technique defend Latin because this is the only difference they have; the *agrégés* who have nothing beyond their *agrégation* defend it to the death, though Nobel prize-winners might mock it!

Is there then a point, a final difference – Nobel prize or Collège de France – at which particular interest no longer obtains? To put it another way, are the authors of the 'Proposals' not caught in the very institution that you describe, trapped in its antagonisms? On the other hand, what were the first reactions that this report aroused among those whom it directly affected?

The professors at the Collège de France do have interests, clearly, but these do not lead them to conceive the educational system in the logic of a corporate defence. This is because it is only to a lesser extent than others that they owe their authority to this position, and above all because they are not involved in the reproduction of the teaching corps. As for reactions, what strikes me as interesting is that, with some rare exceptions, there has been nothing in the way of insults or polemics. People have felt called to raise problems in a different way, and above all to bear in mind the position in the educational institution from which they speak. In the discussions, they even sometimes laugh at their own objections . . . That is a considerable pedagogic effect.

This does not seem to have reached the government. Jean-Pierre Chevènement is far from speaking the same language as the Collège de France.

You will see how the conclusion to the report mentions all the obstacles that there are to the application of its 'Proposals'. My professional pride as a sociologist was involved here . . . It is true that, for the time being, the government has not really grasped what – given the symbolic authority of the Collège – could have been a considerable instrument of transformation. That said, however, I believe that this text will act as a kind of buffer, an obligatory reference point which can serve as an obstacle to regression and abuse of power.

A refusal to be cannon-fodder for the bosses[*]

The present movement of university and lycée *students seems to have surprised their elders . . .*

In the 1960s, a number of people, including sociologists in France and the United States, proclaimed 'the end of ideologies'. A few years later, 1968 saw one of the most extraordinary explosions of 'ideology' that the world has known. In 1986, the same people – or their descendants – noted the end of the 'ideas of 1968','the great laundering . . .'. And here we have the sudden rise of movements that are lively, intelligent, funny and deeply serious, which overthrow the ideology of the end of ideologies. Those who are so keen to see the 'end of ideologies', by which they mean, more or less, a return to 'realism', to the realities of business, productivity, the balance of trade, the 'imperatives' of French foreign policy (such as arms sales or *Rainbow Warrior*) and the rejection of illusory hopes of equality, fraternity and solidarity, speak like bourgeois fathers addressing their sons – in other words, like old men. The end of ideologies means a collective social ageing, resignation to the order of things, the 'wisdom' which makes a virtue out of necessity.

The left in power – what an old men's trick! The anti-institutional and libertarian left has been excluded from power (or has excluded itself), and the apparatchiks have set themselves to preach ideological modernization (often by their own example), in other words renunciation of the 'illusions' that brought them to power. Everything that the right so stubbornly repeated, without actually making people believe it, this left has now said and repeated – not that it has made people believe it either. But people have stopped believing in this left . . .

The students of today say that they're not political . . .

Indeed, and in a certain sense they're right. First of all because, differently from their predecessors of 1968, they do not have the baggage of great political models: the decline of the PCF and the arrival of the Socialists in power has changed a good many things. Besides, their political apprenticeship

---

[*] Interview with Antoine de Gaudemar, published under the title 'À quand un lycée Bernard Tapie?', *Libération*, 4 December 1986.

was less often in the cells of the PCF or the Trotskyist groups, and more from observing around them the unemployment of graduates and the devaluation of educational qualifications, as well as by listening to Coluche or Bedos, who offered them, in the language of parable, the equivalent of some very subtle analyses of racism, trade unionism, the world of politics, etc. They did also learn a lot from the left. The Kabyles say of someone who habitually lies: 'He gives you East for West.' The apparatchiks of the left have given us right for left. The university and *lycée* students might not have much sense of direction, but this simply means that they're like everyone else. What for example divides Devaquet from Chevènement? The revanchist teachers who surround the former from the *normaliens* bent on restoring the hierarchies of their youth who advise the latter?

The renunciations and denials of all these people lead others to believe that this time we are finally through with aspirations – if not to liberty, then at least to solidarity, let alone generosity. Those who govern us today believed that they could carry through to the end what their predecessors had made such a good start with. Because the politicians of the left had praised business (and the army), the right believed that everything was okay, that it could go ahead. It failed to see that the so-called left no longer expressed progressive aspirations, especially those of young people, who have not forgotten the broken promises.

In other words, when the right returned to power it felt that the attempts of the left authorized it to follow its own logic through to the end.

Education policy is like a projective test in which a directing group projects its aspirations for the future of society. Now, what have we seen sketched out here? We've seen neither Marx nor Jesus, as the book put it, but also neither Baudelaire nor Manet, not even Pasteur or Marie Curie – just Berlusconi and Bernard Tapie.[9] Perhaps we'll soon have a *lycée* called after Bernard Tapie, instead of Claude Bernard or Marie Curie. The exalting of business that has gained so much ground – just think of all the TV and radio broadcasts on this theme – has led to the go-ahead boss, sometimes even the combative boss, being offered to young people as a human ideal.

Is this the system of values that the students are rejecting today?

[9] A businessman who embodied the 'spirit of enterprise' praised in the 1980s – President Mitterrand even made him minister of urban affairs – Bernard Tapie was celebrated for his investment in industry and sport, widely echoed in the media, especially as he himself presented television broadcasts on this subject. [Ed.]

To offer business and competition as the ideal, after the American or Japanese model, means establishing a vacuum at the heart of our system of values. We know the aberrations that an educational model like the Japanese can lead to, with the whole pedagogic undertaking subordinated to the logic of competition and selection by exams. We are already not so far from this system, and I believe it is the infernal logic of the struggle of all against all, of unbridled competition for high marks, a good stream, the right subject, the right *grande école*, etc., that the students are denouncing. This is why they exalt the values of solidarity and generosity. There is nothing more divisive and isolating than the handing-out of corrected class essays, or even more so, the search for a university place, for students who know little or nothing about how the system operates, let alone hierarchies that never stop changing.

These young boys and girls tell us that the last will be first. They want to introduce in school the philosophy of the Restos du Coeur.[10] They want to escape the logic of competition and the unbridled individualism it encourages, which in an earlier age was more or less confined to the competition classes of the great Parisian *lycées*, from spreading bit by bit, as is the case today, until it reaches even the smallest secondary school in the provinces.

Isn't this a kind of utopianism?

Yes, of course. And in this sense, the *lycée* students of 1986 are indeed the heirs of the students of 1968. But utopianism contains both information and strength. Teaching has been abandoned to the educational lobbies, corporate pressure groups and ministerial advisers, not to speak of politicians. It is high time that the great scientists and scholars of the Sorbonne and the Collège de France no longer disdained discussing the curricula of primary and secondary education, as indeed Lavisse did in his time, or even writing textbooks for village schools. The professors of the Collège de France did a similar work of this kind a year or two ago. You know what the very authorities who requested this report did with its proposals . . .

You mean that the objectives of the education system have to be rethought from top to bottom. But wouldn't that simply lead to one more reform?

Not at all. I think that what is outstanding about these successive reforms is how they betray the lack of any genuine educational project. At their centre is a black hole: they don't say what kind of person they want to create, or for what kind of social world. This is something that the school and university

---

10 [A charity that distributes food at low prices or free to people in need.]

students have sensed very well. And certain of them speak, quite correctly, of opposing an alternative educational project to that of the minister.

What lies at the heart of the project that the minister proposes – apart from re-establishing the prerogatives of titled professors? To adjust the production of graduates to economic demand. Apart from the fact that this is something that no one knows how to do, given the inevitable lag between the timescale of educational production and changes in the economy, I am not at all certain that it is even desirable. I could mention all the economic, scientific and social inventions that have been born, either directly or indirectly, from an 'overproduction' of graduates: for instance the entire artistic avant-garde of the nineteenth century, now celebrated as a cult at the Musée d'Orsay, arose from an overproduction of painters and daubers!

This is not the essential point, however. What is so insufferable for the students, I believe, is the project of *normalisation*[11] hidden behind this concern for adjustment to the labour market. When a bourgeois or even petty-bourgeois mother talks of her son deciding to read history, you'd think she was announcing a catastrophe. Not to mention philosophy or literature. Students in the humanities have become useless mouths. And not only for 'government circles' of both right and left, but for their families as well, and often even for themselves.

What then do you see as at the centre of this system of absent values?

In my view, it is the disqualification of any kind of gratuitous research, whether in the arts or sciences. Especially when this might produce critical effects, as with the social sciences. Dead artists are celebrated, but as always, they are better loved dead than alive. This rejection of gratuitous research is the rejection of *generosity*. It is the rejection that a generous age rejects: the whole wretched series of petty gestures offered by our guardians of moral order, our ministers of justice, police and education, the most exemplary of which is the expulsion of the Malians. And it would be possible to show that this disqualification of gratuity and generosity is not even identifiable with a genuine concern for *profitability*.

But the students are putting forward precise demands, such as no fees for studies, against selection, etc.

I believe that this all flows from a fundamental refusal to be cannon-fodder for the bosses. And from rejection of the morality implied in the establishment of the reign of competition in education. In the absence of a

---

[11] [In the sense here of the École Normale Supérieur.]

genuine *collective project* for education (and thus for society), all that remains are the individual strategies of reproduction. As in all situations of panic and despair, everyone looks after themselves, there's a struggle of egoisms. People fight to rescue themselves and their friends, and are quite ready to jump into an overflowing boat.

Laissez-faire in matters of education, as embodied by our minister-entrepreneur, is an alibi for the absence of thought, the absence of any project. As far as education is concerned, nothing great can be done without a mobilization around the idea of man and society. That is something that the students of universities and *lycées* say and feel; they feel that they have no real place in a society that is incapable of conceiving the future. And for this reason, the present movement is not just a flash in the pan. Even if it disappears in its present form, it will continue to exist as long as the questions it raises, which I have tried to formulate, have not been explicitly and resolutely confronted.

But isn't there something unrealistic in the fact of rejecting selection?

The effect of any situation of overt crisis, like that which we are now in, is to bring to light, to consciousness, things that were previously hidden. Rejecting selection, in a rather utopian fashion, forces people to discover sooner or later that this already exists. The same can be said about fees. Do you believe that the son of a postman in Luchon, who wants to study in Toulouse, can do so free of charge – in the way that the student at the Lycée Dauphine who lives in Rue de la Pompe can? All this has simply been concealed by the successive reforms.

Politicians make an issue out of education because they have no *project*. They think that education is too important to be left to young people. In fact, the young remind us that we don't know what we want; that we don't know what we want to make them into. We have a thousand ways of making them feel that they are unwanted. And unemployment is not the least of these. That is one of the reasons why they feel solidarity with all those who have constantly been reminded, often brutally, that they are unwanted, such as immigrants and their children.

Should we really be speaking just about competition, rather than selection and unbridled liberalism?

Clearly. Besides, in the proposals of the Collège de France, if you read them closely, you will find an anticipatory condemnation of unbridled liberalism, the return of which was easy to predict. This says that extreme competition already exists and generates cruel inequalities. (Do you think that humanities students at Villetaneuse don't realize that their degree is worth less than a degree from Paris I?) It says that it is up to the state to control and regulate this competition and to neutralize its negative effects.

The school and university students will not take long to understand that it is less a question of rejecting competition – which clearly does not just have negative effects – but rather to demand the means, *all* the means, for competing on an equal basis, as well as inventing new forms of competition that are more in keeping with solidarity. But that would presuppose, once again, a genuine collective project. The son of a worker from Saint-Étienne should be able to go on to studies that are genuinely (and not just formally) free of charge, at a university that can genuinely offer him the best qualifications, and offer teaching that genuinely corresponds to what he wants – whether philosophy, cinema or fine arts. There is no reason why the privilege of freedom from charge, in the full sense of the term, should be reserved for those who have the means of paying.

Principles for a discussion of the contents of education[*]

Towards the end of 1988, the minister of national education set up a commission to study the contents of education. This was chaired by Pierre Bourdieu and François Gros, and its members were Pierre Baqué, Pierre Bergé, René Blanchet, Jacques Bouveresse, Jean-Claude Chevalier, Hubert Condamines, Didier DaCunha Castelle, Jacques Derrida, Philippe Joutard, Edmond Malvinaud and François Mathey. It was charged with proceeding to a revision of the subjects taught, with a view to strengthening their coherence and unity.

In the initial phase, the members of the commission set themselves the task of formulating principles that would govern its work. Aware and concerned about the implications of these principles, and especially their practical applications, they sought in establishing them simply to obey the intellectual discipline that resulted from the intrinsic logic of the knowledge available, as well as from anticipations or questions that might be formulated. Since it was not their mission to intervene directly or in the short term in the definition of new programmes, they sought rather to sketch the broad orientations of the gradual transformation of teaching contents that is indispensable – even if it necessarily takes time – in order to follow and even anticipate as far as possible the development of science and society.

Specialized working groups formed according to these principles will continue or begin a work of deeper discussion on each of the main regions of knowledge. They will seek to propose, in provisional findings that are scheduled for June 1989, not an ideal programme for an ideal education, but rather a series of precise observations, drawing out the implications of the proposed principles. These proposals, which will bear essentially on the restructuring of divisions between subjects and redefining the conditions of their transmission, on the elimination of notions that are outdated or of little relevance and the introduction of new subjects as demanded by advances in knowledge as well as by economic, technological and social change, are to be presented and discussed at a conference bringing together international experts.

If, in the educational system as elsewhere, considered change is a permanent requirement, there is obviously no intention to make a clean break with the

[*] Report of the commission chaired by Pierre Bourdieu and François Gros, Ministère de l'Enseignement Nationale, de la Jeunesse et des Sports, March 1989.

past each time. In fact, several of the many innovations introduced in recent years are fully justified. If it is important to avoid uncritically repeating everything inherited from the past, it is not always possible to discern, at each moment and in every field, what is 'outdated' and what is still 'valid'. However, the relationship that can and must be established between the necessary continuation of the past and the no less necessary adaptation to the future must be constantly taken as an object of discussion.

The necessarily abstract and general form of the principles presented below will only be justified, in due course, by future work that is duly rigorous, whilst putting them to the test so as to determine and differentiate their contents.

First principle
Programmes must be subjected to a periodic questioning with the aim of introducing the subjects required by advances in science and changes in society (first among these, European unification), with any addition being compensated for by suppression.

To restrict the scope, let alone the difficulty, of a programme is not a matter of lowering its level. On the contrary, a restriction of this kind, effected with due care, should make it possible to raise the level, to the extent (and only to this extent) that it makes it possible to work for a shorter period but better, replacing passive apprenticeship by active reading – whether using books or audiovisual aids – by discussion and practical exercise, and thus restoring full place to creativity and the spirit of invention. This implies among other things that the control of apprenticeship and the mode of assessment of the progress accomplished are profoundly transformed. Assessment of the level reached should no longer be based simply on an onerous examination in which chance plays too great a part, but should rather combine continuous assessment with a final exam that bears on essentials and aims to measure the ability to put knowledge to work in a completely different context from that in which this has been acquired – in the case of the experimental sciences, for example, practical tests permitting inventiveness, critical and 'practical sense' to be assessed.

Second principle
Education should privilege all teaching capable of offering modes of thought endowed with a general validity and applicability over teaching that proposes subjects capable of being learned in an effective enough (and sometimes more agreeable) manner by other means. Particular care should be taken that teaching does not leave lacunae that are unacceptable because prejudicial to the success

of the pedagogic enterprise as a whole, particularly in terms of ways of thinking or fundamental know-how that, assumed to be taught by everyone, end up not being taught by anyone.

Decisive privilege must be given to teaching charged with ensuring the considered and critical assimilation of fundamental ways of thinking (such as deduction, experiment, and the historical approach, as well as reflective and critical thinking which should always be combined with the foregoing). In a concern for balance, it is particularly necessary to make more clearly perceptible the specific character of the experimental way of thinking, by a resolute valuation of qualitative reasoning, a clear recognition of the provisional nature of explanatory models, and ongoing training in the practical work of research. It is also necessary to examine whether and how each of the main sectors of knowledge (and each of the 'disciplines' into which these are translated in a far less adequate fashion) can contribute to the transmission of the various ways of thinking, and whether certain specialities are not better placed than others, by their whole logic and translation, for ensuring successful apprenticeship in one field or another. Finally, care must be taken to give major place to a whole series of techniques that, despite being tacitly required by all teaching, are rarely the object of methodical transmission: use of dictionaries and abbreviations, rhetoric of communication, establishment of files, creation of an index, use of records and data banks, preparation of a manuscript, documentary research, use of computerized instruments, interpretation of tables and graphs, etc. To provide all students with this technology of intellectual work, and more generally instil them with rational working methods (such as how to choose between tasks imposed, or to distribute them in time), would be one way of contributing to the reduction of inequalities bound up with cultural inheritance.

Third principle
Programmes should be open, flexible and revisable, a context and not a straitjacket: they should be steadily less constraining in the higher levels of instruction; their elaboration and practical application needs collaboration between teachers. They should be progressive – vertical connection – and coherent – horizontal connection – both within a particular specialism and at the overall level of knowledge provided (i.e. the level of each particular class).

This programme is not any kind of imperative code. It is designed to function as a guide for teachers and students – as well as parents – who should find in it a clear presentation of the objectives and requirements of the respective level of teaching (teachers could be asked to communicate this to students at the start of the year). This is why it must be combined with *presentations of themes* that indicate the 'philosophy' behind it, the objectives sought, and the conditions of its application, also including examples of this.

The objectives and contents of the various levels should be noted and defined in an interdependent way. Programmes should *explicitly* foresee all the specifications (and *only these*) that are indispensable to ensure assimilation of the basic contents of knowledge. While it may be useful to tackle the same question from different points of view (perspective, for example, from the point of view of both mathematics and art history), the fact remains that we should work to abolish all undesirable overlaps, at least when they have been shown not to be useful, both between successive levels of the same speciality and between different subjects at the same level.

To be in a position to obtain continuous and coherent teaching, programmes should envisage, in as precise a manner as possible, *the level required at the start of a course* (avoiding in particular vague headings that leave room for elastic interpretation) and the level required at the *end*. These must be tested, with a view to being realizable without special prowess in the time limits given. (In order to promote a successful application, they should also be combined with indications as to the respective time allotted for each of the main steps.) All the basic specialities should be the object of an apprenticeship whose trajectory over several years should surpass the stage of simple initiation and lead to a sufficient mastery of ways of thinking and the requirements that are particular to these.

Coherence and complementarity between the programmes of different specialisms must be methodically sought at every level. Where commissions by speciality are needed, it is necessary to envisage a *joint* commission of programmes (by level), to ensure coherence and eliminate duplication.

Without falling into a servile imitation of foreign models, critical inspiration should be found in a methodical comparison with programmes in use in other countries, European ones in particular. This is a way of bringing to light things that have been forgotten and ignored, and the comparison should make it possible to weed out survivals bound up with the random past of a historical tradition. Besides contributing to increase the comparability between the French and other European systems, and reducing handicaps in relation to possible competitors, this would in any case have the effect of substituting a logic of conscious and explicit choice for that of automatic and tacit perpetuation of established programmes.

Fourth principle
Critical examination of the contents required must always reconcile two variables: their necessity and their transmissibility. On the one hand, the mastery of a particular knowledge or way of thinking is more or less indispensable, for both

scientific and social reasons, at a particular level (in such and such a class); on the other hand, its transmission is more or less difficult, at this level, given the students' capacities for assimilation and the training of the teachers involved.

This principle should lead to exclusion of any kind of premature transmission. It should also lead to mobilizing all the resources needed (especially the time devoted to transmission, and pedagogic resources), in order to ensure the effective transmission and assimilation of knowledge that is difficult but deemed absolutely necessary. (To get a more precise idea of the real transmissibility, at a given level, of a particular knowledge or way of thinking, account should be taken of the results of research that assesses the mastery that students at different levels and of different social origins have of the knowledge taught in the different specialities.)

The possible transformation of the contents of courses, and the definitive establishment of a change in a programme, should only be effected after a work of experimentation accomplished in an actual situation, with the collaboration of teachers and after transformation of the training (both initial and continuous) of those charged with teaching. The effort of adaptation that would be required of teachers should be supported by awarding sabbatical terms or years, and by organizing protracted training sessions that would enable them to initiate themselves in new ways of thinking or knowledge, acquire new qualifications and possibly change their orientation.

In a more general sense, bodies should be set up with the mission of gathering, grouping and analysing the reactions and reflections of teachers charged with applications, suggestions, criticisms and desired improvements, proposed innovations, etc. (The Minitel network could be used for this purpose.) A constant effort of pedagogic research could be established that is both methodical and practical, associating teachers directly engaged in the work of training.

Fifth principle
Concerned to improve the successful transmission of knowledge by diversifying the forms of pedagogic communication, and sticking to the amount of knowledge actually assimilated rather than that proposed in theory, we shall distinguish, both among the specialities and within each specialism, what is obligatory, optional or facultative, and alongside lectures, introduce other forms of teaching, such as directed work and collective teaching that groups together teachers in two or more specialisms and can take the form of investigations or observations on the ground.

The increase in knowledge makes any encyclopaedic ambition vain: it is impossible to teach all specialisms and the whole of any specialism. Besides, specialisms have emerged that combine basic science with technical application (as is the case with computing at all levels of technology teaching at *collège*[12]). Their introduction into the teaching system cannot be a mere addition: it has to have the effect of imposing a redefinition of the divisions of teaching in the more or less long term.

It is necessary to substitute for the present teaching that is encyclopaedic, additive and divided, a system that articulates obligatory teaching designed to ensure a considered assimilation of the common minimum of knowledge, optional teaching directly adapted to the intellectual orientation and level of students, and facultative and interdisciplinary teaching that depends on the teachers' own initiative. This diversification of pedagogic forms, and the status of different kinds of teaching, should take into account the specificity of each subject, while permitting an escape from simply reckoning by 'discipline', which is one of the major obstacles to any genuine transformation of the content of teaching. A redefinition of forms of teaching that alternated lecture courses and practical work, obligatory lectures and those that are optional or facultative, teaching in small groups (or individualized help for students) and larger groups would have the effect of reducing the number of hours allotted to students without increasing the number of classes allocated to each teacher. It would increase the autonomy of teaching so that, in the overall context defined by the programme, teachers could organize their own study plans before the start of the school year. It should also lead to a more flexible and intensive use of instruments and buildings (the relevant territorial authorities – region, department, commune – should construct or renovate school buildings, in association with the teachers, in such a way as to offer the school system premises that are adapted to their purpose in both number and quality).

Collective and multidimensional activities would undoubtedly work better in the afternoons. This is the case for example with the teaching of languages. Combining as this does the study of usage in oral and written discourse with images, it stands at the intersection of a number of specialities; it leads to connections with outside partners (artists, image industries, etc.) and requires production as well as commentary.

Sixth principle
Concern to strengthen the coherence of teaching should lead to promote teaching given in common by teachers from different specialisms, and even to reconsider the divisions between 'disciplines', examining certain groupings that are historically inherited, and effecting – always in a gradual fashion – certain rapprochements imposed by the development of science.

[12] [*Collège* refers here to the lower level of secondary education, roughly equivalent to junior high school.]

178

Everything should be done to encourage teachers to coordinate their actions, at the very least work meetings designed to exchange information on the contents and methods of teaching, and to give them the desire and resources (in the form of suitable premises, equipment, etc.) for enriching, diversifying and expanding their teaching outside of the strict borders of their specialisms, or by joint teaching. (It would be desirable if certain teachers could be officially authorized to devote part of their allocated teaching hours to the indispensable tasks of coordinating and organizing meetings, copying documents, transmitting information, etc.)

Teaching sessions that group together teachers from two (or more) different specialisms, according to their affinities, should have the same standing as lecture courses (each hour of this kind of teaching counting in practice as an hour for each of the teachers who take part in it). Students here would be grouped according to a different logic from that of the present courses, rather by level of aptitude or as a function of their common interest in particular themes. A particular allocation of annual hours could be officially reserved for this, with its employment freely decided by the whole number of teachers concerned. All available means – libraries that are renewed, enriched and modernized, with audiovisual aids – should be mobilized to strengthen their attractiveness and efficacity. The absolutely necessary effort to reconsider and overcome boundaries between 'disciplines' and the corresponding pedagogic units should not be to the detriment of the identity and specificity of basic teaching; it should on the contrary display the coherence and particularity of the problematics and ways of thinking that are characteristic of each specialism.

Seventh principle
The quest for coherence should be combined with a quest for balance and integration between the different specialisms, and, as a result, between the different forms of excellence. It is particularly important to reconcile the universalism that is inherent to scientific thought with the relativism taught by the historical sciences, which are attentive to the plurality of ways of life and cultural traditions.

Everything should be done to reduce (whenever this seems possible and desirable) the opposition between the theoretical and the technical, the formal and the concrete, the pure and the applied, and to reintegrate the technical dimension into basic teaching. The need to balance the parts reserved for what can be called for convenience the 'conceptual', the 'sensory' and the 'corporeal', imposes itself at each level, but most of all in the earliest years. The respective weight given to technical and theoretical requirements must be determined as a function of characteristics that are specific to each particular level and branch, taking particular account of the professional careers available, and the social and educational characteristics of the students concerned, i.e. their capacities for abstraction as well as whether they are set to enter working life earlier or later.

Modern teaching should in no case sacrifice the history of languages and literature, cultures and religions, philosophies and sciences. It should on the contrary constantly reflect and work on these histories, in an increasingly subtle and critical fashion. But for this very reason, it cannot be governed by the representation sometimes given of these by those who reduce 'humanism' to a fixed image of the 'humanities'. The teaching of languages can and must be, just as much as that of physics or biology, an opportunity for initiation into logic: the teaching of mathematics or physics, just as much as that of philosophy or history, can and must prepare students for the history of ideas, science and technology (on condition, of course, that teachers are trained accordingly). In a more general fashion, access to scientific method passes by way of apprenticeship in basic logic and acquisition of the habits of thought, techniques and cognitive tools that are indispensable for conducting rigorous and considered reasoning. The opposition between 'science' and 'humanities' that still dominates the organization of teaching today, as well as the mentalities of teachers and parents, can and must be overcome by a teaching able to profess both science and the history of sciences or epistemology, to induct students into art and literature as well as aesthetic or logical consideration of these subjects, to teach not only mastery of language and literature, philosophical and scientific discourse, but also active mastery of the logical and rhetorical procedures that these involve. To strip these considerations of their abstract appearance, it would be enough to demonstrate by a class jointly taught by a professor of mathematics (or physics) and a professor of languages or philosophy, that the same general skills are required for the reading of scientific texts, technical notices and arguments. A similar effort should be made to articulate the ways of thinking specific to the natural and the human sciences respectively, in order to inculcate the rational and critical way of thinking that all the sciences teach, whilst recalling the historical roots of all scientific and philosophical work, and leading students to discover, understand and respect the diversity of civilizations, ways of thinking and cultural traditions in time and space.

It will fall to the Conseil National des Programmes d'Enseignement to put into practice the set of principles presented above. Its members should be selected as a function of competence alone, and act in a personal capacity rather than as representatives of bodies, institutions or associations. It should work on a permanent basis (which assumes that its members are freed from part of their other responsibilities) for a term of five years, but the modifications that it hopes in due course to make to the current programmes should only be applied every five years. Its competence should extend to every level and kind of teaching.

Letter to the lycéens of Les Mureaux*

You have asked me to speak on the *lycée* movement. I am very happy to do so, but also very embarrassed. In fact, I refuse to speak of '*lycée* students' in general, let alone in the name of such students. And if I have one thing to tell you, it is that you have to distrust people who do this: even when these representatives speak for you and in your support, they speak in your place.

I just want to raise a few questions that you might be interested in asking yourselves. To start with, can one speak of '*lycéens*' in general? And is there not an abuse of language – the kind used to disguise an abuse of power, actual or virtual, already accomplished or projected – in speaking of '*lycéens*' in general, and above all in the name of '*lycéens*' in general? One particular question that a number of *lycéens* ask – I know this from having asked them and listened to them – is that of the diversity – not to say disparity and inequality – among *lycéens*. Do the '*lycéens*' of the 'second S' class at Louis-le-Grand, who are more or less assured of being accepted in due course by one or other of the scientific *grandes écoles*, have anything in common with the students of an LEP[13] at Villeurbanne or Villetaneuse?

But there are other principles of differentiation that hide beneath the generic concept of '*lycéen*'. And I could show that the quality *lycéens* most indisputably have in common, i.e. that of 'youth', which offers a pretext for facile and hasty speeches on the relationship between generations, is itself extremely diversified. To make myself understood, I will simply say that the famous 'wreckers', who I am careful to distinguish from regular demonstrators, are 'young' in the same sense as '*lycéens*', and they raise the question of what separates them from '*lycéens*' not only in their way of demonstrating their discontent, but also in their conditions of existence (in particular, their relationship to the education system).

The warning about 'spokesmen' or representatives that I mentioned above is based among other things on a reference to this diversity and inequality. I think that it is essentially an act of force to claim to speak for *lycéens* as a whole. But representatives almost always do speak in the name of all, pretty well by definition.

How can we get beyond this situation? It would be necessary for you, *lycéens* of Les Mureaux or elsewhere – but do you have the time, the desire,

* November 1990; archives of the Collège de France.
13 [Lycée d'Enseignement Professionel, a secondary school designed to offer technical training, but with definitely lower status than a *lycée* proper.]

etc.? – to question yourselves as to what your own discontent actually is, the discontent you are trying to express, and to present the reasons or causes behind it. Why don't you try and write – write to me – either individually or collectively what in your view is wrong with your own *lycée*? I could then reply and try to help you pursue this exploration as far as possible.

Such work risks being long and difficult, and being concluded only after the battle is over. But we can be sure that if the battle is waged in the confused way it is today, it will only start up all over again. And it would be important then to discover that the loud cries of representatives and the peremptory assertions of 'commentators' had unjustly drowned out the small voice of the *lycéens* of Les Mureaux.

1988–1995

The priority of priorities should be to raise critical awareness of the mechanisms of symbolic violence that act in politics. This means finding the symbolic weapons able to ensure all citizens the means to defend themselves against this symbolic violence, and if need be, free themselves from their 'liberators'.

7

Disenchantment with Politics, and a Realpolitik of Reason

> We can substitute for the question whether virtue is possible, the question whether it is possible to create worlds in which people have an interest in universality.
>
> Lecture at the Collège de France, 1988–89

At the end of the 1980s, after his involvement as a state expert, Pierre Bourdieu launched a new collective project, The Weight of the World, *which appeared in 1993 and very soon became a work of reference for the social movements. This book enjoyed an immense public success. More than 80,000 copies were sold, it was adapted for the stage, and the sociologist agreed to take part, along with Abbé Pierre, in Jean-Pierre Cavada's TV programme 'La Marche du Siècle' (France 3, 15 April 1993).*

The 'Postcript' to The Weight of the World *directly challenges the closure of the political world on itself, and its forgetting of social reality; and the book's original title seems to reply to Prime Minister Michel Rocard who, under the electoral pressure of the Front National, declared in* Le Monde *on 24 August 1990: 'France cannot take in all the misery of the world, but it must faithfully know how to play its part.'*

The extent of the break involved in undertaking the direction of this investigation can doubtless be measured by the analysis that Bourdieu had offered two years earlier (see p.188) on the political solution that Michel Rocard's government had just offered to the independence claims of the Kanaks:[1] a moment of retreat in 'a formidable crisis of political representation and delegation' (see pp.191–6). It was

---

[1] The struggle for the independence of New Caledonia underwent a bloody episode between the two rounds of the presidential election, when Prime Minister Rocard and President Chirac ordered an assault on the grotto of Ouvéa where independence campaigners had holed up with their hostages; this led to the massacre of FLNKS fighters. Cf. Jean-Marie Tjibaou, *La Présence kanak* (Paris: Odile Jacob 1996); Alban Bensa and Jean-Claude Rivière, *Les Chemins de l'alliance. L'organisation sociale et ses representations en Nouvelle-Calédonie* (Paris: SELAF 1982); and – for Bourdieu's own position – 'Quand les Canaques prennent la parole. Entretien avec Alban Bensa', *Actes de la Recherche en Sciences Sociales* 56, 1985, pp. 69–83. [Ed.]

the very principle of political representation that, according to Bourdieu, was in question; or, more precisely, the 'legitimate usurpation' of every public responsibility, the 'mystery of the ministry', this power that the political mandatory draws from delegation.

This analysis of the exercise of power did not, in Bourdieu's opinion, lead to passivity or resignation. If social groups have been able to work for the establishment of a state based on law, the idea of public service and the general interest, it is because they find a certain benefit in universality.[2] An effective and realistic policy would consist in widening this principle of interest in universality to other social worlds, and inventing institutional structures that would give politicians an interest in virtue.

> Political morality does not fall from heaven, and it is not innate to human nature. Only a realpolitik of reason and morality can contribute favourably to the institution of a universe where all agents and their acts would be subject – notably through critique – to a kind of permanent test of universalizability. [. . .] Morality has no chance of entering politics unless one works toward creating institutional means for a politics of morality. The official truth of the official, the cult of public service and of devotion to the common good, cannot resist the critique of suspicion that will endlessly discover corruption, clientelism, ambitiousness, and at best a private interest in serving a public purpose.[3]

The role of public criticism thus proves determinant in forcing politicians to be what their social function enjoins them to be, i.e. reducing 'the gap between the official and the unofficial' and 'creating conditions for the establishment of the reign of civic virtue'.[4]

Nevertheless, this critique of national bureaucracies did not just lead to revealing the social suffering generated by the neoliberal policies conducted by the left itself (see p.197). It was accompanied by a consideration of the conditions for political action of intellectuals, whose autonomy was threatened by the grip of a 'technocracy of communication' that strengthened the monopoly of the political professionals on public debate.

> The problem I always raise is that of knowing how to bring into public debate this community of scholars who have things to say on the Arab

---

[2] For a more detailed presentation, cf. 'Rethinking the State', in *Practical Reason* (Cambridge: Polity 1998). [Ed.]
[3] Ibid., p. 144.
[4] Ibid., p. 145.

question, the suburbs, the Islamic scarf. For who actually speaks [in the media]? It is sub-philosophers whose sole competence derives from vague readings of vague texts, people such as Alain Finkielkraut. I call them the poor whites of culture. They are semi-scholars, not very cultivated, who set themselves up as defenders of a culture they don't possess, to mark their difference from those who have still less culture than them. These people appropriate the public space and chase out those who have things to say. Before speaking of the 'banlieue disease', before offering all the stupidities that we hear French intellectuals say, we have to move forward. Those who pronounce verdicts of this kind do harm, as the things they say are irresponsible. And at the same time, they discourage people from intervening who actually are there on the ground, who are working and have things to say. At the present time, they present one of the major obstacles to an understanding of the social world. They share in the construction of social fantasies that make a screen between a society and its own truth. [This is one of the reasons why I established the magazine *Liber*], which has correspondents in the majority of European countries, appears simultaneously in five languages, and seeks above all to be the product of a genuine international dialectic. Its aim is to bring different national cultures a bit closer together, so that we don't discover the Frankfurt School thirty years late, or that Germans stop speaking about structuralism in a facile manner. The idea then is to accelerate communication so as to synchronize the space of discussion. *Liber* also has the purpose of bringing scholars into public debate, so that it is not always those who know least who speak most.[5]

When international equilibrium was overturned by the fall of the Berlin Wall and the construction of the European Community – which necessarily became the new context of work – the struggle of intellectuals, in Pierre Bourdieu's view, had a greater need than ever to be collective and international (see p.205).

(see p.205).

---

[5] 'Les intellectuels ont mal à l'Europe', interview with Michel Audédat, *L'Hebdo*, 14 November 1991. [Ed.]

Civic virtue*

The world of politics is the site of two tendencies with opposing directions: on the one hand, it is ever more enclosed on itself, its games and their stakes; on the other hand it is ever more directly accessible to the view of the ordinary citizen, with television playing a determining role in both cases. The outcome is an increasing distance between professionals and laypeople, along with an awareness of the specific logic of the political game.

There is no need today to be an expert in political sociology to realize that a number of declarations and actions of politicians – not only their 'little phrases' on 'grand designs' or the great debates over petty differences between leaders of 'currents', but also the most serious political decisions – often have their roots in interests born out of competition for such and such a coveted position, that of general secretary, prime minister or president of the republic, and this goes for every level of political space. The discordance between the expectations of sincerity or requirements of disinterestedness that are inscribed in the democratic delegation of powers, and the reality of microscopic manoeuvres, contributes to strengthening an active indifferentism as symbolized by the movement around Coluche, which is very different from the anti-parliamentary Poujadism that those who contribute to arousing it try to defend themselves by reducing it to.

This is why the repeated reversals of leaders who are more clearly inspired by the concern to maintain themselves in power than by the interests of those whom they profess to defend, play no small part in the fact that the Front National often recruits today in the former strongholds of the Communist party, which profited more than any other from the trusting or resigned surrender to representatives – we know in fact that this disposition increases in frequency, the further down one goes in the social hierarchy. And if alliances with parties of the right are so advantageous to the Front National, it is less – despite what is often said – by the touch of respectability that they grant it, than by the discredit they inflict on those who denounce their own denunciations while showing themselves ready for anything that ensures their own reproduction.

The disenchantment with politics thus results almost automatically from the dual movement of the world of politics. On the one hand, those engaged in the political game enclose themselves ever more in their hermetic pursuit,

* Published in *Le Monde*, 16 September 1988.

often with no other communication with the outside world except polls that produce responses by the very questions they impose, and a number of them, moved solely by a concern to simply exist (like pretenders) or survive (like dethroned champions), mutually determine one another in actions that, far from being based on ethical conviction or devotion to a political cause, are no more than reactions to the reactions of others. The peak of perversion is reached when, with television performance becoming the measure of all things, communication advisers guided by opinion pollsters train politicians to mime sincerity and play at conviction.

Television, on the other hand, by one of its effects that is most systematically ignored by those who blame it for all the misfortunes of the century – formerly the 'massification' of the 'masses' and today the degradation of culture – has opened a window on the closed world in which politicians play out their game with the prince, in the illusion that they are unperceived. Like small groups of familiars in the ancient democracies, or in the Greek city as imagined by Hegel, mandatories are now under the extended view of the group as a whole: for anyone who has observed them in interviews, declarations or election debates, the protagonists of the political game have no more secrets to hide, and the most unaware of their number would lose much of their pride if they could read the psychological portraits of rare acuteness that the television audience – even the most culturally deprived – make of them when they are questioned. Everyone knows that, as Hugo put it, 'when the mouth says yes, the look says maybe'. And the citizen become television viewer, without needing to possess the art of deciphering the imponderables of infra-linguistic communication, finds him- or herself able to exercise the 'right to view' that (s)he has always more or less consciously claimed.

The 'openness' that electors approved at the last presidential election is not the kind that excites and divides party apparatuses or political commentators; this is an 'openness' that only reinforces the tendency of the political microcosm to close in on itself, i.e. on forms of the usual tricks that are simply a bit more complicated. It is rather the kind that would open the political world to the critical view of all citizens, preventing the political corps from interposing the screen of its particular interests and preoccupations, those that one might rightly call politicians' interests, since they have no other rhyme or reason but the defence of the political corps. The whole world has understood that there are too many real problems to leave politicians the bother of inventing the false problems that they need for their own perpetuation.

The solution that the government of Michel Rocard has brought to the problem of New Caledonia is in this sense exemplary – tackling a problem that had become the object of exploitation by political circles with no other object than to get it out of the way. This showed very clearly how the decision to attack the Ouvéa grotto had been an act of cynical instrumentalism. Genuine political courage, rather – as Mendès France taught in a different age – consists in putting oneself at the service of problems, at the risk of not surviving, rather than making use of problems so as to continue in office at any price. And the success of the negotiations showed that civic virtue, perhaps because it is so rare, perhaps because it calls for virtue, is sometimes a highly effective political weapon.

The feeling arises that, by establishing this mode of political action, the political world is in the process of making up for the delay that it fell into, by closing in on itself, in relation to the expectations of citizens, and particularly in relation to the moral demands that have been voiced so many times over the last two decades, in actions or demonstrations such as those of SOS Racism, or of the students and *lycéens*.

Those politicians who are most free, objectively and subjectively, in relation to the demands of the political game and the constraints of party apparatuses, can make themselves understood when apparatchiks are temporarily reduced to silence. And perhaps the conditions are arising for certain rules, both written and unwritten, to be durably established, or, better still, certain objective mechanisms able to impose on politicians in practice the disciplines of civic virtue. It is up to all citizens, and especially those who, like intellectuals, have the free time and means to exercise their right to survey the political world, to see that a mode of exercising power that is sometimes denounced as a kind of naive moralism (which is indeed what people mean when they talk of 'boy-scoutism'), is actually the creative anticipation of a state of the political world in which those with political responsibility, who are constantly under the gaze of all, are compelled to establish the kind of direct democracy that is made possible, paradoxically, by the transparency and openness of the political field that a democratic use of television would ensure.

Much has been said about the silence of intellectuals at a time when denouncing the failures of civic virtue at every moment only risked serving the most cynical designs. Perhaps the moment has now come for them to speak out, not to celebrate the powers that be, as they are usually asked to do, but rather to participate, along with others, and particularly journalists, in the exercise of civic vigilance which, by criticism and revelation as much as by praise and tacit complicity, would contribute to bringing about a political world in which those with political responsibility had an interest in virtue.

Basing criticism on a knowledge of the social world*

How would you analyze the break between society and the world of politics?

One major reason is the self-sufficiency of a state nobility that draws the most absolute assurance of its competence and legitimacy from its titles of educational nobility. It is well known how an ever greater proportion of those politicians who count – ministers and members of ministerial offices from both right and left, not to mention high civil servants and bosses of big companies, both private and public – emerges from the great educational competitions and see themselves as an elite of 'intelligence'. It is significant that the most arrogant of these new mandarins believe themselves authorized to intervene in an intellectual game that is increasingly dominated by the media-political logic of cultural fast food and the bestseller; and that they sometimes succeed in imposing their symbolic shows of force with the complicity of court 'intellectuals' who rival them in their grip on the media, and purvey today's fashionable commonplaces in televised debates or spectacular colloquia in the weeklies. (Those spaces where men of power short of ideas meet up with 'intellectuals' short of power, reviews or clubs that make connections between Hautes Études en Sciences Sociales and Sciences-Po, conferences, seminars – European, by preference – have kept on proliferating, and there is not a single day when you don't see the same flock of interchangeable protagonists exchange interchangeable statements on the subjects of the day.)

This media circus of Tout-Paris, for all its ostensible openness to the problems of the world, and very often convinced it is making History, is in fact narrowly trapped in its own petty affairs. How could it be otherwise? All these people who never stop talking about 'civil society' actually have no desire, and especially no means (apart from the daily reading of daily papers and opinion polls) of knowing the social world that they claim to understand or govern. How many times, to sum up some 'work' or other destined to take its place for a few weeks on the bestseller list, do you not find that all you need to know is that its roots lie in a quarrel between some petty media masters about the end of 'structuralism', the return of the 'subject'

* Interview with Louis Roméo, published under the title 'La saine colère d'un sociologue', in *Politis*, 19 March 1992.

or the threat of cultural relativism, the nth version of a challenge to the social sciences? (Those who wonder at the novelty of 'postmodern' ideas should re-read Bergson's *Two Sources of Morality and Religion*.)

The chief function of these thinkers without thoughts (and generally without genuine works) is to make believe that they have some thoughts, and thus fill the gap in political and intellectual debate. By imposing the omnipresence of their insignificance, thanks to their quasi-monopoly of the instruments of mass communications (as well as the censorship, often very strict, that they exercise in the name of liberalism and the needs of a struggle against the vestiges of 'Marxism'), they impose at the same stroke problems which have no other raison d'être except their own avid pretensions to the status of master-thinker. They are thus, without even wanting it or realizing it, the natural allies of those who, at the border of the political and intellectual fields, oppose the screen of their wooden economic-financial language to all attempts to bring a bit of reality into the closed field of their rivalries.

Doesn't the climate of 'sinistrosis'[6] that reigns today have less to do with historical reality, and more with the representation that journalists make of this?

What we actually have is a tremendous crisis of representation (in every sense of the term) and delegation, the foundations of democracy. Lacking the ability to express itself directly, or find recognition in political representation, the very deep discontent that haunts a whole section of society (without sparing the traditional clientele of the parties of the left, such as the teaching profession and all the lower and middle categories of public official), can find a safety-valve in national-racist ideologies fuelled by resentment and despair born out of the experience of social, individual or collective decline (whether that of a social category such as engineering workers, for example, or a whole region or nation). I certainly have in mind the material and moral suffering of all the unemployed, all those on the minimum wage, all those with only temporary work. But on top of this there is all the suffering of a quite new type that arises from disappointment in the educational system, whether because those involved have not obtained from school what they expected (for themselves and their families), or they have not obtained on the labour market all that their school qualifications promised them. (Graduate unemployment appears particularly scandalous to those affected and their milieu.) There is also the suffering that derives from deterioration in working conditions (fostered or authorized by the weakening

---

[6] [Rather than the medical sense of the term, this 'climate of sinistrosis' suggests a more general sense of disaster.]

of trade unions and the rise of casual employment), as well as from housing conditions (which in no way spares those who, having realized their dream of a little bungalow, often pay in financial burdens and transport time for a privilege that does not always offer shelter from difficult neighbours – real or imaginary). Those who condemn racism should condemn just as strongly the conditions that promote or authorize racism, delinquency, violence, isolation, the break-up of solidarities – everything that generates fear, withdrawal on oneself – and also, of course, the conditions that promote this conduct of despair, such as housing and employment policy. Virtuous states of mind, moralistic anti-racist preaching, and the anti-Le Pen confessions of faith of certain politicians, do just as much to promote this kind of crisis of confidence in the words of representatives, this deep suspicion towards intellectuals, this kind of generalized anti-clericalism that has always played into the hands of fascism.

One reason for the distress that leads to such desperate solutions as voting for the Front National is that people no longer know what saint to worship; they feel that the ills they experience are neither seen nor known, not understood or recognized by those with the power to speak.

The state itself, this ultimate recourse and temporal Providence (I won't repeat here the demonstration I made by reference to Kafka, but the state still occupies the place of God, whether you like it or not), is transformed into a bad god who, through henchmen with neither faith nor law, renounces the *sacred debt* of the nation to its members – in other words, breaks the contract of citizenship. It is no accident that despair focuses on the question of foreigners. And those whose only slogan is struggle against a party that is seen as able to restore the contract that they themselves are suspected to have broken are certainly the least well placed to root out this conviction . . .

Is this where you see the link between the Front National and certain forms of social suffering?

Certainly. To emphasize the *national* in opposition to the *foreign* means asserting the desire to control the redistribution (of assistance, allowances, insurance, support, etc., and certainly also of work) that is properly the function of the state, by giving absolute priority in this matter to *nationals*. The success of the 'nationalist' message with 'poor whites' who have nothing left but their membership by right of a state that abandons them is very understandable. But what is harder to grasp is that the parties of the left have let themselves get into a position of taking up, against a whole tradition of internationalism and universalism, the dichotomy national/foreigner and indigenous/immigrant, and making it their main principle of vision and division, to the particular detriment of the opposition between rich and poor, who include nationals as well as foreigners . . .

You showed the limits of economism in your book Réponses[7]: *there was a time when people talked about self-management and tried to change the rules of the game; and now, if you don't talk about management, you are perceived as old-fashioned . . .*

I think that economism, which can also be found on the left, in the Marxist tradition, as well as on the right, has the effect of subjecting economic reality in the full sense of the term to a tremendous mutilation, abstracting from a whole dimension of costs and benefits that is absolutely crucial. Not being able to demonstrate this completely here, and to go quickly to the essential point, I will say that the full consequences of a politics conceived simply as managing economic parameters ('equilibrium' in the narrow sense of the term) are paid for in a thousand ways, in the form of social and psychological costs, in the form of unemployment, sickness, delinquency, abuse of alcohol and drugs, suffering that leads to resentment and racism, to political demoralization, etc. A genuinely complete accounting of social costs and profits would make clear how sociology proposes an economics that is no less rigorous and faithful to the complexity of reality than the partial economics of pure management; and that the logic of well-understood interest makes it essential to break with liberal laissez-faire as well as with the determinism of naturalized social laws. And to re-assert the role of the state: against the two forms of submission to the necessity of economic laws that flow from these two forms of economism, we need the state to be armed with an understanding of demographic, economic and cultural laws, so it can work to correct their effects by policies that use the resources (legal, taxation, financial, etc.) that the state has at its disposal. Ethical and political justice on the one hand, and technical correctness on the other, are certainly less antithetical than a short-term calculation of narrowly economic profit and loss leads one to believe. Far from calling for the 'withering away of the state', we have to demand that it exercise a regulatory action able to counteract the 'fatality' of economic and social mechanisms that are immanent to the social order.

It is clear here that your sociology has a political bearing. You are often accused of being hermetic, that it is not all that clear how your work can concretely 'aid liberation' . . .

[7] *Réponses* (with Loïc Wacquant) (Paris: Seuil 1992). [Ed.]

I believe that the reproach often made to sociology (and to myself in particular) of encouraging fatalism – or, what comes to the same thing, a pessimistic resignation – rests on a complete misunderstanding (undoubtedly unconscious, but this does not mean innocent) of the status of social science and the regularities or laws that it aims to establish. Is there any need to remember that social laws are not natural laws, inscribed for all eternity in the nature of things, and that scientific laws are not prescriptive norms, imperative rules of conduct, but rather regularities that are empirically confirmed and validated? It follows from this that these (statistical) regularities in no way impose themselves as an imperative or a fate that we have to submit to. Social regularities present themselves as probable chains of events that can only be combated, if this is deemed necessary, on condition of their being recognized. (If I insist on recalling such elementary truths, it's because some of my critics situate themselves at this level of incomprehension – and incompetence – as well as obscurantism, so that I have to return to the A + B of philosophy of science . . . .)

Do you think that sociology can contribute to a renewal of politics? Do you believe it can contribute to founding or arming the critical counter-power of intellectuals that you often say you want to see?

The knowledge of the social world that sociology provides is certainly one of the most indispensable conditions for a genuinely responsible critical thought. I have mentioned the need to break with economism and promote a regulatory action that takes into account all the constitutive elements of an economics that would be oriented towards happiness rather than just the values of productivity, profitability and competitiveness. But I believe that an economics of this kind, which should give a prominent place to the symbolic, can only be conceived concretely, in its means and above all in its ends, on condition that we are able to establish new forms of delegation and representation. The crisis of representation, which lies at the root of the discredit that politics has fallen into, is undoubtedly linked with the organizational logic of mass parties and trade unions – and particularly with a social technology that was invented in the nineteenth century in order to ensure, at least in principle, communication between leaders and rank-and-file: that of programmes, platforms, resolutions, congresses and mandates. A radical critique of the present forms of circulation of information and elaboration of collective desires should enable us to escape from this demobilizing disenchantment and orient ourselves towards new forms of mobilization and reflection.

Paradoxically, political apparatuses that were conceived as instruments of liberation, individual and above all collective, have very often operated as instruments of domination, particularly by way of the symbolic violence that is exercised both within them and by them. That is why the top priority seems to me to be that of raising critical awareness of the mechanisms of symbolic violence that act in and through politics; and this means broadly distributing the symbolic weapons able to ensure all citizens the means of defending themselves against symbolic violence – liberating themselves, if need be, of their 'liberators'.

Our wretched state[*]

Speaking about this France that generally remains silent about its social suffering, do you think that the presence of the left in power has brought it more in the way of solidarity?

The policies we have seen at work for the last twenty years present a remarkable continuity. Initiated in the 1970s, at the point when the neoliberal vision taught at Sciences-Po began to impose itself, the retreat of the state has since been increasingly sharp. The Socialist leaders, by the way that they rallied to the cult of private enterprise and profit in 1983–84, orchestrated a deep change in collective mentality that led to the generalized triumph of 'marketing'. Even culture has been contaminated. In politics, the constant appeal to opinion polls serves as the basis for one of the most perverse forms of demagogy. One section of intellectuals have lent themselves to this collective conversion – which has succeeded only too well, at least among the leaders and in privileged circles. By practising a tactic of amalgam and indulging in a confusion of thought, they have worked to show that economic liberalism is the necessary and sufficient condition of political liberty; and conversely, that any state intervention bears the threat of 'totalitarianism'. They have taken a good deal of trouble to establish that any attempt to combat inequality – which they deem inevitable – is first of all ineffective, and furthermore can only be undertaken to the detriment of freedom.

Thus they question the essential functions of the state?

Precisely. The state as we know it – but perhaps we should talk in the past tense here – is a quite particular social world, whose official purpose is public service, service to the public and devotion to the general interest. You can pour ridicule over all this, invoke notorious cases of embezzlement of public funds and public purposes. It remains however that the official definition of state office – and of officials, who are mandated to serve, not serve themselves – is an extraordinary historical invention, an advance for humanity, in the same sense as art or science. The conquest is fragile, and always threatened with regression or disappearance. And it is all this that is now rejected as outmoded and belonging to a past era.

[*] Interview with Sylvaine Pasquier about *La Misère du monde*, published in *L'Express*, 18 March 1993.

How is the retreat of the state inscribed in social realities?

This began in the 1970s in the field of housing, with a policy choice of withdrawing support for social housing and promoting access to property.[8] Here again, this was on the basis of false equations that associated collective housing with collectivism and saw petty private property as the basis for political liberalism. No one asked how we might escape the alternative between individual and collective, owning and renting: for example by offering individual houses for rent, as is done elsewhere. Imagination has not been in power under the left any more than under the right. And we have reached a result that our eminent technocrats did not foresee: these sites of relegation where the most disadvantaged sections of the population are concentrated, all those who lack the resources to move to more attractive locations. Under the effects of economic crisis and unemployment, we see the development of social phenomena that are more or less pathological, and which are now the object of study by new commissions of technocrats.

What common ground is there between two youngsters of different ethnic origin in a housing estate in the Nord, or between a worker of Tunisian origin and a post office employee, between a literature teacher and a trade unionist?

Even if the most visible social suffering is met with among the most deprived, there are also less visible forms of suffering at all levels of the social world. Modern societies – and this is one of their main features – are differentiated into a multitude of sub-spaces and social microcosms, each separate from the others. Each of these has its specific hierarchy, its dominant and dominated. It is possible to belong to a prestigious world but occupy only an obscure position in it. To be the musician lost in the orchestra that Patrick Süskind describes in *Double Bass*. The relative inferiority of those who are inferior among superiors, last among the first, is what defines positional misery – not reducible to conditional misery, but just as real and deep. These relative miseries cannot simply be relativized.

Can the sociologist really understand the suffering or revolt of those he investigates?

On condition that he understands the place that his interlocutor occupies in the social world – more precisely, in the social microcosm that his energies, his passions, the things that matter to him, are invested in. That might be

[8] This refers to an investigation published in March 1990 in *Actes de la Recherche en Sciences Sociales* 81/82, and reproduced in the broader context of *Social Structures of the Economy* (Cambridge: Polity 2005). [Ed.]

a firm, a service, an office, a residential district, an apartment block . . . On condition that he makes the effort to think in this place, to really put himself in his place.

Why do these things matter?

Because these miseries generate, just as much as extreme poverty if not more so, representations and political practices that are often incomprehensible in appearance, such as those of racism and xenophobia, and to which the only usual response is indignation or preaching. And also because those who experience them are the chosen victims of demagogic and criminal politicians – starting with the Front National – who live from exploiting suffering, disappointment and despair.

How do people fall into racism? Your investigation shows neighbours plunged in the same difficulties, but living in a mutual state of siege. On the pretext that one family, of North African origin, supposedly has noisy cats . . .

The example par excellence of these 'relatively disinherited' is that of those who were known in the colonies as 'poor whites', all those who, persuaded of being members of an elite, with a monopoly of genuine and exclusive rights, demand a monopoly of access to the economic and social advantages bound up with their being 'nationals' as opposed to 'immigrants'. You can read in this book the pathetic testimonies of small farmers and shopkeepers indignant at the treatment given to immigrants – of whom they have no direct experience – and more broadly, to those who benefit – undeservedly in their eyes – from state aid, such as delinquents, prisoners, etc. Even if these criticisms of the welfare state are dressed up in seemingly more rational guise, they undoubtedly owe their success to the fact that they are so often rooted in impulses or representations of this kind. What has happened to the forces able to counteract the xenophobic delirium that those most directly confronted with 'foreigners' – in competition for work or housing – fall prey to? There are certainly anti-racist movements, but they speak above all to a milieu that is highly educated. What has become of the internationalist principles of the old political or trade-union education? The collapse of the civic ideals of solidarity has left the field free for those triumphant egoisms encouraged by the absence of any political message able to propose any other reason for life apart from personal success measured in salary or monetary value.

Does this argument still stand in a situation of shared destitution?

In places of great suffering, such as the housing estates, the big blocks of flats, the 'difficult suburbs', even the social workers charged by the state or local authorities to ensure the most basic public services, without disposing of the resources needed for this, are caught up in formidable contradictions. I have in mind here, for example, the secondary-school principal who had the most generous and lofty notion of his mission, but found himself forced to spend the greater part of his time struggling against violence (sometimes even by violent means). He experienced this as a breach of contract, and he is not alone here. You have educators, teachers, police, lower-level magistrates who all experience the contradictions of their institutions and the missions they are charged with in the form of personal dramas.

Because they feel that the state has failed, and they take it on themselves to remedy this?

You meet extraordinary individuals who devote themselves body and soul to these poorly paid, poorly conceived and even self-destructive activities – bureaucratic saints in a way – but whose lives are a constant struggle against these bureaucracies. From the standpoint of a junior executive who lives through the latest stock-exchange figures, they are simply mad. I have in mind a social worker whom I had an appointment with, and who arrived that morning quite exhausted, with dark rings under his eyes. He had spent part of the night dealing with drug addicts who had been arrested at the police station. These minor social officials are the advanced antennas of a state whose right hand doesn't want to know what the left hand is doing. Worse – the titled members of the high state nobility, ENA graduates of whatever political persuasion, look down from a great height on this lower nobility and love to teach them a lesson. They fail to understand how these people play a key role in maintaining a minimum of social cohesion. They should remember that the Revolution was triggered by a revolt of the lower nobility against the high nobility . . .

You mean that the lower state nobility is today in revolt?

It is the lower nobility that calls for civic virtue, and denounces the treason of the pharisaic defenders of the 'values' and rights of man. Today they are undoubtedly the guardians of the whole tradition of public service, devotion and disinterestedness that have been handed down by two centuries of social struggles that have served as a laboratory for the invention of such institutions as social security, the minimum wage, etc., as well as virtues and ideals.

Isn't this disillusion aggravated by seeing the left in power renege on its principles?

The great responsibility of this government of the left is to have made acceptable, by practising them, the very policies that its mission was to challenge. And to have succumbed to all the failures and lacks that it formerly denounced. Besides the problem of unemployment, which everyone understands largely escapes political action alone, what it is reproached for is the demoralization of the state, in the double sense of loss of both morals and morale.

Much has been said about the silence of intellectuals. Would you admit that they could have exercised a critical counter-power?

The powerful who are short of thoughts call on support from thinkers who are short of power, and the latter rush to offer them the justificatory notions that they need. And so it all works out for the best, in the best of media and political worlds.

As for scholars who establish knowledge capable of enlightening political action, the results of their works are scarcely noted. Historians, sociologists and economists have brought to light some of the mechanisms and tendential laws that govern societies in the long run. The law of cultural transmission, for example, tells us that the chances of success on the educational market depend to a large extent on the cultural capital that a family possesses. If the intention genuinely is to 'democratize' access to school and culture, it is not enough to undertake superficial and spectacular actions designed to make an impact on newspaper headlines. Mechanisms as powerful as these, which govern our cultural practices, can only be fought if they are properly understood, but it is also necessary, and above all, to accept that a great deal of energy would be needed to have even a very weak effect in the short term. Our leaders prefer demagogic proclamations of the kind: 80 per cent of their generation to *baccalauréat* level by the years 2008!

What are the consequences?

In order to satisfy the demands of a mere slogan, access to senior *lycée* classes has been facilitated for an influx of students who would have previously been barred from this. This was carried out without anything being done to help them overcome their existing difficulties, let alone those that their presence there brought about. More seriously still, the gap between the levels of representation of categories of different social origin was not even reduced at the highest levels of secondary education. The school continues to exclude, but it keeps those whom it excludes inside the system, relegating them to devalued subjects and sending them out at sixteen or eighteen years of age with the stigmata of defeat.

What is the impact of educational policy in the working-class milieu?

For the last thirty years, in the working class but also among small shopkeepers and in the countryside, we have seen the appearance of a generational conflict that is actually a conflict between educational generations, i.e. between those who went into the factory at around fourteen years old and those who spent a longer period at school. Young people from the housing estates, who have all the characteristics of sub-proletarians with no future and no projects, but are affected by the aspirations or rejections that the school has developed in them, are suited to jobs offered by companies on a casual basis. And the break between permanent and temporary deeply divides the world of work, making any kind of collective action difficult. All the more so, in that certain bosses take advantage of the submission that fear of dismissal arouses. The forms of oppression they exercise mark a return to the worst moments of nascent capitalism.

Faced with explosions of violence like that at Vaux-en-Velin, are the media wrong in seeking their reference points in the United States?

Certain acts of delinquency or vandalism can be understood as an embryonic form of civil war. The French '*banlieues*', however, are far from having reached the state of the great American ghettoes. You have to read the very realistic descriptions that Loïc Wacquant and Philippe Bourgois have given of daily life in Chicago and Harlem, to discover what are the concrete consequences of a total retreat of the state. In the name of liberalism, a society with no historical precedent has been allowed to establish itself at the heart of one of the most developed countries of our time, abandoned to the law of the jungle; the state, after destroying all the mechanisms and structures (clans, families, etc.) that might have a limiting effect on violence, leaves behind, after its collapse – like today in Yugoslavia – violence in the pure state, a war of all against all, such as previously existed only in the imagination of Hobbes. The vision of the devastated centres of the great American cities shows us the limits of unlimited liberalism better than any theoretical critique.

How do you see the role of the state?

We cannot rest content with this kind of minimal state whose action is confined to protecting the natural rights of individuals. Let alone with an ethics that replaces public virtue with the private interest of isolated individuals. The ideal republic, according to Machiavelli, is a regime in which citizens have an interest in virtue. I could equally well cite Kant – so readily invoked by those who situate themselves at the opposite pole to Machiavelli's 'sociological' realism – when he says, in substance, in his essay on 'Perpetual Peace', that egoistic interests have to be organized in such a fashion that they mutually counterbalance each other in their devastating effects, so that a man, even when he is not good by nature, is forced to be a good citizen.

Are there any examples that are close to this ideal?

The worlds of science. If they want to succeed here, individuals who are driven, like everyone else, by emotions, passions and interests, have to do so in the due forms. They cannot kill their rivals or attack them with their fists. They have to oppose them with refutations that conform to the prevailing truth regime. The objective should be to establish in the worlds of bureaucracy and politics regulations of the same type, able to inflict an immediate sanction on those who break the rules. Journalists have a key role to play here, one going far beyond denunciation of 'scandals', and so do intellectuals, especially scholars in the social sciences. On condition, of course, that both of these are themselves subject to similar controls, and that recourse to certain procedures such as slander or degradation of others, so common in critique, leads those indulging in it to be immediately disqualified. A mere code of practice is not enough, contrary to the view of 'ethical committees'. But mechanisms able to impose themselves with a rigour analogous to that of a natural order have still to be invented.

And what about the function of the state?

It is only possible to define this by rejecting the usual alternative between liberalism and socialism – one of those damaging dualisms that impede thought. Both systems, at least in their strict and radical definition, have in common that they reduce the complexity of the social world to its economic dimension, and put government at the service of economics. You need only consider the social costs, which in the last analysis are economic and political as well, of policies inspired by an exclusive consideration of productivity and economic profit; this measures the deathly mutilation that economism inflicts on a full and fully human definition of social practice.

The price of unemployment, poverty, exploitation, exclusion and dehumanization is paid for in suffering but also in violence, which can be directed against both others and oneself, with alcoholism, drugs and suicide.

Is this the message of The Weight of the World?

Among other things . . . I believe in fact that if our technocrats took up the habit of bringing suffering in all its forms – economic and otherwise – into the national accounts, they would discover that the saving they thought they were achieving was often a very bad calculation.

8

For Struggles on a European Scale

Reinventing a Collective Intellectual

Liber *magazine was founded as part of an international collective project, and represented an attempt to reactivate at a European level the tradition of the intellectual after the model of the encyclopaedists of the Age of Enlightenment. Pierre Bourdieu already formulated the premises of this undertaking in 1985, in the context of the Collège des Artistes et des Savants Européens, envisaging the creation of a 'European Review of Books' that would be governed by the specific norms of intellectuals. The original ambition of* Liber, *an 'international review of books', was to present avant-garde works of literature, art and science to a wide readership, with the object of counteracting the closure of these worlds on themselves and attenuating the break with the broad public by 'overcoming temporal gaps and misunderstandings bound up with linguistic barriers and the slowness of translation . . . as well as the inertia of scholarly traditions'.[1] Various initiatives were envisaged: to generalize accounts of works published in other languages (see p.233), and investigate the particularisms of national institutions under a rubric of European ethnography – military service in Switzerland, English clubs, Finnish firemen, etc.*

Appearing first of all as a supplement to the Frankfurter Allgemeine Zeitung, L'Indice, Le Monde, El País *and the* TLS, *the first series, which reached nearly two million readers, consisted of five issues between October 1989 and December 1990.* Liber *subsequently became a supplement to* Actes de la Recherche en Sciences Sociales *until this closed in 1999,[2] asserting the continuity of its project by the need to go against 'the un-discussed beliefs of academic orthodoxies, which are so powerful in these times of restoration'.[3]*

Liber*'s editorial line stood out by the place it gave to artists and writers whose*

---

[1] *Liber* 1, October 1989. [Ed.]
[2] An announcement for the magazine stated that '*Liber. Revue Internationale des Livres* has been published in a dozen European countries and languages thanks to the constant efforts of individuals and institutions devoted to the cause of intellectual internationalism.' [Ed.]
[3] '*Liber* continue', *Liber* 7, September 1991. [Ed.]

works bore a political critique.[4] *The end of the Soviet Union, the fall of the Berlin Wall and German reunification were thus privileged themes of the review: the German philosopher Jürgen Habermas analyzed the damaging effects of the reunification process;*[5] *Bourdieu examined the collapse of the Soviet system, the operational reality of a regime that had initially been the bearer of an emancipatory project, and the 'false alternatives' (socialism versus liberalism) used for purposes of political restoration (see pp.218 and 222).*

The intention was to use history, sociology and literature as instruments of self-understanding, so as to disarm the regressive impulses that sometimes underlie the political action of artists, scientists and philosophers. The collective socio-analysis that Pierre Bourdieu called for was designed to disarm the traps that history had bequeathed, and their sediments in everyday language: to win margins of freedom by overcoming the obstacles bound up with past international conflicts, and put in place structures of communication able to promote the instauration of universality.

This 'realpolitik of reason' was the inspiration behind the appeal for a 'corporatism of universality' published as a conclusion to The Rules of Art *(see pp.209–17). Pierre Bourdieu's concern was to strengthen the autonomy of the intellectual field that had been constructed in the late nineteenth century against the powers of religion, politics and economics, and was now under threat from the increased interpenetration of the worlds of art and money, the generalized resort to sponsors for financing university research, and the growing weight of commercial constraints on the undertakings of cultural production and distribution. New forms of struggle had to be invented, including the creation of an 'International of intellectuals', to which Bourdieu devoted himself in the first half of the 1990s.*

To establish a 'critical counter-power' of this kind by organizing 'a concrete solidarity with threatened writers', and to constitute 'a site of reflection on new forms of commitment' – this was the object of the appeal launched in Strasbourg in November 1993, initiated by Pierre Bourdieu and signed by Jacques Derrida, Edouard Glissant, Toni Morrison, Susan Sontag and Salman Rushdie (see p.238). In February 1994, Rushdie was elected president of the International Writers' Parliament, a body of fifty members with both deliberative and executive function. This foundation was accompanied by a charter defining the principles, obligations and forms of action of the organization: independence from established powers, recognition of the diversity of historical traditions in order to escape from the 'prophetism of the old universal consciousness' denouncing the 'great problems of

---

[4] Hans Haacke, for example, with whom Pierre Bourdieu published *Libre-échange* in 1994, and who brought into his work conflicts bound up with the grip of the business world over society, particularly in terms of cultural patronage. [Ed.]

[5] 'Une union sans valeur', interview with Jürgen Habermas, *Liber* 10, June 1992. [Ed.]

the day' as defined by the media, anonymous and collective contributions, etc. We need only mention the setting up of an international network of 400 refuge-towns divided among thirty-four states, and the organization of international press conferences on Rwanda, Algeria, Sarajevo, the right of asylum, etc.

This was an ambitious project, within which Pierre Bourdieu always opposed the 'figure of the intellectual as self-proclaimed bearer of universal consciousness' with the role of 'functionary of humanity' (Husserl), which can be understood in a far more modest sense.[6]

---

[6] 'L'intellectuel dans la cité', interview with Florence Dutheil, *Le Monde*, 5 November 1993. [Ed.]

*For an international of intellectuals**

I would like to propose a series of orientations for a collective action of European intellectuals, basing myself on as realistic an analysis as possible of what an intellectual is and can be.

The intellectual is a *paradoxical* being, who can only be conceived as such by being understood across the classical alternative between autonomy and commitment, pure culture and politics. This is so, because the intellectual was historically constituted *in and through the transcending of* this opposition: writers, artists and scientists asserted themselves as intellectuals when, at the time of the Dreyfus affair, they intervened in political life as such, i.e. with a specific authority based on their membership of the relatively autonomous world of art, science and literature, and on all the values associated with this autonomy, such as disinterestedness, competence, etc. The intellectual is a two-dimensional character, who exists and persists only in so far as there exists and persists, on the one hand, an autonomous intellectual world (i.e. one independent of religious, political, economic and other powers) whose specific laws he respects, and on the other hand, in so far as the specific authority that develops in this world in favour of autonomy is committed to political struggles. Thus, far from there being an antinomy between the quest for autonomy (such as characterizes art, science and literature described as pure) and the quest for political effectiveness, as is ordinarily believed, it is by increasing their autonomy – and hence, among other things, their freedom of criticism towards the powers that be – that intellectuals can increase the effectiveness of a political action whose ends and means find their origin in the specific logic of the field of cultural production.

We need only repudiate this old alternative that we all have at the back of our minds, and that periodically has a resurgence in literary debates, to be able to define what could be the broad orientations for a collective action by intellectuals. But this kind of expulsion of forms of thought that we apply to ourselves when we take ourselves as the object of thought is formidably difficult. That is why, before putting forward these orientations, and in order to do so, we have to try and make as fully explicit as possible the unconscious – and in particular principles of vision and division such as the opposition between pure and committed art – that has been deposited, in each intellectual, by the very history of which intellectuals are the product.

* Lecture given in Turin in May 1989, published in *Politis* 1, 1992.

There is no more effective antidote to the amnesia of origins that lies at the root of all forms of transcendental illusion, than the reconstruction of forgotten or repressed history under the paradoxical form of those forms of thought that appear to be ahistorical and yet structure our perception of the world and of ourselves.

This is an extraordinarily repetitive history, since the constant changes only conceal the form of a pendulum motion between two possible attitudes towards politics – commitment or withdrawal (at least until this opposition was transcended by Zola and the Dreyfusards). The 'commitment' of '*philosophes*' that Voltaire, in the article of his 1765 *Dictionnaire philosophique* titled 'the man of letters', opposed to the scholastic obscurantism of the decadent universities and academies 'where things are said by halves', found its extension in the participation of 'men of letters' in the French Revolution – even if, as Robert Darnton has shown, the 'literary bohème' grasped the revolutionary 'disorder' as the occasion for revenge against the most stubborn successors of the '*philosophes*'.[7]

In the era of post-Revolutionary restoration, 'men of letters', because they were held responsible not only for the movement of revolutionary ideas – by the role of 'opinion makers' that the proliferation of newspapers in the first phase of the Revolution had conferred on them – but also for the excesses of the Terror, were viewed with mistrust or even contempt by the young generation of the 1820s – and especially so by the Romantics, who, in the first phase of this movement, discarded and rejected the claim of the 'philosopher' to intervene in political life and propose a rational vision of the historical process. However, with the autonomy of the intellectual field being threatened by the reactionary policies of the Restoration, the Romantic poets, who had been led to assert their desire for autonomy in a rehabilitation of religious sensibility and sentiment against Reason and the critique of dogma, did not delay in themselves claiming freedom for the writer and scientist (Michelet and Saint-Simon in particular), and assuming in fact the prophetic function that had been that of the eighteenth-century '*philosophe*'.

In a new swing of the pendulum, though, the populist Romanticism that seemed to have taken hold of the quasi-totality of writers in the period preceding the 1848 revolution, failed to survive the defeat of the movement and the establishment of the Second Empire. The collapse of the illusions that I deliberately call *quarante-huitardes* (to evoke the analogy with the *soixante-huitardes* illusions whose collapse still haunts us today) led to the extraordinary disenchantment, so strikingly conjured up by Flaubert in

---

[7] Robert Darnton, *The Literary Underground of the Old Regime* (Cambridge, MA: Harvard University Press 1982).

Sentimental Education, that provided favourable ground for a new assertion of the autonomy of intellectuals, this time in a radically elitist form. The defenders of art for art's sake, such as Flaubert or Théophile Gautier, asserted the autonomy of the artist by not only opposing both 'social art' and the 'literary bohème', but also the bourgeois art that was subordinated, both in matters of art and also the art of living, to the norms of a bourgeois clientele. They opposed the nascent new power of the culture industry by rejecting the usages of 'industrial literature' (except by way of a substitute for a private income, as in the bread-and-butter work of Gautier or Nerval). Accepting no other judgement than that of their peers, they proclaimed the self-sufficiency of the literary field, but also the writer's renunciation of descent from his ivory tower to practise any form of power at all (breaking here with the role of poet *vates* à la Hugo, or prophetic scholar à la Michelet).

In an apparent paradox, it was only at the end of the century, at a time when the literary, artistic and scientific fields acquired autonomy, that the most autonomous agents in these fields could intervene in the political field as intellectuals – rather than as cultural producers converted into politicians, in the style of Guizot or Lamartine – i.e. with an authority based on the autonomy of the field and all the values associated with this, such as purity of motive, competence, etc. In concrete terms, specifically artistic or scientific authority was asserted in political acts such as Zola's 'J'accuse' and the petitions presented in its support. This new type of political action tended to maximize the two constitutive dimensions of the intellectual's identity, the identity of a category that was invented through them – 'purity' and 'commitment', giving birth to a politics of purity which is the perfect antithesis to raison d'état. They imply in fact the assertion of the right to transgress the most sacred values of the collectivity – that of patriotism, for example, with the support given to Zola's article attacking the army, or, much later, during the Algerian war, the appeal to support the enemy – in the name of values that transcend those of the city, or, if you prefer, in the name of a particular form of ethical and scientific universalism that can serve as the basis not only for a kind of moral pedantry but also a collective mobilization for the combat intended to promote these values.

One need only add to this overview of the major stages in the development of the figure of the intellectual some indications on the cultural policy of the Second Republic or the Commune, to sketch a picture of the possible relationships between the cultural producers and the established powers, as these can be observed either in the history of a particular country,[8] or – as

---

[8] Cf. Christophe Charle, *Les Intellectuels en Europe au XXe siècle: essai d'histoire comparée* (Paris: Seuil 2001).

can also be done – in the present political space of European states, from Thatcher to Gorbachev. History brings an important lesson: we are in a game where all the strokes played today, on every side, have already been played before – from rejection of politics and return to religion through to resistance to the action of a political power that is hostile to intellectual activity, not excluding revolt against the grip of what certain people today call the media, or the disabused abandonment of revolutionary utopias.

But the fact of finding ourselves in an 'end game' does not necessarily lead to disenchantment. It is clear in fact that the intellectual was not constituted once and for all time with Zola, and that those who hold cultural capital can always 'regress' towards one of other of the positions marked out by the historical pendulum, i.e. the role of pure poet, artist or scholar, or that of political actor, journalist, politician, etc. Besides, contrary to what the vaguely Hegelian vision of intellectual history obtained by accumulating selected characteristics would lead one to believe, the claim to autonomy inscribed in the very existence of a field of cultural production must reckon with obstacles and powers that are constantly renewed, whether these are external powers such as those of the church, the state and major economic enterprises, or internal powers, particularly those given by control of specific instruments of production and distribution (press, publishing, radio, TV, etc.).

In each case, and contrary to appearance, the *invariants*, being the basis for a possible unity between intellectuals of every country, are more important than the *variations* that arise from the state of present and past relations between the intellectual field and political powers, or the forms taken by the specific mechanisms developed to obstruct the impulse of cultural producers to autonomy in the country in question. The same *intention to autonomy* can in fact be expressed in opposite positions being taken (for instance, secular in one case, religious in another), depending on the structure and history of the powers against which this tendency has to assert itself. Intellectuals of different countries must be fully aware of this mechanism if they wish to avoid letting themselves be divided by conjunctural and phenomenal oppositions rooted in the fact that the same desire for emancipation encounters different obstacles. I could cite here the example of the most prominent French and German philosophers, who, because they oppose the same concern for autonomy to opposing historical traditions, appear to be in opposing camps in their positions towards truth and reason. But I could also take the example of a problem like opinion polls, in which certain people in the West see an instrument of domination, whereas in the countries of Eastern Europe they can be seen as a conquest of freedom.

In order to understand and master the oppositions that risk dividing them, intellectuals from different European countries should always have in mind the structure and history of the powers against which they have to assert themselves in order to exist as intellectuals. For example, they should be able to recognize in the statements of their various interlocutors – and particularly in what might be disconcerting or shocking in these statements – the effect of historical or geographical distance from such experiences of political despotism as Nazism or Stalinism, or from ambiguous political movements such as the student revolts of May '68 – or, in the field of internal powers, the effect of the present and past experience of intellectual worlds that were very unequally subject to the open or concealed censorship of politics or economics, of the university or academy, etc. (When we speak as intellectuals, i.e. with the ambition of universality, at every moment the historical unconscious inscribed in the experience of a particular intellectual field speaks out of our mouths. There was a time when a great deal was said about the communication of consciousnesses. I believe that we are engaged in such communication in everyday life, if of course imperfectly and unhappily, and that we only have any chance of reaching a genuine communication of consciousnesses on condition that we objectivize and master the different historical unconsciouses that separate us, i.e. the specific histories of the intellectual world of which our categories of perception and thought are the product.)

I want to turn now to presenting particular reasons that today give particular urgency to the mobilization of intellectuals and the creation of a genuine *International of intellectuals* attached to defending the autonomy of this field. I do not want to indulge in an apocalyptic vision of the state of the field of cultural production in the various European countries, if I say that its autonomy is very seriously threatened – or, more precisely, that threats of a quite new kind today weigh on its operation; and that intellectuals are ever more completely excluded from public debate, both because they are less inclined to intervene in this, and because the possibility of successful intervention is ever less frequently offered.

Threats to autonomy: interpenetration between the worlds of art and money is increasingly great in the various Western countries. I have in mind the new forms of patronage, and new alliances established between certain businesses, often the most advanced – such as Daimler-Benz and the banks in Germany – and cultural producers; as well as the way that university research has increasingly frequent resort to sponsors or the creation of courses directly subordinate to business (such as the *Technologiezentren* in Germany, or the French business schools). But the grip or empire of business over artistic and scientific work is also exerted actually within the field, by control of the means of cultural production and distribution, even instances of consecration. Producers attached to the big cultural bureaucracies (newspapers, radio, TV, etc.) are increasingly compelled to accept and adopt norms and constraints (for example in terms of their pace of work) which they tend more or less unconsciously to make into a universal measure of intellectual accomplishment (I'm thinking for example of the 'fast writing' and 'fast reading' that have become the law of journalistic production and criticism). We may ask whether the division into two markets, which has been characteristic of fields of cultural production since the mid-nineteenth century, with the restricted field of producers for producers on the one hand, and the field of large-scale production and 'industrial literature' on the other, is not threatened with disappearance, as the logic of commercial production tends to increasingly impose itself on avant-garde production (notably, as in the case of literature, by way of the constraints that weigh on the book market). And it would also be necessary to show how a state patronage that seems to make possible an escape from the immediate constraints of the market, imposes via the mechanism of commissions and committees a regular *normalisation*[9] of research, whether scientific or artistic. *Timeo Danaos, et dona ferentes.*[10] We have to work to raise awareness and vigilance towards the poisoned chalice that any kind of patronage can represent.

Exclusion from public debate. This exclusion is the result of the combined action of a number of factors, certain of which spring from the internal development of cultural production – such as the ever greater specialization that leads scholars to deny themselves the total ambition of the old-style intellectual – while others are the result of the increasing grip of a technocracy that dismisses citizens by promoting 'organized irresponsibility', in Ulrich Beck's term, and finds immediate complicity in a technocracy of communication, increasingly present via the media in the world of cultural production itself. On the first point, we should for example develop the analysis of the production and reproduction of the power of those who have been called the 'nucleocracy', i.e. those members of the state nobility who are the object of an almost unconditional delegation. It goes without saying that, in order to understand the tacit complicity these 'nucleocrats' – who are only the limiting case of technocrats – enjoy, especially in France and even all those in the Socialist party today who tend to reduce politics to a problem of administration, it is not enough to invoke, as Beck does, the dormitive virtue

---

[9] [See p.170, n.11]
[10] 'I fear the Greeks, even when they bear gifts.' Virgil, *Aeneid*, II, v, 49. [Ed.]

of an expert discourse able to put responsibility to sleep: we have to take into account, as I did in my book on *The State Nobility*, the whole logic of an educational system that confers on the chosen ones a legitimacy with no historical precedent.

The high technocracy wins immediate complicity from the new technocracy of communications, the group of professionals in the art of communication who monopolize access to the instruments of communication, and who, having only very little to actually communicate, establish the vacuum of media background noise at the heart of the communications apparatus. The organic intellectuals of the technocracy monopolize public debate to the detriment of the professionals of politics (parliamentarians, trade unionists, etc.); and to the detriment of those intellectuals who are subject in their own particular world to a specific kind of media putsch – what are called 'media coups' – such as journalistic investigations that aim to produce manipulated classifications, or the countless awards that newspapers publish on the occasion of birthdays, etc., or again the regular press campaigns that aim to credit or discredit authors, works, and schools of thought.

It has been shown how any successful political action is increasingly action that has succeeded in rendering itself visible and manifest, in the press and above all in television, thus imposing on the media responsible for its success the idea that it has succeeded – which is why the most sophisticated forms of action are often steered, with the help of communications advisers, towards the media that are to report them.[11] In the same way, an ever larger part of cultural production, when this is not the product of people who work in the media and whose signature is solicited because they are assured of having the support of the media, is defined in its date of appearance, its title, its format, its volume, its content and its style, in such a way as to fill the expectations of the journalists who make it by talking of it.

There is nothing new in the existence of a commercial literature, or the fact that the requirements of commerce impose themselves within the cultural field. But the grip of the holders of power over the instruments of circulation – and hence also of consecration, at least up to a certain point – has certainly never been so widespread or deep; nor the border between a pioneering work and a best-seller so muddied. This muddying of borders to which media producers are spontaneously inclined (as witness the fact that journalistic awards always mix together the most autonomous and the most heteronomous producers, Claude Lévi-Strauss and Bernard-

---

[11] Cf. Patrick Champagne, *Faire l'opinion* (Paris: Minuit 1990).

Henri Lévy) undoubtedly poses the worst threat to the autonomy of cultural production. The heteronomic producer, whom the Italians call the *tuttologo*, especially when he embarks on the terrain of politics but without the authority or autonomy given by a particular competence, is certainly the Trojan horse through which heteronomy penetrates the field of cultural production. The condemnation that can be made of the doxosophists – who appear to be scientists or are scientists of appearance, as Plato put it – follows from the idea that the specific force of the intellectual, even in politics, rests on the autonomy given by the ability to respond to the internal requirements of this field. The Zhdanovism that still flourishes among failed authors is simply one attestation among others that heteronomy still prevails in a field by way of those producers least capable of succeeding according to the field's own norms.

The paradoxical and seemingly contradictory nature of the intellectual means that any political action that aims to strengthen the political effectiveness of intellectuals is driven to take up slogans that appear to be contradictory: on the one hand, to reinforce autonomy, especially by sharpening the break with heteronomous intellectuals and struggling to ensure that cultural producers have the economic and social conditions needed for autonomy (first of all in matters of publication and assessment of the products of intellectual activity); on the other hand, to release cultural producers from the temptation of their ivory towers and encourage them to struggle to take control at least of their instruments of intellectual production and validation, and enter secular life to assert there those values associated with their autonomy.

This struggle can only be a collective one, since some of the powers to which intellectuals are subject owe their effectiveness to the fact that intellectuals confront them in a dispersed fashion, competing with one another. And also because attempts at mobilization will always remain dubious, and condemned to fail, as long as they are suspected of being in the service of struggles for leadership by one intellectual or a group of intellectuals. It is only possible if, abandoning once and for all the myth of the 'organic intellectual', cultural producers agree to work collectively for the defence of their own interests, something that can lead them, in the context of a nascent Europe, to assert themselves as a power of criticism and supervision, even of proposition, vis-à-vis our technocrats, or – out of an ambition that is both superior and more realistic – to commit themselves to a rational action in defence of the economic and social conditions for the autonomy of these privileged social worlds in which the material and intellectual instruments of what we call Reason are reproduced. This 'realpolitik of reason' will undoubtedly be suspected of corporatism. But it is up to those who champion it to show, by the goals in whose service they provide the hardly won means of its autonomy, that this is a corporatism of universality.

History rises in the east*

For a politics of truth. Neither Stalin nor Thatcher

Many people believed for a long time that we had reached the end of history. The social movement that bore the hopes of humanity during the whole of the nineteenth century, and the first half of the twentieth, gradually dwindled away amid the failures and horrors of a bureaucratic tyranny. The world entered the Brezhnev age. A caste society arose where we hoped to see a classless one. An oligarchy totally closed upon its privileges was able to find, in the double language that assured it the usurped monopoly of a revolutionary rhetoric, the means to conceal, even from itself, the wall of incomprehension that divided it from ordinary citizens. The tragic fate of this world with no historical beyond was like a heavy weight on the whole of progressive humanity. And not simply because this socialism with an inhuman face provided conservatives of all countries with the best of all justifications for the status quo.

We have just seen the end of a dictatorship; yet whatever one might say, this was not simply a dictatorship like any other. It was established and exercised in the name of the people, and it was brought down by the people; in the name of truth, and it was defeated by truth; in the name of liberty and equality, and it was defeated in the name of liberty and equality. A tremendous celebration of the Revolution of 1789! This revolution against all the crimes committed in the name of the revolution is exceptional in not being counter-revolutionary. The collision of words – freedom against freedom, truth against truth, equality against equality – could possibly lead to nihilism, in the wake of a terrible semantic devaluation. But what are these peoples doing, after being bullied, oppressed, locked up and imprisoned in the name of these words reduced to slogans, in the name of truth converted into a state lie, but putting into practice the poet's programme of giving a purer sense to the words of the tribe. It is natural that poets and writers, whether their names are Mircea Dinescu, Václav Havel or Christoph Hein, should discover their original role as representatives of their group, or more modestly, the role of public writer. These are the people who teach that the grand words in which the dreams and ideals of humanity are deposited can emerge

* Published in *Liber* 2, December 1989.

purer and stronger from the radical doubt to which history has subjected them; and by setting out to defend them against an abuse of language that is always pregnant with abuse of power, they recall that the politics of truth is certainly more realistic, even in politics, than any form of realpolitik.

This is why intellectuals in all countries should organize today to continue the struggle launched in this way. We are through with the 'organic intellectual' who believed he was compelled to bend his reason to the verdicts of raison d'état, or the 'fellow-traveller' in the image of Sartre, who to wipe out his 'original sin' sought to 'stupefy' himself so as to rank with the 'thinkers' of the Party. There can be no compromise in matters of truth. Let no one say to us that we need to prepare a 'common market of the spirit' for 1992. The culture that Europe needs, for itself and the world, and particularly the world's Third Estate, will not emerge from the negotiations of experts or the discussions of technocrats. The question is to make the rigorous use of reason, and thus of language, a political virtue, indeed the first of all political virtues, and thus to give intellectuals the sole power that they have a right and a duty to claim, that of exercising a ceaseless and effective vigilance against the abuse of words – and grand words most of all.

The revolutionary élan that the peoples of the East have infused into the languid history of Europe is something to seize. All the professionals of political discourse are trying to grab it for their own use. They come back with their false alternatives: Stalin or Thatcher, socialism or liberalism, Karl Marx or Milton Friedman, Moscow or Chicago, state or market, planning or laissez-faire, hiding the fact that behind each of these words lurk their own interests and fantasies, or, more simply, their inability to think freely. They will try and swing the pendulum back from one economic and political absurdity to another. And the collusion of complicit adversaries makes it hard to discover the higher ground, which is neither a golden mean nor, as the ideologists of revolution claimed, a 'third way'. Those who have discovered the ideals of truth, freedom, or even equality and fraternity against the perverted distortions that were made of them, and still are, by 'socialist' state nobilities, are paradoxically the best placed to teach us to free ourselves once more from the words and ways of thinking that have been left in our unconscious by megalomaniac thinkers and irresponsible engineers, always ready to sacrifice peoples on the altar of their projects or equations.

We must also however prevent at any cost the manipulators of phobias and fantasies from reawakening old terrors, reviving old blames, so easy to distort into perverted or desperate self-assertion, from playing all those games of fright that always risk leading to real terror, just as they do when played by children. We should on the contrary rejoice that a powerful and weighty Germany, ever more inclined to go to sleep, despite the stimulus of the alternative movements, on the soft pillow of its economic success, finds itself placed at the centre of this test of truth, at the heart of the practical confrontation between the realities of the 'capitalist paradise', a mere inversion of the old Eastern mirage, and the aspirations or demands that have been left in the minds of its eastern citizens by socialist rhetoric, and above all perhaps by the everyday revolt against the negating privileges of the proclaimed ideals.

So history did not really stop in Moscow in the 1930s. And the demands and hopes that the new revolutionary movement bears, above all the tremendous contradictions that this seemingly dead time of history has bequeathed us, can be, if we are able to confront them without mincing words, a principle for setting a liberatory thought and politics again in motion.

The political language of conservative revolutions[*]

Philosophical discourse, just like any other form of expression, is the result of a transaction between an expressive intention and the censorship exercised by the social universe in which this is necessarily produced. Thus to understand the work of Heidegger, in its truth that is inseparably both philosophical and political, we have to retrace the work of euphemization that enabled him to reveal political impulses and fantasies in the very act of disguising them. We have to analyze the logic of double meaning and suggestion that enabled words from everyday language to operate simultaneously in two registers that are deliberately both combined and separated. To put something in a philosophical form was a way of expressing a form of politics; it meant presenting in a philosophically acceptable form, by making it unrecognizable, the fundamental themes of the thought of 'conservative revolutionaries'. To reconstruct the different variants of the world view that was crudely expressed by essayists in Weimar Germany, and with these the logic, inseparably both intellectual and social, of the philosophical field that is the real operator of the transmutation of the *völkisch* mood into existential philosophy, is therefore the condition for understanding the political ontology of Martin Heidegger without making cleavages that are only too convenient between text and context, or between the Nazi rector and the 'shepherd of Being'.

* Written for the back cover of *L'Ontologie politique de Martin Heidegger* (Paris: Minuit 1988)

Mental walls[*]

We live in an age of lost illusions, and a kind of radical doubt is incumbent on us. Today is therefore a time for celebration, particularly here in Berlin. What can we do? What task or mission can we set ourselves as philosophers, sociologists, writers and artists? What *realistic* task, in other words one that can be realized collectively?

The first objective of a modest programme of intellectual work would be to subject political language, and especially words denoting collectives (people, nation, national, etc.) to a radical critique. As I have shown in relation to Heidegger, our everyday language, and still more so supposedly scientific language, is pregnant with a political ontology. In the past, those who claimed a critical view of the social world, from orthodox Marxists through to the Frankfurt School, were among the greatest producers of concepts charged with political ontology. But the first target of criticism must be the words of criticism themselves. This is what I call the principle of reflexivity. We should not understand by this simply the exhortation for a return of the knowing subject on itself, in the tradition of subjective philosophy. What is involved is rather a genuine socio-analysis, and this can only be a collective undertaking. Intellectual life (and no doubt political life too) would be deeply changed if each speaker, such as myself at this time, felt constantly exposed to a critique that sought to grasp not only the reasoning of their discourse but also its possible causes, its unconscious social determinants, dispositions and interests bound up with the occupation of a particular position in the social world, and more particularly as far as intellectuals are concerned, in the academic or intellectual world.

This is a point we have to dwell on. I will certainly be accused of sociologism, reductionism, and held responsible for demeaning reason. I have said a hundred times, and say it again, against all the forms of rationalist absolutism – of which the most enlightened representative today is undoubtedly Jürgen Habermas – that reason is historical through and through, and all we can do is work to create the historical conditions in which it can be deployed. This is what I call a realpolitik of reason. To fight for reason, for the undistorted communication that makes possible the rational exchange of arguments, etc., means fighting very consciously against all forms of

---

[*] A lecture given at the Institut Français in Berlin on 2 October 1992, in the context of a meeting of the Friends of *Liber*, and published in the special issue of *Liber* of January 1993.

violence, starting with symbolic violence. We have to work resolutely and collectively to bring to light the mechanisms of this insidious violence, which is exercised through competition for positions, honours, titles, and can be observed in a particularly clear fashion here and now, in this country.

I believe that the weapon par excellence of critical reflexivity is historical analysis: paradoxically, the methodical historicization of the instruments of rational thought (categories of thought, principles of classification, concepts, etc.) is one of the most powerful means of removing these from history. Popper spoke very incautiously of the poverty of historicism; I am increasingly convinced that we should rather speak of the poverty of ahistoricism: so many of our purest theoretical debates only exist and subsist because they present opposing de-historicized notions, products of the transfiguration of historical constructions into transhistorical essences.

Perhaps all this seems somewhat abstract. But I am afraid of seeming too concrete, or even a little down to earth, if I transpose these reflections onto the ground of everyday practice, making use of the freedom – or irresponsibility – that is conferred by my foreigner status, which exposes me to the naivety and arrogance, pretentious and antipathetic, of the giver of lessons. For example, the use that some people make of reference to the past, particularly in debates over intellectuals in the former East Germany, is a perfect illustration of everything that the sociology of intellectuals, who are often taxed with historicist pessimism, brings to light: how can one not see the role of specific interests in the practices and discourse of all those who make a Zhdanovite (or McCarthyite) use of the denunciation of Zhdanovism in order to seize positions in the East, thus reproducing exactly what they denounce?

Revolutionary crises often present the spectacle of similar confusions of bad faith (in the Sartrean sense of self-deception). One should re-read Robert Darnton on the role of minor intellectuals in the French Revolution. And those who are so keen today to judge and condemn without really understanding should also re-read what an American historian quite recently wrote about the mechanisms of censorship in East Germany, and meditate on the phrase with which he concluded his description of a meeting with two 'censors' in the GDR: 'But I was also very much aware that nothing was simple in this strange world the other side of the wall.' (I could just as well have cited the little book, *Total Fears*,[12] in which Bohumil Hrabal relates his encounters with his censors, with a good deal of lucidity and courage.) The weapons of scientific analysis, which grasps transhistorical invariants, are indispensable if we are to escape the logic of denunciation, which spares

[12] [English edition: Prague 1998.]

itself the work needed to understand behaviour by relating this to the social conditions that makes it possible and sometimes even inevitable.

Perhaps you will accuse me of scientism, but I would like to be able to take part here, in Berlin, in a rigorous and hence liberatory analysis of the almost experimental situation that presents itself to anyone who wants to study the variations of behaviour and strategies as a function of such different social variables as citizenship (East/West), discipline, age and status. Not to apportion blame and praise, in the manner of a criminal trial which historians are often so keen on. But rather to understand, to show reasons, and remind those who judge and condemn that the people they condemn are like them, very much so in their actual history, i.e. what they themselves could have been had they been subject to the same conditions. This shows why it is necessary to historicize. I am one of those in France who were scandalized when they heard German pacifists shout: 'Better red than dead', and I struggled as best I could, with a good many others, to break the symbolic isolation of intellectuals in the Eastern countries. So I have all the more right to judge rather severely those who are so severe in judging those who had no other choice but to be red rather than dead.

The Germans have shown a good deal of courage in confronting their past history – perhaps they had no other choice. Innumerable books have cast light on the historical mechanisms that led to that horror. Today we need to be just as intrepid in confronting the past and the present. It is no longer a question of conceiving the whole or everything, rather of constantly conceiving the limits of thought. More than ever today, the critical sociology of intellectuals is a precondition for any research on intellectuals and any political action by them. Only intellectuals with no illusions about intellectuals can undertake a 'responsible' and effective intellectual action.

We should pursue and generalize the work of historical anamnesis. To avoid being puppets of the past, i.e. of the unconscious (it was Durkheim who said that 'the unconscious is history'), we have to reappropriate the past for ourselves. The rhetoric of unification tends to conceal the fact that though the Wall has ceased to be a physical and political reality, it continues to exist in the mind as a principle of vision and division. I said in 1989, in an interview with *Der Spiegel* (which was not published at the time, presumably because it seemed too pessimistic, but has now been published), that just as the Vendée was still divided from the rest of France, two centuries after the Revolution, by an invisible boundary, so a lasting division remained between the two Germanys. We can see today, on the second anniversary of reunification, that habits (in the sense of habitus) can readily survive the social conditions that produced them. Especially when they are reinforced by objective conditions (such as unemployment, the contempt of '*Wessis*', the *Abwicklung* of the welfare state,[13] all following pell-mell).

That said, this mental wall should not be pulled down only to make way for the restoration of others. I have in mind here all those historic walls, often built by intellectuals and especially the 'proletaroid intelligentsia', the 'dangerous class' par excellence, which have divided nations, those 'imagined communities' that end up by being real ones.[14] Here again, history is the most effective weapon against the particular form of fetishism that is nationalism, but a critical history (critical in the sense of the Frankfurt School, but also that of Kant), in other words a reflexive history that takes itself as its own object and subjects this celebratory history, this history that constructs fetishes, to historical anamnesis. (I am particularly thinking here of the history of literature in its traditional form, which is one of the foundations of national and nationalist religion, and the imposition of belief in 'national identity'; but the same could be said, or almost so, of the history of other arts and even the history of philosophy.)

This history that creates fetishes should be substituted by a history geared towards research into those historical transcendentals that are the historical categories of understanding – and here we have to reconcile, which is hard less for theoretical reasons and more for social ones, the tradition of Durkheim with that of Kant, as represented particularly by Cassirer. We could show in this way that the historical opposition between France and Germany has served as a basis (unconscious and repressed) for a certain number of grand alternatives (for example culture versus civilization), and that it is necessary to de-fetishize, or what comes to the same thing, denaturalize. I take here the example of one of the most central of these oppositions – at least to my eyes – that dividing the 'imperialism of universality' issuing from the philosophies of the Enlightenment and the French Revolution from the national populism associated for me with the name of Herder, but present in a whole tradition of German literature and philosophy, through to Heidegger. It is important to see that the thought of Herder, and more generally thought à la Herder, though like much conservative thought (for example that of Burke) a reaction to French-style thought, inasmuch as this is 'revolutionary', progressive and universal, was also a reaction (though not necessarily reactionary) to an imperialism or nationalism that (as can best be seen in French colonial undertakings) invoked the universal (rights of man, etc.) in order to impose itself. There is something a little disturbing (at least for me) in Herder's type of thought, in notions such as the 'spirit of the people' or 'soul of the people'

[13] *Abwicklung* was the word used for the dismantling and liquidation of the socialist state after the collapse of the GDR. [Ed.]
[14] Cfc. Benedict Anderson, *Imagined Communities* (London: Verso 1983)

that provide the basis for a kind of anti-universalist organicism, as in the exaltation of language as the condensate of the experience and authenticity of nations, and thus as possible foundation for national claims and nationalist annexations. And without endowing scientific clarification and the reach of consciousness with an effectiveness that they certainly do not have, one can expect that if the Germans took cognizance both of the ambiguity of the Herder tradition that is periodically reasserted, and of the fact that it is based on the ambiguity of *Aufklärung* in the French mode – an ambiguity that escapes both its champions and its adversaries – they would certainly be less disturbing both to themselves and to others. In the same way, French intellectuals would give their universalism fuller force if they were able to strip it of the whole unconscious substratum of particularism, or even more or less sublimated nationalism, that makes their present support for the construction of Europe so ambiguous. (These somewhat abstract considerations lie at the root of the foundation of *Liber*, and more particularly, of the section titled 'European ethnography', which publishes texts that aim to make explicit certain traditions and constitutive presuppositions of the national unconscious, i.e. these particularities or particularisms born from history that are often imputed a kind of nature, as 'national characters'.)

It is thus on condition that they ceaselessly work towards this historical exploration of their historical unconscious that artists, writers and scientists can enter without danger either to others or themselves the struggle for which they are the best armed, symbolic struggle against symbolic violence. Their task in fact is to forge instruments of defence and critique against all those forms of symbolic power that have undergone such a tremendous development, both in the economic world and in that of politics, to the point that critical thought is certainly several wars behind. And to give a symbolic force to this critique of symbolic violence by drawing on artists who, like Hans Haacke, know how to place all the resources of artistic invention at the service of acts of disclosure. It is particularly by seeing their mission, without recreating the myth of the organic intellectual, as that of acting as public writers and bringing into public space the private discourses of those deprived of public discourse.

I spoke at the start of a modest programme. The first condition for a realistic action is knowledge of its own limitations. Intellectuals can represent an unchallengeable force, a critical power, a counter-power, on condition that they struggle collectively to win control of their instruments of production (against economic and political power) and the assessment of their products (against journalism). It is here that international solidarity, based on the construction of transnational instruments of exchange and communication, can play a decisive role in liberating the cultural producers from the negative effects associated with the closure of national cultural and linguistic fields, and the effects of domination exercised by political, economic and cultural powers (particularly those of the university) with a national base. We know from experience that free intellectuals have often found refuge abroad, in the Netherlands in the age of absolutism, then in France, where many pioneering literary and artistic movements as well as political ones had their birth in the nineteenth century, more recently in Britain and the United States with the rise of Nazism. Foreign countries have often provided a site of freedom, dissidence and rupture, and it is by struggling for the unification of the global intellectual field and the removal of all obstacles to the international circulation of cultural producers and their products, that intellectuals can best contribute to the progress of liberty and reason.

Intellectual responsibilities*

The words of war in Yugoslavia

Yugoslavia. The silence is certainly a guilty one. But in order to have a good conscience or be seen to be doing what should be done, do we have to speak out at all cost, without being really effective and at the risk of saying no matter what? Conviction alone is not enough, generous as it might be. And when this is combined with ignorance, it says more about those who speak and the intellectual world in which they are situated than the object they think they are speaking about.

When there are centuries of history behind each word, as is the case here, we risk being manipulated by the words that we manipulate, to take sides without knowing it on the questions that these words hide (for example, an entire vision of Bosnia and its population is implied simply by calling the Muslims of the region 'Bosniaks'). Questions of words are often questions of life and death. Words are an issue in symbolic struggles, and words kill because, transformed into mobilizing slogans, appeals and orders, they constitute the populations with particular characteristics that they denote into dehistoricized and naturalized essences: names of languages, names of religions, names of ethnic groups, names of regions, etc., so many historical creations, to which intellectuals have contributed, and which the same intellectuals, or others, make into weapons in their struggles for hegemony, for domination in the state or for the construction of states that they hope to dominate.

Intellectuals have a tremendous responsibility in these matters. It is little writers without real talent, enclosed in the national limits of their brains, who – as Danilo Kis shows in the terrible charge-sheet of *The Anatomy Lesson*,[15] profit from the conditions offered by authoritarian, national-socialist or national-Communist populisms to settle, on the terrain of politics, literary, artistic or philosophical conflicts in which they are otherwise doomed to defeat. This happens in the context of the collapse of the bureaucratic structures of great empires or states, which, as Rogers Brubaker has shown,[16] authorizes and promotes a regression towards that degree zero of politics

---

* Published in *Liber* 14, June 1993.
[15] Danilo Kis, *La Leçon d'anatomie* (Paris: Fayard 1993).
[16] Rogers Brubaker, 'L'éclatement des peuples à la chute des empires', *Actes de la Recherche en Sciences Sociales* 98, June 1993, pp. 4–19.

which is return to primitive solidarities and loyalties, often justified in the language of blood and genetic purity, and asserted in blood and operations of 'ethnic cleansing'.

What can intellectuals do in such circumstances – I am not speaking of those on the ground, powerless and desperate – but take advantage of their (provisional?) externality to assist the camp of reason, which is necessarily weakened in time of crisis? And ceaselessly mobilize all intellectual weapons available against those in their ranks who, in ordinary situations of intellectual life, resort to political or economic weapons in order to triumph at all cost in intellectual struggles, in this way often preparing very real wars in which they can continue these intellectual struggles by other means.

How to escape the circle of fear?*

Juan E. Corradi, Patricia Weiss Fagen and Manuel Antonio Garreton, *Fear at the Edge: State Terror and Resistance in Latin America* (Berkeley: University of California Press, 1992)

The politics of fear as the basis for despotism is a singular object, and little discussed since Montesquieu. In four countries in the south of Latin America: Argentina, Brazil, Chile and Uruguay, military regimes in the 1970s practised a state terror designed to 'dissolve or isolate civil institutions able to protect citizens against the power of the state'. In a strange inversion, the state that tends to ensure the maintenance of order, the security of individuals, and in Max Weber's terms the 'predictability and calculability' of the social world, became the origin of a kind of radical insecurity and an almost total unpredictability. These dictatorships that 'promised to do away with fear, actually generated new fears by profoundly breaking social routines and habits, making daily life unpredictable'; they aroused a feeling of impotence, and the familiar environment itself seemed inhabited by strange and hostile forces: the obsession with survival prevented people from living.

Terrorism and state terror, or the different possible combinations of the two, establishes uncertainty at the heart of the social system (especially when the state, which as Norbert Elias says somewhere was constituted against the logic of racketeering, becomes – as we have seen in several recent examples – a mafia that organizes racketeering and murder). Legal definitions of criminal activity are vague; information is imprecise or inaccessible, and communication difficult; physical violence is openly practised in association with semi-clandestine activities such as torture and illegal execution. Acts of public intimidation (such as kidnapping accompanied by a heavy deployment of force, or public executions) establish the most extraordinary insecurity at the heart of the most ordinary existence. In such conditions, 'the ability to rationally calculate the consequences of an action is deeply altered'.

But the most dreadful effect of terrorism and state terror is the atomization of groups, the destruction of all solidarity between isolated and frightened individuals. As well as the return to primitive solidarities, and a kind of 'amoral familialism' that reinforces the tendency to break solidarity with

---

* Published in *Liber* 17, March 1994.

those who resist, from fear that this will attract repression. Inaction seeks justification in a mutual transfer of responsibilities that appears as a 'social exchange of excuses': those with any influence pass the buck to ordinary citizens 'who have nothing to lose', and ordinary citizens pass it back to people with influence 'who don't risk anything'. One says that he is finishing his studies, another that he doesn't want to create problems for his family or his boss, or that he's afraid his passport won't be renewed (also reminiscent of Bohumil Hrabal's *Total Fears*); young people say they are too young, and old people that they are too old. Worse still, it is not rare to observe 'a regular hatred towards those who give the example of courage', thus facing others with a difficult moral choice. The fear that everyone has of all others gradually isolates those individuals and groups who are most active in resistance to power. Appeal to necessity, whether pessimistic or cynical, provides a powerful system of defence against appeals to action. Despair leads to a kind of 'social autism' (in Bruno Bettelheim's term) and retreat into silence. Public threats and private intimidation combine with rumour in condemning individuals who are isolated and unable to verify their subjective impressions by confronting them with those of others with more or less unrealistic beliefs, where the borders between the fantastic, the possible and the desired are often muddied. If, incidentally, it is not so hard to understand this 'logic of collective inaction', which finds the conditions of its full flourishing in the extraordinary circumstances created by the politics of terror, the same thing is met with every day in all total institutions, such as prisons, psychiatric hospitals and boarding schools, as well as in the routines of bureaucratic existence or intellectual life, where the diffuse fear of uncertain sanctions very often suffices to trigger countless infinitesimal acts of cowardice that make possible abuses of power both great and small.

Is it possible to break the circle of fear? Comparative analysis of different historical situations shows that the major precondition for such an outcome is the existence of organizations able to break the monopoly of communications controlled by the state, providing material and legal assistance, supporting efforts of resistance and gradually imposing the conviction that the future is not permanently closed. This enables the great majority of people to convince themselves that heroic exceptionalism is not the only possibility of action, and take assurance by discovering that many others think and act as they do, likewise that important personalities (both at home and abroad) support their action and strengthen protective barriers. To put it another way, the most effective strategies are those that lead the silent and terrorized majority to discover and demonstrate their collective strength, by way of actions that are relatively ordinary and have little risk, but which, practised at the same time by a great number of people together (such as a whole population silently moving into the city centre, or the simultaneous closing of all houses and shops) produce a tremendous symbolic effect, first of all on those who perform them, but also on those against whom they are directed.

Declaration of intent, **Liber 25, 1995**

To contribute effectively to the realistic internationalism that is its raison d'être, *Liber* has initiated two complementary strategies. On the one hand, it has sought to offer its Turkish, Greek, German and Bulgarian readers the possibility of familiarizing themselves with English, Scottish, Czech and Irish authors, works and institutions – and vice versa – and make known on the international scale particularities bound up with national traditions (this is the particular function of issues devoted to a single country, or analyses and descriptions of singular features and characteristics of a historical tradition under headings such as 'Untranslatable' or 'European ethnography'). On the other hand, it has set out to bring together and compare different analyses of the same particular object (in this case intellectuals) as it presents itself in different national cultures, showing in this way, against the presuppositions and stereotypes of superficial journalism, facts and effects that are to be found on all sides, invariants that are denied or ignored just as infallibly by the vague or pompous assertions of international meetings and reviews, as by descriptions limited to a single nation. By thus enabling readers from different countries to read in their own language texts that are free of the anecdotal particularities that fill national newspapers and reviews, and filled with information that on the contrary is absent because it is taken for granted by those familiar with it, we hope to contribute, patiently but constantly, to leading them out of the limits of their national universe and creating a kind of collective intellectual, freed from the idolatry of those cultural idioms that are too often identified with culture.

In the service of historical forms of universality[*]

Intellectuals do not generally have a good press. The words that describe them are almost everywhere pejorative. This is undoubtedly because it is intellectuals themselves, whether great or small – but most likely small – who invented them. Anti-intellectualism of all kinds, just like all forms of racism, has almost always had its origin in resentment, often bound up with collective decline (that of the former great empires, especially the English, Austrian, French and Portuguese), or else the *déclassement* of individuals, whether in social space as with the decline of the petty bourgeoisie, or in the microcosms of art, literature and science, where social decay and dereliction are also rife (not to forget journalism, the site of many disappointed illusions and lost hopes). The worst form of anti-intellectualism, whether intellectual or not, finds countless justifications today in the anomic practices promoted by the decline of the autonomy that the worlds of cultural production had conquered over several centuries of struggle against temporal powers, the church and the market. Commerce and journalism (itself increasingly subject to the sanction of the market by way of television, which tends ever more to impose its domination over it, and is dominated by presenters and the rule of ratings) constantly have a tighter grip on the production, circulation and assessment of books.[17] We can see all sorts of consequences arising from this. For example the development of 'world fiction', a literature designed from the start for the global market, which, because the logic of the book trade gives it first place on the bestseller lists in every country, is sometimes equated, with the conscious or unconscious complicity of editors and critics, with the great works of universal literature which only slowly won the recognition they everywhere enjoy today, almost always against the powers of commerce.[18] Likewise the appearance of characters from the media-political scene who, like a double or under-study caught in the trap of their own role, as in the film *Kagemusha* by Akiro Kurosawa, mimic the figure and role of the intellectual. Lacking the work and authority that the intervention of the writer as intellectual on the political scene presupposes, they can only deceive people by way of a constant presence in the field

[*] Published under the title 'Et pourtant . . .' in *Liber* 25, December 1995.
[17] Cf. L'emprise du journalisme', *Actes de Recherche en Sciences Sociales* 101/102, March 1994, pp. 2–9.
[18] Cf. Pascal Casanova, 'La *world fiction*, une fiction critique', *Liber* 16, December 1993.

of journalism (it would be better to give names here, but none of them are known outside their own country); they import into it practices that in other fields would be called corruption, misappropriation, embezzlement, traffic in influence, unfair competition, collusion, illicit understanding or abuse of trust, the most typical of which is called in French 'renvoi d'ascenseur' (returning the lift).

The very deep demoralization that arises from this decline in autonomy of the literary, philosophical and scientific microcosms is reinforced by the crisis of millennial utopias and the break in the enchanted relationship that united a fraction of the intellectuals, often the most generous of them, with – if not the people, then at least a more or less fantastic image of the people. It has become good form to view with condescension, if not commiseration, everything that might evoke any form of 'commitment', and the same indulgence is sometimes extended to all the trajectories that led so many uncompromising revolutionaries to coveted positions in the literary, political or journalistic establishment, and to the tranquilly conservative political positions that go together with these.

Yet those who we find on all sides announcing the end of intellectuals and their function or mission, to use a big word, are seriously deceived; perhaps, quite simply, because they take their desires for reality, attesting in this way that they still find the very idea of the intellectual disturbing. It is true that, thanks in particular to the advance of social science, we have today a far more realistic view of intellectuals, but one that is not only opposed to the naively hagiographic exaltation to which so many biographers and commentators readily subscribe, but also to the denigration of disappointed love and ambition practised by the critique of resentment.

The microcosms in which cultural works of universal ambition are produced and circulate (law, science, art, literature or philosophy), and where the material or symbolic profits they procure (such as celebrity) are disputed, are in one sense, and in a certain connection, social worlds like any others, with relations of force and struggles to preserve or transform these, profits and powers. In a different connection, however, they are profoundly distinguished from these: the relations of force and the struggles of which they are the site assume here a specific form, and are in a position to impose their own law (*nomos*), all the more completely to the extent that they are independent from external economic forces (those of the national and international market for cultural goods and services) and political ones (particularly those of the national state and nationalism). This means in concrete practice that it is only possible to accomplish anything here, and be not only known but also recognized (by one's peers), inasmuch as one respects the specific law of this field, that of art or literature for example, to the exclusion of any other, in particular that of commerce or power.

This realistic view of intellectual worlds need in no way lead to disenchantment, as we shall see. It can even serve as the basis for a rational utopianism, founded on the defence of autonomy and of all the advances this has made possible. But if they want to set themselves up as effective guarantors of a 'ban on regression' (*Regressverbot*, as the Germans say), intellectuals cannot rest content with the prophetic denunciations of the total intellectual in the manner of Sartre, nor again with the critical analyses of the 'specific intellectual' as defined by Foucault. They have to mobilize and organize themselves on an international scale (perhaps using the new technologies of communication), in such a way as to constitute a genuine collective intellectual: transdisciplinary and international, able to form an effective counter-power vis-à-vis the economic, political and media powers, both national and supranational, and put new forms of action at the service of the different historical forms of universality which are indissociable from their existence and their specific interests.

This function of mandatories of universality that certain intellectuals can sometimes claim is inscribed in all fields of cultural production – legal, scientific, literary, artistic – as both rationale and ideal norm, able, even if it is constantly transgressed or more simply just forgotten, to exert powerful social effects. (Paradoxically, the almost parodical actions of media intellectuals provide evidence of this effectiveness, as a hypocritical homage of vice to virtue inspired by a quest for the symbolic profits awarded to respect for universality.) It is in the name of this ideal or myth that we can still seek to mobilize today against the enterprises of restoration that have sprung up almost everywhere in the world, even within the fields of cultural production themselves; it is in the name of the symbolic force that it can give, despite everything, to 'true ideas', that we can seek to oppose with some chance of success the forces of intellectual regression, moral and political, and particularly those aroused by past and present imperialisms and the consequences these have generated, such as xenophobic and racist violence towards immigrants issuing from societies that are economically and politically dominated within the new 'world order'. But the first task of this new enterprise of *Aufklärung*, which should serve as foundation for a new internationalism, is undoubtedly to submit to criticism the illusions of reason and the abuses of power that are committed in its name: those who wax so indignant against fanatical violence should turn their rational criticism against the imperialism of universalism and the fanaticism of reason, whose violence, as implacable as it is impeccable (that of the quite formal 'rationality' of the dominant economics, for example), might well lie at the root, paradoxically, of the most irreducible forms of irrationalism.

The object of a writers' parliament[*]

Since its foundation in Strasbourg in November 1993, the International Writers' Parliament has been the focus of a number of attacks. It strikes me as important, on the eve of this Strasbourg meeting, to indicate the discussions that have occupied us over the past year.

To exist collectively, as a force of solidarity, contestation and proposition, but first of all to rise above linguistic and national particularisms, the action of the International Writers' Parliament should be based on three principles:

One. Independence from political, economic and media powers, as well as from any kind of orthodoxy. The Parliament's action must have the objective of defending the autonomy of creation and thought everywhere that this is threatened, of restoring to writers full control of their means of production and definition of their works, and of defining for themselves a 'creation policy' independent of state 'cultural policy' and indifferent to the pressure of market and medias.

Two. A new internationalism, based on knowledge and recognition of the diversity of historic traditions.

This certainly means always struggling for universal causes whilst guarding against the 'imperialism of universality', whether this takes the form of a cosmopolitanism limited to the borders of Europe, a humanitarianism of bad conscience or a prophetism of the old universal consciousness, set on denouncing great scandals of the day or taking ethical positions on the 'important problems of the hour', i.e. the questions posed and imposed by the media.

Far from promoting exchange between intellectuals on a global scale, a false European universalism has contributed to arousing distrust and withdrawal on the part of intellectuals outside of Europe, without encouraging them or genuinely helping them escape from subjection to the former colonial metropolises or their own political authorities (themselves very often dominated by the great central economic and political powers, particularly through the grip of the IMF).

[*] Published in *Libération*, 3 November 1994

Three. New kinds of activism.

The Parliament should not be one of those groupings like academies and clubs that draw great symbolic profit from organizing the defence and collective promotion of the advantages and privileges of their members, without asking anything in exchange. It is rather a new type of movement, based on a radical critique of the representation that intellectuals often give of their function in history. A movement able to demand and obtain an activist commitment, i.e. contributions (subscriptions, gifts of time and work) that are unrewarded (hence anonymity, collective work) and respectful of singularities. The Parliament's objectives and those of the permanent bodies it will gradually endow itself with (secretariat, commissions, etc.) should be decided on jointly by all members. This presupposes that places and times of discussion are gradually established, plenary meetings (Lisbon, Strasbourg, Amsterdam) as well as 'regional' ones, and forms of organization that are simple and open, with the aim of ensuring the continuous orchestration of information. We should seek therefore to:

– intensify, in the face of the proliferation of attacks on the freedom to create and think, the consciousness of common interests, and lead the necessary task of collectively organizing the defence of these interests;

– defend creators and the conditions of creation everywhere against established powers, i.e. not only those creators who are threatened, persecuted or censored, but also the conditions for free creation, in particular minority or oppressed languages and cultures (teaching, access to publication, etc.), genuine freedom of expression, and of the instruments of production and distribution (publishing houses, magazines, translation policy);

– act as a critical body against all measures likely to threaten the exercise of the function of criticism, starting with the widespread reach of instances of manipulation of minds, political and religious propaganda;

– orient and organize a continuous and deepening work, associating writers and specialists, on important political, economic and cultural problems that are often excluded from the media's day-to-day vision (scientific criticism of the political uses of science or scientific authority; analysis of a critical situation – Rwanda, Haiti, East Timor, Algeria, etc. – with the aim of presenting and distributing an informed, rigorous and complex representation of this situation and formulating proposals);

– organize, through a functioning network, the concentration and redistribution of information: each participant gathering and transmitting to all others, either directly or by the intermediary of a common organ of concentration and redistribution (newsletters) the pertinent information on all problems of general interest (function of an independent press agency).

Intellectuals have scarcely invented anything new in the way of forms of action since the Dreyfus affair. It is significant that their collective actions only deploy to a very small extent their particular abilities – as distinct from what happens in the world of fine arts. All those useless petitions, mechanically signed, all those platforms over-heated with hypertrophied egos . . . One of the most pernicious threats among those currently bearing on the intellectual and collective autonomy of writers is the stranglehold of a media-intellectual complex that imposes its view of the world, its problematics, its culture of urgency. This complex is a real Trojan horse, seeking to introduce into intellectual life and public space the logic of show business, a cynical quest for visibility at any price and a traffic in symbolic capital. It does so by the way it exploits cases of spectacular distress and presents the posture or pose of commitment, reduced to the moralizing indignation of the good European soul and its vague retrospective sense of guilt (colonialism, Holocaust, etc.). It is also because they are fed up with being condemned to silence and taken hostage by media intellectuals, who claim to speak in their name and in their place, and disfigure the image of the intellectual, that the most aware and rigorous of writers have beaten a retreat, and refuse to participate in discussions whose terms they have not been allowed to define.

We must set in motion all the means needed to break the isolation of writers, by:
– simultaneous press conferences;
– free platforms orchestrated in newspapers of all countries;
– actions geared at the governments of different countries.

As well as this, the International Writers' Parliament should promote the publication of White Papers presenting the results of the work of 'commissions of specialists' (accompanied by contributions from writers) and serving as a basis for demands or practical recommendations that are collectively defended in the press and by representation to national and international political authorities; also works by writers who are censored or persecuted in their own countries.

By way of an international network of 'refuge-towns' (which already include Strasbourg, Amsterdam, Berlin, Gorée, etc.), it will seek to develop an active, constant and discreet solidarity in support of writers, artists and scholars who are threatened, persecuted or condemned to exile. To sum up, the International Writers' Parliament should invent forms of action that are both effective, conform to intellectual dignity, and appeal to the imagination and to artistic forms rather than to the traditional petitions and media 'interventions'.

The Writers' Parliament will be what writers themselves make of it, on condition that they never stop asking what it should be in its composition and function, on condition that they accept only to define it provisionally in terms of what it does. It will be what it does, because this is a necessary task that no one is doing; because it can only be done by writers gathered together to do something that they could not do individually.

It will be what writers do who have come together to speak, in their own specific language, of what they want to do, to raise the questions that they want to raise – and these alone –, to exchange information about actions they are conducting or planning, to seek together the means to give these actions their full force. The gathering will produce its own effects: when some speak of their action over Rwanda, others will think what they are doing or could do about Algeria. And each, strengthened by the information and inspiration they have received from the others, will be able to amplify the action of all in their own particular world.

9

Towards a Collective Intellectual

Two initiatives launched in the early 1990s on problems of higher education and on Algeria enabled Pierre Bourdieu to put into practice his conception of the collective work of intellectuals.

    In March 1992, an appeal to the community of scholars and academics led to the creation of a collective, the Association de Réflexion sur les Enseignements Supérieurs et la Recherche (ARESER), chaired by Pierre Bourdieu and with the historian Christophe Charle as secretary. The 'appeal to the community of scholars and academics', launched on 26 March with the foundation of the Association, was signed by around a hundred academics and scholars from every discipline. ARESER proposed here to promote a genuine academic and scientific community that could take its own future in hand: 'Of all the faults that higher education and intellectual life in France has suffered from for a long time, one of the most serious is the lack of a broad collective discussion on the goals and modalities of an academic and scientific life adapted both to the development of knowledge and to the transformations of the student body. Up to now, this function of discussion has been fulfilled either by organizations that are supposedly representative, but which as we know are now in crisis, or else by pressure groups or specialist organizations that currently tend to enclose themselves in disciplinary objectives or narrow corporatism.'

    Against the dysfunctions affecting the decision-making process, and in particular the loss of control of specialist bodies, which left 'scientific administrators' with the power to set the objectives and modalities of teaching, the action of ARESER consisted in gathering documents and producing texts designed to establish 'some diagnoses and emergency remedies for a university in danger' – as indicated by the title of a book that the collective published in 1997.[1] Summed up in the proposal for a 'law on university programming', the reflections of this collective sought to provide the means for struggling against the reinforcement of a two-speed teaching system, not just by the commitment of the financial and human resources required for the pedagogic training of student bodies that were increasingly heterogeneous, but above all by a reorganization of forms of work and a

---

[1] ARESER, *Quelques diagnostics et remèdes urgents pour une université en péril* (Paris: Raisons d'Agir 1997). [Ed.]

strengthening of self-administration. In parallel with this proposal, ARESER organized a number of round tables with the participation of foreign academics, and intervened in the public debate with articles discussing ministerial policies: for instance the simulated 'national consultation' of fifteen- to twenty-five-year-olds, launched in 1994 by Prime Minister Edouard Balladur for electoral purposes (see p.246); or again the 'trompe-l'oeil' *reforms proposed by the ministers François Bayrou (see p.253) and subsequently Claude Allègre.[2]*

The 'Algerian question' was perceived by Pierre Bourdieu as an 'extreme limit of all the social and political problems that a scholar and an intellectual might encounter', and became for him the context of a collective work with the Comité International de Soutien aux Intellectuels Algériens (CISIA), founded in June 1993 to support intellectuals who had been the object of attack and murder since the start of the Algerian civil war – for example, the sociologist Djellali Labes, the journalist Tabar Djaout and the playwright Abdelkader Alloulla (see p.259).

In association with the Writers' Parliament, the CISIA set out first of all to facilitate emigration for those intellectuals who were most at risk, then to break the isolation of those who had been cut off from all information by the prevailing violence. As the committee's charter declared (Paris, 1 July 1993):

> It is intelligence that is being murdered. Algeria's entry into political modernity and pluralism is taking place with a terrible violence. The violence of the bloody repression of the riots of October 1988; the violent protest of Islamist preachers; the violent interruption of the electoral process; the violence of machine-gun fire against those seeking to overthrow the established power; repeated violations of human rights; terrorist violence and the violence of the state's security forces, engaged in a ferocious duel leading to civil war, against the background of economic disaster . . . When people are killed whose work is to produce ideas, analyses, and works of art, or to care for human life, it is the head, the heart and the voice of a country that is under attack.

The CISIA set itself the objective of alerting public opinion, in 'complete independence from governments, institutions and parties', of the dangers to life and liberty, and took up a position in support of a 'party of civil peace' (see p.256), which the presidential elections of November 1995 that brought Liamine Zeroual to power seemed to be leading to: 'Algerians have voted for their leaders. But

---

[2] Claude Allègre was minister of education in Lionel Jospin's first government, and referred to by Pierre Bourdieu as an 'illiterate sociologist'. Bourdieu discussed his departure in a joint contribution with Christophe Charles and members of the ARESER bureau (see p.302). [Ed.]

they have also voted above all for the requirement of civil peace, immediately, in other words transition from armed violence to political confrontation.'[3]

The CISIA also had the further goal of providing, equally removed from both 'cold political analysis' and the 'indecent humanist preaching' of media intellectuals,[4] *tools for understanding the present situation, especially by showing that 'Islam is not inherently incompatible with a state based on law'.*[5] *Against the collective repression that arose from the colonial situation, a work designed to explore the 'historical unconscious' showed that the collective lie of the Algerian governing class, bound up with the regression into barbarism for which France had provided the model in the repressive responses of the Algerian war, had its roots, following the end of the colonial era, in the subordination of culture to politics: against the culture installed 'in the name of true religion, science, the spirit of the people or the logic of the market', we should work for the establishment of a 'consensus of compromise', a culture based 'on the multiplicity of concrete experiences'.*[6] *To the extent that 'the dominant cultural model' had been imposed not on the basis of traditional Islam but rather that of a 'modernist ideology' mixing old and new in a coherent whole calling for 'conversion', what was needed was to struggle for the establishment of political and cultural freedoms.*

The texts produced by Pierre Bourdieu with Marie Virolle, Jean Leca (who chaired CISIA during these years) (see p.263) and Jacques Derrida (see pp.259 and 261) repeatedly declared this support, while criticizing the measures of the French government on matters of immigration.

---

[3] 'Le parti de la paix civile' (with Marie Virolle), *Alternatives Algériennes* 2, November-December 1995. [Ed.]
[4] 'Avec les intellectuels algériens' (with Jean Leca), *Le Monde*, 7 October 1994. [Ed.]
[5] Charter of the Comité International de Soutien aux Intellectuels Algériens (CISIA), Paris, 1 July 1993. [Ed.]
[6] 'Avec les intellectuels algériens', op. cit. [Ed.]

An example of 'rational demagogy' in education*

A demagogic questionnaire

The questionnaire that M. Balladur put to young people between the ages of fifteen and twenty-five presents the great advantage of concentrating in a small piece of folded paper the essential features of those great errors that should be avoided at all costs in any investigation of this kind. In this respect, it provides an irreplaceable document for all *lycée* and university students, whether under or over twenty-five, who wish to familiarize themselves with research techniques. Let us hope that it succeeds at least to that extent. From a scientific point of view, however, all conditions are in place right from the start to guarantee that no significant result can ever be obtained from this consultation.

The survey presents itself as a census, as the questionnaire was sent to everyone through the post. Reply if you want to! This procedure prevents any control of the age and socio-demographic structure of the respondents. Whatever the response rate might be, the completed questionnaires cannot be properly used, as no one will ever know who has replied and who has not, an indispensable condition for making proper use of any questionnaire, and interpreting the biases introduced by non-responses.

All the more so, given that in a political consultation of this kind it is impossible to rule out all ambiguous and facetious replies – 'I fill in a lot of questionnaires', 'I have socio-demographic features that are not those of my age', etc. A survey conducted on a random sample whose structure had been carefully controlled would have provided results with a genuine meaning and at less expense.

As soon as such an ambitious objective is proposed as asking young people to express themselves on their 'own experiences', their 'view of life', their 'conception of the future', it would be a basic precaution to offer them every chance to express themselves in their own words. This questionnaire, however, which is in the main a closed one, is based on scales of attitudes ('completely agree', 'moderately agree', 'moderately disagree', 'completely disagree'), with the optimum ('completely agree') referring to a social model that is quite stereotyped, and very unevenly distributed among the population (I feel

---

* These two texts were jointly signed with Christian Baudelot and Catherine Lévy, and published in *Le Monde* on 8 July and 27 September 1994. They accompanied publication of the results of the 'Balladur questionnaire', and expressed the point of view of ARESER.

European; I have confidence in the future; my family has enough money to live on; I feel well in myself; when I feel bad I know who to turn to; school gives a good preparation for working life; etc.).

There is no conception at all here that many young people might have nothing to say on these points, but a good deal to say about life, work, housing estates, cops, bosses, suburbs, etc. The few open questions, ostensibly stereotyped, that are interspersed from time to time, in no way compensate for this gap, as they presuppose a certain mastery of written language, and a confidence in writing and in the organizers of the survey that are far from existing. As for the variables by which young people are characterized here, they show a disturbing poverty.

What is most scandalous about this operation is that reputable polling institutes and sociologists have compromised themselves by a manipulative undertaking that can only discredit them, without even trying to apply the minimum level of professional principles that would assure such a study a minimum objectivity. The objective pursued, which is that of obtaining a maximum number of responses from the given age group, is similar in form to a referendum (in its primary sense of consultation rather than vote), such as the recent consultation of secondary school administrators, teachers and parents organized by the minister of national education.

The government seems to expect these national consultations to appease the protest movements against their new legislative projects (16 January and anti-CIP[7] demonstrations). This direct pseudo-democracy, a regular parody of the *cahiers de doléances* that were written collectively at meetings called for this purpose in the run-up to the États Généraux of 1789, is simply a form of rational demagogy. It is no kind of apprenticeship in democracy, nor an exercise of the rights of the citizen, to enrol people in an anonymous dialogue where the subjects address themselves to the 'prince' to let him know their desiderata; a collection of individual opinions (even admitting that these had been combined and interpreted) has nothing in common with collective projects, and a people (or a section of them) is not reducible to a mere addition of subjects.

Less than one young person in five

France today has nine million young people aged between fifteen and twenty-five. Out of this total, 1,539,000 returned the questionnaire, i.e. a response rate of 17.1 per cent. Even if three times more than the organizers expected, this response should not hide the most important fact: more than four young people out of five abstained from taking part in this national consultation

[7] [Contrat d'Insertion Professionelle, a new standard employment contract.]

addressed to them. There is no reason to suppose that the respondents are representative of the total consulted.

This should temper the overflowing enthusiasm of the organizers and the commissioning minister, powerfully relayed by the media, who have spent the whole summer counting up the replies like so many million francs in the Téléthon. On the pretext that this reached and then surpassed the magic figure of a million, they already started speaking of a 'massive response', a 'high tide', etc. Quite apart from the heap of paper received having no real value, the response rate was actually modest, very close to what is obtained from a postal survey with no follow-up on subjects that have no strong appeal for the population questioned.

As for the results, they were on a par with the questions asked – disturbingly banal. They only confirmed what had long been established by less onerous and more fruitful studies conducted by sociologists, demographers, psychologists and statisticians . . . Results that the press and media have already broadcast widely. The fact that the family, in a period of unemployment and uncertainty, is the ultimate refuge for a large number of young people, has been emphasized for a long time by family sociologists and demographers; and specialists in education have repeated for nearly twenty years that school and university are perceived both as a site of integration and as a pitiless mechanism of selection. We also knew very well that firms do not recognize educational qualifications, and that young people accuse their bosses of not trusting them: this is apparent from the differential rates of unemployment by age group. As for fear and uncertainty about the future, how could this be otherwise in a gerontocratic society riddled with unemployment and subject to so much restructuring over two decades? One need only lend an ear to the cries of last March's demonstrators.

The organizers of the consultation now tell us that they did not intend a sociological investigation. Indeed! But what then is the status of this undertaking, a consultation organized by the government of the day? The 'high tide' here is one of abstention; if the government wanted to organize a consultation, it should have obtained the resources needed and put in place the elements of a national debate. Collective discussion and the confrontation of ideas are always richer than individual responses that are foreclosed by the questions themselves.

A trompe-l'oeil university reform[*]

The most remarkable effect of what people call the Bayrou reform, and indeed the only effect at all, is the positive response it has met with among university administrators and students, who are usually critical or reserved. And yet an unprejudiced examination of the minister's proposals forces us to conclude that this supposed reform is not a reform at all, particularly when compared with those projected or carried out in previous years.

The first chapter of the measures announced bears on the organization of the first year into semesters and the creation of an orientation semester. This reform, however, has been inscribed in law since the decree of 26 May 1992! It was a cornerstone of the educational reform that was projected when Lionel Jospin was minister of national education, but poorly received at that time and put on the back burner, until it was taken up and made official by Jack Lang and carried out in the universities. Something that these establishments have been practising for the last five years is thus presented as a novelty. The only new feature is that the authors of the previous initiative, being more concerned for the flexibility and autonomy of the universities, deliberately left the initiative to the institutions themselves. The real question now is not to introduce this reorganization but rather to assess its effects, as it has already been tried out for long enough. As far as the information available permits us to conclude, however, these effects appear modest at best. It seems that only a few students have taken advantage of the possibilities of orientation that are offered. This miraculous remedy for failure rests in fact on a false assumption, that failure arises chiefly from a lack of information and motivation on the part of the students. This is to forget that students have only a limited margin of choice after the *baccalauréat*, as a function of their ranking, and that the highest failure rates pertain to students in those classes that offer neither the choice nor the intellectual weapons to tackle the most general DEUGs.[8] One major problem that is raised today in the universities is that of their adaptation to a changed student body. To reduce the origin of these difficulties to individual errors of orientation is to make a misdiagnosis and consequently to adopt inappropriate remedies.

---

[*] Jointly signed with Christian Baudelot, Christophe Charle, Jacques Fijalkow, Bernard Lacroix and Daniel Roche for the ARESER collective, and published in Le Monde, 1 April 1997.

[8] Success rates of 24.3% and 33.1% were recorded for the DEUG in technical classes (F, G and H), against 61% to 68.6% for general classes (figures from the ministry of national education, cited in Le Monde, 29 January). [DEUG is the abbreviation for Diplôme d'Études Universitaires Générales, the basic two- or three-year course that provides a foundation for the higher degree of licence or maîtrise.]

The second point that the ministerial catalogue highlights is 'profession-alization'. We should recall that professionalization has been a prominent tendency in a number of branches (AES, MASS, MIAGE,[9] communications, etc.), sometimes by way of optional modules known as '*pré-pro*' – for example in the training of teachers. Arrangements bearing on professionalization increase the burden of education without anything in exchange, particularly by transforming teachers into canvassers for business apprenticeships, to the detriment of what is supposedly their essential task, i.e. teaching and research.

The four measures highlighted that bear on premises and buildings also display the art of trompe-l'oeil; an additional construction plan, creation of a modernization agency designed to support the ineffective presidential teams; possibility of recourse to the legal formula of a foundation to increase the number of universities. Finally, the university buildings, which are currently the property of the state, will be given to the universities themselves with full possession, in accordance with a proposal already contained in the Laurent report. In fact, the additional construction plan is simply a re-run of the emergency catch-up plan that was taken out following the strikes of December 1995, but with no additional means. To give universities their existing premises means turning over to them the management and renovation of ageing buildings without any guarantee that budgets will be increased accordingly, and the state abandoning responsibility in matters of accident or obligatory upgrading.

As far as research and personnel policy are concerned, these proposals offer the same mixture of poverty and ambiguity. Is the minister familiar with the functioning of the institutions that he is responsible for? We can only agree with assessing the results of research, taking into account the pedagogic activity of teachers, revising the service obligations of certain over-burdened categories and promoting mobility. The problem is that these arrangements have theoretically been in place already for a good while. Assessment is already the task of the Comité National d'Évaluation, which reports on the strengths and weaknesses of the various research units in each establishment. And taking pedagogic activity into account has long been one of the recruitment criteria of the commissions of specialists and the Conseil National des Universités. The most important thing, however, would be to take into account the multifunctional character of academics in terms of teaching, research and management in the course of a single career, something that the rigidity of current norms ignores. Finally, to focus new categories of teachers such as those qualified for secondary schools but

---

[9] [Respectively, Administration Économique et Sociale (a *licence* qualification), Mathématique pour Sciences Sociales (a DEUG specialisation), and Maîtrise d'Informatique Appliquée à la Gestion (information technology for management).]

teaching in higher education, whose number is growing in order to save on expenditure, is no more than a response made under pressure from the interested parties themselves to a difficulty created by a short-sighted recruitment policy; we see now that it is not possible to eternally add more 'auxiliary lecturers' in higher education. The real direction that needs defining is rather the long-term consideration of recruitment flows, given that retirement will accelerate in the years ahead, and of the balances to be observed between different categories of personnel, to avoid a further balkanization of universities – in which, to save on state finance, there has been far too great a proliferation of 'acting' positions.

The most concrete measure, which has made it possible to obtain the provisional support of certain student organizations, concerns rationalization of the system of scholarships. Here again, all this involves is dressing up in new clothes a traditional system of awards in which the increase in funds for each beneficiary will be offset by a reduction in the number of individuals aided by the present system. It is also notable that the discussion has been postponed until 1998, an election year when government action in favour of students can be highlighted, without making any guarantee – since there will certainly be a new government, and even if this is of the same political colour, it can always argue that a new economic situation forces a revision of budgetary options (remember 1995).

In sum, the balance is a meagre one, especially at the end of two years' consultation and major media operations to give the impression that work is going on in high places. Higher education policy can be summed up by the metaphor of Balzac's wild ass's skin: from a referendum on education buried by Chirac when he was a candidate, to the report of the Fauroux commission, discarded in practice, and the law on programming, conceded in autumn 1995, reasserted in March 1996, and abandoned on 28 June 1996, we have a whole catalogue lacking both imagination and any real project, in which laissez-faire and pretence go hand in hand. While all studies show that a good long training is the best weapon against unemployment, this absence of university policy justified by the pretext of budgetary constraint[10] represents a failure to assist young people in difficulty and a charge on the future in a ten-year time frame. Such short-sighted electoralism is as unacceptable in this domain as it is in others.

---

[10] The Fauroux report gave a detailed list of the minimal measures required to bring French universities up to European standard. The lack of attention this text received, despite being commissioned by the government, is significant of the financial blockage.

One problem can be hidden by another*

The question of the 'Islamic' scarf

The debate under way apropos the wearing of the 'Islamic' scarf, as it is arbitrarily called, reveals the current state of political debate in France. The grip of the media, concerned only with sensation, the grip of opinion polls that make it possible to transform false problems raised by the media into objects of 'democratic' consultation, the government's attempt to reduce politics to administration, the withdrawal into itself of the Socialist party, which thinks and acts less with regard to political reality than as a function of the issues involved in its internal competition for succession – a whole series of factors have combined to steer public debate into questions that are more or less futile, or worse, real questions reduced to futility.

This is the case with the debate over the problem posed by three girls from Creil who came to school with a cloth over their heads . . . Projecting onto this minor and soon forgotten event the veil of grand principles – freedom, secularism, women's liberation, etc. – those people who always stake a claim as *maîtres à penser* have revealed, as if it were a projective test, their unavowed positions on the problem of immigration. The apparent question, whether or not to accept the wearing of the so-called Islamic veil in school, hides the latent question, whether or not to accept in France immigrants of North African origin, and enables them to answer the latter in a way that would otherwise be unacceptable.

In revealing their hidden thoughts in this incautious way, they contribute to raising the level of anxiety that a good many French people feel towards this phenomenon, and the irrationality such anxiety generates. They only delay the moment when the need to mobilize resources to give immigrants who are generally quite 'de-Islamicized' and decultured (the majority of them have no knowledge of their language and culture of origin) the possibility of fully asserting their dignity as human beings and citizens will be coura-geously asserted. The moment has come, for European intellectuals, to demand that national governments and European bodies conceive and put into practice a broad common programme of economic, political and cultural integration for immigrants.

* Archives of the Collège de France.

Stay the hands of the murderers!*

Abdelkader Alloula, the playwright, director and inspiring figure of an avant-garde theatre in the Arabic language, has just been murdered. He was one of those symbolic figures who make the connection between international culture and the voice of the Algerian people. He was one of those independent spirits who reject authoritarian tutelage and indoctrination. This is why he died; it is all of this that his murderers sought to kill.

Abdelkader Alloula, murdered like so many others: Ahmed Asselah, director of the school of fine arts in Algiers, along with his son, a student; Tahar Djouat, writer, journalist and poet; Mahfoud Boucebci, professor of psychiatry; Djilali Belkhenchir, professor of pediatrics; Mohand Oubélaïd Saheb, engineer; Smaïl Yefsah, television journalist; Larissa Ayada, painter, of Russian nationality; Monique Afri, an employee of the French consulate; Rachid Tigrizi, economist; Raymond Lousoum, optician, of Tunisian nationality; Youcef Sebti, poet and agronomist; Joaquim Grau, known as 'Vincent', bookseller, friend of culture and the arts.

We condemn without appeal those who, within Algeria and outside the country, and within or outside the state, arm the murderers in the name of or under cover of Islamism, who give the order to shoot, cut throats, decapitate and mutilate defenceless citizens, known or unknown, men, women and even children; those who, establishing a reign of terror, aim to destroy civic solidarity, break democratic defences and lead an entire people to lose their reason.

Katia Bengana, 17 years old, *lycée* student, killed because she did not wear the hijab; Rachida Oubelaïd, murdered with her husband in front of their young daughters; Oum el-Kheir Haddad, fortune-teller, five months pregnant, shot; Fadela Ikhlef, housewife, brutally murdered; Aïcha Bouchlaghem, mother of nine children, brutally murdered; Aouïcha Allel, shopkeeper, shot; Aïcha Meloufi, housewife, shot; Mimouna Ricouèche, mother of five, decapitated in front of her family; Tamma Mansour, housewife, shot; Keltoum Boudjar, 94 years old, murdered; Safia Lounis, 73 years old, murdered; Bernabia, shot as he was driving his car. And still more, mothers, wives and sisters of policeman, civil servants, imams . . .

We declare that no political cause, no ideological or religious motive,

* A message read at the Panthéon by Ariana Mnouchkine on 16 March 1994, during a meeting organized by the CISIA.

254

can justify resort to the criminal strategy that is being practised in Algeria. We proclaim our solidarity with all those who continue resisting the dictates of terror by the sole weapons of reason, speech, writing and peaceful determination.

Abdelkader Alloula, murdered like so many others: Djilalli Liabes, sociologist; Laadi Flici, doctor and writer; M'hammed Boukhobza, sociologist; Hafid Senhadri, trade-union official; Rabah Zenati, television journalist; Radouane Sari, nuclear physicist; Saad Bakhtaoui, journalist; Abderrahmane Chergou, economist; Omar Arar, imam; Rabie Allauochiche, *lycée* director; Olivier Quemeneur, French journalist.

We call on all those who have united with us in this action, in Germany, Belgium, Canada, Spain, Great Britain, Italy and the Netherlands, to mobilize for the purpose of convincing their fellow citizens, the media in their countries, and their governments, that the suffering in Algeria is now a challenge to the conscience of the world.

We solemnly ask the French government to end its policy of national isolation and wretched security concerns, and renew the tradition of hospitality that has always been that of France, by granting visas on a broad scale to those men and women who seek refuge here.

We ask it to break with a cautious wait-and-see attitude and guarantee its active support and economic aid to those who take as their programme the re-establishment of pluralism of expression, the perspective of democracy and the struggle against all forms of exclusion in Algeria.

Abdelkader Alloula, murdered like so many others: Rachid Djellid, sociologist; Karima Belhadj, 17 years old, social worker; Djamel Bouhidel, archaeologist; Ahmed Traïche, teacher of the Koran; Mustapha Abada, television journalist; Hamoud Hambli, professor of Islamic law; Abdelhamid Benmenni, journalist; Rabah Guenzet, professor of philosophy, trade unionist; Zhor Mezjane, secondary school principal. And dozens of teachers, magistrates, lawyers, doctors and nurses, officials, engineers, technicians, journalists, civil servants, imams, trade unionists, former liberation fighters, athletes, members of voluntary associations . . .

We proclaim again our sympathy and solicitude for all Algerians who mourn their dead and suffer. We are also at their side in their efforts to save the intelligence and culture of their country from extermination, and to preserve the social cohesion and creative energy of their people.

For a party of civil peace*

What gives us the right to speak? Yet how can we keep silent? This is a contradiction that we feel deeply today, we who are present in this hall.

If we have no illusion about what we can do against violence by the mere strength of our speeches, we feel none the less bound to do something, imperatively, to combat the despotism of terror. And I am sure that you feel this contradiction too.

We know that the roots of this tragedy lie in the whole violence that the French nation was guilty of, for more than one hundred and fifty years, and we still feel responsible for this; but we also know that this guilt, collective or individual, whilst certainly one of the emotions that both mobilizes and paralyses us, does not justify any kind of intrusion, and that we must not try to put it to sleep by vague humanist litanies.

I could continue to list the contradictions that unite and divide us, introducing division between us and within each one of us, making us choose between violence, terrorism and state terror, between compromise and resignation; in fact, the very invitation to speak appears to some people as a concession to the criminals, and the appeal to democracy as an abdication in the face of despotism and terror. This is why I believe it is quite justifiable to speak of a tragedy.

I will however just mention one last contradiction, and indeed the most terrible of all: how, without abandoning the duty of analysis and understanding, which would undoubtedly lead to saying that all sides are wrong, or that all sides are right, can we take a stand in an active way, with at least a little effect, at the same time *against* all those who contribute to the reign of terror, and *for* the party of civil peace, which certainly exists in Algeria, in other words in support of the majority of men and especially women whom the reign of terror condemns to solitude and silence?

The CISIA, an international committee in support of Algerian intellectuals, which brings together intellectuals from many countries, a good number of them specialists in North African societies, has set itself the task, among other things, of trying to introduce the logic of analysis in a field abandoned to partisan passion and sectarian incomprehension. At the risk of seeming to indulge in a naively scientistic utopianism, I would like to recall here the conclusions of certain scientific analyses of the mechanisms of terrorism and

* Talk given at the Sorbonne on 7 February 1994.

state terror, and the social effects these produced in the various countries of Latin America that they ravaged, in different combinations, in the course of the 1970s [see p.230]. In situations of radical unpredictability and total insecurity, where, as can be seen from the evidence that we shall hear, the street appeared a place full of menace, where information became imprecise and inaccessible, where fear made communication difficult even within the family, where open violence and acts of public intimidation, kidnapping, executions, etc. were combined with more or less clandestine actions such as torture and arbitrary execution, where anxiety was heightened by rumour, where – in a word – the concern for survival prevented any real life, in these situations of extreme insecurity, it was always noticeable how groups became atomized and solidarities collapsed, leaving individuals isolated and afraid, withdrawing in on themselves in what Juan Corradi has called an 'amoral familism'.

But this analysis also shows that it is possible to escape from the circle of fear, and how this is possible. The first condition is the existence of organizations able to release individuals demoralized by terror from the alternative between heroism and resignation, and organize actions designed to give back morality and morale to all those whom fear had condemned to isolation. This can be done by helping them discover that many others think like them, and that important individuals and institutions, both in their own country and abroad, support their actions and are offering them increased protection. The most effective strategies are those that lead the silent majority to discover and show their collective strength, in actions that are relatively simple and have little risk, but produce a tremendous symbolic effect, above all on those performing them, but also on those they are directed against, if they are performed at the same time by a very large number of people together – such as a silent march to an agreed meeting-place, or the closure of buildings and shops, etc. Such actions have taken place in Algeria on many occasions, but they have always been partly neutralized by being annexed for partisan objectives, real or supposed.

I am therefore convinced that our appeal for civil peace can be something quite different from a platonic and vaguely humanist declaration by a group of intellectuals of good will. What is needed for this is that in Algeria itself, men and women of unchallengeable authority – of whom there are a large number – intellectual, moral, religious and political authority – decide to unite their symbolic strength and appeal – possibly with the international backing that the CISIA and the International Writers' Parliament could offer them – for a mobilization of the forces of peace in a party of civil peace that would bring together the silent majority, today atomized, demoralized and condemned to impotence by the regime of terror. By restoring confidence among all who have the desire to resist violence, this party of peace would unite and combine the strength of all those who, in their work and their everyday lives, have not ceased, despite the threats that are quite particularly directed against them, to act in support of civil peace, at the price of a daily struggle against intimidation and fear. And this force would be able accordingly to denounce and effectively counter-act the demagogic manoeuvres of those sorcerers' apprentices who, with seeming impunity, seek to exploit the anxiety and despair of the immense sub-proletariat generated by economic crisis and international exploitation.

You will doubtless think that I am lapsing here into utopianism, and forgetting the antinomies that I started off by listing, and all the censoring these imply. If there is any naivety here, it is a function of the anxiety that I feel, with a great many others, in the face of the threat of civil war in its most horrible forms. My response is thus the idea of actions that are more limited but more secure, those for which the CISIA has been founded. We must start with what depends on us, i.e. our own governments. Other speakers will explain the approaches we plan to make to European governments, with a view to obtaining cancellation of Algeria's crushing debt – your support for the petition we have drafted will give more strength to such interventions. Then there are the tasks of assistance for those who have had to flee the violence. Need we say, against prevailing rumours, that we have never made any selection among the victims, and that we do not ask those who approach us to pass a language test? We will explain the initiatives we have taken with a view to obtaining appropriate legal status for those who seek refuge in France. Initiatives that are particularly difficult, though particularly needed, given the current ideology of national security. We are working together with the provincial branches of the CISIA and other associations to find jobs, housing and funds for those who request our support. Here again, we have need of you. Those who believe they can help us with one or other of the points I have mentioned can let us know, either here today on their way out, or by letter, giving their name and address, and the kind of assistance they can offer.

I will confine myself to these very specific indications. The extreme seriousness of the situation in Algeria, which justifies neither rhetorical complacency nor moral exhortation, imposes on us both restraint and dignity.

Failing to assist an endangered person*

Decrees putting an end to the special status that Algerians enjoyed as regards their right to remain in France have recently been published in the *Journal Officiel*; these amount to the crime of failing to assist an endangered person. This policy of 'closed counters' means turning our back on the universal hospitality that founded the very identity of this country of the rights of man. It is time to move to civic resistance.

The laws of July and August 1993 were designed, we were told, to 'control' the flows of migration, and consolidated – one could say armour-plated – the same year by the constitutional reform that restricted the right of asylum. They are now showing their sinister consequences: individuals legally established here experience a more precarious fate than ever; children born in France, now known as 'young foreigners', are excluded from French nationality, the applications policy demonstrates its arbitrary character. And so on. Up to now, Algerians could benefit from a special status at least as far as their right to remain in France was concerned, though not their right of residence. The decrees published on 20 December in the *Journal Officiel* have now deprived them of this.

The government dares to present this gesture as just one measure among others, just a return to the standard regulations for foreigners. As if the closing of French consulates in Algeria was not enough! As if the detour through the Nantes office was not enough, an interminable procedure that in 80 to 90 per cent of cases ends in failure! As if it were not yet enough to make a selection among those holding visas and wanting, for obvious reasons, to remain for more than three months!

Hundreds of testimonies agree in describing the inhuman and shameful policy that the majority of administrations involved practise towards applicants. Now the state abdicates its responsibilities in favour of local mayors, giving them the possibility, in a completely arbitrary fashion, of issuing or rejecting as they see fit the entrance and reception authorizations for foreigners.

The situation is still more painful for Algerians inasmuch as it is determined by the civil war that is under way there, in which France plays a contradictory role and assumes questionable responsibilities. However such responsibilities are judged, in the name of what principles can we refuse to accept innocent

* Jointly signed with Jacques Derrida and Sami Naïr, and published in *Le Monde*, 29 December 1994.

victims and all those fleeing from a civil war? No one can feign ignorance today, or even pretend that this tragedy is the business of other people on the other shore of the Mediterranean. The cynicism of these decrees is blatant, at a time when tens of thousands of Algerians are exposed to the risk of death.

We denounce the crime of failure to assist an endangered person. We denounce the ignominy of racial laws disguised as a return to standard regulations. Each time that France has sought to be the country of human rights, the land of the right of asylum and universal hospitality for the victims of tyrannies, it has had to combat xenophobic hatred and the sordid egoism that hides behind a patriotic mask. Those who condemned Dreyfus opened the way to those who supported Pétain.

We address ourselves here to all those who no longer recognize themselves in a France of repressive – and above all hypocritical and demagogic – conservatism, in a France of police controls, administrative investigations, certificates of accommodation and similar mechanisms. We call them to join with us in a broad movement of civic resistance, which, together with other associations, will have to list all the failures of republican law in matters of the right of asylum and citizenship in order to combat them. Our immediate aim lies in one single demand: the abrogation of discriminatory measures and return to the republican practice of the right of asylum.

M. Pasqua, his adviser, and foreigners*

Under the title 'When intellectuals lack rigour', M. Barreau accuses us of not respecting the facts, even if he at least grants us as 'intellectuals' (but what about others?) 'the right to oppose a policy they disapprove of'. The question is a political one: who is it directed at? And it should be no surprise that an adviser to M. Pasqua has difficulty in following us. In rejecting this policy, and distinguishing between the rigour of harshness and the rigour of precision, we challenge M. Barreau's argument on the five points that his embarrassed reply raises.

1) Is it now forbidden to declare that we disagree with the law of nationality? This deprives certain 'young foreigners' of rights that they previously enjoyed; it forces them into procedures that no one would have proposed if their purpose was not to discourage those concerned.

2) We never said that the closing of consulates in Algeria 'was intended to annoy the Algerians'. We simply noted that along with a number of other similar measures, this added to the already considerable difficulties of requesting and obtaining a visa, in the present tragic situation when such application is often a last resort when faced with the risk of death.

3) When we regret that the state has abdicated its responsibility in favour of local mayors, we are told that 'the prefects have the final decision'. This legal phrase does not change the situation that mayors do have the power to decide, except in special circumstances, after difficult legal procedure and discouragement in advance. We wanted to emphasize the risks of arbitrariness in a delegation of this kind.

4) A further political disagreement: for historical reasons that are only too evident, and taking into account France's responsibilities in the terrifying Algerian situation (responsibilities that can be differently interpreted, but not denied outright), we do not believe that to return Algerians to the standard regulations needs no explanation or is just in today's circumstances. 'Moroccans and Tunisians manage with this', M. Barreau tranquilly says. This is a shocking argument, just like saying that the Évian agreements are past history.

If, as we are reminded, the 'ministry of the interior and the ministry of foreign affairs' were doing the 'maximum' to receive threatened Algerians, or wanted to do so, why the rigour of these new decrees? The point we make is that this is where the whole question lies.

* Jointly signed with Jacques Derrida, and published in *Le Monde*, 10 June 1995.

5) M. Barreau should be aware that not all foreigners (even non-Europeans) need a visa to enter France. This is what we call discrimination. We are not calling for an unlimited opening of the border, in this time and situation. We are protesting against the new 'rigour' (a rigour that we find distasteful) of a certain immigration policy, of which the recent decrees show the true face. And at least as regards the visa requirement, we are protesting against the unprecedented and terribly harsh conditions that the new decrees place on Algerians – and many others – who wish to request and obtain a visa.

If this was not the declared intention of this repressive policy, then please let us know what is the sense and purpose of decrees such as these?

No ghettoizing of Algeria!*

In 1989, the ministry of foreign affairs granted 800,000 visas to Algerians who wanted to spend a certain time in France, for whatever reason. The number of these – despite the restriction brought by the establishment of an obligatory visa requirement – simply reflected the density of human and economic relations between the two countries.

In 1994, less than 100,000 visas were granted to Algerians, even though the requests were similar in number and in kind to those of the previous years. In 1995, scarcely a tenth of the visa requests were granted. This amounts to a virtual closing of the frontier between the two countries.

Naturally enough, we must demand that those women and men who seek to save their lives by emigrating should be able to do so as a matter of urgency, and should find a decent reception from the French authorities – which is not currently the case. We struggle day after day alongside our Algerian friends, and come up against obstacles that are all the more repugnant in that these reception measures only affect a few thousand individuals. Has France become so weak, so timid, so forgetful of its ambition to be the country of the rights of man?

We declare that it is indispensable to avoid aggravating the situation of millions of Algerian women and men who intend to remain in their country, amid such perils, so that Algeria can continue to live, create, produce and prepare a future for itself. To prohibit them from travelling to France – or another country – means exposing them to greater risk, driving them to despair and discouragement, it means blocking social respiration and more surely compromising the perspectives for democracy and escape from the present crisis.

To plunge the country into isolation means playing the game of violence, ostracism and intolerance. It also means driving into a longer and less reversible exile those who would not choose this route, since no one can now be assured that if they return they will be able to exit again, even if they find themselves at risk of death.

Are Algerians no longer proper citizens of the world? Do they no longer need to go and see their relatives and friends, to travel, go to meetings, work with fellow professionals or exchange ideas with other people? France bans them from international travel on the pretext of terrorism. Don't we all

* Jointly signed with Jean Leca, and published in Le Monde, 25 March 1995.

realize that terrorists manage to travel perfectly well across the world without 'proper' visas?

Once again, it is ordinary Algerian society that pays: caught in a vice between the violence of armed Islamic groups and military-police repression, it is also hostage to French security fantasies. In this sense, the French policy of refusing visas is criminal.

It is also short-term and narrow-minded in terms of trans-Mediterranean exchange. Official France has become deaf to the legitimate demands of a population settled on both sides of the Mediterranean; by confining one section of these in a territorial ghetto, it facilitates the task of those who want to confine them in a political and religious ghetto.

In order for Algerians to be able to continue to live in their country and preserve it from the worst, we ask the French authorities to resume the normal delivery of visas (a minimum number of rejections, a shorter and simpler procedure); the granting and renewal of long-term, multiple-entry visas for categories of people who are at risk and do not envisage exile; and the delivery of emergency visas for those applicants threatened with death.

A national demonstration will be held in Nantes on 25 March, in front of the office of the ministry of foreign affairs that deals with postal requests from Algerians for visas – which means for the most part sending form letters of refusal. Those who see the Algerian situation as one of the great dramas involving the future of the whole region, and who wish for a civil, peaceful and democratic outcome, can only alert the public powers about the blindness of their policy as regards the movements of Algerian citizens.

Reveal and divulge the repressed*

The roots of the Algerian problem can only be grasped by going back a very long way. In the wake of independence, there was a kind of collective repression of colonization, colonial repression and the violence associated with the war of liberation. I believe it is necessary now to analyze the strategies of bad faith – in the sense of lying to oneself, of self-deception – that those who had been colonized, collectively but differentially according to their position in Algerian political space – practised in order to repress the fact of colonization, and the profound traces this has left in things and in minds. To contribute to this exploration of the historical unconscious, we need a social history of the differential relations that Algerians had and continue to have with the French language. The central site of repression and self-deception has been all questions to do with Arabization as against the perpetuation of French. (The problem of the French language has always been tackled in a shamefaced manner, passively, as if the Algerian leaders thought that Arabic was fine for the dominated, whereas French – or even Latin and Greek – was better suited to the dominant; the same could be said about Islam.) The lie was a collective one, for which we are perhaps in the process of paying the price today. Unfortunately, historical faults are committed by some people, but their punishment inflicted on all. These problems must all be tackled historically. Clearly, we can see in this case how history is not a pure and academic science; more precisely, it *is* a pure and academic science, but the more pure and academic it is, the more it is committed and political.

This colonial unconscious also includes something of the war of liberation – the truth of the war of liberation. I have read two or three theses on the war, which I believe have remained unpublished, and these have made me appreciate how this was one of the most tragic histories that humanity has ever known. The history of successive purges (by the FLN, within the FLN, by the French army, etc.) has been buried under the ritual praise for the *moudjahidin* in which everybody has joined. Thus the 1954 declaration, which has become a commonplace of anniversary celebrations, if you read it again today, has many good qualities, but these are obscured by anti-colonialist rhetoric. Marx somewhere denounces the retrospective cult of past revolutions.

* Intervention at the conference 'Algeria–France–Islam' organized by the Centre Français de l'Université de Fribourg en Brisgau and the Centre de Sociologie Européenne du Collège de France on 27–8 October 1995, published by L'Harmattan in 1997.

The Algerians are past masters of retrospective revolutionism (something they learned from the French, a part of their colonial unconscious), and this has very often served as an alibi for the establishment of conservatism. The Soviet model also played a part, of course. There is superfluity of choice for this kind of thing today. So many revolutions have been misled that there is not even any need to reinvent a pseudo-revolutionary rhetoric. We need only dip into the arsenal of failed revolutions.

It is also necessary, in a balance-sheet of the repressed, to include the history of the repression of the Algerian revolution, which is one of the great shameful sicknesses of the French conscience; I could tell dozens of anecdotes about the tragic memories that many French people have of the Algerian liberation war. There is a French suffering about Algeria, as Joseph Jurt put it, which we still need to draw on if we are to consider and act seriously. Unfortunately, this French suffering also generates very damaging impulses of collective paranoia, and you need only walk around one of the Paris railway stations today to have the sense of seeing a remake of a film about Algeria from the 1960s. In other times, France was a model for a certain number of things (including human rights), but it is in the process of becoming a model for collective regression into barbarism – and, as there are barbarians in all countries, this negative model risks becoming universalized. We must fear that other European states will seek justification from the bad example that France is now giving, and similarly renounce their generous politics on questions of immigration. And unfortunately, if you go along the Kabyl coast today, you also get the impression that the Algerian army is repeating what the French army did at that time, so that the Algerian war is being replayed in a dramatic fashion on both sides of the Mediterranean, with the same phobias, the same madness, the same primitive reflexes of military barbarism.

In this colonial unconscious that has to be brought into the light of day, there is among other things the effects of a kind of servile imitation of the French state. Touring Algeria immediately after independence, I was struck (as I wrote at the time) by seeing all kinds of people replaying scenes of everyday colonialism, for example in the offices of the colonial administration, or a high civil servant with all the external signs of arrogance that are so typically French. All this of course in the name of the anti-colonial struggle. This relationship to the state seems to me to merit a much deeper analysis. How did the French state model come to impose itself in this way? How was it imitated even without the conditions of its operation being ensured? The historical conditions of operation of a modern state that is the product of a long historical development are not immediately given, they can only be produced by the work of the educational system, by a civic education, by a struggle against the vestiges of feudalism, against the traditions of nepotism inherent to a certain state of family structures, etc. Otherwise you end up with feudal-socialist models (in which, as my friend and student M'hammed Boukhobza, recently murdered, showed, bureaucratic structures and socialist rhetoric serve to mask and support the perpetuation of the great privileged lineages). All these things are very well known to specialists, but they have to be made public; they should not remain the privilege of the scholarly community.

Another site of repression is the problem of intellectuals. I believe that part of this kind of civil war that we are facing derives from the fact that Algerian intellectuals continued their intellectual struggles by other means. In general, intellectuals are reduced to using symbolic weapons for their battles, but as soon as they have the opportunity and the resources, they move on to other weapons. We know the role that they play in national civil wars – the case of Yugoslavia, for example. It is always said that intellectuals are good for nothing. In fact, when they want to act against the tendencies immanent in society, they are powerless; but when they act for the worst they are very effective, as they offer an expression and legitimization for a society's dark and shameful impulses. This means that an intellectual world that is badly analyzed, badly self-analyzed, is very dangerous. And if I had to indicate a 'dangerous class', in the nineteenth-century expression, I would say that it is intellectuals, and particularly those whom Max Weber called 'proletaroid intellectuals': such as the defrocked petty clergy who led the millennial movements of the Middle Ages, or the revolutionary agitators of 1789. Intellectuals have a very big responsibility, and in the repression I refer to, Algerian intellectuals played an enormous role. Here again, there is no great sense in speaking in general: the intelligentsia is a field in which there are dominant and dominated, there are struggles, people who fight against obscurantism, against repression, etc. But by and large, the overall results, to speak as statisticians do, are pretty devastating. We should therefore work towards a historical sociology of intellectuals in their relationship with language, state, nation, the Berber problem, the problem of Arabization, etc. It is impossible to tackle any problem properly without breaking through the smokescreen that intellectuals produce, and without first of all studying what they have said. The historicization that Joseph Jurt has described is not at all academic. It is not just a question of restoring historical truth, but of using history to restore a truthful relationship to history. The work of anamnesis of the historical unconscious is the major instrument for gaining mastery of history, and therefore of the present that is an extension of history. It is clearly not a question of criminalizing people (even if at times, to avoid an academic tone, I may have been a little polemical), hunting out and denouncing the guilty (which is still an effect of bad faith). Nor of shifting the guilt onto others, as retrospective revolutionaries or prosecutors. Rather of demanding that history is assumed in its reality and its consequences. And the condition for this is to establish it, something that only the scholarly community can do.

I have moved on very naturally, it seems to me, from problems of knowledge to problems of action, and I believe that, as I said just now, the Algerian problem raises the question of the specific responsibility of scholars in a particularly sharp way. There is a whole tradition of commitment in France, initiated by Zola, which strikes me as perfectly respectable. The duty of communicating the truth is part of the business of the scholar; here again you can appeal to Max Weber. There is a responsibility of scholars, above all in a situation like that of Algeria, where we are dealing with a problem that is largely a historical artefact, constructed essentially by the media. If it is true, as I genuinely believe, that social reality in modern societies is to a very large extent constructed by the media, which are the dominant means of production of the dominant discourse on the social world, we are less disarmed than we are in fighting economic forces. We are better equipped to combat the multinationals of symbolic production that produce the celebrated 'social problems', on condition that we have even a small ability to organize ourselves so as to give some effectiveness to the truth, knowing as we do that this does not have a spontaneous effectiveness. I often quote Spinoza, who said that 'there is no intrinsic force in the true idea'. This is one of the saddest sentences in the entire history of thought. It means that the truth is very weak, lacking in strength. As a result, those of us working to produce the truth, who tacitly believe that it is important to produce the truth, and that it is important to distribute the truth because we teach, talk, write it, etc. – do we not have to try to reflect on the need to unite in order to collectively give a bit of social force to truth, if we are to be in agreement with ourselves, to avoid being too contradictory and too desperate?

1995–2001

We have to reject a false and hypocritical neutrality, and above all the depoliticized political philosophy that leads straight to the MEDEF[1] table.

[1] [Mouvement des Entreprises de France, the French employers' federation.]

10

Supporting Social Struggles

From December 1995 to Raisons d'Agir

Conservative discourse always hides behind the name of good sense
Choses dites, 1987

The social movement of December 1995 arose from the conjunction of several crises: a student contestation accompanied from November by a mobilization of activist networks in higher education; a public transport strike in reaction to the announcement of a state plan for the SNCF and a reform of the pension system, which helped to block traffic and activities in the big conurbations; and finally, following the announcement on 15 November of the 'Juppé plan' for reforming social security, envisaging the reduction of public expenditure in the name of a struggle against exclusion, the development of various forms of resistance for which the mobilizations of the day offered a privileged expression.[2]

In reaction to these mobilizations, the inspirers of the Fondation Saint-Simon[3] *and* Esprit *magazine launched a petition in support of the government, 'Pour une réforme de fond de la Sécurité sociale', which stigmatized as archaic both the existing health-care system and those who rejected the proposed reform. In support of the strikers, Pierre Bourdieu participated in drafting an appeal at the initiative of academics close to activist circles, which was published in* Le Monde *on 5 December 1995.*[4] *The demonstration of 12 December, which brought out over a million people, ended with a meeting at the Gare de Lyon during which Bourdieu spoke in defence of the public services threatened by*

---

[2] Cf. René Mouriaux and Sophie Béroud, eds, *Le Souffle de décembre* (Paris: Syllepse 1997). [Ed.]

[3] *The Fondation Saint-Simon* was established in December 1982 by François Furet, Pierre Rosanvallon, Emmanuel Le Roy-Ladurie, Simon and Pierre Nora, Alain Minc and Roger Fauroux. It brought together academics, businesspeople and senior civil servants, and 'performed an ideological work of dissimulating political work . . . to construct the "narrow path" followed by political leaders towards market democracy as the "end of history" and social-liberalism as the insurpassable horizon for our societies'. Cf. in particular Keith Dixon, *Les Évangélistes du marché. Les intellectuels britanniques et le libéralisme* (Paris: Raisons d'Agir 1998); Vincent Laurent, 'Enquête sur la fondation Saint-Simon. Les architectes du social-libéralisme', *Le Monde Diplomatique*, September 1998; Serge Halimi, 'Les boîtes à idées de la droite américaine', *Le Monde Diplomatique*, May 1995. [Ed.]

[4] Cf. Julian Duval, Christophe Gaudert, Frédéric Lebaron, Dominique Marchetti and Fabienne Pavis, *Le Décembre des intellectuels français* (Paris: Raisons d'Agir 1998). [Ed.]

neoliberal policies; he particularly denounced the action of 'a state nobility who preach the withering away of the state and the undivided rule of the market and the consumer'.[5] Against the experts who based their authority on economics, Bourdieu thus proclaimed his support for those whom the technocratic elites present as a people dominated by their 'impulses', to whom rational policies have to be dictated from above – as suggested by the philosopher Paul Ricoeur (Le Journal de Dimanche, 10 December). Bourdieu's analyses focused on the social mechanisms by which neoliberalism had been imposed in France since the 1980s (see pp.288, 294 and 300).

Pierre Bourdieu's criticisms directly bore on successive French governments: immigration policy, with the Pasqua-Debré laws (1993–95) that authorized discrimination on the basis of appearance (see p.286); the refusal to regularize immigrants without proper documentation (see p.284), which led in 1996 to a major mobilization of voluntary organizations that continued the movement of December 1995; then the silence of the left in the battle of homosexuals for equality before the law (see p.282); and again, the 'advertising effects' of the minister of education, Claude Allègre (see p.302). Bourdieu sought to lend the full weight of his scientific celebrity, often in association with other intellectuals, in support of activists situated in the 'vanguard' of contestation;[6] as well as of all those, from 1997 on, who saw the politics of the Jospin government as departing from the ideals of the left (see p.296).

In January 1998, Pierre Bourdieu publicly intervened in support of the movement of unemployed, whose forms of direct action, under the impulse of a mobilized minority of activists, had captured media attention. The occupation of the École Normale Supérieure gave him the opportunity to stress the 'social miracle' constituted by the mobilization of those whose situation tends to atomize and disorganize them.[7] The cause of the unemployed enabled him to denounce the generalized precariousness maintained by liberal policies (see p.294); the 'objective insecurity' of the world of work lay at the root of the 'subjective insecurity' that affected both permanently employed and casual workers, making it possible to apply policies of flexibility and establish new modes of domination.[8]

As well as particular interventions of this kind, Pierre Bourdieu sought to create an ongoing framework for his action. Since the 'general assembly' project had no further sequel after 1996 (see p.280), he put into practice his idea of the 'collective intellectual' by bringing together researchers with a similar orientation

---

[5] Speech published under the title 'Against the Destruction of a Civilization', *Acts of Resistance* (Cambridge: Polity 1998), pp. 24–8. [Ed.]
[6] Cf. 'Some Questions on the Gay and Lesbian Movement', in *Masculine Domination* (Cambridge: Polity 2001), pp. 118–24. [Ed.]
[7] Cf. 'The Protest Movement of the Unemployed, a Social Miracle', *Acts of Resistance*, pp. 88–90. [Ed.]
[8] 'Job Insecurity is Everywhere Now', *Acts of Resistance*, pp. 81–7. [Ed.]

to his own. This was the collective Raisons d'Agir, designed to place the analytical skills of researchers at the service of movements resisting neoliberal policies, and thus counterbalance the influence of conservative think-tanks.[9] Starting from the basis of the public success of The Weight of the World *and the collective work this inspired, the group engaged in symbolic struggles against the imposition by experts, especially economists, of neoliberal dogma. Sociological work, in the form of making visible what was hidden in the customary perceptions of the social world, then served as a foundation for political interventions by the collective in the press and through public lectures and debates.[10]*

For the distribution of 'intellectual weapons of resistance', Pierre Bourdieu also founded a collection of low-price books, selling at between 30 and 40 francs – Liber-Raisons d'Agir – designed to offer works of social sciences to a broad public in an accessible form, along with analyses that were blocked by the media censorship, especially when these bore on the media themselves.

Liber-Raisons d'Agir intends to present the most advanced state of research on current political and social problems. Conceived and realized by researchers in social science, sociologists, historians and economists, but also sometimes by writers and artists, all inspired by an activist desire to distribute the knowledge indispensable for political discussion and action in a democracy, these booklets, small but dense and well-documented, are designed to add up to a kind of international popular encyclopaedia.

The first two titles in the series, which attracted great attention and public debate,[11] began the distribution of a critique of the field of journalism, which Pierre Bourdieu and his collaborators had begun to analyze several years earlier.

---

[9] A counterpart on the left to the many right-wing think-tanks was the Fondation Copernic, established to renew and defend the gains of the welfare state. [Ed.]

[10] As well as regular publication by the collective in *Le Monde Diplomatique*, Pierre Bourdieu coordinated a special issue of *Les Inrockuptibles*, 'Joyeux bordel' (December 1998–January 1999), giving voice here to trade unionists and activists in voluntary organizations, as well as researchers, artists and philosophers. [Ed.]

[11] *Sur la télévision* (1996) sold over 140,000 copies, and Serge Halimi's *Les Nouveaux chiens de garde* (1997) reached 100,000 in less than six months. [Ed.]

A look back at the December 1995 strikes*

In both Germany and France, many intellectuals and political figures stigmatized the strikes of December 1995 as retrograde and corporatist. Could one not consider them, on the contrary, as movements reacting to the neoliberal policies that required a withdrawal of the state in conformity with the Maastricht criteria?

The subordination of certain intellectuals towards political and economic forces has never been so visible as it was in the context of this movement, which was surprising in both its scope and its duration. Not content to describe it as a kind of reactionary movement, retrograde and archaic, even nationalist and racist (as Michel Weivorka[12] claimed in a *Le Monde* article), some of them – especially journalists, whose often exorbitant privileges are well-known, including 'journalist philosophers' – denounced the privileges of the strikers, especially those of the SNCF, those 'affluent' workers bent on defending gains that were purely and simply equated with privileges. Despite all the signs to the contrary. For example, at the demonstration at the Gare de Lyon, when I expressed the solidarity of intellectuals (or, more exactly, a section of them), the strikers were applauded like mad by the crowd – as well as the representatives of various trade unions (especially the new SUD union, those who split away from the CFDT when it supported the government and attracted a number of authors of the so-called 'text of experts' in favour of the government), representatives of the movements in support of the homeless (Droit au Logement), of illegal immigrants threatened with expulsion, and of immigrants more generally. This solidarity by workers with unemployed and immigrants has since been repeatedly asserted, for example in the context of the movement of 'civil disobedience' opposed to the strengthening of the 'racial laws' promulgated by Pasqua. Those among the journalists and journalist-intellectuals who described this movement as 'populism', seeking to make an amalgam between it and Le Pen's Front National, are either stupid or dishonest, if not both (I have in mind Jacques Juilliard, better known as editorialist on *Le Nouvel Observateur* than as a historian, who tried to lump me together with Pasqua in his book on the

---

* Interview with Margareta Steinrücke, published in *Sozialismus* 6, 1997.
[12] Michel Wievorka , a sociologist and director of CADIS, a workshop established by Alain Touraine, signed in December 1995 the position in support of the Juppé government's policy. (Cf. Julien Duval et al., *Le Décembre des intellectuels français*, op. cit.)

1995 events). This kind of amalgam lies at the root of the conservative critique of all the criticisms made of Maastricht-style Europe, and the neoliberal policy practised in its name. In every case the aim is to rule out the very possibility of a left-wing critique of the reactionary economic and social policy that covers itself with liberal or even libertarian language ('flexibility', 'deregulation', etc.), with the myth of 'globalization' presenting this forced liberty that is proposed to us as an inevitable destiny.

It seems that the 1995 strikes in France played a role of precursor in Europe. Protest movements have subsequently developed in other countries, especially Germany with the miners and steelworkers, and the mobilizations against the dismantling of the welfare state. Does that not invalidate the theme of the end of history (as class struggle) developed by conservatives after the fall of the so-called Communist regimes?

The French movement has certainly had tremendous repercussions throughout Europe (rather like 1848); it has undoubtedly contributed to accelerating an awakening consciousness, and above all to showing that, despite mass unemployment and the precarious position of all manual and intellectual workers, a movement is possible.

Nothing has given me greater pleasure (and I am not alone in this) than the innumerable messages of solidarity addressed to the movement of December 1995, as well as the explicit reference that the German workers on strike made to the French movement. But the most important thing is that people have understood everywhere that what lies concealed beneath the appeal to economic necessity is a return to a modernized form of naked capitalism, via the demolition of the welfare state. I believe in fact that the collapse of the so-called 'Communist' or 'socialist' regimes – not that this has anything to do with an end of history (which would suppose, paradoxically, that these regimes had genuinely been communist or even socialist) – has given the dominant a temporary advantage in their struggle to impose conditions most favourable to their interests. And we have seen the reappearance of forms of exploitation that are worthy of the nineteenth century, or even worse in a certain sense, to the extent that they put the most up-to-date strategies of management at the service of the maximization of profit.

What spurred you to show solidarity with the strikers, as against the many French intellectuals who remained very reserved or even hostile towards the movement? What led you to give this speech to the railway workers at the Gare de Lyon, and thus appear (for example in Germany) as the only point of criticism to the European liberalism of Maastricht?

It was certainly my research – and I have particularly in mind *The Weight of the World* – that prepared me to understand the significance of this movement of revolt against the withdrawal of the state. Whereas the majority of French intellectuals sing the praises of liberalism, I was able to measure the catastrophic effects that these initial measures in a liberal direction produced – in the field of housing, for example. I could see the consequences of the 'casualization' of employment, in both the public and private sectors; I have in mind here, for example, the effects of censorship and enforced conformity that insecurity at work produces, particularly in cultural production and broadcasting, among people working in radio and television, among journalists and increasingly also among teachers. As distinct from the majority of 'intellectuals' who speak in the media, my work made me informed about the reality of the social world – without being too distorted, as many economists are, by a faith in formal constructions. I believe that the authority of economics and economists is undoubtedly one of the factors responsible for the complicity that a number of intellectuals have extended to the dominant discourse – or at least the reserve that they have maintained, convinced that they had neither the necessary competence to adequately assess discourses on 'globalization' or on the economic constraints associated with the Maastricht treaty. Intellectuals are always prey to the effects of theory, but so too, more subtly, are the leaders of social movements and workers themselves (particularly by way of the economic doctrine that radio and television constantly pour out, and to which minor intellectuals with a sprinkling of economic training have given their support – as in the French case the essayists of the Fondation Saint-Simon, *Esprit* and *Le Débat*). This all makes particularly necessary the intervention of researchers who are well enough informed and equipped to be able to combat on an equal basis those fine speakers who are often very poorly trained, and appeal to the authority of a science that they have not mastered to impose a completely political vision of the world of economics.

In fact, this dominant discourse is extremely fragile, and only a little work is needed to see this – but in these matters, intellectuals are more keen to repeat the impressions of public opinion or the verdict of journalists. I remember for example having felt (and expressed) doubts about the credo of 'globalization' (and 'delocalization' which is a *marxisant* variant of the term) by observing that the share of European imports coming from non-European countries, while rising very slightly over the last thirty years (by about 1 per cent) remains relatively very low (less than 10 per cent of GDP). Trade between Europe and the newly industrialized countries, such as those of South-East Asia, represents rather less than 1 per cent of European GDP. You can see here how the myth of Hong Kong and Singapore is a new variation of the old 'yellow peril' that has been brandished to us (like the myth of Japan to the Americans) in order to justify as necessary, inevitable and fatal, policies designed to demolish the social gains of the workers. A fact such as this, which everyone can grasp with a little effort, and which, once the self-evidence of *doxa* is broken (a para-doxical break such as is incumbent on any genuine researcher), is increasingly current today (though without yet reaching newspapers and journalists!), is enough to spoil all fatalistic discourses and stop blaming 'globalization' for all the evils of the day, starting with unemployment. It even allows us to discover that a common European policy aiming to prohibit social dumping, which tends to pull all countries down to the level of the most disadvantaged in terms of the social gains of the workers, could neutralize the harmful effects of competition; and, more precisely, that a policy designed to achieve a reduction in working hours without a reduction in wages could bring a solution to unemployment without leading to the catastrophic consequences that are invoked by those opposing such a measure.

You can see that I was not so irresponsible and unrealistic when I maintained in December 1995 that the issue at stake in the strike was the defence of the social gains of a section of workers, and through this, of a whole civilization embodied and guaranteed by the welfare state, able to defend the right to work, the right to housing, the right to education, etc. And it is in the same logic that I could oppose to what I have called 'Tietmeyer thought'[13] (very close in its fatalism to what in other times was called 'Mao Tse-tung thought'), the need to create, in opposition to the European central bank, political institutions and a European welfare state able to manage the European economic and social space in a rational fashion (with a rationality quite distinct from the short-term rationality of service economists, and able above all to release the various states from the mad competition for competitivity by strengthening 'wage rigour' and 'flexibility'). This would stimulate them to a reasoned cooperation in policies of reducing working time along with stimulating demand and investment in new technologies, policies that are impossible or ruinous, according to our false experts, these 'semi-smart' fellows, as long as they are pursued simply by one country in isolation. (There is no need for me to say that a policy of this kind, by its very success, would make conceivable and realizable an action designed to transform power relations at the level of the global economic field, and reverse at least partially the effects of imperialism – of which immigration is not the least.)

---

[13] After the president of the German Bundesbank, presented by the press of that time as the 'high priest of the deutschmark'. (Cf. 'The Thoughts of Chairman Tietmeyer' (1996), reprinted in *Acts of Resistance*, pp. 45–51.) [Ed.]

The Raisons d'Agir collective emerged from this experience of solidarity with the strikers. What are its objectives and its modes of action? What have been its effects?

The working group Raisons d'Agir, which we established immediately after the December strikes to try to give practical embodiment to the kind of 'collective intellectual' for which I had been calling for many years, was born out of a concern to produce instruments for a practical solidarity between intellectuals and strikers. We met on a regular basis and brought out very cheap booklets presenting the results of the most advanced research on important political, social and cultural problems, along with concrete proposals for action as far as this was possible. The first in this series was my own booklet *Sur la télévision*, which was extraordinarily successful (sales have now reached nearly 100,000), enabling us to finance the subsequent booklets without a problem – I forgot to say that we actually established a publishing house.

So that this work could be really serious and effective, it had to be accomplished on an international footing. We set up (with your assistance in Germany) a network of researchers and research groups, which we hope to be able to mobilize around various subjects (for example, we sent all members of the network a kind of questionnaire on the subject of immigration policy), and whose works we hope to be able to produce in French. One of the functions of this network is to familiarize ourselves with studies already published that deserve to appear in French in the collection 'Raisons d'Agir' (we will need funds to pay properly for the translations) and to produce original texts suitable for publication in a number of languages (several publishers – German, Greek, Italian, American, etc. – have agreed to publish virtually the whole series). This will gradually constitute a kind of great international popular encyclopaedia in which activists from all countries will be able to find the intellectual weapons needed for their struggles. It is a difficult undertaking; the social sciences have made tremendous progress, and it is only at the price of a quite special effort, in which only convinced activists can participate, that we shall be able to find in each case the simple and effective mode of expression that will make it possible to transmit the results of research without loss or distortion.

Appeal for a general assembly
of the social movement[*]

What society do we want to live in, and what society do we want our children to live in? This is indeed the question that the social movement of November–December 1995 raised, and this is certainly the reason why a very large majority of the population saw it as legitimate. The big problems indicated by the strikers and demonstrators are in fact problems for all women and men.

What struggle against unemployment and exclusion, for a society of full employment, in particular through a reduction in working time?

What public services, guarantors of equality and solidarity, close to citizens and creating jobs?

What different Europe for tomorrow, turning its back on liberalism – a Europe that is democratic, ecological and social?

The social movement very forcefully raised the question of effectively equal rights for all, men and women, nationals and immigrants, urban and rural. How is it possible to fight for the rights of women, and conquer genuine political and social equality? How can we defend access to knowledge and employment for young people, and guarantee public education open to all? How can we combat exclusion, establish a right to housing, and new rights for the unemployed, the excluded, and casual workers?

The challenges imposed by globalization, in each country and in all countries, call for a global response, which cannot consist in submission to the laws of the market. The social movement, in its way, has already brought elements of such a response. No one however can claim that definite responses have been provided to all these different questions. They will emerge from debate and discussion, with all affected having their voice, rather than from the verdict of pseudo-experts.

In December, intellectuals, trade unionists of all kinds, activists in the women's movement, associations of unemployed and homeless already made common cause. We propose today that they should come together, in a form open to all, in each town in France, to develop their responses to the questions raised, starting from everyday problems and involving all citizens. We propose setting up in this way, right away and throughout 1996, a broad general assembly, pluralistic and decentralized, at which grievances can be noted and

* Collective text, Archives of the Collège de France.

proposals developed. We propose the circulation of texts and documents, reports and questionnaires. We propose that all these decentralized approaches should be the object of a general discussion on 24 October 1996, the anniversary of the start of the railway workers' strike. This is also something for us to do together.

We invite all women and men who identify with this appeal to take every initiative for discussion and joint work, and to make these widely known.

In support of the march for homosexual visibility[*]

I would have liked to be here this evening and extend my support. I have long been aware of the efforts that homosexuals have ceaselessly made, as you are doing today, to obtain full and complete recognition of their existence, their rights, their right to existence. I am also aware of the resistance provoked by such action – even in its most 'respectable' forms – and demands. One of the contradictions that all struggles by victims of symbolic violence encounter is this: either to bend themselves to the norms of good behaviour that are imposed on them even in their revolt against the injustices, humiliations and stigmatizations imposed on them in the name of good behaviour; or else to transgress these norms, by provocative actions of symbolic subversion that may win the sympathy of people of good will, but at the same time risk reinforcing stigmatization and contempt. Every day gives illustrations of this pincer effect. I do not however believe that this should condemn you to inaction, or condemn us to inaction.

I believe it is time to create a wide movement, grouping homosexuals and heterosexuals, in solidarity with all organizations engaged in struggle against symbolic violence and discrimination, i.e. all forms of racism by gender (or sex), ethnicity (or language), and class (or culture).

The appeal launched by 234 personalities that was published in *Le Nouvel Observateur* on 9 May 1996 is a first step in this direction. Its object was to organize a struggle against all forms of legal discrimination based on non-recognition of the homosexual couple: absence of inheritance rights including the right to inherit housing leases, absence of the status of supporter of a family (which implies exemption from military service), refusal of the advantages granted to heterosexual couples by airlines, etc. The defects of the law, apart from the fact that they reveal an archaic state of collective thinking, offer countless weapons – like the Pasqua laws in other areas – for all those inhabited by anti-homosexual racism. We must thus struggle by every means to obtain genuine *legal equality* for homosexuals.

But this is not enough. We need a proliferation of symbolic actions, uniting heterosexuals and homosexuals, both large-scale actions like this

[*] A text read on the platform at the Place de la Nation for the rally at the end of the march for homosexual visibility organized by Lesbian and Gay Pride on Saturday, 22 June 1996. This intervention gave rise to a text jointly signed with Jacques Derrida, Didier Éribon, Michelle Perrot, Paul Veyne and Pierre Vidal-Nacquet, which was published in *Le Monde* on 1 March 1996 under the heading 'Pour une reconnaissance du couple homosexuel'.

march, and small-scale actions in the context of the workshop, office, or business, designed to roll back, by way of vigilance and assistance at every point, both shame and guilt, and contempt, derision and insult.

That is what I wanted to say, undoubtedly a little clumsily. And please know that in any case, I am with you with all my heart.[14]

---

[14] The Pacte Civil de Solidarité (PACS), adopted in October 1999 on the proposal of the Socialist minister of justice, Élisabeth Guigou, met the greater part of the demands that this text makes. [Ed.]

Combat state xenophobia[*]

There is a lot that could be said, and said again, on the policies of the government over this summer, and not just on the question of the reception of foreigners. But the latest measure of M. Debré is exemplary in its absurdity, and reveals the blatant incoherence and demagogic crassness of his policy.

Instead of regularizing the situation of the 300 'sans-papiers' who occupied the church of Saint-Bernard in Paris, and have struggled since last March to obtain residence cards, the minister of the interior forcibly hospitalized on 12 August the ten foreigners who had been conducting a hunger strike for nearly forty days, on behalf of the whole group. According to medical advice, their state of health was not yet serious. So this was simply a show of force designed to demonstrate the government's repressive determination.

This intervention is absurd. It disregards the distress of thousands of foreigners who are not clandestine simply because they lack the right papers. These are people who came from countries suffering violence and requested political asylum, the spouses and children of foreigners in a regularized situation who are refused the right to live with their families, people who have lived legitimately in France for many years and who have made multiple requests to obtain residence cards and work. Since spring this year, some twenty occupations of offices and hunger strikes, across the whole of France, have brought to public attention the distress of these men and women, who only took such extreme action after exhausting all other recourse.

There is no possible outcome today except a regularization of the situation of these foreigners who have gradually over the past twenty years been caught in the trap of laws that are ever harsher, based on the unrealistic and liberticidal myth of a closure of French borders. How can the government be forced to break with this policy, criminal in both its motivation and its stupidity, a policy that involves us all? How can we combat the state xenophobia it establishes, which by the effect of habit risks steadily imposing itself as a dogma? How can we prevent the most shameful form of demagogy from establishing itself in power by proxy?

The appeal to fasts in solidarity, conducted all over France with the aim of obtaining a regularization of the Saint-Bernard 'sans-papiers' and other

[*] AFP press release of 14 August 1996, regarding the publication in Libération, on 3 May 1995, of the results of an investigation by a group set up to examine how the election programmes of the various political parties tackled the question of foreigners resident in France; a theme continued in the text 'Le sort des étrangers comme schibboleth', published in Contre-feux, pp. 21–4.

foreigners in similar situations seems to me to offer a preliminary response to these questions. Solidarity with foreigners threatened in their rights, dignity, and their very existence, can be the basis for a new solidarity with all those determined to resist the politics of baseness.

Enough state racism!*

We've had enough of the prevarications and procrastinations of all those in positions of 'responsibility', elected by us, who claim they are 'not responsible' when we remind them of the promises that they made us. We've had enough of the state racism that they authorize. Today again, one of my friends, a Frenchman of Algerian origin, told me the story of his daughter, who went to register at university, and was asked by an official there to present her papers and her passport, simply on seeing that she had an Arab-sounding name.

To put an end once and for all to these insults and humiliations, which would have been unthinkable a few years ago, we have to make a clean break with a hypocritical legislation that is no more than an immense concession to the xenophobia of the Front National. To repeal the Pasqua and Debré laws, of course, but also put an end to the hypocritical statements of all those politicians who – at the very moment when the compromises that the French bureaucracy made over the deportation of Jews are under the spotlight – are giving more or less free rein to all those in the bureaucracy who are in a position to express their most stupidly xenophobic impulses, like the university official that I mentioned above.

It is pointless to get drawn into grand legal debates as to the comparative merits of this law or that. The question is to abolish completely a law that, by its very existence, legitimizes discriminatory practices by officials high and low, and contributes to casting global suspicion on foreigners – and of course, not just any foreigners. What kind of citizen are you, if you have to prove your citizenship at every turn? (A number of French parents of Algerian origin wonder what names they should give their children to spare them trouble of this kind. And the official who harassed my friend's daughter was astonished that her first name was Mélanie . . .)

I say that a law that authorizes any official to question someone's citizenship on the basis of their face or their family name alone, as is the case a thousand times a day today, is a racist law. It is regrettable that there is not, in the very civilized government that M. Jospin has offered us, a single person bearing one or other of these stigmas destined for the irreproachable arbitrariness of the officials of the French state, a dark face or an Arab-sounding name, to remind M. Chevènement of the distinction

* Published in Les Inrockuptibles 121, 11–14 November 1997.

between law and custom, and that there are legal dispositions that authorize the worst of customs.

I leave all this for the consideration of those who, silent and indifferent today, will in thirty years' time express their 'repentance', at a time when young French people of Algerian origin have names such as Kelkal.[15]

---

[15] Following a wave of attacks starting on 25 July (explosion in a suburban railway carriage at the Saint-Michel station, causing eight deaths and eighty-four wounded), a manhunt led on 29 September to the shooting by gendarmes of Khaled Kelkal, a young man from Vaux-en-Velin (Rhône) who was presumed to be a terrorist and suspected of being involved in the summer attacks. In an atmosphere 'worthy of the Far West, with posters of persons wanted and parachutist costumes', images were widely broadcast of a body 'riddled with eleven bullets and a twisted head'. (Henri Leclerc, 'Terrorisme et République', Le Monde Diplomatique, February 1996.) [Ed.]

Neoliberalism as conservative revolution*

I am grateful to the Ernst Bloch Institute and its director Klaus Kufeld, the town of Ludwigshafen and its mayor Wolfgang Schulte, and to Ulrich Beck for his very generous *laudatio* that made me believe we can see at a time not far off the realization of that utopia of the European collective intellectual that I have for a very long time been calling for.

I am aware that the honour that is done me by placing me under the aegis of a great champion of utopia, a place that is today discredited, despised and ridiculed in the name of economic realism, is a stimulus and justification for trying to define what the role of intellectual can and should be today, in its relationship to utopia and especially the European utopia.

We stand at a time of neo-conservative restoration. But this conservative revolution is taking an unprecedented form: it is not as in other times a question of evoking an idealized past by the exaltation of blood and soil – agrarian and archaic themes. This new type of conservative revolution appeals to progress, reason and science (economics, in this event) to justify restoration, and seeks in this way to dispatch progressive thought and action to an archaic past. It erects into norms for all practice, and thus ideal rules, the actual regularities of the economic world abandoned to its own logic, the so-called law of the market, in other words the law of the strongest. It ratifies and glorifies the reign of what are called financial markets, and thus the return to a kind of radical capitalism, with no other law than that of maximum profit, capitalism with no restraint or disguise, but rationalized and driven to the limit of its economic efficiency by the introduction of new forms of domination such as management, market research, marketing and advertising.

If this conservative revolution is deceptive, it is that it seems no longer to have anything in common with the old pastoral Black Forest of the conservative revolutionaries of the 1930s;[16] it is decked out with all the signs of modernity. Does it not come from Chicago? Galileo said that the natural world is written in the language of mathematics. Today, we are led to believe that the economic and social world is made up of equations. It is by arming itself with mathematics (along with media power) that neoliberalism has become the supreme form of conservative theodicy, proclaiming itself since the end of the 1960s under the name of the 'end of ideologies' – or, more recently, the 'end of history'.

---

* Speech made on the occasion of the award of the Ernst Bloch prize 1997, published in K. Kufeld, ed., *Zukunft Gestalten. Reden und Beiträge zum Ernst-Bloch-Preis 1997* (Talheimer 1998).
[16] A reference to Martin Heidegger – see. p.221 above. [Ed.]

What is proposed to us as an unsurpassable horizon of thought, and the end of critical utopias, is nothing more than an *economistic fatalism*, to which we can apply the criticism that Ernst Bloch addressed to the economism and fatalism that lurked within Marxism:

> [T]he same man who drove the fetish character out of production, who believed he had analyzed, exorcised every irrationality from history as merely unexamined, uncomprehended and therefore operatively fateful obscurities of the class situation, who had banished every dream, every operative utopia, every *telos* circulating in religion from history, plays with the 'forces of production', with the calculus of the 'process of production, the same all too constitutive game, the same pantheism, mythicism, upholds for it the same ultimately utilizing, guiding power which Hegel upheld for the 'Idea', indeed which Schopenhauer upheld for his alogical 'Will'.[17]

This fetishism of the productive forces leading to fatalism can be found today, paradoxically, among the prophets of neoliberalism and the high priests of monetary stability and the deutschmark. Neoliberalism is a powerful economic theory, which reinforces, by the particular symbolic power bound up with its theory effect, the power of economic realities that it is deemed to express. It ratifies the spontaneous philosophy of the heads of the big multinationals and the agents of high finance (particularly the managers of pension funds), which is echoed throughout the world by politicians and high officials, both national and international, and above all by the world of major journalists, almost all of whom are equally ignorant of the underlying mathematical theory, and thus becomes a kind of universal belief, a new ecumenical gospel. This gospel, or rather the woolly vulgate that we are offered on all sides under the name of liberalism, is made up of a series of terms that are poorly defined, such as 'globalization', 'flexibility', 'deregulation', etc., and that, by their liberal or even libertarian connotations, can contribute to giving the outward appearance of a message of freedom and liberation to a conservative ideology that sees itself opposed to all ideology.

In actual fact, this philosophy has no other purpose than the ever increasing creation of wealth – and, more secretly, its concentration in the hands of a small privileged minority; and this leads it to struggle with all means, including the destruction of the environment and the sacrifice of human beings, against every obstacle to the maximization of profit. The champions of laissez-faire, Thatcher and Reagan and their successors, actually have no intention to

---

[17] Ernst Bloch, *The Spirit of Utopia* (Stanford: Stanford University Press 2000), p. 241.

'*laisser faire*'; to free the terrain for the logic of the financial markets, they have to wage total war against trade unions, the social gains of past centuries, in short, against the whole civilization associated with the welfare state.

Neoliberal politics can be judged today by results that are familiar to all, despite the falsifications based on manipulation of statistics and crude trickery, which make believe that the United States and Great Britain have attained full employment. There is mass unemployment in these countries, and a growing proportion of citizens, even in the middle class, are subject to the precariousness of casual work and above all constant insecurity; there is deep demoralization bound up with the collapse of basic solidarities, especially those of the family, with all the consequences that ensue from this state of anomie, such as juvenile delinquency, crime, drugs, alcoholism, the resurgence of fascist-style movements, etc; not to mention the steady destruction of social gains, the defence of which is described as archaic conservatism. On top of this we see today the destruction of the economic and social foundations of humanity's most precious cultural gains. The autonomy of the world of cultural production from the market, which had previously been steadily increasing thanks to the struggles and sacrifices of writers, artists and scholars, is now increasingly threatened. The reign of commerce and commercialism imposes itself more each day on literature, particularly through the concentration of publishing, ever more directly subject to the constraints of immediate profit, of cinema (one might well ask what will be left of avant-garde cinema in ten years' time, if nothing is done to offer its producers means of production and perhaps still more so of distribution); not to speak of the social sciences, condemned to serve the directly self-interested commands of business bureaucracies and the state, or else die from the censorship of money.

What then do intellectuals have to do with all of this? I will not try to list here all the forms of resignation, let alone collaboration – that would be too long and too cruel. I shall simply mention the discussions of so-called modern or postmodern philosophers, who, when they are not content to let things go, occupied simply with their own scholastic games, either enclose themselves in a verbal defence of reason and rational dialogue, or worse, propose a 'radical chic' variant of the ideology of the end of ideologies, with its condemnation of 'grand narratives' and nihilistic denunciation of science.

In the face of all this, which is scarcely encouraging, how can we escape demoralization? How can we give back life and social force to the 'reflective utopianism' that Ernst Bloch spoke of in relation to Bacon?[18] First of all,

---

[18] Ernst Bloch, *The Principle of Hope* (Oxford: Blackwell 1986).

what should we understand by this? Giving a rigorous sense to the Marxian opposition between 'sociologism' in the sense of pure and simple submission to social laws, and 'utopianism', the adventurous challenge to such laws, Ernst Bloch described the 'reflective utopian' as one who acts 'by virtue of a perfectly conscious presentment of the objective tendency', i.e. the objective and real possibility of his 'time', which in other words 'psychologically antic- ipates a possible reality'. Rational utopianism defines itself simultaneously against the 'pure wishful thinking that has always discredited utopia', and against 'the philistine platitude essentially occupied by the Given';[19] it is opposed both to the 'heresy, in the last analysis a defeatist one, of an objectivist automatism, according to which objective contradictions are sufficient in themselves to revolutionize the world that they affect', and 'activism *en soi'*, pure voluntarism, based on an excess of optimism.[20]

Thus against the fatalism of bankers, who want us to believe that the world cannot be otherwise than it is, i.e. in complete conformity with their interests and desires, intellectuals, and all who are genuinely concerned with human happiness, must restore a utopian thought that is scientifically sound, both compatible with objective tendencies in its goals, and with means that are also scientifically tested. They must work *collectively* on analyses able to serve as the basis for realistic projects and actions, closely tuned to the objective processes of the order that they aim to transform.

The rational utopianism that I have just defined here is certainly what is most lacking in Europe today. To the Europe that bankers' thinking seeks at all costs to impose on us, we have to oppose, not, as certain people wish, a nationalist rejection of Europe, but rather a progressive rejection of the neoliberal Europe of the banks and bankers. They have an interest in making out that any rejection of the Europe they offer is a rejection of Europe as such. To reject the Europe of the banks means rejecting the bankers' thinking that, under cover of neoliberalism, makes money the measure of all things, of the value of men and women on the labour market, and ever more closely in all dimensions of existence, and which, by establishing profit as the sole principle of valuation in matters of education, culture, art and literature, condemns us to the philistine platitude of a civilization of ratings, the best- seller, and the TV series.

Resistance to the bankers' Europe, and the conservative restoration this is preparing for us, can only be on a European scale. It can only be really European, i.e. freed from national interests and assumptions, prejudices and habits of thought, if it is the work of a concerted grouping of intellectuals

---

[19] Ibid.
[20] Ibid.

from all European countries, trade unions from all European countries, and the widest range of organizations from all European countries. The most urgent thing today, therefore, is not to draw up European programmes, but rather to create institutions (parliaments, international federations, European associations of this and that: whether lorry-drivers, publishers, teachers, etc., but also defenders of trees, fish, mushrooms, clean air, children, and so on) within which European programmes can be discussed and elaborated. The objection will be made that all this already exists: in fact, I am certain that the opposite is the case (you need only think what the European Trade Union Confederation is today), and that the only European international that is really in the course of construction and endowed with a certain effectiveness is that of the technocrats, against which I have nothing to say – I would indeed be the first to defend it against simplistic challenge, which most often is stupidly nationalist, or worse, Poujadist.

Finally, to avoid sticking to a general and abstract response to the question I raised at the start, that of the possible role of intellectuals in the construction of the European utopia, I would like to mention the personal contribution that I want to make to this immense and urgent task. Convinced as I am that the most crying gaps in European construction lie in four main fields, that of the welfare state and its functions, that of the unification of trade unions, that of the harmonization and modernization of education systems and that of the articulation between economic and social policy, I am currently working, in collaboration with researchers from a number of European countries, on conceiving and constructing the indispensable organizational structures for conducting the comparative and complementary research that is needed to give utopianism in these matters a reasoned character, particularly by bringing to light the social obstacles to a genuine Europeanization of institutions such as the state, the education system and the trade unions.

The fourth project, and the one particularly close to my heart, is that of the articulation between economic policy and what is called social policy – or, more precisely, the social effects and costs of economic policy. The question here is to try to trace the underlying causes of the different forms of *social poverty* affecting men and women in European societies – which most commonly means economic decisions. This is a way for the sociologist, who is generally brought in only to repair the damage done by economists, to recall that sociology could and should be involved at the level of political decisions, which are increasingly left to economists or inspired by economic considerations in the narrowest sense. By detailed description of the suffering generated by neoliberal policies (the kind of description that we already offered in *The Weight of the World*), and by systematically relating economic indexes, including the social policy of businesses (dismissals, forms of training, wages, etc.) with more typically social indexes (industrial accidents, occupational diseases, alcoholism, drug use, suicide, delinquency, crime, rape, etc.), the question I want to raise is that of the social costs of economic violence, as a way of laying the foundations for an economics of happiness, which takes account in its calculations of everything that the managers of the economy, and economists, leave out of the more or less fantastical accounts in the name of which they aim to govern us.

By way of conclusion, I would just like to raise the question that should be at the centre of any rational utopia concerning Europe: how to create a *really European Europe*, i.e. one freed of all dependence on all imperialisms, starting with that exercised, particular in matters of cultural production and distribution, by commercial constraints, and likewise free of all the national and nationalist vestiges that still prevent it from accumulating, increasing and distributing what is most universal in the tradition of each of the nations that compose it? To end with a 'rational utopia' that is completely concrete, I would suggest that this question, which is so essential in my view, could be placed on the programme of the Ernst Bloch Centre, and the international of 'reflective utopians' of which this might be the headquarters.

An upsurge of action by the unemployed[*]

Those women and men who today are customarily referred to as 'excluded' – excluded temporarily, provisionally, for the long term or definitively from the labour market – are almost always also excluded from collective speech and action. What is happening then, when after several years of isolated and seemingly unrewarding effort on the part of a few activists, necessarily a minority, a collective action finally succeeds in breaking the wall of media and political indifference?

First of all, the ridiculous anger and scorn, hardly disguised, of certain professionals of language – journalists, trade unionists, and politicians of both sexes – who only see the demonstrations of unemployed as an intolerable challenge to their petty interests, their monopoly of authorized speech about 'exclusion' and the 'national drama of unemployment'. Faced with this unexpected mobilization, these professional manipulators and full-time television personalities could only see it as a 'manipulation of distress', 'an operation intended for the media', the illegitimate action of a 'minority', or even an 'illegal' though peaceful action.

There followed the extension of the movement and the eruption of a minority of mobilized unemployed onto the media-political stage: the first gain by the unemployed movement was the movement itself (which helped to divert a disoriented popular electorate from the Front National). The unemployed movement, i.e. the simultaneous initiation of a collective organization and the chain reactions that had led to it and that it contributed to producing: from isolation, depression, individual resentment and vindictiveness towards scapegoats, to collective mobilization; and from resignation, passivity, withdrawal and silence, to making oneself heard; from depression to revolt, from the isolated unemployed individual to the collective of unemployed, from misery to anger. This is how the slogan of the demonstrators became true: 'If you sow misery, you harvest anger.'

But also, a reminder of some basic truths of neoliberal societies, which had led to the movement of November–December 1995 and which the powerful apostles of 'Tietmeyer thought' bent their efforts to concealing. Starting with the indisputable relationship between unemployment rate and rate of profit. The two phenomena, the frenzied consumption by some and the poverty of others, are not just concomitant – some grow rich even while sleeping, others are impoverished a bit more each day – they are interdependent: when the

* Jointly signed with Géraud Mauger and Frédéric Lebaron, under the aegis of the Association Raisons d'Agir, and published in Le Monde on 17 January 1998.

stock exchange puts out the flags, the unemployed suffer, the enrichment of some going hand in hand with the pauperization of others. Mass unemployment, in fact, remains the most effective weapon that the bosses have at their disposal to impose a freeze or a fall in wages, the intensification of work, the degradation of working conditions, the introduction of new forms of domination at work and the dismantling of the labour code. When firms dismiss workers, by one of those 'social plans' that the media announce with great fanfare, their shares soar. When a reduction in unemployment is announced in the United States, stock prices on Wall Street go down. In France, 1997 was the year in which all records were broken on the Paris stock exchange.

Above all, however, the unemployed movement challenges the divisions methodically maintained between the 'good' poor and the 'bad', between the 'excluded' and the 'unemployed', between the unemployed and those at work.

Even if the relationship between unemployment and crime is not a mechanical one, no one today can fail to see that 'urban violence' has its origins in unemployment, generalized social precariousness, and mass poverty. Those condemned in Strasbourg 'to give an example', the threats to reopen houses of correction or to suppress family allowances to 'failing' parents of trouble-makers are the hidden face of neoliberal employment policy. And under Tony Blair we see young unemployed forced to accept no matter what wretched job, and the US-style 'security state' replacing the welfare state.

Because it forces us to see that all unemployment is virtually long-term unemployment, and long-term unemployment is exclusion on reprieve, that exclusion from UNEDIC[21] also means being condemned to assistance, to social support, to charity, the movement of unemployed challenges the division between 'excluded' and 'unemployed': to send unemployed people to the social security office means withdrawing their unemployed status and driving them into exclusion.

But it also forces us to discover, and this above all, that those in work are potential unemployed, that generalized precariousness (especially that of young people), and the organized 'social insecurity' of all who live under the threat of a social plan, makes every worker potentially unemployed.

Expulsion *manu militari* will not solve 'the problem'. Because the cause of the unemployed is also that of the excluded, those in casual work and those wage-earners whose jobs are at risk. Because a moment will perhaps come when the reserve army of unemployed and casual workers, which condemns to subjection those at risk of being excluded, rebounds against those who based their policy (oh! the Socialists) on a cynical trust in the passivity of the most dominated.

---

[21] [Union National Interprofessionel pour l'Emploi dans l'Industrie et le Commerce (UNEDIC) is the official association of the 'social partners', i.e. employers and trade unions, that oversees the operation of unemployment insurance.]

*For a left that is left**

Two weeks after the Black Friday of the elections for regional presidents, witch-doctors of all kinds have rushed to the bedside of the Republic. For one of them, a change in the electoral law could enable democracy to rediscover its nice moderate colours; for another, a famous lawyer, a revision of the electoral system would put a paralysed democracy back on its feet; for a third, a former minister and fine strategist, it is the absence of a 'centre' that has transformed the state into a drunken boat, swaying from right to left and back again, at the risk of collapsing to the far right.

The highest figure in the state, in the role of noble father that is somewhat too big for him, chides the parties as quarrelsome children, and promises a change in the rules to enable the game to start up again without the skinheads. A former presidential candidate, with a belated flash of lucidity, wonders whether the electors are not fed up with seeing the same show for thirty years. Experts in election results measure to the percentage point the electoral potential of new coalitions being formed.

The three regional presidents just elected are already trumpeting on the television stage: far from being hostages, they are ramparts; they only embraced the Front National the better to stifle it; they all but invite their regional councils to vote the rapid erection of their own statues, as a support for local artists, regional culture and republican spirit.

But derision is not a sufficient response to the sad spectacle of these politico-media diagnosticians. The 'new' response they claim to bring to the fascization of a section of the political class and French society is as superficial as they are themselves. They restrict the circle of awkward questions to the habitual vademecum of the future candidate for the next election. How to avoid losing the European elections? How to prepare for legislative elections, if the Assembly is dissolved again? What new party is best to join? And soon it will be how to rally the votes of the disaffected centre, etc. It is this conception of politics that for several years now has been the best ally of the Front National: instrumental and cynical, more attentive to the interests of elected representatives than to the problems of electors, and not looking anywhere else for a solution than in manipulation of the rules of the electoral and media game.

---

* Drafted in the context of the Association Raisons d'Agir, and jointly signed with Christophe Charle, Frédéric Lebaron, Gérard Mauger and Bernard Lacroix, this was published in *Le Monde*, 8 April 1998.

The real questions are of a quite different order: why, in less than a year, has the plural left lost the dynamic of the victory it narrowly seized, when it does not even have the excuse of bad economic indicators? Why has it aroused such disappointment, of which the election results that are interpreted as victories give only a weak idea? Why, for example, did so many people vote for organizations that claim to be outside the political game? Why did a part of the right in its disarray prefer radicalization, when it is already in power through a left that is carrying out all its dreams? With its extremist temptation, the right is replaying a game already lost by the German centre and right in the early 1930s under the Weimar Republic. The impotence of the state only arouses in the electorate a massive indifference towards the Republic: it is clear that people don't go to the polls just to distribute offices, brush scandals under the carpet, sell public services to the highest bidder, or hand themselves over to bureaucracies that are immovable and inaccessible, both national and international.

By its implosion, the French right has returned to the disturbed origins of the regime that it established. When conservatives no longer know what to conserve, they are ready for any kind of conservative revolution. The persistent electoral success of a party such as the Front National, whose programme if put into practice would mean the ruin of its most deprived electors, often expresses nothing more than aversion towards a political personnel who are stubbornly deaf and blind to the distress of the popular classes. The false pretences of the plural left disappoint the left electorate, demobilizing activists and sending the most exasperated to the far left. It is hardly surprising that the first people to protest have been those who were the first to be swindled by the plural demagogy of a left that was in actual fact singular – i.e. the *sans-papiers*, the unemployed, and teachers.

Electoral reform would not be enough to calm the demands that ministers respond to by ostentatious charity, calculated sprinkling of favours, and clever tricks. When they do not refrain from arrogant verbal or demagogic utterances, the very opposite of the enthusiastic generosity of a mobilizing message, or even practices tragically similar to those of their predecessors. The official left finds it hard to cast off the dubious heritage of Mitterrandism; it irritates its supporters without being able to expect the least sign of satisfaction from its enemies; it profits temporarily from the mediocrity of its opponents without proposing anything else than a politics of day-to-day expedients that changes nothing essential in the everyday life of the great majority of citizens. When the day of reckoning approaches, which may well be closer than it believes, with the newly available threat of dissolution, what can it appeal to in order to mobilize abstentions and dissuade them from voting for the Front National? Jobs for some young people, the 35–hour week which is ever less of a reality, uninterrupted austerity, an educational reform transformed into a ministerial show, the forward flight towards a bankers' Europe? Do they believe they can keep on deceiving the expectation of a social Europe with a 'European plural left' inspired by the troika of Blair, Jospin and Schröder?

The rank-and-file left still believes in the welfare state; it is time for the 'Jospin-Chevènement-Hue-Voynet' quartet to remember that left majorities have led to disaster every time that they have tried to apply the policies of their opponents and taken their electors for amnesiac idiots. The proper responses to rampant or declared fascization can only arise from the social movements that developed from 1995 on. On condition that we are able to understand and express them instead of working to deflate them by public defamation or the velvet glove of former party apparatchiks now converted into state apparatchiks. They have themselves suggested certain political perspectives and even sometimes put forward detailed projects and programmes. Local pressure in some regions of the left contributed to bring to reason the less blind elements of the right. The demonstrations against the Front National bear witness to an activist capacity that seeks to defend causes more ambitious than simply the rejection of fascism. The movement for the renovation of public services – and particularly for a fairer national education, as expressed today in Seine-Saint-Denis[22] – is the very opposite of an identity-based retreat to an archaic institution. It proclaims the need for public services that are effective and egalitarian both in their operation and in their effects. The movement of *sans-papiers*, an object of public obloquy for those in 'responsible' positions on all sides, is a collective resistance to the obtuse policy that, in the name of a struggle against Le Pen, often takes from him its ideas and weapons (with the success that we know so well . . .). The movement of unemployed appears as a struggle that has to be constantly renewed against the destructive effects of generalized precariousness. The recent movements against the Multilateral Agreement on Investments and for capital taxation[23] show the rise in the forces of resistance to neoliberalism, a resistance that is international by its very nature.

These forces, which the professionals of manipulation suspect of being controlled by outside manipulators, are still a minority, but they are already deeply rooted, both in France and in other European countries, in the

[22] A reference to the spring 1998 strike movements of teachers in this department. (Cf. Sandrine Garcia, Franck Poupeau, Laurence Proteau, 'Dans la Seine-Saint-Denis, le refus', Le Monde Diplomatique, June 1998.) [Ed.]
[23] An international mobilization of information on the contents of the Multilateral Agreement on Investments succeeded in preventing this being signed by the G8 states. In connection with this mobilization, ATTAC, which was initially founded to promote the Tobin tax on capital movements, took a central place in the international mobilization against the liberal policies of deregulation. [Ed.]

practice of activist groups, in the trade unions and voluntary organizations. It is they who, by linking together on an international scale, can start to oppose in practice the alleged fatalism of 'economic laws' and to humanize the social world. The horizon of the social movement is an international one of resistance to neoliberalism and to all forms of conservatism.

An age of restoration[*]

We have to develop new forms of struggle to counteract by appropriate means the violence of symbolic oppression that has established itself bit by bit in the Western democracies. I have in mind the hidden censorship that increasingly affects the critical press, and, in the major official newspapers, also critical thought. We experienced this very directly when we opposed the Gulf war. The so-called progressive press rejected our texts or saw that they were combined with texts supporting the war. Several British papers refused to publish the very fine poem written by Harold Pinter that denounced the war (we published it later in *Liber*).

Both political and intellectual life are ever more subject to media pressure – starting with television – while the media themselves are under pressure from their presenters or quite simply from an obligation of good conduct that excludes any possibility of criticism.

The conservative international, with its centre in the United States, exerts pressure on all the spaces of free expression, such as museums, and represses pioneering research by controlling the award of public subsidies on the pretext of pornography or threat to public order.

We find ourselves in an age of restoration. Mediocre critics and insignificant writers denounce modern art as pure deception, and call for the novel to be brought back in line with traditional narrative forms. Not to speak of the social sciences, which always bear the weight of suspicion. The debate on the French Revolution (analyzed very well by Kaplan's book)[24] has brought the old anti-revolutionary ideologies back in fashion. The individualist and ultra-subjective tendencies that dominate economics and are in the course of conquering the entire field of the social sciences (with Gary Becker in particular)[25] seek to undermine the very foundations of social science.

It is in the intellectual sphere that intellectuals have to wage their struggle, not just because this is the terrain where their weapons are most effective, but also because it is most often in the name of an intellectual authority that the new technocracies succeed in imposing themselves. The new demagogy appeals chiefly to opinion polls to legitimize the repressive measures

[*] Published in *Les Inrockuptibles*, May 1998 supplement.

[24] Steven L. Kaplan, *Farewell, Revolution* (Ithaca: Cornell University Press 1995).

[25] A professor at the University of Chicago, and awarded the Nobel Prize for economics in 1992, Gary Becker was the inventor of the notion of 'human capital', designed to extend the model of the 'rational agent' and 'free market' to every field of human activity. (Cf. Pierre Bourdieu, 'Avenir de classe et causalité du probable', *Revue Française de Sociologie* 15, January–March 1974, pp. 3–42.) [Ed.]

taken towards foreigners, or cultural policies hostile to the avant-garde. This is why intellectuals must have autonomous means of expression, which do not depend on public or private subsidies, and must organize collectively, to put their specific weapons at the service of progressive battles.

One minister doesn't make a summer[*]

His fall was expected, but we cannot spare ourselves the pleasure of seeing the departure of a man who did not spare his efforts to make himself hateful to an entire profession, including the students in the name of whom he claimed to be acting. This satisfaction, however, will be very short-lived: the effects of his policies will be felt long after he has returned to his laboratory; and besides, were the policies really just 'his'? The attention that he personally attracted – some people wondered whether his policies had any other aim – risks concealing the fact that all he essentially did was continue or extend the policies of his predecessors, sharpening still further the challenge to the university system by incessantly demanding reforms, in the spirit of the whole succession of ministers we have seen over the last fifteen years, and seeking to adapt it to the great market in educational services that is under construction, without abandoning, come what may, its regular scientific tasks.

The tone was rapidly set. He spoke of 'trimming the fat off the mammoth', setting absentee teachers back to work . . . It was a very festival of contempt, forgotten only by those who profess astonishment that the name of Allègre is brandished today at all demonstrations.

No one expected the minister of education to be the minister of teachers. But we have at least the right to expect an employer to show a minimum of respect for his staff – teachers were not the only victims of the verbal excesses of 'their' minister. Excesses that were deliberate, since repeated and immediately justified in the name of *lycée* and university students. He was going to put them at the centre of the educational system, and if his typically populist proposals, which commentators found so ravishing, had the power to shock, it was because they rubbed against the interests and conservatism of the teachers. Discovering the existence of a class struggle, the minister courageously took the side of the oppressed: the desks against the dais, families against 'corporations'.

There was in fact nothing so new with the slogan about putting students at the centre. Allègre's predecessor made exactly the same speeches, though in less flowery language. Besides, this supposed concern with the 'users' of the educational system was all too reminiscent of the obsession with the

---

[*] Jointly signed with Christophe Charle and the members of the ARESER bureau, and published in *Le Monde*, 8 April 2000.

customer that lies at the root of the new managerial fashions developed since the early 1980s in the wake of the prophets of managerial 'excellence', Thomas Peters and Robert Waterman. Beyond the incantation, however, we saw a reinforced differentiation among these 'users', exactly parallel with the segmentation of customers in the world of commerce. This was the theme of the burdensomeness of programmes, the stacking-up of knowledge, which the minister illustrated, with a street-hawker's cunning, by inviting a journalist who interviewed him on a Sunday evening television show to weigh a carrier bag full of textbooks. As if anyone expected students to memorize the contents of textbooks, which are designed above all as collections of documents on which class work is based. No matter! – they had to be lightened. On the pretext that some school or university students lacked the resources to accede to such knowledge, the teaching dispensed had also to be adapted, reducing it to essentials and aiming at utility.

Despite the ministerial proclamations, the *lycée* students whose side the minister claimed to take felt placed not at the centre of the system, but rather at its periphery. In 1998 they took to the streets along with their teachers, to demand more resources for their schools. The shock was a rude one; once again young people showed their ignorance and ingratitude. Happily the minister could appeal to their parents – not ordinary parents, but officials from the two big 'representative' federations, which up till then had been in competition, but now defended the same positions as his own. Until actions mushroomed that brought teachers, students and parents out together . . .

Faced with the negative reactions aroused by Allègre's verbal sallies and irresponsible attacks against one discipline or another – language teaching to be more practical, mathematics cut back because of pocket calculators – the minister did not change his tone, but made sporadic efforts at discussion. Here again, there was no innovation from the practice of his predecessor, except perhaps in form. Whereas Bayrou had launched a 'general assembly', Allègre used a different semantic register, that of 'charters': a charter to build the school of the twenty-first century, a charter for the reform of *lycées*, a charter for theses, a charter for deconcentration, a charter for student life, a charter for the quality of school construction and renovation, a charter for school transport, etc . . . The kind of charter, in other words, that is granted from above, with a simulacrum of discussion being organized strictly within this context.

Allègre has gone, and will not be regretted. There is a risk, though, that we might be satisfied with this. For beyond any formal considerations, this minister, who people try to make us believe was the victim of his bold reforms, was stuck in the political continuity of his department's projects.

It is now to be feared that, in the absence of mobilization, the liberal orientation of his educational policy, broadly conceived in a European context and continually inspired by the American example, will be strengthened still further. In this respect, higher education stands in the front line: its adaptation to the market, and even its actual transformation *into* a market, have already been significantly begun.

From the mid-1980s on – and it is undoubtedly 1983 that marks the break – the theme of the lack of adaptation of academic teaching to the needs of business, never precisely defined, and as if business were the only 'customer' for graduates, found its way into government discourse on both left and right. While unemployment rose, and the conversion to neoliberalism meant renouncing macroeconomic policies of reflation, the attack on teaching in general and universities in particular made it possible to shift responsibility and make out that youth unemployment was simply a question of lack of proper training, so that young people themselves internalized the legitimacy of their growing exclusion from the labour market.

A further convergence among the governing class, across political divisions, was how the need for a 'massification' of higher education imposed itself even on those who had previously maintained an elitist discourse of selection for university entry; it was necessary to respond to the ever stronger social demand for schooling, while asking the university to play the role of an instrument for managing unemployment by delaying entry onto the labour market. This new boom in university staff – who more than doubled in fifteen years – after the boom of the 1960s, may well be a French particularity, but it has deepened inequalities between branches rather than suppressing these. To struggle against this specific tendency of the French dual system, it would have been necessary to commit budgetary resources that went beyond simply catching up after the stagnation of earlier years, and a long-term reform that no minister, in a context of changing governments and student movements, either could or would undertake. If this 'massification' made possible economies of scale, the democratization of teaching could only be at a growing (individual) cost.

All the higher education policies put into effect since the mid-1980s, from Jospin to Allègre, by way of Lang, Fillon and Bayrou, sought to take advantage – electoral in particular – from the increase in staff, even while trying to keep down costs. This was the perspective within which the rhetoric of bad adaptation was mobilized, and a trompe-l'oeil professionalization developed. In the universities, with resources held constant, 'professional' branches – the latest avatar of which is professional degrees – could only be added to the detriment of existing branches, termed 'classic' and declared maladapted.

This false professionalization is in actual fact a Trojan horse for the privatization of higher education. It favours or authorizes the growing intervention of representatives of the 'world of economics' – a euphemism used to describe employers without arousing too much opposition in the 'university community'. It justifies the lightening of disciplinary knowledge to the benefit of the acquisition of vague skills that no one even knows will be of any use in a professional context. What will become, for example, of people with a degree in scriptwriting? Finally it challenges the notion of national diplomas and state certification of university degrees. Yet it is brandished all round, even where one might have expected different references, for example when access to an occupation, which already exists and so has no need to be established, is by way of competition.

The project to reform the CAPE[26] that was published in February 2000, and more broadly to recruit and train teachers, is exemplary in this respect. This new arrangement makes it possible to pre-select as early as September, on debatable criteria – 'professional vocation', for example, will be assessed in a necessarily brief oral that goes together with the assessment of files – those to be prepared for competitive examination in the context of the Instituts Universitaires de Formation des Maîtres. A preparation reduced to the minimum, just four months, and sanctioned by supposed tests of admissibility. The logic is clear: what matters in this new conception of recruitment, and for the whole profession of teacher, is certainly not disciplinary knowledge.

The new educational 'professional', whose job is essentially one of 'socialization', especially in so-called 'difficult' establishments, will have to count above all, in order to respond to the demand – now differentiated according to whether students attend schools in educational priority zones or city centres – on the tricks and fudges of a pedagogy that is disembodied by being cut off from any disciplinary foundation and often derived from such pseudo-sciences as neuro-linguistic programming or transactional analysis, which now have official popularizers in the institutions of 'professional' training for both future and established teachers. Higher education has likewise been besieged by the language of the market, which the ministry of national education has sought in a number of ways to inscribe in both facts and minds: by encouraging teachers and researchers individually, through the law on innovation, to launch themselves in business start-ups; by pushing universities concerned to renovate or expand their premises – in the context of the Université du Troisième Millénaire plan – to build ties with the local

[26] [Certificat d'Aptitude au Professorat des Écoles Maternelles et Primaires, the teaching diploma for primary and nursery school teachers.]

economic environment; by organizing, along with the Édufrance 'agency' created by Claude Allègre and destined to survive him, the sale of 'French educational know-how' abroad, as a way of experimenting with the projected transfer to the market of the provision of educational services; by preparing, through the Agence de Modernisation des Universités, the transformation of universities pressed to buy the management software it produces – particularly software for accounts and human resources management, which of course are sold at market price – and thus invited, under the auspices of the computer fairy, to familiarize themselves with management criteria drawn from the private sector. It is likely that the forces pressing for deregulation, despite the defeat of the Seattle attempt, will return to the charge very soon.

After three years of absurd agitation and false reforms that were scarcely begun, the theatrical talents of the new minister will not suffice to make up for the time that has been wasted. In any case they will be unable to resolve or even disguise the crucial problems that remain for the future of universities and research, the most urgent of which we shall list below, hoping that this minister will find the time to read these precise and realistic reform proposals, the outcome of a long work of discussion conducted by a group of teachers of all ranks and from all disciplines:

– nothing or nearly nothing, apart from vague recommendations of advisers, to ensure a rapprochement between the universities and the *grandes écoles*;
– the solidarity pact between researchers and researcher-teachers, off to a bad start with the aborted reform of the CNRS, remains to be concluded and put into practice, this time with both presiding ministers;
– the future of young doctors – despite the magic formulas about training in research through research, and no longer actually for research – is under a cloud because the ministry has chosen (under pressure from the ministry of finance) to prefer temporary positions, or those with heavy schedules, to the detriment of combined research and teaching posts;
– formulaic incantations about software learning programs have led to forgetting the consideration that is needed about a new balance between lectures and groups with limited numbers that are used by all foreign universities that are really effective;
– up to now, the Europeanization of higher education has only given rise to meetings between ministers against the backdrop of our oldest universities (Sorbonne, Bologna), with long-term harmonization schedules.

Certain people have dreamt at this time, with the opening of borders, of subjecting the uncontrolled use that is now made of the new communication technologies to the Social Darwinist forces of generalized competition, allegedly good always and everywhere, without seeing that, in a field where France does not have the lead, an unrestrained competition of this kind could only benefit those best endowed, or those nations that are economically and linguistically dominant. The construction of a European university space will only be real and advantageous to all if the university community, instead of simply bending to the decisions of regional, national or European technocracies subject to practical or financial imperatives, engages in a process of collective intellectual discussion. In calling for a genuine parliament of universities – open to European higher education – and long-term commitment by the state on objectives that are collectively debated, ARESER has proposed indicators in this direction, to break with the false ritual consultations of post-crisis periods that the French university system has known for the last thirty years.

New techniques of teaching and distributing knowledge could enable European universities to draw closer to the demanding and universalist ideal on which they were founded. But it is up to all of us, academics, students and administrative staff, not to our ephemeral ministers and their fashionable advisers, whether this can be realized without sacrificing either the autonomy of knowledge, or the plurality of points of view, or accessibility to the greatest number.

The contemporary relevance of Karl Kraus*

A textbook of struggle against symbolic domination

Karl Kraus did something quite heroic, by questioning the intellectual world itself. There are intellectuals who question the world, but there are very few intellectuals who question the intellectual world. This is understandable if we bear in mind the paradox that this is the more risky undertaking, because it is where our own stakes are involved. Others are well aware of this, and hasten to remind us at every opportunity, turning our own instruments of object-ification against us. Besides, this leads to putting oneself on the stage – as could be seen with Karl Kraus's 'happenings' – and thus putting oneself person-ally in play. To theatralize one's actions, as Kraus did, to dramatize one's ideas and enact them, put them into practice, is something quite different from writing a scholarly article that puts forward a thesis in abstracto. It requires a kind of physical courage, perhaps a certain exhibitionism, as well as the talent of an actor, and a disposition that is not part of the academic habitus. But it also means taking risks, because putting yourself in play to this point does not just mean commitment in the conventional Sartrean sense of the term, i.e. on the terrain of politics and political ideas; it is yourself that you commit, you give yourself as hostage, with your whole person and personal properties, and you must consequently expect shocks in return. Rather than giving 'expositions', as at the university, you 'expose' yourself, which is eminently different. Academics expose a lot of things in their lectures, but they don't expose themselves very much. You have to expect personal attacks, called personal precisely because they aim at the person (was Kraus not accused of anti-Semitism?), ad hominem attacks that aim to destroy the very basis, the integrity, veracity and virtue of the person who, by their interventions, sets him – or herself up as a living reproach, even if irreproachable.

---

* Extract from a talk given at the conference 'Actualité de Karl Kraus. Le centenaire de la *Fackel* (1899–1936), Paris, 4–6 November 1999, published in *Austriaca* 49, December 1999, pp. 37–50. Karl Kraus was born in Gitschin (Bohemia) in 1874, and died in Vienna in 1936. A great German writer and essayist in the early decades of the twentieth century, he was highly influential both intellectually and politically, especially through *Die Fackel* (*The Torch*, 1899–1936), a satirical magazine which he founded, soon becoming its sole author. Kraus subjected the culture and politics of the Austrian bourgeoisie to a pitiless and radical criticism, above all for its involvement in the slaughter of the First World War; he focused on the key role of the press as corruptor of language and thought, and the liberal press in particular for its support for the world of business. Cf. Karl Kraus, *Les Dernier Jours de l'humanité* (Marseille: Agone 2000); *Dits et contre-dits* (Paris: Ivréa 1993), and Jacques Bouveresse, *Schmock ou le triomphe du journalisme. La grande bataille de Karl Kraus* (Paris: Seuil 2001). [Ed.]

What terrible thing did Kraus do to arouse such a fury? (All the newspapers agreed not to mention his name, though this didn't protect him from slander.) One thing in particular, which he summed up in a sentence that I see as containing the essence of his programme: 'Even if I have done nothing more than recopy or transcribe each day what they say and do, they treat me as a detractor.' This splendid formula explains what could be called the 'paradox of objectification': what does it mean to look at the everyday facts from outside, as an object, or in Durkheim's term, 'as things' – and more precisely, to look at the intellectual life of which you are part, in which you take part, in this way, breaking with the bond of tacit complicity that you have with this and arousing the revolt of persons objectified in this way, and of all those who recognize themselves in them? What is this operation that consists in rendering scandalous something that has already been seen and read every day in the papers? (This is rather like what we did with *Actes de la Recherche en Sciences Sociales*, which has a number of common features with *Die Fackel*, e.g. the way that a document, a photo or an extract from an article stuck into an analytical text completely changes the status of both text and document; what would otherwise be the object of a rather distracted reading can then suddenly appear astonishing or even scandalous. Pretentious editorials you can see every week – to be really Krausian, one should give proper names –, but if, one fine day, you cut one of them out and stick it in a magazine, the whole world finds that unsupportable, insulting, injurious, slanderous, terrorist, etc.) To stick something on paper and offer it to the public, to make public what is generally said only in the secret of gossip or unverifiable scandal-mongering, like the little nothings of university, publishing or journalistic life, known by everyone yet highly censored, by declaring yourself personally the guarantor responsible for their authenticity, means breaking the relationship of complicity that unites all those who are in the game, suspending the relationship of connivance, complacency and indulgence that each person grants the other, and that makes for the general functioning of intellectual life. It means condemning yourself to appear a badly behaved lout, claiming to raise to the dignity of scholarly discourse mere malicious tattle – or worse, a spoiler of the game or a traitor who gives the game away.

If recourse to objectifying quotation is immediately denounced and put on the index, it is because it is understood as a way of pointing the finger and putting on the index. In the particular case of Karl Kraus, however, those whom he put on the index were those who generally put others on it. In more universal terms, he objectivized those who held the monopoly of public objectification. He made power – and abuse of power – visible by turning this power against those who wielded it, and he did so by the simple strategy of pointing. He made journalistic power visible by turning against journalistic power the power that journalism wields against us on a daily basis.

This power of construction and constitution wielded by mass publication and mass disclosure is one that journalists exercise every day, by the very fact of publishing or not publishing facts or statements that come to their attention (to mention a demonstration or pass it over in silence, to report a press conference or ignore it, and if they do report it, to do so in an accurate manner, or one that is inaccurate, distorted, favourable or unfavourable), or again, on a wholesale basis, by the use of headlines and titles, by the more or less arbitrary use of professional labels, by excess or default (we could discuss their uses of the label 'philosopher'), by making into a problem something that is not, or vice versa. They can go further, however, with total impunity, as regards individuals and their actions and works. One could say without exaggeration that they have a monopoly of legitimate defamation. Those who have been victims of defamatory statements of this kind, and have tried to rebut them in print, know that I am not exaggerating. Quotation and collage have the effect of turning back against journalists an operation that they carry out on a daily basis. And this is a perfectly irreproachable technique, being in a certain sense anonymous. That being said, not all intellectuals and artists are up to inventing techniques of this kind. One of Kraus's interests was to provide a kind of textbook for the perfect combatant against symbolic domination. He was one of the first to understand in practice that there is a form of symbolic violence that is exercised over minds by manipulating cognitive structures. It is very hard to invent suitable techniques of self-defence to mobilize against symbolic violence, and harder still to teach them.

Karl Kraus was also the inventor of a technique of sociological intervention. As distinct from the kind of pseudo-artist who claims to do 'sociological art' but is neither artist nor sociologist, Kraus was a sociological artist in the sense that his actions were sociological interventions, i.e. 'experimental actions' that aimed to make hidden properties or tendencies of the intellectual field reveal, disclose and unmask themselves. This is also the effect of certain historical conjunctures that lead certain individuals to betray in broad daylight what their previous acts and especially their writings disclosed only in a highly veiled form – I am thinking for example of Heidegger and his rectorial address. Kraus made these masks drop without waiting on historical events. To do this, he resorted to 'provocations' that pushed people to mistakes or crimes. The virtue of provocation is that it offers the possibility of 'antici-pating', by making immediately visible, what only intuition or knowledge enables one to predict: the fact that the everyday submissions and conformities of everyday situations prefigure extraordinary submissions and conformities.

Jacques Bouveresse has referred to the famous example of the false petitions, genuine sociological 'happenings' that gave an occasion to verify sociological laws. Kraus drew up a false humanist and pacifist petition on which he put the signatures of some sympathetic figures, genuine pacifists, as well as signatures of former militarists now converted to pacifism. (Imagine for example what could be done today with those revolutionaries of May 1968 who are converts to neoliberalism.) Only the pacifists protested against the use of their names, while the others said nothing, evidently because this enabled them to do retrospectively what they did not do when they should have done. That is experimental sociology!

Kraus extracted a certain number of sociological propositions that are at the same time moral propositions. (I deliberately reject here the opposition between descriptive and prescriptive.) He had a horror of 'good causes' and those who took advantage of them: in my view it is a sign of moral health to be furious against those who sign symbolically profitable petitions. Kraus denounced what is traditionally called pharisaism. For example the revolutionism of opportunist litterateurs, which he showed is simply the equivalent of a former epoch's patriotism and exaltation of national sentiment. Anything can be mimicked, even avant-gardism and transgression, and those intellectuals whom Kraus parodied already evoke our 'parody intellectuals' – as Louis Pinto calls them – for whom transgression (easy enough, and most commonly sexual) is the rule, along with all the conformist forms of anti-conformism, the academicism of anti-academicism, which the Paris media circus makes such a speciality of. We have intellectual roués, even intellectual perverts, semiologists converted to novelists like Umberto Eco or David Lodge, artists who more or less cynically practise tricks and procedures taken from avant-garde works of an earlier time, such as Philippe Thomas, who gets his works signed by collectors, and will sooner or later be copied by someone else who plays at getting his works signed by the same collectors. And so it goes, on and on. In the same way, Kraus denounced all the intellectual profit bound up with what we call 'returning the lift', the economy of intellectual exchange. He showed how the rule of exchanging favours made any serious criticism impossible, and how theatre directors did not dare to reject plays by a powerful critic such as Hermann Bahr, which could run in every theatre.[27] We have the equivalent today, with all those literary critics whom publishers commission to edit series, or whose books they vie for, and I could give some incredible examples of 'returning the lift' in which university positions are also involved.

---

[27] Hermann Bahr, a Viennese critic and playwright, was one of Kraus's favourite targets – 'the tireless and prolix major-domo of the New'. [Ed.]

If we can see ourselves already in Kraus, it is because to a large extent the same causes produce the same effects. The phenomena that Kraus observed have their equivalent today. As for knowing why some of us love Kraus – writers and artists in all countries, but particularly German-speaking ones –, the reason is somewhat more complicated. We occupy certain positions, and what we like may be connected with these positions. It is important to try and understand Kraus's position in his world, if we are to understand what in this might be similar or homologous to our own situation, leading us to find ourselves in the positions he took up. Perhaps the fact that he was an intellectual of the old school, trained in the old way (you need only read his German, his diction, etc.), who felt threatened by the new kinds of intellectual; on the one hand, that meant journalists, who in his eyes embodied subordination to the market; on the other hand, administration intellectuals, including those of the war administration, and apparatus or party intellectuals, who played a very important role in his struggle. He had against him an alliance of apparatchiks and journalists. Here again, *mutatis mutandis*, there are several analogies with today. Perhaps the fact that, like today, the boundaries between the intellectual field and the journalistic field are in the process of shifting, and relations of force between these two fields in the process of changing, with the rise in number and symbolic weight of 'mercenary' intellectuals who are directly subject to the constraints of competition and the market.

The fact that we recognize Kraus is certainly bound up with an affinity of temperament. But we might ask whether, to be a little bit 'moral', it is perhaps necessary to feel rather bad in one's situation, in the world in which one finds oneself; to be perturbed, even shocked or scandalized, by things that everyone finds normal and natural, and lacking in any case the benefits of conformity and conformism that spontaneously fall to those who are spontaneously conformist; whether it is perhaps necessary, in a word, to have some *interest* in morality (which should not be concealed). But the weakness of Kraus – and of any temperamental critic – is that he is not very good at grasping structures; he sees their effects, he points them out, but most commonly without grasping their origin. Criticism of individuals, however, cannot take the place of criticism of structures and mechanisms – which enables the reasons of temperament, good or bad, to be converted into the reasoned and critical reason of analysis. That said, analysis of structures does not mean depriving social actors of their freedom. They have a little bit of freedom that can be increased by the knowledge they are able to gain of the mechanisms in which they are caught. That is why journalists are mistaken to see the analysis of journalism as a 'criticism' of journalism, when they should see it as an indispensable instrument to gain knowledge and awareness of the structural constraints in which they are caught, and thus get a little more freedom.

Sociology, as we know, invites people not to moralize but to politicize. By bringing to light the effects of structures, it casts a large doubt on professional ethics, and on all the forms of journalistic pseudo-criticism of journalism, or television critique of television, which are no more than so many ways of improving ratings and restoring good conscience, while leaving everything as it is. In fact, it invites journalists to find political solutions, i.e. to seek in their own world the means to struggle with the particular instruments of this world, to control their instruments of production and oppose all the non-specific constraints imposed on them. And to do so by organizing collectively, and creating – particularly thanks to the internet – international movements of critical journalists; in other words, inventing, in place of the so-called 'ethics' that certain journalists like to spout, a genuine ethics of action (or struggle), in and through which journalists would denounce as journalists, in the way that Kraus did, those journalists who destroy the profession of journalism.

I I

The Media in the Service
of Conservative Revolution

*Pierre Bourdieu's first works on the emergence of 'journalist intellectuals' date from
the 1970s (see. p.319), and those on the submission of journalism to the demands
of the market from the 1980s (see. p.321). On the occasion of a critical retrospective
on the first Gulf war, journalists from Reporters Without Borders invited Bourdieu
to take part, and he analyzed their unwitting contribution to naturalizing the
dominant view of the social world (see. p.326). The publication of* On Television[1]
*triggered a particularly violent polemic, mobilizing the major daily papers and
weeklies over a number of months, during which time Bourdieu's book remained
high on the best-seller list. His analysis of the constraints bearing on journalistic
work (urgency, competition, etc.), which contributed to the 'disenchantment with
politics', in fact followed on from his analysis of the threat that media intellectuals
pose to public debate, with their production adjusted to the demands of audience
figures. But while Bourdieu's scientific writings had been relatively little read,* On
Television *broke down the barrier of scholarly esotericism.*

The situation did not quieten down, particularly after the publication in
Libération, *on 17 January 1995, of a piece titled 'Sollers tel quel', in which
Pierre Bourdieu denounced the backsliding of the avant-garde, as expressed in
Philippe Sollers's apology for the then prime minister and favoured presidential
candidate in 'Balladur tel quel'.[2] This work of unveiling was complemented by
the publication in 1997, likewise by Raisons d'Agir, of* Les Nouveaux chiens
de garde, *a book in which Serge Halimi, a journalist on* Le Monde Diplomatique, *described the networks of 'connivance journalism' and the installation of
market ideology in the opinion press; a work continued, in the same collection,
by a collective publication authored by young researchers from the Centre de
Sociologie Européenne,* Le Décembre des intellectuels français, *on the political
cleavages that the movement of December 1995 had revealed between those*

[1] *Sur la télévision*, published by Raisons d'Agir in 1996 [*On Television* (New York: New Press 1998)],
reprinted two lectures at the Collège de France that were filmed in March 1966 by the cable channel
Paris Première, along with an article 'L'emprise du journalisme' that had appeared in March 1994 in
Actes de la Recherche en Sciences Sociales 101/102. [Ed.]
[2] Sollers's article was published in *L'Express*, 12 January 1995; 'Sollers tel quel' is reprinted in *Acts of
Resistance*, pp. 11–14. [Ed.]

intellectuals who supported the Juppé plan and those who sided with the resistance of the strikers, and on the decisive role played by the media in the construction of the public debate.[3]

Besides the paradoxical effects of the 'publicity' that the violent criticism of leading editorialists generated, the resonance of these publications can be explained by the revival of social struggles, as well as the growing attention that focused on the drift of the media – as confirmed by the launch of ACRIMED (Action-Critique-Média), 'for democratic action in the field of the media', in the wake of the social movement of November–December 1995;[4] followed in 1998 by the mobilization behind the distribution of the film by Pierre Carles, Pas Vu Pas Pris.[5]

The growing visibility of Pierre Bourdieu after the publication of The Weight of the World, *and his highly publicized support for the strike of December 1995, were now followed by the polemic between him and Daniel Schneidermann on the subject of his appearance on the programme 'Arrêt sur Images' (Channel 5, 23 January 1996). In the course of this programme – the object of which was a critique of certain television productions – Bourdieu explained that no genuine deciphering of television could be done on television, because 'the mechanisms of television impose themselves even on critical programmes' (see. p.336). What should have been discussed as an analysis was taken as an attack, especially when the sociologist sought to explain in what way the constraints of the journalistic milieu established a 'cynical vision' of politics, reduced to a microcosm cut off from the public and depicted as simply a confrontation of egoistic ambitions.*[6]

Political disillusion, marketing technique, and submission to the competitive market, were also subjects that led Pierre Bourdieu to involve himself during autumn 1999 in an action initiated by ACRIMED 'for the defence of France Culture'; a criticism of the collapse of programming that had followed the nomination of Jean-Marie Cavada to the head of Radio France, and of Laure Adler to the head of France Culture. A 'regular liquidation', this reform of programmes by importing '"recipes" supposedly successful for private and public radio alike', transformed public radio, in the view of ACRIMED, into a 'scarcely disguised advertising tool for the most commercial books, records and films'.[7]

---

[3] As well as virulent criticisms from *Esprit* and magazines such as *Marianne*, *L'Événement du Jeudi* and *Le Nouvel Observateur*, Pierre Bourdieu's sociology was also attacked by one of his former collaborators, Jeannine Verdès-Leroux, in *Le Savant et la politique* (Paris: Grasset 1998). But the culmination of this reaction was the series of 'points of view' commissioned by *Le Monde* on 18 September 1998, with the participation of Olivier Mongin for *Esprit*, Philippe Sollers for *L'Infini*, Alain Finkielkraut for *Le Messager Européen*, Bernard-Henri Lévy for *La Règle du Jeu*, and Claude Lanzmann and Robert Redeker for *Les Temps Modernes*. [Ed.]
[4] This group was launched by Patrick Champagne and Henri Maler [Ed.]
[5] Commissioned by Canal Plus but then rejected, this documentary on the connivance between journalism and politics, which asked the question: 'Can everything be shown on television?', became a film, rejected by television, on the limits of self-criticism in television. [Ed.]
[6] 'Return to Television', *Acts of Resistance*, pp. 70–7. [Ed.]
[7] ACRIMED, 'Manifeste pour la défense de France Culture', *L'Humanité*, 5 November 1999. [Ed.]

Bourdieu's attention to the way the dominant media functioned in the service of market thinking especially focused on the fact that this power was an obstacle to progressive struggles.

One of the major obstacles to the constitution of forces of resistance is the fact that the dominant control the media as never before in history . . . In our day, all the major French newspapers are completely controlled. Even seemingly independent papers such as *Le Monde* are in fact joint stock companies dominated by the great powers of money.[8]

Beyond a critique of the media, it was the social movement as an 'international of resistance to neoliberalism and all forms of conservatism' that lay at the root of the questions Pierre Bourdieu addressed to the 'masters of the world, these new powers that are the combined forces of money and media' (see. p.340).

---

[8] Interview with Lino Polegato (14 December 2001), for the review *Flux News* (Liège, Belgium) 27, December 2001–January 2002. [Ed.]

Libération, *twenty years on**

The evolution of *Libé* is a favourite subject of distinguished conversation today: '*Libé* has become the paper of business intellectuals'; '*Libé* is *Le Parisien Libéré* for yuppies'. Everyone bases their judgements on observations that fuel spontaneous statistics: *Libé* readers seen in the bus or Métro, the paper's contents, new contributors, new sports headings, stock exchange. Changes in readership are inferred from the supposed changes in the contents, or vice versa, ascribing the deplorable novelties to intentions or desires. And as soon as this question is raised, some trendy 'sociologist' or other, of the kind that fashionable weekly and monthly magazines like *Lui* or *Globe* – not to mention *Le Nouvel Observateur* – periodically launch on the market, relentlessly explain to us the whole problem: rise of individualism, end of intellectuals, great clean-out of 'mandarins', and other self-fulfilling prophecies dear to those who take their desires for reality. They have an easy time of it: the sociology without tears that they offer has every chance of being received with relief by all who feel on firm ground with ready-made analyses of this kind, in which they recognize a number of their own amateur sociological intuitions.

I regret that the idea I have of sociology bars me from such facile verdicts, forcing me to stick to the grumpy image of sociologist without apostrophes, kill-joy, bore, stuffed with statistics and concepts, serving as a foil for those sociologists with apostrophes who would also like to be 'philosophers', with their 'fragmented' or rather raggedy discourse, glaring rather than shining. I regret not being able to write a fashionable advertising blurb, saying that *Libé* is the paper of those who were twenty years old in 1968, and are still enjoying an extended youth today, that what was the rallying point for long-haired and bearded cool kids has become the 'indispensable' reading of modern executives with strong purchasing power, intelligent city-dwellers and innovators open to modernity. And all this in language situated 'some-where' between *Libé* headline and chic advertising slogan. But though this would no doubt bring great pleasure to those who take media windbags for philosophic lanterns, it would not help much towards understanding a phenomenon that, after all, is not so devoid of interest.

To learn something about *Libé* and ourselves: old-established readers; early

---

* This was commissioned by *Libération* in 1988, to accompany readership statistics for advertising purposes. The paper never published the text, but an abridged version appeared in *Actes de la Recherche en Sciences Sociales* 101/102, March 1994.

admirers, now disappointed; or new converts – more precisely, converts of the first, second or eleventh hour –, we would need the means to examine whether and how the gradual shifts in the contents of the newspaper are connected with concomitant shifts in the characteristics of its readers: whether the disappearance of such things as typographer's comments, the scathing criticism of the television page, emergency inquiries about a young Arab bludgeoned by a big store's security guards or a meeting of Usinor workers at Dunkirk, and the appearance of the very 'Sciences Po'-style commentary of the financial pages, 'straight' analysis of American football, or banner headlines about the circus of cohabitation or the presidential elections, has anything to do with the extension of the readership towards the 15–24 and 24–35 year-old age groups, with the almost doubling of the relative share of 'business and senior executive' readers (from 22 per cent to 39 per cent), or the very marked increase in the share of urban readers with tertiary education or an annual income over 120,000 francs, those active in sports, big travellers, and 'recent shareholders'.

But does this mean that recent shareholders are necessarily more reactionary, or that the 'sophisticated consumers and early adopters' who are well placed to seduce advertisers herald the triumph of sophisticated pioneers, ready to accompany the reconversions and conversions effected by the survivors as against the liberated libertarians with whom *Libé* started?

These are the first questions that come to mind, and they certainly conceal others far more complex, which would have to be gradually elaborated, constructed and confronted with the data. But all this, which would take a great deal of time and trouble (in every sense of the word), is something that will not actually be asked of me. Because at bottom, the role of sociologist without apostrophes is undoubtedly to say without circumlocution those things that no one wants to know.

Questions of words[*]

A more modest view of the role of journalists

I do not want what I am going to say to be taken as a critique of journalism, at least in the sense that is generally given to this term, i.e. an 'attack' on an activity and those who practise it.

My intention is simply to contribute to a process of self-reflection that journalists are themselves conducting. And to do so first of all by recalling the limits that such self-reflection necessarily comes up against. Every group produces a representation of what it is and what it wants to be; and this is particularly true for the specialized agents of cultural production. This representation clearly owes a great deal to the interests, conscious and unconscious, of those who produce it, and who notably sin by omission or by indulgence towards themselves. If Marx said that 'mankind only poses problems that it can solve', one could say here that 'groups only pose the problems that they can stand'. They have escape strategies, especially that of posing extreme problems bound up with limit situations, in order to avoid everyday problems. The debate about medical ethics is an example of this: to pose the problem of euthanasia is a way of avoiding that of the nurses, of daily life in the hospitals, etc. I would warn therefore against the danger to which a group such as the one here is exposed: we shall speak a great deal about the Gulf war, a situation in which journalistic freedom was reduced almost to zero, and avoid raising those problems where the freedom of journalists is weak but still real. The first step towards ethical reflection consists in defining the zones of freedom where genuine responsibilities and real possibilities of action are involved.

How can one raise these ordinary problems that consideration of extra-ordinary problems tends to obscure? How can we avoid shifting discussion from those regions of practice that depend on us – as the Stoics put it – towards those that do not depend on us, so that we are exempt by definition from any responsibility and any action? We must start by returning to a far more modest view of the role of journalists. What actually does lie in their power? Among those things that do depend on them, there is the handling of words. It is thus by controlling their use of words that they can limit the effects of symbolic violence that they may exert willy-nilly. Symbolic violence is a violence practised in and through ignorance, and all the more readily in that those who practise

* An intervention at a conference organized by Reporters Without Borders, and published in Les Mensonges du Golfe (Paris: Arléa 1992), pp. 27–32.

it are unaware they are doing so, and those experiencing it unaware they are experiencing it.

This statement has an abstract air, but here is a concrete example. This morning I heard a trailer for a programme by Jean-Marie Cavada, in the course of which a philosophy of the social history of relations between the sexes was put forward as if this could simply be taken for granted: 1970s, sexual liberation; 1980s, moralism; 1990s, the return of sentiment – something like that. When I hear things of this kind – and God knows how many one hears every day, it's 'the return of the subject', 'the end of structuralism', 'the return to democracy', 'the end of history', etc. – I always wonder: 'How do they know?' In the world of journalists, however, which is the site par excellence of the production, reproduction and circulation of this vulgate, the strange fact is that no one asks this question. You read on the front page of *Le Nouvel Observateur* about 'the return of sentiment', or in a headline of *Le Quotidien de Paris* 'the end of the sexual revolution'. These media coups are symbolic coups de force that are struck in all innocence, and all the more effective for being unconscious. There is a sense in which this can only be done because the people who practise this violence are themselves victims of the violence that they practise, and this is where we get the false science of the half-educated that likes to give the appearance of scientific ratification to the intuitions of common sense (we could call this the 'Cofremca[9] effect'): typologies based on projecting the social unconscious of these new magicians link up with the unconscious of those who commission such things (businessmen or politicians) and those who receive their commissions (journalists). And the responsibility of journalists comes from their involvement in this circulation of unconscious material.

This is an example of those symbolic effects that often take the form of the well-known paralogism: 'The king of France is bald'. When someone says 'The king of France is bald', two senses of the verb 'to be' are involved, and an existential proposition (there is a king of France) is hidden by a predicative statement (the king of France has the property of being bald). Attention is attracted to the fact that the king is bald, while in reality, the idea that there is a king of France is smuggled in as self-evident. I could cite countless statements about the social world that are all of this type, especially those that have collective nouns as their subject: 'France is fed up', 'The people will not accept', 'The French support the death penalty', etc. In the opinion polls, instead of asking first: 'Do you think there is a moral crisis at the present time?', and then: 'Is it serious, very serious, etc.?', people are simply asked: 'Is the present moral crisis serious, very serious, etc.?'

Among the most powerful tacit propositions are all those that bear on those

[9] [Cofremca is a leading market-research institute for the media.]

oppositions, that are principles of vision and division, such as rich/poor, bour-geois/common people, on which the struggle of the workers' movement was based and which are still present in the unconscious of the majority of us; but also today, oppositions like nationals/foreigners, indigenous/immigrants, us/them, etc. This is a tremendous change. People might take completely different positions on what should be done about immigrants, but even those with opposing views tacitly agree – consensus within dissent – that the opposition between indigenous and immigrants has predominance and priority over every other kind of opposition, starting with that between rich and poor – within which there can of course also be indigenous and foreigners. This realizes the dream of all bourgeoisies, to have a bourgeoisie without a proletariat. From the point that there are only nationals, rich and poor together, everything is well sorted out, at least for the rich. A number of words that we use without even thinking about them, and particularly all these pairs of adjectives, are cate-gories of perception, principles of vision and division that are historically trans-mitted and socially produced and reproduced, principles that organize our perception of the social world, and especially of conflicts; and political struggle essentially aims at maintaining or transforming these principles, reinforcing or changing our view of the social world. Journalists therefore play a central role, because among the producers of discourse it is they who wield the most powerful means for circulating and imposing these. They thus occupy a privileged position in the symbolic struggle to make things seen and believed. This is why intel-lectuals have an ambiguous position towards them. They are envied by some intellectuals who would like to be seen ('did you see me?'), and envied also by less garish intellectuals who would like to be heard. Those who know something about the social world would certainly like to be able to say it, but they come up against those who control access to the means of communication, and are therefore in a position to select who can have access to a mass audience.

To sum up, I would say that the strongest part of communication is its unconscious aspect, the underlying communication between unconsciouses – which in Aristotle's sense are particularly those 'things with which we commu-nicate, but about which we never communicate', those fundamental oppositions that make discussion possible, yet are never the object of discussion. What I am preaching here is the necessity of communication about the unconscious of communication. If this is not simply to remain a pious wish, we would need to conceive and create a critical instance able to sanction and punish – at least by means of ridicule – those who overstep the limits. I know that I am indulging in utopia, but I would like to imagine a critical programme bringing together scholars and artists, singers and satirists, with the aim of putting to the test of satire and laughter those journalists, politicians and media 'intellectuals' who fall in too glaring a fashion into abuse of symbolic power.

*From miscellany to a matter of state**

On the unintended effects of the right to information

It is possible to get an idea of the contribution of journalism to the genesis of an 'active and effective public opinion' by following the chronological development of a quite ordinary case, that of 'little Karine', which would have remained confined to a short report in a regional newspaper, but was gradually transformed into a regular matter of state by the constitution of collective, public and legitimate opinion, and finally ratified by a law providing for life imprisonment.

This started with the Perpignan *Indépendant* reporting the disappearance of a little girl on 15 September 1993, the 'emotional appeal' of her mother (16 September), the accusation of a 'suspect', a family friend who had 'already been condemned twice by the assize court' (20 September), and the confession of the murderer (22 September). Then, on 23 September, came a change of tone: a declaration by the victim's father appealing for the restoration of the death penalty, a similar declaration by Katrine's godfather, and an editorial suggesting that the facts leading up to the murder 'should have led to definite measures to prevent further recidivism'. On the 25th, an appeal from the family for a demonstration in support of a draft law increasing sentences for the rape and murder of children, the announcement of the creation of an Association des Amis des Parents de Karine in a small neighbouring village, and an appeal to the minister of the interior from another village. On the 26th, a demonstration with banners demanding the restoration of the death penalty or at least life imprisonment. *La Dépêche de Toulouse* closely followed the same movement, though an editorial on the 26th spoke of 'a man who remains one of us' and called for moderation. On 27 September, *L'Indépendant* announced that the government would bring to the Assembly in the autumn session a draft law to increase sentences for the murder of children. A number of politicians spoke at this point, first of all members of the Front National, then from other parties (in particular, the Socialist mayor of Perpignan).

From this point on, the debate moved into the national arena. *L'Indépendant* announced on 6 October that the Association Karine, which now had the services of an lawyer, would be represented throughout the case, and that it had called for a demonstration and for people to write to deputies; on 8 October the Association met with the minister of justice; on the 9th it called for a rally;

* An addendum to 'L'emprise du journalisme', *Actes de la Recherche en Sciences Sociales* 101/102, March 1994, p. 8,

on the 10th a demonstration for 'genuine life imprisonment' was held. On the 16th, a further demonstration at Montpellier; on the 25th, a meeting attended by 2,700 people. The 28th, new visit to the minister of justice. The 30th, 137 right-wing deputies demand the restoration of the death penalty. On 17 November, television forcefully intervenes, Charles Villeneuve presenting a programme titled 'Le Jury d'Honneur' on which 'Karine's mother and Maître Nicolas' appear, as well as the minister of justice, representatives of various associations and lawyers, on the subject: 'What should we do with child killers?', a question in which every word is an appeal to vengeful identification. The Paris newspapers only get involved rather belatedly, and not very strongly. Except *Le Figaro*, which from the end of September has a piece by a lawyer, the author of *Ces enfants qu'on assassine*, who demands an end to indulgence and appeals for a referendum, making several subsequent appearances in favour of reforming the law (as does *Le Quotidien de Paris*). The announcement on 4 November that the Council of Ministers has decided to present a law establishing life imprisonment triggers resistance from the main organizations of magistrates, and an advocates' association notes that 'by pursuing a media goal, the project goes against the serenity of legislative work' (*La Croix*, 4 November).[10]

In the first month of the case, therefore, journalists played a determining role. By offering it the possibility of access to public expression, they transformed a wave of private indignation that would have remained impotent into a public – *published* – appeal, licit and legitimate, for revenge and mobilization, which then served as the basis for a public and organized movement of public protest (demonstrations, petitions, etc.). The brevity of the time span, less than four months, between the death of the young girl and the legislative decision restoring life imprisonment, has the merit of making clear the effects that journalists are able to produce, each time that, by the simple act of *publication*, i.e. a disclosure that implies ratification and making something official, they stoke up or mobilize popular impulses. And as for the intervention of television in this affair, its subjection to audience ratings and the logic of competition for market shares leads to fawning on the most widespread expectations, thus strengthening the propensity to let the unknown effects of publication have free rein, or even multiplying them by the demagogic excitation of basic passions. The responsibility of journalists certainly lies in a laissez-faire irresponsibility that lets them have unpredictable effects in the name of a right to information, which, constituted into a sacrosanct principle of democracy, sometimes provide demagogy with its best alibi.

---

[10] 'Convicted of the rape and murder, on 13 September 1993, of little Karine, then eight years of age, Patrick Tissier was condemned to life imprisonment followed by a period of supervision of thirty years, at the assize court of Perpignan, Pyrénées-Orientales on 30 January 1998.' (*Le Monde*, 2 February 1998.) [Ed.]

The misery of the media*

Why do you see the question of Algeria as so important at this time?

It seems a priority to me in both moral and political terms. From a cynical standpoint, that of our own interest as properly understood, Algeria is today the number one problem for France. Neither the government nor politicians of any persuasion (we tend to forget that it was Joxe who opened the way for Pasqua)[11] have understood this, let alone journalists. The civil war in Algeria could spill over to France at any time, with its murders and bombings,[12] and the people responsible will not always be those whom journalists like to point to, i.e. Islamists . . . This is why we need to support in every way possible the Rome agreement between the democratic parties and the representatives (I believe them to be genuinely representative) of the FIS.

At bottom, behind the question of Algerian refugees you see that of republican values?

The policing policy of the French government is a threat to democracy, which up to now has been protected by republican public spirit; it establishes racist practices towards all those who do not have a properly French face, or surname, or ancestors. The measures taken towards foreigners threaten France's universalist and internationalist traditions.[13] They reveal, in certain social categories, the latent disposition to racism. The police don't have to be told to check people according to their appearance, they do so unless you tell them otherwise.

In this work in support of Algerians, and of republican values, do you feel helped by the media?

The difficulty is that this association of researchers, the CISIA [see. p.243] is a tiny number of volunteers, with no infrastructure, and we don't have an immoderate desire to be seen in the media. To the point that a radio

---

* Interview with François Granon, published in *Télérama* 2353, 15 February 1995.
[11] Pierre Joxe and Charles Pasqua were both interior ministers, for governments of the left and right respectively. [Ed.]
[12] Bombings took place in France in July the same year. [Ed.]
[13] A reference to the Pasqua laws (see pp. 261 and 272). [Ed.]

producer recently said: 'Oh, the CISIA, they're not doing anything; you never see them.' All this because there was an afternoon devoted to Algeria, but we were busy with something else . . .

To exist means you have to be on radio or TV?

No one today can launch any action without the support of the media. It's as simple as that. Journalism ends up dominating the whole of political life, as well as scientific and intellectual life. Bodies need to be created where it is possible to work together, where researchers and journalists can mutually criticize one another. Journalists, however, are one of the most susceptible categories: you can talk about bishops, the bosses, and even teachers, but about journalists it's impossible to say even things that are completely objective . . .

This is a good time to say them!

The underlying paradox is this. It's a very powerful profession made up of very fragile individuals. With an enormous disparity between a considerable collective power and the fragility of the status of journalists, who in this respect are in a position of inferiority vis-à-vis both intellectuals and politicians. Collectively, journalists can overwhelm, but individually, they are constantly endangered. It is a trade in which, for sociological reasons, life is hard (it is no accident that you find so much alcoholism), and the junior managers are often dreadful. Not only are careers broken, but often consciences as well – though that's also true elsewhere, I'm afraid! Journalists suffer a lot. By the same token, they become dangerous; when there is suffering of this kind, it always ends up being transferred elsewhere, in the form of violence and contempt.

Is it a milieu able to reform itself?

The conjuncture is very unfavourable. The field of journalism is a site of fierce competition, in which television exerts a terrible hold. You can give countless signs of this, such as the appointment of TV journalists to edit newspapers, or the growing place of TV pages – and their docility, not to say servility – in the press. It is television that sets the rules: the subjects that can be spoken of and those that can't, those individuals who are important and those who are not. Television, however, though alienating for the rest of journalism, is itself alienated, since it is subject to the direct constraint of the market like scarcely any other space of cultural production.

You can joke about it, but today it is only the Guignols[14] who say so publicly. (In a general sense, if a sociologist wrote a tenth of what he hears when he talks with journalists – on '*ménages*',[15] for instance, or the fabrication of programmes – he would be denounced by the journalists themselves for his partisanship and lack of objectivity, not to mention his insupportable arrogance . . .). If you drop two points in the ratings, you're out. This violence that weighs on television contaminates the whole field of the media. It even contaminates intellectual, scientific and artistic milieus, which were built up on a disdain for money and a relative indifference to mass consecration – can you imagine Mallarmé expecting to be recognized in the street or applauded at meetings? But those little worlds like literature or the sciences, where you can live unknown and poor as long as you have the esteem of a few and do things worthy of being done, are currently under threat.

Do you believe that in the present conditions of competition, the media can hear your plea?

I know that I have the air of a professor with his head in the clouds, who appears to preach morality at a time when the boats are burning, and the boss of *Libération* has to wonder each morning if he'll have enough advertisers to publish the next issue. But it is precisely this crisis, and the violence it exacerbates, that makes certain journalists begin to tell themselves that the sociologists are not as crazy as they seem. Among journalists, as everywhere else, it is especially the young ones and women who are most affected; I would like them to understand a bit better why this is happening to them, that it's not necessarily the junior manager's fault – he may not be very bright, but that's precisely why he was chosen – it's the structure that's oppressing them. This kind of awareness could help them put up with violence and organize themselves. It de-dramatizes and offers the instruments for collective understanding.

You have described the fields of art and science as worlds that gradually found appropriate rules. How is it that the field of journalism has not found rules of its own?

In the world of science, there are social mechanisms that oblige scientists to behave morally, whether they are 'moral' or not. The biologist who accepts money from a laboratory to write a junk article risks losing everything. He

---

[14] [A TV programme with 'news puppets' rather like *Spitting Image*.]
[15] These are lucrative 'presentations' of conferences by leading journalists, or 'debates' organized by big companies for promotional purposes. [Ed.]

is excluded and discredited. Whereas, in the journalistic milieu, where can you find a system of sanctions and rewards? How can you show esteem for a journalist who does his job well?

You are accused of wanting to see a state-controlled system, a central committee for the media . . .

I know. But the very opposite is the case. The autonomy that I champion would increase difference, whereas dependence makes for uniformity. If three leading French magazines – *L'Express*, *Le Point* and *Le Nouvel Observateur* – tend to be interchangeable, it's because they are subject to pretty much the same constraints, the same polls, the same advertisers; their journalists move from one to the other, and they pinch subjects and cover each other's stories. If they could win greater autonomy from their advertisers – from sales figures, which are equivalent to ratings – from television, which defines what are important issues – today you 'have' to report on relations between Balladur and Chirac[16] – they would immediately differentiate themselves more. I suggested, for example, that to limit the damaging effects of competition, newspapers should create common bodies, analogous to those set up in extreme cases, such as a child kidnapping, when everyone agrees a news blackout on certain information. In these extreme cases, the media overcome their competitive interests in order to preserve a kind of common ethic. On other subjects that are only covered because others do the same, such as the 'headscarf affair' [see p.253], you could equally imagine a kind of moratorium. In the case of books, this kind of follow-my-leader is striking. Many cultural journalists are forced to discuss books that they despise, simply because others have written about them. This does a lot for the irresistible success of volumes like the latest Alain Minc or other stupidities of the same kind . . .

Faced with media that dislike you, you seem to choose an attitude that one might criticize as disdainful. Why?

It's rather an attitude of reserve. But it doesn't really suit me. I don't know of any major scientist, or artist or writer, who does not have a difficult relationship with the media. It's a big problem, since citizens have the right to hear the best. The mechanisms of invitation and exclusion, however, mean that television viewers are almost systematically deprived of the best.

---

[16] This interview was conducted shortly before the election. Édouard Balladur and Jacques Chirac, both members of the RPR, were rivals for their party's candidacy in May 1995. [Ed.]

So you're keener on changing television than newspapers?

The tool itself is certainly not in question. It would permit the very opposite of what is done with it today. It could be an instrument of direct democracy, but it is transformed into an instrument of symbolic oppression. To change television, a great amount of work would be needed; this would be a genuine democratic task – not at all the old style of politics.

Aren't you rather exaggerating here? Why do we see Pierre-Gilles de Gennes on the television, who seems to be less reticent than you, but not Bourdieu?

The problem with de Gennes on television is that he can talk about anything, because he is the only person allowed to talk about things that he doesn't actually talk about.

I don't follow . . .

Indeed. He's allowed to say things that are a little naive, but nice, like when he suggests irrigating the Sahara . . . But you never hear de Gennes talking about physics. He can talk admirably for lay people; he uses metaphors, he acts as if everyone has understood, but in the end he never really talks about physics: because after three seconds – the ratings! The upshot is that, under a rubric that he doesn't follow, he says no matter what in fields where he has nothing to say.

Do you encounter an additional difficulty as a sociologist, in that the broad public sees you as 'less scientific' than a physicist or biologist?

You have to compare things that are comparable. In relation to nuclear physics, the comparison is too unfavourable to sociology because this is not established to the same degree, nor formalized, etc. But let's compare it with history. That is a science far less advanced than sociology, and its findings are far less important from the point of view of managing existence, both individual and collective. But no one questions a historian about being scientific, like they do us. Not only do we deal with burning issues – whereas the problems historians discuss are dead and buried – but we are still competing with people who claim to say, on our own subject, things that are equally definitive in the name of other principles of validation. My own principle of validation is the same as a physicist's, but it is opposed by a different principle, that of the politician: the argument from authority or plebiscite by numbers. It is as if the validity of a theory was judged by universal suffrage.

You basically mean that sociology has the same object as politics, but the same rules of validation as science . . .

That's it. And rules of validation for politics are applied to it on the pretext that its object is political. If I were a Byzantine specialist, I would have a position rather like that of Lévi-Strauss, and be listened to with reverence – and indifference. But because I work on the present, and might chance to speak about Balladur or Tapie, or journalists – a taboo subject par excellence – this authority is challenged, even though what I have to say is far better founded and more complex than the run-of-the-mill media intellectual whom the majority of journalists run after, even though rather despising them, and who arrives with three pat formulas pre-adapted to television, i.e. simplistic and suited to reinforcing common opinion. In his case, they agree to put themselves at his service so as to let him tell his stories, which they think will improve their ratings. But if I were to ask the same for myself and others, they would denounce my arrogance. [. . .]

When the truth is complicated, which is often the case, it can only be said in a complicated way, unless you speak of something completely different, as Pierre-Gilles de Gennes does . . . Our work is not only to go against common opinion and against our own social blinkers, but to do so using a language that opposes the disclosure of scientific truth, which is always subversive. Even words are fashioned so as to prevent our speaking about the world such as it is.

Questions about a misunderstanding*

Why is it so hard to be understood by journalists when one speaks about journalism? Why is it impossible to write anything about this profession without having to justify oneself, sometimes even before the courts, and without exposing oneself to an abuse of power in the form of requests to insert comments and a right of reply without appeal? Why is it so dangerous today to tackle these subjects that certain very good writings by journalists on questions of television fail to find a publisher?

Why do those with a virtual monopoly of the mass distribution of information not tolerate analysis of the mechanisms that govern the production of information, and still less, distribution of the least information on this topic? Why is a book that – at this time of writing – has not been mentioned at all in a daily paper proud of its serious reputation, yet has already sold more than 70,000 copies,[17] its readers certainly less convinced of the transparency of journalism than are journalists themselves, been the object of a haughty disdain?

Who has ever denied that there are great journalists, though certainly more on the side of investigation than writers of editorials or entertaining columnists? But what necessity lies in the fact that, identifying the most objective description of mechanisms with an attack on individuals, journalists rise as one man against any iconoclastic analysis? And that even those who are most sensitive and have greatest integrity, those most concerned for the genuine image and ideal reality of journalism, take up the cudgels on behalf of the entire profession – including the most indefensible of their colleagues, as they are best placed to know?

Why in this highly differentiated field of journalism, which like the school or the church is riven by competition and conflict between people whose work is very different or who do the same work in very different ways, does the ruse of social reason, which has a thousand tricks up its sleeve, see to it that the exemplary worker-priest or devoted parish vicar take up arms to defend prevaricating cardinals or corrupt bishops against adversaries who are in reality his allies, and who, like heretics, do no more than remind the profession of the pure ideals of its origins?

---

* Published in *Le Monde Diplomatique* (February 1998), this text replied to an article by Edwy Plenel, 'Le faux procès du journalisme', a remonstration by the editor of *Le Monde* who set himself up as advocate for the hewers and drawers of his profession against Pierre Bourdieu's *Sur la télévision* and Serge Halimi's *Les Nouveaux chiens de garde*, perceived as attacks on journalism.

[17] By the end of 2001, *Les Nouveaux chiens de garde*, then in its 22nd impression, had sold more than 220,000 copies; *Le Monde* never published a review of this book. [Ed.]

Can television criticize television?*

An account of an appearance on screen

I wrote these notes in the days following my appearance on the programme 'Arrêt sur Images'. I already had at the time a feeling that my trust had been abused, but I did not envisage making this public, thinking that would be unfair in some way. A further programme in the same series, however, quite obstinately showed four extracts from my intervention, presenting this retrospective settling of accounts as a bold critical self-reflection by the programme itself. A fine kind of courage, which hardly bothered to oppose any 'opposing' voice to the three ruffians charged with the critical execution of my statements.

At least, in the face of so clear a breach of the trust that should obtain between host and guest, I now feel free to publish these observations, which anyone can check by viewing the recordings of the two programmes.[18] Those who might still have doubted, after seeing the first programme, that television was a formidable instrument of domination, should now be convinced: Daniel Schneidermann, the producer, gave proof of this despite himself in showing how television was a space where two presenters could triumph with no trouble at all over any criticism of the television system.

'Arrêt sur Images', La Cinquième, 23 January 1996. The programme perfectly illustrated what I wanted to demonstrate: the impossibility of giving a coherent and critical speech about television in the medium itself. Seeing in advance that I could not deploy my argument, I decided as a second-best to let the journalists play their habitual game (cuts, interruptions, distractions, etc.), and simply say, after a while, that they were perfectly illustrating my thesis. I should have had the force and presence of mind to be clear about this in my concluding remarks – instead of making polite concessions to 'dialogue', imposed by the feeling of having been too violent and having needlessly offended my interlocutors.

Daniel Schneidermann had asked me on several occasions to appear on his programme, but I had always refused. In early January he repeated his request, very insistently, for a programme on the theme: 'Can television discuss social movements?' I hesitated a great deal, but did not want to let

* An earlier version of this text was published in *Le Monde Diplomatique* of April 1996, under the title 'Analyze d'un passage à l'antenne'.
[18] 'Arrêt sur Images', La Cinquième, 23 January and 13 March 1996.

slip an opportunity for giving, *on television*, a critical analysis of television, for which this was an exemplary occasion.

After having agreed on principle, subject to a preliminary discussion of the arrangements, I remember Daniel Schneidermann explaining at the very start that there would have to be a 'opponent', as if this went without saying. I don't remember very well the arguments he used, if indeed there were arguments – for him it was all taken for granted. I agreed out of a kind of good manners: not to accept debate, in no matter what conditions and with no matter whom, would be a lack of democratic spirit. Daniel Schneidermann mentioned possible interlocutors, in particular an RPR deputy who had spoken against the way in which the television channels had reported the strike. This seemed to imply that he expected me to take the opposite position (asking me for an analysis – which tends to show that, like the majority of journalists, he equates analysis and critique).

I then proposed Jean-Marie Cavada, as he is the head of the channel on which the programme was to be broadcast, also because he strikes me as typical of a softer and less visible kind of violence: he gives every appearance of formal equity, while using all the resources of his position to exert a constraint that strongly steers discussions; my analyses would thus be worth that much more. Though Daniel Schneidermann explained that the fact that I wanted to challenge the director of the channel was no problem, and that I did not have to restrain my 'criticisms', he ruled out Jean-Marie Cavada in favour of Guillaume Durand. He asked me to propose extracts from previous programmes that could be presented in support of my analysis. I gave him an initial list (including several references to Messrs Cavada and Durand), and to justify these choices, I was led to disclose my intentions.

In a second conversation, I perceived that several of my proposed extracts had been replaced by others. In the final run-through, I noticed the appearance of a lengthy segment devoid of interest that sought to show how viewers could say the most opposing things about the television presentation of strikes, thus relativizing in advance the 'criticisms' I would be making (to recall the eternal first lesson of all teaching on the media: editing can do anything with images). In a further conversation, I was told that Jean-Marie Cavada had finally decided to come, and he could not be refused this right of reply, since he was being 'challenged' himself.

Right from the first conversation, I had expressly asked for the positions I had taken during the December strikes not to be mentioned. This was not the subject, and such a reminder could only make sociological analysis appear as biased criticism. At the start of the broadcast, however, the journalist Pascale Clark announced that I had publicly supported the strikes, and been 'very critical of the representation of these given by the media' – though I had said nothing at all on that subject. She repeated this with her first question, on the reasons why I had not spoken on television during the strikes.

Faced with this new retreat from the promise that had been made to obtain my participation, I hesitated for a long time, wondering if I should leave or reply. In fact, from this intervention on, which faced me right from the start with the alternative between resigned submission to manipulation or an abrupt breach of the rules of 'democratic' debate, the theme that my two 'opponents' incessantly harped on throughout the programme was, how could I claim to be objective about the representation of an event towards which I had taken up a partisan position?

During the telephone discussions, I had also made the point that there were now two of these 'opponents', and both professionals (it will appear, when I make a brief attempt to analyze the situation I found myself in, that there were actually four). I had expressed the desire that they should not abuse the advantage this gave them. In fact, carried away by the arrogance and certainty of their rightful position, they constantly interrupted me and cut me off, while offering ostentatious flattery. I believe that in this programme, in which I was supposed to present a sociological analysis of a televised debate, as the main speaker, I spoke for twenty minutes at the most, and less to present my own ideas than to do battle with interlocutors who rejected the whole work of analysis.

Daniel Schneidemann spoke to me several times, up to the day of the broadcast, and I spoke to him with complete trust (this being the tacit condition, at least for me, of participation in a public dialogue), revealing my full intentions. He said nothing to me at any time about the intentions of my 'opponents'. When I asked him whether he intended to show them, in advance, the extracts I had selected – which would mean revealing my entire arsenal – he said that if they asked for this he could not refuse . . . He spoke vaguely to me of a segment on an ill-defined subject filmed in Marseille. After the programme, he expressed his satisfaction, saying how happy he was that a 'major intellectual' – flattery! – had taken the trouble to closely watch and discuss television, but especially how he admired my 'opponents' for having 'played the game' and courageously accepted being criticized . . .

The day of the broadcast, at about 2 p.m., just when I was getting ready to leave, Daniel Schneidermann called to tell me that he was very upset at hearing that I intended to be accompanied by Pierre Carles, who was making a film about me.[19] He told me that this film-maker, whom he knew well,

[19] *La Sociologie est un Sport de Combat* (C-P Productions, 2001) presented Bourdieu's sociology through some aspects of the sociologist at work (1998–2001). A further film by Pierre Carles, *Enfin Pris!*, examined this appearance on television and analyzed the 'Schneidermann-style pseudo-critique' that Bourdieu saw as 'a way of improving ratings and polishing his conscience' ('Karl Kraus et les médias', in G. Stieg and J. Bouveresse, eds, *Actualité de Karl Kraus*, loc. cit., pp. 37–50.) [Ed.]

would not miss the slightest opportunity to use any images he could take to make fun of myself and my interlocutors, and suggest a suspicious view of our interactions and relations. I told Pierre Carles to call him; Daniel Schneidermann did not dare forbid him access to the studio, and we left together. While we were waiting at the entrance, Daniel Schneidermann himself came out, somewhat embarrassed, to tell Pierre Carles that he was not allowed in.

Before the programme, the 'opponents' and presenters left me alone on the set for nearly an hour. Guillaume Durand came and sat opposite me, and complained at what he saw as my complicity with the Socialists (he was not well informed . . .). I replied with a certain exasperation, and he then remained silent and very embarrassed. The presenter, Pascale Clark, tried to relax the atmosphere. 'Do you like television? – I hate it.' We remained at that level. I wondered if I shouldn't leave. I remembered Pierre Boulez faced on screen with an embittered and pitiful essayist, a former acolyte of Jack Lang whose name I have forgotten. I remembered all the scientists that François de Closets had summoned as 'witnesses' and who had been questioned by 'opponents' simply to make a spectacle.

If I had at least managed to convince myself that what I was about to do might have some kind of use, or that I had come there to communicate something about this new instrument of manipulation . . . In actual fact, my dominant impression was that I had only succeeded in putting myself in the position of a dissolving fish to be thrown in the water.

The arrangement on the set: the two 'opponents' seated on either side of the male presenter, like china dogs (or guard dogs), with me on the side, facing the female presenter. I was given the 'run-through' of the broadcast: only two of my statements had been retained, and four new 'subjects' added, including two lengthy segments and reports, all designed to show the relativity of 'criticisms' and the objectivity of television. The two statements of mine that were dropped, after I had already been shown them, were designed to show the violent feelings of the strikers towards television.

Conclusion (which I wrote before the broadcast): it is impossible to criticize television on screen because the mechanisms of television impose themselves even on programmes designed to criticize the medium. The programme on the treatment of strikes on television reproduced the very structure of programmes about the strikes.

WHAT I WOULD HAVE LIKED TO SAY

Television is both an instrument of communication and a censoring instrument (hiding even whilst showing), subject to a very strong *censorship*. I could appeal to the instruments of distribution in order to demonstrate the monopoly of television (television is the instrument that makes it possible to speak to the largest number, beyond the limits of the field of professionals). But this attempt might make it seem as if one were making use of television, as media people do, in order to act in this field, and gain symbolic power by virtue of a celebrity (badly) acquired with lay people, i.e. outside the field. It would still need to be verified whether one goes on television in order to (and only in order to) benefit from the specific characteristic of this instrument – the fact that it makes it possible to speak to the largest number – and thus to say things that deserve being said to the greatest number (for example that it is impossible to say anything on television).

INSIDE THE MACHINE: THE MOST VISIBLE AND THE MOST HIDDEN

The role of the presenter:
He imposes the problematic, in the name of respect for formal rules with a variable geometry and in the name of the public, by way of summarizing ('The fact is . . .', 'Let's be clear . . .', 'Answer my question . . .', 'Explain yourself . . .', 'You still haven't answered . . .', 'You are not saying what reform you want . . .') that actually places the interlocutor in a defensive position. To lend his words authority, he makes himself the spokesperson of the viewers: 'The question everyone is asking', 'It matters to all French people . . .'. He can even appeal to 'public service' to put himself in the position of 'users' in describing the strikes.

He allocates speech and signs of importance (respectful or disdainful tone, paying attention or impatient, titles, order of speakers from first to last, etc.).

He establishes urgency (and uses this to impose censorship), cuts off speech, refuses to let people speak (in the name of the public's supposed expectations, or rather the idea that the audience will not understand, or more simply, of its political or social unconscious).

These interventions are always differentiated: for example, trade unionists are always the object of injunctions ('What do *you* propose, then?'), in a peremptory tone and hammering the syllables; the same attitude in cutting people off ('We've just been speaking about this . . . Thank you, madam, thank you'), a dismissive thanks, as against the fawning thanks addressed to an important figure. Overall behaviour is quite different, according to whether it is someone 'important' (Alain Peyrefitte) who is being addressed, or just some casual guest: body language, look, tone of voice, verbal continuity (impatient 'yes . . . yes . . . yes', sceptical noises that hurry up and discourage), the terms in which the interlocutor is spoken to, titles, order of speaking, time allotted (the CGT delegate spoke for a total of five minutes during the ninety-minute programme 'La Marche du Siècle').

The presenter acts as lord and master of the set ('my programme', 'my guests': the brutal interjection he makes to those who challenge his way of conducting the debate is applauded by the audience on the set who act as a kind of claque).

The composition of the set:
This is the outcome of a whole preliminary work of selective invitation (or refusal). The worst censorship is absence; the words of the absent are excluded in an invisible fashion. Hence the dilemma: invisible (virtuous) refusal or the trap.

It obeys a concern for formal balance (for instance, equality of speaking time allotted in 'face-to-face' debates), but this serves as a mask for actual inequalities. In the programmes on the December 1995 strikes, you had on one side a small number of actors perceived and presented as committed and partial, and on the other side observers presented as arbiters, completely neutral and well-behaved – i.e. those *presumed guilty* (of harming users of public services) summoned to *explain themselves*, to impartial arbiters or experts whose function is to judge and *explain*.

The appearance of objectivity is ensured by the fact that the partisan positions of certain participants are disguised (by playing with titles or high-lighting expertise: for example, Alain Peyrefitte is described as a 'writer' and not as an 'RPR senator and chair of the editorial board of *Le Figaro*', Guy Sorman as an 'economist' rather than 'adviser to Alain Juppé'.

The logic of the language game:
The game is rigged in favour of the professionals of speech, of authorized speech.

Democratic debate conceived after the model of a ball game enables a ratings device (the 'face-to-face') to be presented as a model of democratic exchange.

Affinities between a section of the participants: those in the media share the same world (among themselves and with the presenters). Familiar with the media and with its people, they offer every guarantee: not only is it known in advance that they appear well on screen (they are 'good customers', as the professionals say), but above all that there will be no unpleasant surprises. The most successful kind of censorship involves giving voice to people who have nothing to say except what is expected of them – or better still, have nothing to say at all. The titles given them help give their speech authority.

The different participants are not equal in these situations: on the one hand, professionals of speech, with the aptitude of manipulating sustained language that is needed; on the other hand, people less well armed and with little experience of situations of public speaking (trade unionists, and, still more so, workers who are questioned, and stammer into the camera, or speak too quickly, get in a muddle, or show off as a way of extricating themselves, even though a few minutes earlier, in a normal situation, they expressed themselves perfectly clearly and forcefully). To ensure true equality, we would need to favour the disfavoured (help them with gestures and looks, give them time, etc.), whereas everything is actually done to favour the favoured.

The presenters' own unconscious, their professional habits. For example, their cultural submission as semi-scholarly or autodidact cultural intermediaries, inclined to recognize the due academic signs of recognition. They are the mechanism (i.e. the ratings) made flesh: when they cut off statements that they believe are too difficult, they doubtless do so sincerely, in good faith. They are the perfect relays of the structure, and if they were not, they'd be fired.

In their view of strikes and strikers, they engage their unconscious as a privileged group: from one side they expect justifications or fears ('Express your fears', 'What are you complaining about?'), from the other side explanations or judgements ('What do you think?').

Questions to the real masters of the world[*]

I am not going to make myself look ridiculous by describing the state of the world of the media to people who know this better than I do; people who are among the most powerful in the world, with a power that is not just that of money, but the power that money can give over minds. This symbolic power, which in the majority of societies was distinct from political or economic power, is today united in the hands of the same individuals, who hold control of the major communications groups, i.e. the set of instruments of production and distribution of cultural goods.

I would love to subject these very powerful individuals to a questioning of the kind to which Socrates subjected the powerful of his time (in one dialogue, with a great deal of patience and insistence, he asked a general famous for his courage what courage was; in another, he asked a man known for his piety what piety was, and so on; making clear each time that they did not really know these things). Not being in a position to proceed in this way, I would like to raise a certain number of questions, which these individuals certainly never ask themselves (in particular because they don't have the time), and which boil down to just one: masters of the world, do you really know what you are doing, what you are in the process of doing, all the consequences of what you are in the process of doing? Questions to which Plato replied with the celebrated formula, which undoubtedly applies here too: 'No one is bad by choice.'

You will tell us that the technological and economic convergence of audio-visual media, telecommunications and computing, and the proliferation of networks that results from this, make legal protection for audio-visual material ineffective and useless (for instance the rules on distribution quotas for European films); you will tell us that the technological profusion arising from the proliferation of digital channels responds to a potential demand from a great diversity of consumers, and that this 'explosion of media choices' means that every demand will receive an adequate supply – in other words, all tastes will be satisfied. You will say that competition, especially when combined with technological advance, is synonymous with 'creation'. I could back up each of my assertions with dozens of references and quotations, but

[*] Published in L'Humanité and Libération on 13 October 1999, and Le Monde on the 14th, under the title 'Maîtres du monde, savez-vous ce que vous faites?', this intervention on a special broadcast of Canal Plus/MTR (11 October) was delivered before an audience that brought together heads of the largest groups of the communications industry.

these would be quite redundant. A single example, which summarizes almost everything that I have just said, I borrow from Jean-Marie Messier: 'Millions of jobs have been created in the United States thanks to the full liberalization of telecommunications and communications technology. Let this be an inspiration for France! The competitiveness of our economy and the jobs of our children are at stake. We have to overcome our nervousness, and open wide the gates of competition and creativity.'

But you also tell us that the competition of new entrants, far more powerful ones, coming from telecommunications and computing, is such that the audio-visual media find it increasingly hard to resist; that the sums paid for rights, particularly for sporting events, are ever higher; that everything produced and circulated by the new communications groups that are technologically and economically integrated, i.e. including televised messages as well as books, televised films or games – in other words, everything that comes under the catch-all name of 'information', should be treated simply as one more commodity among others, with the same rules applied to it as are applied to any other product; and that this standard industrial product must therefore obey the common law, the law of profit, without any cultural exception being sanctioned by limiting rules (such as the standard pricing of books, or distribution quotas). Finally you tell us that the law of profit, i.e. the law of the market, is eminently democratic, because it sanctions the triumph of the product voted for by the greatest number.

Each of the above 'ideas' could be opposed, not by other ideas, which would run the risk of appearing an ideologist lost in the clouds, but rather by facts: to the idea of the extraordinary diversification of supply, we could oppose the extraordinary uniformity of television programmes, the fact that the various communications networks increasingly tend to broadcast the same type of product at the same time – games, soaps, commercial music, sentimental 'telenovelas', police series that are no better for being French, like *Navarro*, or German, like *Derrick*. So many products issuing from the quest for maximum profit for minimum cost; or, in another field, the growing homogenization of newspapers, especially the weeklies.

To take another example, the 'ideas' of competition and diversification could be countered with the fact of the extraordinary concentration of communications groups – a concentration shown by the most recent merger, between Viacom and CBS,[20] i.e. a group geared towards the production of content and a group geared towards distribution, leading to a *vertical integration that means distribution governs production*. The accumulation of

[20] Or, now that I am re-reading this text for publication (12 October 2000), the no less terrifying merger of the US media giant Time Warner with the leading global internet access provider, America Online (AOL).

production, exploitation and distribution leads to abuse of a dominant position which favours in-house productions: Gaumont, Pathé and UGC are responsible, by themselves or through cinemas whose programming they control, for the projection of 80 per cent of exclusively controlled films on the Paris market; not to mention the proliferation of multiplexes, which represent unfair competition to small independent cinemas, now often forced to close.

The essential thing, however, is that commercial preoccupations, and particularly the quest for *short-term* profit maximization, are increasingly and ever more widely imposed on the totality of cultural production. In the book publishing field, for example, which I have studied closely, editors are forced to orient themselves unambiguously towards commercial success, on account of the very high profit rates that are required, especially when publishing houses are integrated with big multimedia groups. I could cite the example of Thomas Middlehoff, president of Bertelsmann, as reported in *La Tribune*: 'He gave the 350 profit centres two years to meet their targets. [. . .] Between now and the end of 2000, each sector must ensure a profit of more than 10 per cent on the capital invested.'

This is where we have to start asking questions. I spoke just now of cultural production. Is it still possible today, and will it still be possible in the future, to speak of *cultural* production and culture? Those who are making the new world of communications, and who are themselves made by it, love to bring up the problem of speed, information flows and transactions that become ever more rapid, and no doubt they are partly right when they have in mind the circulation of information and the cycle of products. That said, the logic of speed and profit, combined in the pursuit of *maximum short-term profit* (with audience ratings for television, sales figures for books and of course newspapers, and entrance tickets for cinema) strikes me as hard to reconcile with the idea of culture. When what Ernst Gombrich called the 'ecological conditions of art' are destroyed, art and culture soon die off.

As proof of this, I could just mention what has happened to Italian cinema, which was one of the best in the world and now survives only by dint of a small handful of directors, or German cinema, or the cinema of Eastern Europe. Or the crisis that auteur cinema is experiencing everywhere, particularly for lack of distribution circuits. Not to speak of the censorship that film distributors can impose on certain films, the most familiar example being that of Pierre Carles, whose film – not by chance – showed censorship in the media. Or again, the fate of cultural radio such as France Culture, one of the rare sites of freedom from market pressure and editorial advertising, which today has been condemned to liquidation in the name of modernity, audience figures and media connivance.

It is impossible to genuinely understand, however, what the reduction of culture to the state of a commercial product means, unless we recall how the worlds of production of those works we consider as timeless in the field of fine art, literature or cinema were constituted. All the works we see exhibited in museums, all the works of literature that have become classics, all the films preserved in cinémathèques or film museums are the product of social worlds that were steadily constituted by freeing themselves from the laws of the ordinary world, and especially from the logic of profit. One example will make this clear: we know from surviving contracts that the painters of the *quattrocento* had to struggle against their patrons for their work no longer to be treated as a mere product, valued by the surface painted and the price of the materials used; they had to struggle to obtain the right to sign their works, i.e. to be treated as authors, as well as for what has been called – from a quite recent date – author's rights (Beethoven still had to struggle for this); they had to struggle for their rareness, uniqueness and quality, and it was only with the assistance of critics, biographers, professors of art history, etc. that they succeeded in imposing themselves as artists, 'creators'.

It is all this, however, that is threatened today by the reduction of the work of art to a product and a commodity. The current struggles of film directors for the 'final cut' and against the claim of the producer to have ultimate right over their work are the exact equivalent of the struggles of the *quattrocento* painters. It took nearly five centuries for painters to win the right to choose the colours they used, the manner of using them, and finally the right to choose their subject, which is why the disappearance of the subject, with abstract art, was such a scandal for the commissioning bourgeois; in the same way, to have an auteur cinema you must have a whole social world, with small theatres and studios projecting classic films and frequented by students, cinema clubs inspired by cinema-loving philosophy teachers, schooled in these same theatres, understanding critics who write in *Cahiers du Cinéma*, cineastes who learned their trade by seeing films that they wrote up in *Cahiers*, in sum, a whole social milieu in which a certain cinema has value and recognition.

It is these social worlds that are threatened today by the domination of commercial cinema and the big distributors, which producers must reckon with unless they are distributors themselves; these worlds were the culmination of a long development, but today they have entered a process of involution; they are the site of a backward slide, from art work to product, from author to engineer or technician using technical resources, the famous 'special effects', and stars – all extremely expensive – in order to manipulate or satisfy the primary impulses of the spectator (often anticipated thanks to the research of other technicians, i.e. marketing specialists). We know, however, how much time is needed to create creators, i.e. social spaces of producers and receivers, within which they can appear, develop and succeed.

To reintroduce the reign of commerce and commercialism into these worlds that were steadily built up against it means imperilling the highest works of humanity – art, literature, and even science. I do not think that anyone really intends this. That is the reason I quoted Plato's celebrated formula that 'no one is bad by choice'. If it is true that the forces of technology, allied with the forces of economics, the law of profit and competition, are a threat to culture, what can be done to counteract this movement? What can be done to strengthen the chances of those who can only exist in the long term, those who, like the Impressionist painters of an earlier time, work for a posthumous market? Those who work to bring about a new market, in opposition to those who bend to the demands of the existing market and draw great immediate profits from it – material, economic, and also symbolic, in the form of prizes, academies and decorations?

I would like to convince you, but this would doubtless need a great deal of time, that the pursuit of maximum immediate profit is not necessarily obedience to *the logic of well-understood interest*, at least where books, films and paintings are concerned. To equate the pursuit of maximum profit with pursuit of the maximum public means exposing oneself to losing the existing public without conquering another, losing the relatively restrained public of people who read a lot, go often to museums, theatres and cinemas, without necessarily gaining new readers or occasional spectators. Since we know that, in all the developed countries at least, the length of school attendance is still steadily growing, as well as the average educational level, and all those practices strongly correlated with it such as museum or theatre attendance, reading, etc., we can imagine that a policy of economic investment in producers and products described as 'quality' could even be economically profitable at least in the medium term, on condition however that this could count on the services of an effective educational system.

The choice, therefore, is not between 'globalization', i.e. submission to the laws of the market, the reign of commercialism, which is always the opposite of what is almost universally understood by culture, and defence of national cultures or this or that form of cultural nationalism or localism. The kitsch products of commercial 'globalization', the blockbuster film with special effects, or even that 'world fiction' whose authors might be Italian or English, are the opposite in every respect of the products of that literary, artistic and cinematographic international whose centre is everywhere and nowhere, even if for a very long time, and perhaps still today, it is in Paris, site of a national tradition of artistic internationalism, as well as in London and New York. In the same way that Joyce, Faulkner, Kafka, Beckett and Gombrowicz, pure products of Ireland, the United States, Czechoslovakia and Poland, came into their own in Paris, so a number of contemporary film-makers such as Kaurismaki, Manuel de Olivera, Satyajit Ray, Kieslowski, Woody Allen, Kiarostami and so many others, would not exist as they do exist without that literary, artistic and cinematographic international whose headquarters is in Paris. Undoubtedly because it is here that, for strictly historical reasons, the microcosm of producers, critics and attentive audience that is needed for its survival was constituted and managed to survive for a long time.[21]

Many centuries were needed, I repeat, to produce producers who produced for posthumous markets. It is a bad way of posing the question to oppose, as is often done, a 'globalization' and globalism that is on the side of economic and commercial power, as well as of progress and modernity, to a nationalism attached to archaic forms of preservation of sovereignty. What is rather involved is a struggle between a commercial power that aims to extend to the whole world the particular interests of commerce and those who govern it, and a cultural resistance based on defence of the universal works produced by the denationalized international of creators.

I would like to end with a historical anecdote, which also has to do with speed, and will show very well what in my view should be the relationship that an art free from the pressures of commerce could have with temporal powers. We know that Michelangelo followed the due forms of protocol so badly in his relations with Pope Julius II, his patron, that the latter was compelled to sit down very rapidly to ensure that the painter was not seated before he was. In a certain sense, I could say that I have tried here to perpetuate, in a very modest but faithful way, the tradition inaugurated by Michelangelo of a distance from established powers, above all those new powers that are the combined forces of money and media.

---

[21] I draw here on the analysis of Pascale Casanova, *La République mondiale des lettres* (Paris: Seuil 1999).

12

Resisting the Liberal Counter-Revolution

In reaction to the international context of liberal counter-revolution, which brought economics to power, Pierre Bourdieu added a sociology of economics to his analyses of the social effects of economic logic. In Social Structures of the Economy *he brought together and summarized a broad investigation into the housing market that had originally been published in the early 1990s, a text of historical analysis of state policies towards the movement of capital and delocalization of businesses, as well as the 'foundations for an economic anthropology' designed to oppose the 'ahistorical view of economic science'.*[1]

In parallel with this, Bourdieu synthesized his works on Algeria, the 'social genesis of economic habitus' and the 'scholastic bias', themes that run through his texts on the economy of practices from his first critique of structuralism, formulated on the occasion of his analysis of the strategies of Béarn peasants,[2] *and formalized for the first time in* Practical Reason *(1980), before leading on to a systematic critique of scholastic reason in* Pascalian Meditations *(1997).*

Faced with the constitution of a global economic space unified according to the logic of a concentration of capital in the interests of a 'conservative international of directors and managers of industrial multinationals' (backed by the action of international institutions such as the IMF and World Bank), Bourdieu supported movements of struggle against neoliberal globalization on the occasion of the demonstrations in Nice (December 2000) and Québec (April 2001) (see pp.373, 374 and 377).

The relative success of these struggles, however, did not prevent him from turning his attention to other international issues – among which Algeria maintained a special place – and intervening in collective contexts. For example, questioning the complicit silence of national and international bodies in the face of the 'blood bath' authorized and even fomented by the hierarchies of the Algerian state and army (see p.351), and supporting the initiatives against the recurrent wars of the 1990s, first the Gulf war and then the Balkan wars (see p.355). These positions should be seen against the background of his analyses of an international situation in which 'the world community has given carte blanche to the United States to establish a certain order', one in which 'power relations are

---

[1] *The Social Structures of the Economy* (Cambridge: Polity 2005). [Ed.]
[2] 'Les relations entre les sexes dans la société paysanne', *Études Rurales* 5/6 (1962), reprinted in *Le Bal des célibataires* (Paris: Seuil 2002). [Ed.]

crushingly in favour of the dominant', and it is only 'the justice of the strongest' that rules.³ The fact that such a transnational relation of force could be presented as a natural necessity, Bourdieu saw as the result of 'twenty years of work by the conservative think-tanks and their allies in the fields of politics and journalism', who had invented 'a new planetary vulgate' whose intentions and work on people's consciousness it was imperative to disclose (see p.364).⁴

But it was the European level that Pierre Bourdieu saw as the privileged terrain for a renewal of struggle, devoting to this a text published in Le Monde Diplomatique *in June 1999, in which he criticized the process of European construction, which 'at the present time is simply social destruction'.⁵*

The 'Appeal for a General Assembly of the European Social Movement' (1 May 2000) (see p.362), was thus an attempt to bring together anti-capitalist activists at a European level in a structure similar to the social movements of the 1990s, which Pierre Bourdieu had characterized by their rejection of traditional forms of political mobilization, a self-management that facilitated participation by the rank and file and the foregrounding of direct action.⁶

Certain recurring oppositions, such as that made between the libertarian and authoritarian traditions, are simply the transcription onto the level of ideological struggle of the fundamental contradiction of the revolutionary movement, which is forced to resort to discipline and authority, even to violence, in order to combat authority and violence. As a heretical challenge to the heretical church, a revolution against the 'established revolutionary power', the 'libertarian' critique in its 'spontaneist' form seeks to exploit, against those who dominate the Party, the contradiction between 'authoritarian' strategies inside the Party and the 'anti-authoritarian' strategies of the Party in the political field as a whole. And even the anarchist movement, which accuses Marxism of authoritarianism, displays the same kind of opposition, between the 'platform' type of thought concerned to lay the basis for a powerful anarchist organization and rejecting the demand for an unrestricted freedom for individuals and small groups, and the 'synthesis' type of thought that seeks to leave individuals completely independent.⁷

---

³ Interview in *Flux News*, 14 December 2001, p. 24. [Ed.]

⁴ Cf. also 'Les ruses de la raison impérialiste' (with Loïc Wacquant), *Actes de la Recherche en Sciences Sociales* 121/122 (1998). [Ed.]

⁵ 'For a European Social Movement', *Le Monde Diplomatique*, June 1999, reprinted in *Firing Back* (London: Verso 2003), pp. 53–63. [Ed.]

⁶ Cf. 'Les objectifs d'un mouvement social européen' (available together with various other interventions of this time at www.samizdat.net and published under the title 'Contre la politique de dépolitisation'). [Ed.]

⁷ 'La représentation politique' (1981), reprinted in *Langage et pouvoir symbolique* (Paris: Fayard 2001), p. 234.

Based on the rejection of any political recuperation, in the libertarian tradition of the left (see p.127) as reactivated by the 'Appel pour l'autonomie du mouvement social',[8] Pierre Bourdieu's interventions were intended to give impetus to political actions based on practical knowledge, and enable the emergence of a European coordination of social movements and trade unions that would escape the control – and compromises – of institutions like the European Trade Union Confederation. In this perspective, the Vienna and Athens meetings, of November 2000 and May 2001 respectively (see p.380), aimed to establish a new kind of political work that sought to escape both the logic of the political meeting and that of the academic conference.

---

[8] This appeal was launched in 1998 by trade unionists from SUD and activists from the associations that had organized the European marches against unemployment and precariousness; some of its initiators were also among the first signatories of the general assembly of the European social movement. (See in particular Bernard Schmitt and Patrice Spadoni, *Les Sentiers de la colère, 15 472 kilomètres à pieds contre le chomâge* (Paris: L'Esprit frappeur 2000). Preface by Pierre Bourdieu, 'Misère du monde et mouvements sociaux', pp. 15–21. [Ed.]

Open letter to the members
of the UN mission to Algeria*

At the request of the general secretary of the United Nations, a delegation chaired by Mario Soares, and including Simone Veil, I. K. Jurgal, Abel Karim Kabariti, Donald McHenry and Amos Wako, is to visit Algeria on 22 July 1998 for a two-week 'information mission'. As members of the Comité International pour la Paix, la Démocratie et les Droits de l'Homme en Algérie, recently founded in Paris, we can only welcome this initiative. We hope very strongly that it will help to cast light on a situation that is complex, confused and opaque, and in this way contribute to the return of civil peace in Algeria.

The Algerian government requested this mission, and has promised it 'free and complete access' to all sources of information. We do not doubt that its members will be able to meet representatives of the vital forces of the nation. Competent ministers will explain to them that life in Algeria is now normal, even if there is still some 'residual terrorism'. They will indicate that eradication of this is obstructed by the too great tolerance of Western governments towards clandestine Islamist groups that use their countries as rear bases for terrorism in Algeria. And they will insist on the urgent need for a better international anti-terrorist coordination. Above all, they will emphasize that this situation should not obscure the good functioning of the new 'democratic institutions', nor the reality of freedom of expression of the 'independent press'.

This will be confirmed by the great majority of representatives in the National Assembly and Senate, as well as by the editors of the different media, who are fond of emphasizing the freedom that they give proof of each day. In the same way, the president of the Observatoire National des Droits de l'Homme (which reports to the president of the republic), Maître Kamel Rezzag Bara, will acknowledge the existence of 'mistakes and excessive zeal' by the forces of order, but explain that these are limited, and are being systematically prosecuted and punished by the courts. This will also be confirmed by the members of the Conseil Supérieur de la Magistrature, who will stress their role as guarantors of the independence of magistrates.

* This text, written for the Comité International pour la Paix, la Démocratie et les Droits de l'Homme en Algérie, was jointly signed by Majid Benchikh, Tassadit Yacine (Algeria), Patrick Baudoin, Pierre Bourdieu, François Gèze, Pierre Vidal-Nacquet (France), Anna Bozzo (Italy), Inga Brandel (Sweden) and Werner Ruf (Germany). Two other collective texts on similar lines were addressed to the French government in February 2001 and to the European Commission in May 2001.

Finally, the delegation will meet representatives of 'civil society': women's associations, health workers, housing activists, trade unionists from the Union Générale des Travailleurs Algériens. It will certainly be impressed by their freedom of speech, including criticism of the government, and their courage in the face of the dramas provoked by Islamic terrorism and the difficulties of everyday life.

If the members of the UN mission stick to these meetings, they will certainly leave Algeria with the feeling that, while the country is still experiencing a difficult time, it is on the way to a true democracy, as their various interlocutors bear witness. And yet, these represent only a small fraction of Algerian society, that structured in and around the 'real power', the term used by Algerians to denote the heads of the army. If the delegation wants to 'know the full reality of the Algerian situation in all its dimensions', as the Algerian ambassador to the UN, M. Abdallah Baali, has proposed, we invite its members to take him at his word and broaden its investigations.

We invite it for example to meet, in private, the lawyers for the victims of the 'mistakes and excesses' of the forces of order, whom they can contact through the intermediary of the Syndicat National des Avocats, chaired by Maître Mahmoud Khellili, or the Ligue Algérienne de Défense des Droits de l'Homme, chaired by Maître Ali Yahia Abdenour. These will speak to them of judgements handed down by tribunals on the sole basis of confessions extracted under torture, systematic violations of the rights of defence, and extra-judicial executions that have become common currency.

We invite them to meet, in private, representatives of the Syndicat National de la Magistrature, who demand the abrogation of the executive decree of 24 October 1992, which has reduced to practically nothing the independence of judges, and who oppose the recently projected law on the status of the judiciary, which will further aggravate this situation.

We invite them to meet, in private, representatives of the thousands of families seeking relatives who have 'disappeared', kidnapped by elements of the security forces or death squads linked with the government militias.

We invite them to meet, without witnesses, journalists of press organs that have been 'suspended' or banned.

We are convinced that evidence of this kind will help them question their official interlocutors more closely on the denunciations that have been made for the last several years by organizations that defend human rights, and particularly to raise the following questions:

Why does the Algerian army, which according to the constitution does not play any political role, occupy the key place in the political system that is acknowledged by all impartial observers, so that it imposes its choices – openly or otherwise – at every major juncture?

What guarantees has the state given for the necessary repression of terrorist acts being conducted with due respect to the international conventions and agreements on human rights that Algeria has ratified?

Is it possible to visit the fourteen places of detention in the region of Algiers that have been indicated as centres of torture by the International Human Rights Federation?

Is it true that 18,000 political prisoners are currently held for 'acts of terrorism'? In what conditions have they been judged and condemned?

Is the 'ministerial decree' of 7 June 1994, which banned the media from broadcasting any information on the 'security situation' except the 'official communiqués' of the minister of the interior, still in force? Is it true that 'reading committees' of the interior ministry are present at the three printing works that print the Algerian daily newspapers?

Why did the forces of order not intervene in the massacres that took place between summer 1997 and early 1998, even though their units were often stationed close by? Have diligent investigations been made on the basis of evidence collected by Amnesty International, which that organization says 'lends weight to information according to which members of the armed groups that massacred civilians often act in concert with certain army units and security forces, or with their consent'?

Is it true, as Prime Minister Ahmed Ouyahia has indicated, that there are some 5,000 'legitimate defence groups' whose status is defined by the law of 4 January 1997? Is the existence of these groups, which were set up in 1994 and amount to some 150,000 men, compatible with the UN's international agreement on civil and political rights, which was ratified by the Algerian state in 1989? Is it true that these groups take part in offensive actions together with the security forces? What is the legal foundation for this?

What follow-up has the Observatoire National des Droits de l'Homme given to the 1,728 requests for localization of missing persons that it acknowledges receiving between 1994 and 1996? Have there been new requests since then? If so, how many, and what follow-up has it made?

We hope very strongly that the delegation will be able to obtain sincere replies to these questions, and any others it deems useful to raise. In our view, this bears on the credibility and effectiveness of this mission: everything must be tried to avoid the Algerian people being pushed still further into despair by thinking that the international community is intervening only to support the status quo. We also hope that this visit will not be used to exonerate the Algerian state yet again from its cooperation agreements with the competent bodies of the United Nations, commitments tied to the international treaties it has ratified. It is particularly urgent that the government should grant the special rapporteurs of the UN on the subject of extra-judicial executions and torture the authorization to come and investigate in Algeria that they have been waiting for since 1993.

Only policies of openness based on respect for human rights and democratic freedoms can permit the return of peace and the marginalization of extremists, indispensable conditions for the advance of Algeria and for regional stability. We hope you will be able to take note of this message.

European appeal for a just and lasting peace in the Balkans*

The participants in the international meeting held in Paris on 15 May 1999 have echoed a number of convergent appeals, both in Europe and the United States, that have opposed both 'ethnic cleansing' in Kosovo and the NATO bombing of Yugoslavia.

The states that launched or supported this undeclared war, waged outside any international legality, have claimed that it was moral and legitimate because the defence of a people's rights and lives was sufficient justification. They accept that 'mistakes' have been made, and what is called 'collateral damage', but these are only 'wrong steps in the right direction'. Any criticism of the NATO war, we are told, helps to sustain the regime of Slobodan Milosevic, or at best means refusal to act against his reactionary policy.

All this is false. What is the result of several weeks of NATO bombing? A tragedy! Each day that passes, the war aggravates the situation of the civilian population, and makes the resolution of national conflicts in Kosovo and the whole Balkan region that much more difficult. It is impossible to hold as moral and legitimate: a war that provides the pretext for a dreadful aggravation of the fate of the Kosovar people whom it claims to support, rather in fact promoting their exodus; a war that unites the Yugoslav people suffering aggression around the repressive regime of Slobodan Milosevic, blinding them to Belgrade's responsibilities in the ethnic cleansing of Kosovars; a war that strengthens the regime, weakens the democratic opposition to it also in Montenegro, and destabilizes Macedonia; bombings that kill civilians, and destroy infrastructure, factories and schools.

This war contradicts its proclaimed purposes all along the line. It is promoting a catastrophic chain reaction which we have to escape from at the earliest possible date, between, on the one hand, the intensification of bombing pursued to try to save the 'credibility' of NATO, and on the other hand, the brutal and massive expulsion of populations, accompanied by the unleashing of violence with no common measure with the repression that was inflicted before the onset of the bombing.

It is untrue that everything had been tried, that the bombing was an effective response to Serbian repression and an appropriate measure to defend

---

* This collective text, published in *L'Humanité* on 17 May 1999, was the outcome of a meeting on 15 May at the Paris office of the European Parliament.

355

the lives and rights of the Kosovars. Nothing has been done to maintain and expand the presence of the OSCE observers, or involve neighbouring states and the populations affected in the search for solutions. Western governments accelerated the disintegration of Yugoslavia, and never treated the national questions intrinsic to this federation in a systematic way. They confirmed the partition of Bosnia-Herzegovina on ethnic lines that had been jointly organized by Belgrade and Zagreb. And they got drawn into the Albanian question in Kosovo because they had preferred to ignore the expulsion of Serbs in Croatian Krajina.

At the Rambouillet negotiations, they opted for an armed response by NATO instead of proposing an international intervention force that would act on the basis of a UN mandate, though this proposal could have been legitimately imposed in the event of Milosevic refusing: such an intervention force would have been far more effective in protecting the population than were the NATO bombs. What we must demand today is the return of the Albanian population under international protection, placed under the responsibility of the UN General Assembly, and the withdrawal of Serbian forces from Kosovo. The first step towards attaining these objectives is an immediate stop to the bombing.

The reopening of a process of negotiation on such a basis, in a UN context, not only does not imply any trust in Slobodan Milosevic, but would be more destabilizing of his power than the bombs of the last few weeks, which have instead affected the Yugoslav population, including the opposition. A procedure of this kind must be based on a principle, and be accompanied by the necessary resources. The principle is respect for the right of peoples, and in particular the Albanian and Serb populations of Kosovo, to decide their own destiny for themselves, with respect for the rights of minorities. Resources means economic aid to the Balkan states, uniquely and strictly conditional on respect for individual and collective rights; an investigation into the atrocities committed in Kosovo, conducted under the authority of the International Criminal Court; respect for the right of asylum, according to the terms of the Geneva Convention; reception of all refugees who request this, as well as Yugoslav deserters, and their free circulation in all European countries.

We demand, finally, a debate in our countries on the balance-sheet of the NATO action, on the role that the organization now sets itself and on perspectives for European security. This cannot, in our eyes, be based on a logic of war and increased arms expenditure, but rather on a policy of development and eradication of social misery, along with realization of the universal rights of peoples and of human beings, men and women.

For our part, we shall pursue:

Solidarity action with those democratic, political, trade-union, voluntary and feminist oppositions that are resisting reactionary state powers;

Solidarity action with the expelled populations, defending their right of asylum along with their right to return and their self-determination.

The signatories decide: to coordinate their activities for the realization of these objectives in a lasting way; to conduct a work of reflection on this basis and to meet again in June or September in a European capital; to get this appeal signed and submit it to candidates for the European elections.

For an Austria in the forefront of Europe[*]

What can I say to progressive Austrians in the face of what is happening in their country? I risk appearing naive, not being in Austria and not being Austrian, but I would at least like to help them defend themselves against certain definitions of their situation imposed from outside, and against those givers of pharisaic lessons who, constantly harking back to past situations, make it impossible to see and confront the present as it really is. I have in mind the reference so rapidly made to Hitler and Nazism, based on a priori suspicions and unconsidered associations, which is superficial and prevents a grasp of the specificity of what is happening today; this reference is an obstacle to any serious analysis of the ensemble of causes that have made possible the rise of this individual who is both insignificant and odious, and whom I do not want to name. (If I could make one recommendation, particularly to intellectuals and journalists, it would be never to mention his name.)

If analogies are to be sought at any cost, they should be sought not in Germany of the 1930s, but rather in the United States at a far more recent period, with a character such as Ronald Reagan, the handsome B-movie star, always bronzed, always well styled, just like this other man that I don't want to name; like him, the bearer of ultra-nationalist and ultra-reactionary ideologies, and ready, also like him, to play the role of puppet in the service of the most conservative interests and desires of economic forces, the role of chic incarnation – not even chic, rather kitsch – of radical laissez-faire. One could continue with Margaret Thatcher, but to move on quickly, I shall go straight to Tony Blair, with a similar Hollywood smile, who in Lisbon today is taking more reactionary positions on Europe than those of a right-wing French president.

But if we look not just for earlier analogies, which do not explain a great deal, but rather for *causes*, we have to study what is happening in the international political world, with the unrestrained triumph of neoliberalism – a mere mask, simply modernized, of the most archaic conservatism, the old 'conservative revolution' that produced such a mass of demoralized and confused people, ready out of despair to deliver themselves to the first demagogue who comes along, helped by the mystification that the media collude in for ratings purposes.

[*] This intervention was read by a participant at a conference on 'the political value of the culture sector between market and state' (IG Kultur Österreich, Vienna, 31 March 2000), in the wake of the entry of the far-right Freedom Party into the Austrian government.

What can be done in the face of this conservative revolution? We can certainly struggle symbolically, in particular by working collectively to deepen our analysis of the phenomenon, and invent, with the aid of artists, new forms of effective symbolic action. But we can also establish new structures of resistance, and in particular oppose to these foolish nationalisms a new internationalism, an international political resistance. Two months ago we launched the idea, with a certain number of trade unions and movements in various European countries, of bringing together all such movements – trade unions of course, but also movements in support of the unemployed, illegal immigrants, the homeless, etc. – around the elaboration of a Charter for a European welfare state.

At this time, when we suddenly discover that a puppet clown whom no one can take seriously threatens to take power in Austria, I believe that this Austria that has been suddenly awakened can also shake Europe. Naturally, this means that all Europeans have to collaborate. All intellectuals, all leaders of trade unions and community organizations, should set aside foolish slogans of boycott and actively side with the critical and progressive forces that have mobilized in Austria; I particularly have in mind young people. I was struck to see in all the filmed reports the massive representation of young people, who we were told are 'depoliticized', but are in fact just demoralized by politicians, disgusted with politics because of the cynicism and opportunism of politicians. Because if the fascistoid character whose name is constantly uttered is an opportunist par excellence, a chameleon, he is only a limiting case of those politicians who happily go from far left to centre right or even further in a single career, clothing their renegation in a socialist rhetoric. These supposedly demoralized and depoliticized young people are waiting for a political message that is neither, like that of the far right, pure verbalism of the kind 'we only need . . .', and associated with the exaltation of neoliberal laissez-faire, nor that false realism preached by social-democratic zealots of the neoliberalized economy.

What message? I will not try and offer a programme on the hoof here; but we are going to publish this project of a Charter, which I would like to see signed by a large number of Austrians, in all European papers – given that these papers agree, which cannot be taken for granted – on 1 May 2000, a symbolic date. We shall have a meeting in September or October, to fine-tune the Charter, which will be drafted between now and then. We then hope to hold a big meeting in Athens, which would be – these are big words . . . – something like a general assembly of the European social movement, i.e. the constitution of an international political force able to oppose the real enemy, i.e. the brute force of the economy as disguised with neoliberal rhetoric.

That is what I wanted to say. I apologize to those whom I may have surprised or even shocked. In any case, I am convinced that, surprising as it may seem, Austria and progressive Austrians can be the vanguard of that European social movement that we need absolutely to create in order to struggle against the forces that threaten democracy, culture, free cinema and literature, etc., and of which he-whom-I-shall-not-name is simply an insignificant and detestable epiphenomenon.

The manifesto 'for a general assembly of the social movement', which arose out of the discussions conducted over several years in various European countries, aims to create the intellectual and institutional conditions for a regrouping of all critical and progressive forces.

It will be published in the next few days, to coincide with 1 May, in newspapers in Germany, Great Britain, Spain, Greece and Italy, as well as several other European and non-European countries (Argentina, Bolivia, Korea, Japan, etc.).

This makes the start of a broad collective work, inter-disciplinary and international, aiming to define the principles of a genuine political alternative to the neoliberal politics that is tending to assert itself in every country, sometimes under the aegis of social-democracy, and to invent the organizational and institutional means needed to put it into practice.

It will find an initial extension in the elaboration, through a series of working meetings, of a Charter for the European social movement, and the holding of a general assembly for the European social movement in the next few months.

Those who want to join in this project, which has received the support of a large number of representatives of associations, trade unions, and other organizations such as those of artists, writers and scientists, can post their signatures, possibly accompanied by suggestions, proposals and comments, on the site www.raisons.org, where they will find a complete and detailed list of the first signatories.

Pierre Bourdieu

Manifesto for a general assembly
of the European social movement*

In order for the social movements that have sprung up all over Europe in the course of the last few years to be continued and broadened, it is important to bring together the collectives involved, trade unions and community organizations, into a coherent network, initially at the European level, the form of which has still to be invented, which would be able to accumulate energies, orchestrate objectives and elaborate common projects. These movements, despite all their differences and disagreements, have in common, among other things, that they take up the defence of all those left behind by neoliberal policies, and by the same token, the problems left behind by these policies.

These problems are ignored or repressed by the social-democratic parties, which, concerned above all to manage the established economic order in such a way as to preserve their management of the state, accommodate themselves to growing inequality, unemployment and precariousness. A genuine critical counter-power has to be able to put these things constantly on the agenda, using a variety of forms of action that express, as at Seattle, the aspirations of citizens of both sexes.

Since this counter-power has to confront international forces and institutions, including multinational firms, it must itself be international, and to start with, European. In the face of forces geared towards the preservation and restoration of the past, particularly through the dismantling of every vestige of the 'welfare state', it must be a force of movement, which can and must compel international organizations, states and their governments to decree and put into practice effective measures to control the financial markets, and struggle against inequalities within and between nations.

For this reason we proposed holding, before the end of 2000, a general assembly of the European social movement, with the object of elaborating a Charter for the social movement and laying the foundations of an international structure that will bring together every organizational and intellectual form of resistance to neoliberal policies, in complete independence from parties and governments.

This general assembly is designed, first of all, to give rise to an open comparison of different projects of social transformation aiming to counteract

---

* This collective text was published in Le Monde on 1 May 2000, along with the introduction printed above.

the economic and social processes presently under way (the turn to flexibility, precariousness, poverty, etc.), and combat the ever tighter 'security' measures by which European governments seek to neutralize the effects of these; secondly, to establish permanent connections that will make possible rapid mobilization with a view to common action by all the collectives represented – without introducing any form of centralized compulsion, or losing anything of the diversity of inspirations and traditions; thirdly, to define common objectives for national and international actions, aiming at the construction of a society based on solidarity, and the unification and improvement of social norms.

The coming together of all men and women whose daily struggle against the most harmful effects of neoliberal policies has given them practical acquaintance with the subversive potentials these contain could in this way trigger a process of collective response and creation able to offer all those who no longer recognize themselves in the world as it is, the realistic utopia around which different but convergent efforts and struggles could be organized.

The new planetary vulgate*

In all the advanced countries, bosses and international high officials, media intellectuals and high-powered journalists agree in speaking a strange Newspeak whose vocabulary, which appears to have come from nowhere, is on every tongue: 'globalization' and 'flexibility'; 'governance' and 'employ-ability'; 'underclass' and 'exclusion'; 'new economy' and 'zero tolerance'; 'communitarianism', 'multiculturalism', and their cousins 'postmodern', 'ethnicity', 'minority', 'identity', 'fragmentation', etc.

The distribution of this new planetary vulgate – from which capitalism, class, exploitation, domination and inequality are remarkably absent, terms that are peremptorily banished on the pretext of presumed obsolescence or impertinence – is the product of a definite symbolic imperialism. Its effects are all the more powerful and pernicious in that this imperialism is borne not just by the champions of the neoliberal revolution, who under cover of modernization are seeking to remake the world by making a clean slate of the social and economic gains resulting from a hundred years of social struggle, depicted today as so many archaisms and obstacles to the nascent new order, but also by cultural producers (scholars, writers, artists) and even political figures of the left, the majority of whom still see themselves as progressive.

Like dominations based on gender or ethnic group, cultural imperialism is a symbolic violence supported by a relationship of constrained commu-nication designed to enforce submission, and whose particular feature consists in this case in its universalization of certain particularisms bound up with a singular historical experience, misconstruing them for what they are, and interpreting them as universal.[9]

In the same way, therefore, as a number of questions that in the nineteenth century were seen as philosophical – such as Spengler's theme of 'decline' – and discussed throughout Europe had their origin in historical particularities and conflicts specific to the singular world of German academics,[10] so today a number of topics that directly arose from intellectual confrontations bound

* Jointly signed with Loïc Wacquant, and published in Le Monde Diplomatique, May 2000.
[9] We should note right away that the United States has no monopoly of universal claims. A number of other countries – Great Britain, France, Germany, Spain, Japan, Russia – have exercised, and still try to exercise in their own spheres of influence, forms of cultural imperialism that are in every way comparable. There is simply the difference that, for the first time in history, one single country finds itself in a position to impose its point of view on the whole world.
[10] Cf. Fritz Ringer, The Decline of the Mandarins (Cambridge: Cambridge University Press 1969).

up with particularities and particularisms of American society and universities have been imposed on the entire planet in a de-historicized guise.

These commonplaces – in the Aristotelian sense of notions or theses that are used in argument but are not argued with – owe the essential part of their power of conviction to the prestige of the place that they emanate from, and the fact that, circulating from Berlin to Buenos Aires and from London to Lisbon, they are present everywhere at once and are powerfully relayed everywhere by those supposedly neutral bodies of neutral thought that are the great international organizations – World Bank, European Commission, OCDE – as well conservative think-tanks such as the Manhattan Institute in New York, the Adam Smith Institute in London, the Deutsche Bank Foundation in Frankfurt and the former Fondation Saint-Simon in Paris, not to mention philanthropic foundations, and schools of state power such as Sciences-Po in France, the London School of Economics, the Harvard Kennedy School of Government, etc., and the mainstream media, incessant dispensers of a passe-partout lingua franca that is designed to give pressed editorial writers and specialists in cultural import–export the illusion of ultra-modernism.

Apart from the automatic effect of the international circulation of ideas, which tends by its own logic to obscure the conditions and significance of its origins,[11] the play of preliminary definitions and scholastic deductions substitutes the appearance of logical necessity for the contingency of socio-logical necessity, and tends to conceal the historical roots of a whole series of questions and ideas – the 'efficiency' of the (free) market, the need for recognition of (cultural) 'identities', or the reaffirmation and celebration of (individual) responsibility – that are decreed to be philosophical, sociological, economic or political, depending on the place and time of reception.

Planetarized and globalized in a strictly geographical sense, and at the same time stripped of their particularity in time and place, these commonplaces that media repetition transforms into universal common sense succeed in making people forget that they often only express in a truncated and unrecognizable form, unrecognizable even for those who propagate them, the complex and contested realities of a particular historical society, tacitly erected into the model and measure of all things: American society of the post-Fordist and post-Keynesian era. This unique superpower, this symbolic Mecca, is characterized by the delib-erate dismantling of the welfare state and the correlative hypertrophy of the penal state, the crushing of the trade unions and the dictatorship of the notion of enterprise based solely on 'shareholder value' – along with the sociological

[11] Cf. Pierre Bourdieu (with Loïc Wacquant), 'New Liberal Speak. Notes on the New Planetary Vulgate,' Radical Philosophy 105, January – February 2001.

consequences of all this, the generalization of casual employment and social insecurity, made into a privileged motor of economic activity.

This is the case for example with the vague and lazy debate about 'multi-culturalism', a term imported into Europe to denote cultural pluralism in the civil sphere, whereas in the United States it expresses, in the very movement by which it conceals these things, the continued exclusion of Afro-Americans and the crisis of the national myth of the 'American dream', 'opportunity for all' – along with the bankruptcy of the system of public education at a time when competition for cultural capital has intensified and class inequalities are growing vertiginously.

The adjective 'multicultural' veils this crisis by artificially corralling it into the microcosm of the university and expressing it in an ostensibly 'ethnic' register, whereas the real stake involved is not the recognition of cultures marginalized by academic canons, but rather access to the instruments of (re)production of the middle and upper classes, such as the university, in a context of the active and massive disengagement of the state.

American 'multiculturalism' is neither a concept, nor a theory, nor a social or political movement – though it pretends to be all these things. It is a screening discourse whose intellectual status derives from a gigantic effect of national and international allodoxia[12] that deceives those within it as well as those without. It is moreover an American discourse, despite conceiving and presenting itself as universal, inasmuch as it expresses the specific contradictions of the situation of academics who, cut off from any access to the public sphere and subject to a sharp differentiation in their professional milieu, have no other terrain on which to invest their political libido than that of campus quarrels dressed up as conceptual epics.

'Multiculturalism', in other words, wherever it is exported, carries with it three vices of American national thought: 1) a 'groupism' that reifies social divisions, canonized by the state bureaucracy into principles of knowledge and of political demands; 2) populism, which replaces the analysis of structures and mechanisms of domination by celebration of the culture of the dominated and their 'point of view', raised in fact to the level of a proto-theory; 3) moralism, which presents an obstacle to the application of a healthy rationalist materialism in analysis of the social and economic world, and condemns people to an endless and ineffective debate on the 'recognition of identities', whereas, in sorry everyday reality, the problem is in no way located at this level.[13] Whilst

---

[12] The act of taking one thing for something else.

[13] No more than the globalization of material and symbolic exchange does the diversity of cultures date from our century, being coextensive with human history, as was already pointed out by Émile Durkheim and Marcel Mauss in their 'Note sur la notion de civilisation'. (*Année Sociologique* 3/12 [1913]; reprinted Paris: Minuit 1968, pp. 46–50.)

philosophers spout learned twaddle about 'cultural recognition', tens of thousands of children from the dominated classes or ethnic groups are turned away from primary schools for want of places (25,000 this year in the City of Los Angeles alone), and only one young person in ten from households earning less than $15,000 per year gains entry to a university, as against 94 per cent of those from households with more than $100,000.

The same demonstration could be given for the highly polysemic notion of 'globalization', the effect of which, if not its very function, is to dress up as cultural ecumenism or economic fatalism the effects of American imperialism, and make a transnational power relationship appear as a natural necessity. At the end of a symbolic turnaround based on the naturalization of patterns of neoliberal thought whose domination has been imposed over the last twenty years by the work of conservative think-tanks and their allies in the fields of politics and journalism,[14] the remodelling of social relations and cultural practices in conformity with the American overlord – which has been effected in the advanced societies by the pauperization of the state, the commodification of public goods and the generalization of job insecurity – is accepted with resignation as the inevitable end-point of national development, when it is not celebrated with a sheep-like enthusiasm. Empirical analysis of the development of advanced economies over the long term, however, suggests that 'globalization' is not a new phase of capitalism but simply a 'rhetoric' that governments invoke so as to justify their willing submission to the financial markets. Far from being the necessary result of the growth in international trade, as we are incessantly told, de-industrialization, the increase in inequalities of all kinds, and the contraction of social policies, result from domestic policy decisions that reflect the swing in class relationships in favour of the owners of capital.[15]

By imposing on the rest of the world the standardized categories of perception of its own social structures, the United States is refashioning the world in its own image: the mental colonization effected by the diffusion of these ambiguous concepts can only lead to a kind of generalized and even spontaneous 'Washington consensus', as we can observe today in matters of economics, philanthropy or the teaching of management. This double discourse, in fact, based on belief and a mimicry of science, superimposes on the social imagination of the dominant the appearance of reason (economic and political in particular), being endowed with the power of bringing about the realities that it claims to describe, according to the principle of self-fulfilling prophecy: present in

[14] Cf. Keith Dixon, Les Évangélistes du marché (Paris: Raisons d'Agir 1998).
[15] On 'globalization' as an 'American project' that seeks to impose the conception of 'shareholder value', cf. Neil Fligstein, 'Rhétorique et réalités de la "mondialisation"', Actes de la Recherche en Sciences Sociales 119, September 1997, pp. 36–47.

the minds of political or economic decision-makers, as well as the minds of their audience, it serves as an instrument for the construction of both public and private policies, and at the same time for the assessment of these policies. Like all mythologies of the age of science, the new planetary vulgate is based on a series of oppositions and equivalences, which support and reflect each other in depicting the contemporary transformations of advanced societies: the economic disengagement of the state and the strengthening of its policing and penal components, deregulation of financial flows and withdrawal from the labour market, reduction of social protection and moralistic celebration of 'individual responsibility':

MARKET	STATE
Freedom	Compulsion
Open	Closed
Flexible	Rigid
Dynamic, Mobile	Static, Fixed
Future, Novelty	Past, Outdated
Growth	Immobilism, Archaism
Individual, Individualism	Group, Collectivism
Diversity, Authenticity	Uniformity, Artificiality
Democratic	Autocratic ('Totalitarian')

The imperialism of neoliberal reason finds its intellectual culmination in two new exemplary figures of the cultural producer. First of all the *expert*, who prepares, in the shadows of ministerial or directorial corridors, or the secrecy of think-tanks, highly technical documents that are couched as far as possible in economic and mathematical language. Then the *communications adviser*, a renegade from the past world of the university in the service of the dominant, whose mission is to put into academic terms the political projects of the new state and business nobility, and whose planetary model is without a shadow of doubt the British sociologist Anthony Giddens, professor at Cambridge University before being recently placed at the head of the London School of Economics, and father of the 'theory of structuration', a scholastic synthesis of various sociological and philosophical traditions.

And we can surely see the ruse of imperialist reason in the fact that Great Britain, which for historical, cultural and linguistic reasons finds itself placed in an intermediate and neutral (in the etymological sense) position between the United States and continental Europe, has given the world this two-headed Trojan horse, political and intellectual, in the dual person of Tony Blair and Anthony Giddens, self-proclaimed 'theorist' of the 'third way', which, in his own words (and these deserve to be cited quite literally), 'adopts a positive attitude towards globalization', 'tries (sic) to react to new forms of inequality' but warns from the start that 'the poor of today are not the same as the poor of yesterday (any more than the rich are the same as they formerly were)'. Giddens 'accepts the idea that existing systems of social protection and the overall state structure are the source of problems, and not simply the solution for resolving them', 'stresses the fact that economic and social policies are linked together' in order to better assert that 'social expenses should be assessed in terms of their consequences for the economy as a whole', and finally 'is concerned about the mechanisms of exclusion' that he discovers 'at the base of society, but also at the top (sic)', convinced that 'redefining inequality in relation to exclusion at both of these levels' is 'in conformity with a dynamic conception of inequality'.[16]

---

[16] Extracts from the catalogue of social definitions of his theories and political views offered by Anthony Giddens on the FAQ page of his website.

Open letter to the director-general of UNESCO on the threats posed by the GATT agreement*

Monsieur director-general,

When they joined the World Trade Organization by adopting the Marrakesh agreements in 1994, the signatory states, a large majority of whom were also members of the general council of UNESCO, subscribed on the same occasion to the General Agreement on Tariffs and Trade. This agreement, however, constitutes the most serious threat with which UNESCO has ever been faced. GATT and the mechanisms being prepared to put it into practice have profound implications for UNESCO's appointed mission. Every sector of your organization's activity is directly affected. The negotiations that were provided for, five years after the GATT agreement entered into effect, to apply this agreement 'in the direction of steadily raising the level of liberalization', are currently under way. Regular meetings in Geneva, working groups and special sessions of the WTO council for trade and services, have been held since February of this year. Labelling, domestic regulations and policies of subsidy, access to public markets, all aspects of policy are put to the test of 'commercially correct'.

The common desire of the United States and the European Union is to reach a general agreement in December 2002. As an American note of 13 July [2000] makes clear: 'The mandate of this negotiation is ambitious: to suppress restrictions on trade in services and obtain real access to a market subject to specific limitations. Our challenge is to accomplish a significant suppression of these restrictions across all sectors of services, tackling the national mechanisms already subject to GATT rules, followed by those mechanisms that are not presently subject to GATT rules and covering all possibilities of providing services.' The intentions hidden behind the bureaucratic jargon are very clear: to impose, in the 137 states that are members of the WTO, the opening of all services to the laws of free exchange. This implies, in due course, the disappearance of the notion of public service, the destruction of every form of diversity, the negation of fundamental rights. The negotiators at Geneva agreed to exclude 'the protection of general interest' from the set of objectives to be preserved within GATT. The WTO secretariat indicated that 'promoting competition and economic efficiency' is an objective that governments are required to give themselves. The European

* This collective text was published in L'Humanité, 25 September 2000.

negotiator for GATT has recently declared that 'education and health are ripe for liberalization'. On 5 and 6 October [2000] a decisive special session of the council for trade in services will be held at the WTO. This is why it seems urgent to us, Monsieur director-general, to question the members of your general council about the compatibility between the missions assigned to UNESCO, for which they are responsible, and the General Agreement on Tariffs and Trade to which they have also adhered. It is true that GATT does not apply to 'services provided in the context of the exercise of state authority'. But the definition of these is very restrictive, since it exclusively concerns services that are not supplied on a commercial basis, or are not in a situation of competition.

It is also true that, until now, each state maintains the right to apply domestic regulation (prescriptions in terms of personnel, criteria of need, technical norms, licences, government monopolies, subsidies to firms or institutions). But in future, this regulation will be subject to the criteria formulated by GATT: these national measures can in no case 'be more rigorous than is needed to ensure the quality of the service', the WTO being judge of last resort. States are held to submit their national legislation and regulations to the WTO, which, if it does not – yet? – have the power to modify these, will have the power to decree that such norms are contrary to GATT, and have states that fail to modify them condemned. When the United Nations pact on economic, social and cultural rights was adopted, each party agreed that national legislation was an indispensable instrument for putting this into effect. With the WTO, national legislation, an instrument of sovereignty, sees its scope subordinated to the laws of competition. For the countries of the South, suppression of national preference reduces to nothing the hope of a development adapted to national and local particularities and respectful of diversity.

It is true, again, that a series of annexes to GATT provide lists of exemptions that are envisaged, with governments being left to inscribe limits to these exemptions according to sector. But this guarantee is very temporary and fragile against the damages of liberalization. These exemptions are subject to regular revision, and they can be challenged by other agreements sponsored by the WTO. For example, certain exemptions accepted in the context of GATT are forbidden in the context of the agreement on market access.

The GATT principle according to which there cannot be discrimination between providers of services will be imposed in all sectors and at all latitudes. Private service companies will be able to use the laws of the market to transform into commodities and sources of profit, service activities responding to those fundamental rights that are, in particular, education and culture. From now on, the WTO documents speak only of an 'education market'.

Education, training and research will be steadily handed over to the laws of the market, with pupils and students being no longer citizens exercising a right, but simply consumers. Researchers will lose the little scientific independence that remains to them today. The objective of access to free education for all will give way to paid education reserved to those privileged by money.

National policies designed to preserve cultural identity constitute obstacles for the transnational culture industries, which see them as 'barriers to trade'. It should be recognized that the negotiations under way, in the name of the principle of connectivity that challenges all the classifications currently in force, cover services such as the entire range of audio-visual material, libraries, archives and museums, botanical and zoological gardens, all services associated with entertainment (arts, theatre, radio and television services, fun fairs, recreational and sports facilities), press and advertising. Protection of cultural and natural heritage, management of natural parks and biosphere reserves, are all directly threatened by these proposals of liberalization, especially those concerning tourism.

Monsieur director-general, the General Agreement on Services, which the WTO is preparing to apply, radically challenges the mission entrusted to UNESCO in the name of the idea 'that a peace based exclusively upon the political and economic agreements of governments would not be a peace which could secure the unanimous, lasting and sincere support of the peoples of the world, and that the peace must therefore be founded . . . upon the intellectual and moral solidarity of mankind': i.e. to promote cooperation between the nations of the world in the fields of education, science and culture, and more particularly, 'in full and equal opportunities for education for all, in the unrestricted pursuit of objective truth, and in the free exchange of ideas and knowledge'.

UNESCO's actions of protection and promotion necessarily contradict the erection of free market access into an absolute rule. The free competition to which the activities of education, research and culture are being handed over will aggravate inequalities in access to these activities, which are already very deep. The liberalization of these services will mean abandoning a right for all in favour of a privilege for some.

Monsieur director-general, we are persuaded that, in your capacity as the highest official of UNESCO, you cannot subscribe to the exclusively commercial notion of education, science and culture that the WTO seeks to impose. We ask you to draw the consequences of this, and demand with us that GATT be either totally renegotiated or declared null and void.

Social Europe is hanging fire*

I am forced to be in London today, but happy to be able to tell you, thanks to the kindness of Annick Coupé,[17] what I think of the Europe that is being prepared for us, and first of all of the Charter of Fundamental Rights, which is a deception. It is designed to give the illusion of a social 'concern', but remains very vague (the social rights guaranteed are ill defined, and only apply to European citizens); it is not accompanied by any measure or mechanism of enforcement. And this is easily understandable. The social-democratic converts to neoliberalism do not want a social Europe. Social-democratic governments persist in their historical error: liberalism first, 'social' later, which means never, because uncontrolled deregulation makes the construction of a social Europe ever more difficult. Political parties have depoliticized themselves, and contribute to depoliticization. The weakened European trade unions, oriented towards compromise or cynically 'refocused', either cannot or do not want to obtain anything more than an adjustment in neoliberal domination (as witness what in France is called 'social refoundation'). The European Trade Union Confederation is trying to reach a social Europe by way of negotiation, in a relationship of forces that is very unfavourable to it. The result is very low social norms for the developed countries, and tremendous disparities between countries.

In sum, social Europe is hanging fire, whilst neoliberal Europe is advancing in leaps and bounds. The adoption of qualified majority voting for liberalization measures (article 133) will accelerate the already dramatic process of challenging states, public services, culture, etc. We have to put a stop to this process, or at least slow it down and limit it, by maintaining, at least for a time and for defensive purposes, the principle of unanimity, despite its highly ambiguous character.

While neoliberal globalization is accelerating, social Europe cannot be constructed on the basis of a 'Charter of Fundamental Rights', nor by decisions taken on the basis of a qualified majority. This is why progressive trade unions (or the progressive sections of these unions) and social movements (above all the movements of unemployed) of all countries must unite in a broad European Social Movement that will work towards a common platform of demands and an overall project of construction of a social Europe. This is an immense and long-term task, to which all of us, scholars and activists, must contribute, and which meetings such as this are steps towards.

* A declaration read in Nice during the demonstration of 6 December 2000.
[17] A member of the 'Group of Ten' union, Annick Coupé was one of the founders of the trade-union federation SUD-PTT. Very active in the social movement of the 1990s, she was associated with Pierre Bourdieu in several of his interventions from 1995 on. [Ed.]

For a real mobilization of organized forces[*]

I want first of all to thank the organizers of this demonstration for giving me the opportunity to rank myself among the spoilsports gathered here and trying to bait the great media-political show of the 'masters of the world', who, under police protection and surrounded by their court of journalists, are going to tell us how they see the world.

This world that appears to them as involved in an inevitable process of globalization, is in reality, and this is the worst of it, the product of a systematic, organized and orchestrated policy. This policy began in the late 1970s in the United States – to be precise, in 1979, with the measures taken to raise interest rates – and was then extended by a whole series of measures aiming to deregulate financial markets in the big industrialized countries. Its purpose was to stimulate the rates of profit on capital and restore the position of owners in relation to managers.

This series of measures had the effect of favouring an ever greater autonomy of the world financial field, the world of finance, which was put to functioning according to its own inherent logic, that of pure profit, and independently in every way from the development of industry. Finance, indeed, is relatively little involved in the industrial field; we know for example that the contribution of the stock market to investment is extremely weak.

In order to produce this independent financial field, which in a certain sense spins round in thin air, its only recognized purpose being the constant increase of profit – in order to produce this world, it was necessary to invent and establish a whole series of financial institutions designed to promote free financial movement. And it is these institutions that have to be brought under control. It seems to me, however, that we need more than a simple measure of regulation, as those lobbying for the introduction of a Tobin tax seem to think, even though I do of course support this. As I see it, we cannot be satisfied with this kind of measure, and the question I want to raise today is that of the means to establish genuine and permanent control over these processes. The question, therefore, of a genuine political action, based on genuine political mobilization, and aiming at the imposition of such controls.

However necessary it may be, such a mobilization is also very difficult. In fact, the policy of globalization, which has nothing inevitable about it,

[*] Video message broadcast in Zurich on 27 January 2001 on the occasion of the Davos counter-summit.

is accompanied by a policy of depoliticization. The appearance of inevitability that I referred to, and that is normally associated with the idea of globalization, is the product of an incessant propaganda action (no other word is possible), involving the collaboration of a whole series of social agents, from the think-tanks that produce official representations of the world through to the journalists who reproduce and circulate these. We must try therefore to conceive of a political action able to struggle against this depoliticization and at the same time against the policy of globalization that draws support from such depoliticization in order to impose itself.

How will it be possible to establish and exercise genuine and effective controls over monetary mechanisms and great concentrations of capital such as pension funds? As I see it, this could be done by the intermediary of central banks; in particular, since we are in Europe, by the European Central Bank. But to succeed in taking control of these financial bodies, the first requirement is to regain control of political bodies. This can only be done by a broad social movement that can enter into the system of controlling instances of economic forces and impose the establishment of international bodies rooted in a genuine popular movement.

I have spoken of a popular movement. It is true that we are currently in a period in which the dominated are demoralized and demobilized, particularly by the policy of depoliticization that I mentioned earlier. But there is also the fact that for the most deprived, those whom official discourse refers to as 'excluded', very subtle policies of social control have been put in place in every developed country, which in fact are nothing more than the brutal and rather simplistic control, based more or less on policing, of an earlier era. These policies could even be seen as a deliberate project: it all takes place as if a certain number of agents – educators, organizers, social workers – had the function of teaching the most deprived – and particularly those who have been rejected by the education system and thrown out of the labour market – something like a parody of the capitalist spirit, the spirit of capitalist enterprise. A kind of self-help has been organized which is quite in conformity with the Anglo-Saxon political ideal. In order to establish and effectively exercise democratic control, regulations are not enough, nor are polished writings and polite approaches to political bodies. We need to invent a new kind of transnational action. Why do I see it as important to locate this action at the European level, at least initially? Because this is where a whole set of very varied movements, trade unions, community groups, etc. are to be found, which despite their disparate aspect – which is doubtless very well illustrated in this hall –, despite their appearance of disorder and dispersion, their disagreements and divergence, their competition and even conflict, have a great deal in common. They have in common a vision of the social world that could be called libertarian, a desire to find a new way of doing politics. They also have in common a very deep internationalism, of which Third Worldism is simply a particular form. By transcending this diversity we shall be able to mobilize a broad movement capable of exerting constant pressure on national and international governmental bodies; and, to achieve a kind of provisional unification, we must overcome the hegemonic temptations that many social movements have inherited from a former era. It is imperative to exorcise authoritarian temptations, if we are to invent the collective forms of organization that will enable us to build up political forces without letting these cancel each other out in internal quarrels and divisions.

This assembling in a broad and united European movement, bringing together trade unions, community organizations and scholars, could be the social force that, by giving itself flexible forms of organization, as little centralized as possible, will be able to build up European critical traditions in liaison with progressive forces across the world; able to resist the dominant economic forces and propose a new progressive utopia. It would have to take back control of economic forces at a level at which they offer a lever (which is why I referred to European bodies and the European Central Bank), at the same time as putting its utopia into practice.

I think that the European social movement as I conceive it, free from any kind of Eurocentrism and strong in its progressive tradition of anti-imperialism and internationalist solidarity, should be established in liaison with the countries of the Third World, Latin America, Africa and Asia, in such a way as to bring together all the forces needed so that those who are today having their celebrations in Davos are subject at each moment to the kind of sword of Damocles that a social movement present at all times and places, not just for the occasional heroic 'happening', would provide. The point is to constitute a force that would be constantly there, representing a permanent mobilization of people already mobilized and organs of mobilization. No matter how restive we are – and God knows that I am very restive – it is impossible to do without organizations, organizers and professional activists. Calling the organizers of resistance to band together, to unite in a great European confederation, would – in my view – contribute to creating a force of resistance and control at the scale of the economic and political forces gathered in Davos.

For a permanent organization of resistance to the new world order*

Very many of you here are disturbed, indignant, revolted by the world as it is today, the world that is being made for us by economic and political powers. Those powers that, long embodied by the deceptive figures of B-movie stars, have today taken the blinkered and mulish face of George W. Bush.

Very many of you here in Québec, but also in Berlin, Tokyo, Rio, Paris and across the world, are rebelling against the policy of 'globalization' of which the 'summit of the Americas' is a new stage, after Seattle, Seoul and Prague. Because, just as this meeting that aims to establish free exchange on an all-American scale shows very well, the 'globalization' that is presented to us as a *fatality*, the inevitable destiny of advanced societies, is actually a *policy*, a policy that aims to impose those conditions that are most favourable to economic forces.

What actually is this 'free exchange' that they tell us about? It is enough to read the General Agreement on Trade and Services, of which the Montreal agreement is certainly just a variant, to be enlightened and edified. But, let us say in passing, who will have the courage to read these thousands of pages that are deliberately confusing, drawn up by experts in the pay of the big international lobbies? You need only read these pages to understand that what is on the agenda above all is the destruction of all the *defence systems* that protect the most precious social and cultural conquests of the advanced societies; to understand that the point is to transform into commodities and sources of profit all service activities, including those that meet such fundamental needs as education, culture and health. The measures that the WTO is concocting are supposed to be applied to such services as libraries, audio-visual media, archives and museums, and all the services bound up with entertainment, performance, sport, theatre, radio and television, etc. I could, to make clear the effects of the unmitigated reign of money, take the example of theatre or cinema – increasingly abandoned to blockbuster films with special effects that brutalize and stun the whole world –, but I shall stick to the terrain of sport, where the logic of profit (bound up in particular with televised broadcasts of sporting events) has led to the disappearance of

---

* A declaration transmitted by video to the demonstrators at the people's summit in Québec, 4 April 2001.

everything that was connected with a form of amateurism (starting with the beauty of performance) and introduced corruption, doping, the concentration of sporting resources in the hands of a few big clubs with the ability to pay exorbitant transfer fees – I am thinking here of football.

I have spoken of the destruction of *immune defence systems*, and this is precisely what is involved. Is it not readily apparent that a programme like that of the WTO, which treats as 'obstacles to trade' policies aimed at preserving national cultural particularities, and by that fact constituting barriers to the transnational culture industries, can only have the effect of depriving the majority of countries – and in particular those less well endowed with economic and cultural resources – of any hope of a development adapted to cultural particularities and respectful of diversities, in cultural matters as well as in other fields? This is particularly by compelling them to submit all national measures, domestic regulations, subsidies to establishments or institutions, licences, etc. to the verdict of an organization that seeks to confer the appearance of a universal norm on the requirements of transnational economic powers.

The myth of free exchange between equal partners masks, beneath the polite façade of legally guaranteed international agreements, the brutal logic of relations of force that is asserted in fact in the dissymmetry of the double standard, two weights and two measures: this logic means that the dominant, and in particular the United States, can resort to protectionism and subsidies that they forbid countries in the course of development (forbidden for example to restrict the import of products that cause serious damage to their own industries, or to regulate foreign investments). Foreign laws by which the dominant place themselves above the law. The Kabyle people have a name for this kind of contract, which gives the dominated the right to be eaten by the dominant; they speak of a contract between a lion and a donkey.

You are particularly well placed here, in Canada, to observe the effects of free-exchange agreements between unequal powers, and to analyze the effect of domination that integration into inequality involves. As a result of an abolition of protective measures that has left it defenceless, particularly in matters of culture, Canada is in the process of experiencing a regular economic and cultural integration by its southern neighbour. The customs union has had the effect of dispossessing the dominated society of all economic and cultural independence from the dominant power, with the brain drain, the concentration of press and publishing, etc. to the benefit of the United States. It would be useful to have a detailed analysis of the particular part that the French-speaking province of Québec plays in resistance to this process; the language barrier can be a protection (a further example would be the comparison between Britain and France). I see an indication of this in the contribution of the Québécois to the struggle against globalization – for example the role of Québécoise women in drawing up the magnificent World Charter of Women.

Thus, everything that is described by the term 'globalization' – a term that is both descriptive and prescriptive – is the effect not of economic fatality but of a conscious policy. This policy is quite paradoxical, in that it is actually a policy of depoliticization: shamelessly drawing on the lexicon of liberty, liberalism, liberalization, deregulation, yet aiming to confer a fatal grip of economic determinism by liberating this from all control, and obtaining the submission of governments and citizens to the economic and social forces that are 'liberated' in this way. Against this policy of deregulation, we need to re-establish politics, i.e. political thinking and action, and find the correct application point of this action, which is today beyond the borders of the national state, and its specific means, which cannot be reduced to political and trade-union struggles within national states. We must oppose the agreement of the governments of North and South America with a social movement of the two continents, bringing together Americans from North and South – a project that is not so unrealistic as it might appear, if you bear in mind that it is often the United States itself that has provided – with people like Ralph Nader, Susan George and Lory Wallach – the first movements to challenge the policy of globalization. This movement will find a natural ally in the European social movement, which brings together trade unions, community organizations, and critical scholars from all European countries, and is currently in the process of construction.

And one could conceive, therefore, in connection with other international movements such as the World March of Women, the establishment of a permanent organization of resistance, able to oppose its slogans (of boycott, for example), its demonstrations, its critical analyses and symbolic productions (artistic ones in particular) to the faceless violence of economic forces, and to the symbolic powers that bend themselves to the service of these, particularly in the press, television and radio.

Scholars and the social movement*

Intellectual responsibilities

If it is important today, perhaps even necessary, that a certain number of independent scholars have associated themselves with the social movement, this is because we are faced with a policy of 'globalization'. (I deliberately say a 'policy of globalization', and do not speak of 'globalization' as if it were a natural process.) This policy is to a large extent kept secret, as far as its production and distribution is concerned. And a whole work of research is needed at this point, to reveal it before it can be put into effect. Subsequently, this policy has effects that can already be foreseen thanks to the resources of social science, but which are still invisible in the short term to the majority of people. A further characteristic of this policy is that it is partly produced by scholars. The question therefore is to know whether those who anticipate its damaging consequences on the basis of their scientific knowledge can and should remain silent. Or whether this does not involve a kind of failure to assist persons in danger. If it is true that the planet is threatened by serious calamities, do those who believe they understand these calamities in advance not have a duty to overcome the reserve that scientists generally impose on themselves?

The majority of cultivated people, especially in the social sciences, have a dichotomy in their minds that strikes me as quite harmful: the dichotomy between scholarship and commitment – between people who devote themselves to scientific work, which is conducted according to scientific methods for the attention of other scientists, and people with commitment who take this knowledge to the outside world. This is an artificial opposition, and in fact you have to be an autonomous scientist working according to the rules of scholarship in order to produce a committed knowledge, a scholarship with commitment. To really be a committed scientist, legitimately committed, you have to commit your knowledge. And this knowledge is only gained in scientific work, subject to the rules of the scientific community. To put it another way, you have to break with a certain number of oppositions that are in our minds, and are so many ways of authorizing resignation – starting with that of the scholar who withdraws to his ivory tower. The dichotomy

* Interventions made between 3 and 6 May 2001 in Athens, under the aegis of Raisons d'Agir Greece, on the occasion of meetings with Greek trade unions and scholars on such subjects as European trade unionism, culture and journalism.

between scholarship and commitment reassures the scholar of his good conscience, as he receives the approval of the scientific community. It's as if scientists saw themselves as doubly scientific because they did nothing with their science. If applied to biologists, this would be criminal. But it is just as serious if applied to criminologists. This reserve, this flight into purity, has very serious social consequences. Should people like myself, paid by the state for their research, carefully keep the results of this research for their colleagues? It is quite fundamental to give priority to the criticism of colleagues in what one believes to be a discovery, but why reserve for them knowledge that has been collectively gained and checked?

As I see it, the scholar has no choice today: if he is convinced that there is a correlation between neoliberal policies and crime rates, all the signs of what Durkheim would have called anomie, how can he avoid saying so? It is not just that there is nothing to reproach him for in this, he should even be congratulated. (Perhaps I am apologizing here for my own position . . .)

What then should this scientist do in the social movement? First of all, he will not give lessons – after the fashion of certain organic intellectuals who, being unable to impose their wares in the scientific marketplace, where competition is harsh, go and play the intellectual vis-à-vis non-intellectuals, even while saying that intellectuals don't exist. The scientist is neither a prophet nor a *maître à penser*. He has to invent a new role, and a very hard one; to try and assist those bodies that take as their mission – even the trade unions, though ever more weakly, I am sorry to say – resistance to neoliberal policy; he has to take on the task of assisting them by providing them with instruments. Especially instruments against the symbolic effect exercised by the 'experts' engaged by the big multinational companies. Things must be called by their name. The present education policy, for instance, is decided by UNICE,[18] by the Transatlantic Institute, and the like.[19] You need only read the WTO report on services to understand the education policy that we have had for the last five years. The ministry of national education simply passes on the advice elaborated by lawyers, sociologists and economists, which is given a form of legal appearance and put into circulation.

Scientists can also do something newer and more difficult: promote the appearance of the organizational conditions needed to generate the intention to invent a political project, and then for its success – all this would of course be a collective project. After all, the Constituent Assembly of 1789 and the Philadelphia Convention were made up of people like you and me, who had a certain legal baggage, who had read Montesquieu, and invented

---

[18] [Union of Industrial and Employers' Confederations of Europe.]
[19] Cf. *Europe Inc. Liaisons dangereuses entre institutions et milieux des affaires européens* (Marseille: Agone 2000).

democratic structures. In the same way today, we have to invent things . . . We could of course just say: 'There are parliaments, a European Trade Union Confederation, all kinds of institution that are supposed to see to this.' I will not seek to show this here, but the fact is that they do not see to it. So we have to create favourable conditions for such invention. We have to help remove the obstacles to this invention, obstacles that are partly within the social movement that has the job of removing them – particularly in the trade unions . . .

What reason is there to be optimistic? I think that we can talk in terms of reasonable chances of success, and say that this moment is the *kairos*, the opportune time. When we had this discussion around 1995, we were completely ignored and seen as crazy. People like Cassandra, who announce catastrophes, are made fun of; journalists attack them and they are insulted. Now we are listened to a bit more seriously. Why? Because of the work that has been accomplished. There was Seattle and a whole series of demonstrations. And then, the consequences of neoliberal policy, which we predicted in the abstract, have begun to be visible. And people now understand . . . Even the most blinkered and stubborn journalists know that a company making a profit of less than 15 per cent will lay off workers. The most catastrophist prophecies of the prophets of disaster (who were simply better informed than the others) are beginning to be realized. It is not too soon. But it is also not too late. Because this is only a beginning, because the catastrophes are only commencing. There is still time to shake social-democratic governments, for whom intellectuals have a particular blind spot, particularly when they get social advantages of all kinds . . .

Making social movements effective

In my view, a European social movement can only be effective if it includes three components: trade unions, social movements and scholars – on condition, of course, that it integrates these and does not simply juxtapose them. I said yesterday to trade unionists that in all European countries there is a profound difference between the social movements and the trade unions, bearing on both the contents and the means of action. The social movements have raised political objectives that the trade unions and parties had abandoned or forgotten, if not repressed. They have also introduced methods of action that the trade unions had gradually abandoned. Especially methods of personal action: the actions of the social movements appeal to a symbolic effectiveness that depends, on the one hand, on the personal commitment of those expressing them; a personal commitment which is also a physical one. We have to take risks. It is not just a question of parading with linked arms as trade unionists traditionally did on May Day. We need actions, occupations of buildings, etc., and this demands both imagination and courage. But I also want to say, please, no 'union-phobia'; there is a logic to the trade-union apparatuses that must be understood. Why is it that I say to trade unionists things that are close to the view that the social movements have of them, and to the social movements things that are close to the view that trade unionists have of them? Because in order to overcome these divisions, which contribute to weakening groups that are already weak enough, we need each group to see itself as it sees others. The resistance movement to neoliberal policy is globally very weak, and it is weakened by its divisions, like an engine that emits 80 per cent of its energy in heat – in the form of frictions, tension, conflicts, etc. But one that could go much quicker and further, if . . .

The obstacles to creating a unified European social movement are many and varied. There are obstacles of language, which are very significant, for example in communication between trade unions or social movements – bosses and managers speak foreign languages, but trade unionists and activists far more rarely. This makes the internationalization of social movements or trade unions very difficult. Then there are obstacles bound up with habits, ways of thinking, and the strength of social and trade-union structures. What can the role of scholars be here? That of working collectively to invent collective structures for invention, which will give rise to a new social movement, in other words new contents, new goals and new international means of action.

How to effectively establish the critical attitude[*]

> The aristocrats of intelligence believe there are truths that are not good to tell the people. For me, as a revolutionary socialist and sworn enemy of all aristocracies and all tutelage, I believe on the contrary that the people must be told everything. There is no other way of restoring their complete freedom.
>
> Mikhail Bakunin

Fidelity to the philosophy of the Enlightenment, Foucault said, did not mean fidelity to a doctrine but rather fidelity to an attitude. Is it possible to continue this critical attitude and effectively establish it, collectively therefore, in the intellectual and social world? Is it still possible to establish it in a sufficiently effective manner to arouse the fury of the political establishment as we did in 1981, when we launched an appeal against the coup d'état in Poland? (see p.131). I have not forgotten the insults that this appeal brought us. 'Germano-fools' said one person, who subsequently became minister of culture, then of education; 'irresponsible', said another, who became prime minister.

Today intellectuals hardly worry any more. Journalists have taken their place as *maîtres à penser*, and shut them up in the features sections of the newspapers. While others discuss the presidential term, they go on about the racist mouthings of a minor writer. Pierre Nora proclaims for the nth time 'the end of intellectuals'. (It is under his banner that Ferry and Renaut proclaimed the end of '1968 thinking', and a certain Dosse decreed the death of 'structuralism'.)

But one might begin to think that this arbiter of Parisian elegance who plays the intellectual only to announce the 'death of intellectuals' is perhaps right, when we see *Le Débat* publish a contribution to the 'debate' signed jointly by the man whom the papers call the 'second-in-command of MEDEF' and François Ewald, who claims to have been assistant to Michel Foucault, and put his name to the posthumous works of Foucault that were published in the collection that Pierre Nora edits for Gallimard. The same François Ewald who, the papers say, brought to the table of the modernized

[*] The initial version of this text was delivered as a lecture at the Centre Beaubourg on 21 June 2000, in the context of a day devoted to Michel Foucault under the title 'Le philosophie, la science, l'engagement', and published in Didier Éribon, ed., *L'Infréquentable Michel Foucault. Renouveaux de la pensée critique* (Paris: EPEL 2001), pp. 189–94.

bosses' organization a clutch of media-political intellectuals. This article written in collaboration (a less euphemized version of which first appeared in *Commentaire*) is a paean to the 'risk society', no more than an intellectually degraded and vulgarized version of the thinking – already vulgar – of the *maîtres à penser* to Blair and Schröder respectively, Anthony Giddens and Ulrich Beck. This is only comparable, to go back in time somewhat, with Heidegger's condemnations of *Sozialfürsorge* or 'social security' (already at that time!), responsible for 'worry' (*Sorge*), and an 'inauthentic' relationship to the future of *das Mann*, the worker, deadened or stupefied by too much security and a society that offered paid holidays. This trajectory, like those that have led so many intellectuals from the far left to the right, even the far right, is a further symptom, and one of the most frightening ones, of the direction in which the intellectual world has been developing. (One of the social phenomena in relation to which it is particularly hard to respect Spinoza's motto: 'not laugh, not weep, but understand'.) We mourn for the critical intellectual.

We have ended up getting used to these reversals (or *catastrophes*, to use the Greek term), to the point that we no longer even appreciate all that they say about an intellectual world which has, strictly speaking, lost its bearings, by losing its autonomy in relation to economics, politics, and of course journalism, itself the blind servant of all this and actively contributing to this servitude. We are in a catastrophic situation, in which it is more necessary than ever to give new strength to intellectual criticism.

Foucault worked a good deal to define the place and role of the specifically critical intellectual, the role and place that he had to assume in relation to and within the social movement. Concepts, he said, came from struggles and should return to struggles. How should we understand that phrase today? Is it possible to reconcile theoretical investigation and political action? Is there still a place for intellectuals who are both autonomous (in relation to established powers) and committed (against these powers if need be)? Foucault embodied an exemplary attempt to hold together autonomy of research and commitment to political action. Autonomy first of all: he worked to the end to satisfy the demands of the most advanced historical research. A great worker and man of the library, he fought all his life to expand the definition of philosophy, in other words its mission and task. This presupposed a great deal of work, to bring together the demands of two different traditions, those of history and philosophy, instead of making use of one set to escape the others, or vice versa (as is often done today, and sometimes even in his name). Above all, Foucault never put himself at the service of any policy, of either right or left.

Commitment: he was never a pure scientist, proclaiming his indifference to politics, in what I call the escapism of *Wertfreiheit*, flight into neutrality. He always rejected a false and hypocritical neutrality, above all the depoliticized political philosophy (which leads straight to the MEDEF table) and the depoliticized, policed, fashion of talking about politics, as taught at Sciences-Po, the effect of which is to make a science that criticizes the political presuppositions of political 'science' appear as 'political' in the very choice of its methods and objects, not to mention its political implications. So as not to speak in thin air, I would like to cite an example here, which condenses the entire evolution of the intellectual world, and which expresses in striking fashion this tendency to 'Sciences Po-liticization' – or rather depoliticization – that is also incarnated by *Le Débat*, this (empty) intersection between Sciences-Po and the École des Hautes Études. (*Le Débat* was founded by François Furet at the initiative of his friend Pierre Nora, with the assistance of the École des Hautes Études, and perfectly embodies the hegemonic ambitions that this very political historian – even a politician himself – has tried to exert over the intellectual field, giving himself a whole set of instruments of power: the École des Hautes Études, *Le Débat*, the Fondation Saint-Simon, along with 'involvement' of one kind or another in a whole range of periodicals, *Le Nouvel Observateur* of course, but also *Le Monde* and even *Libération*.) The example I referred to is France Culture, one of the rare media sites that had escaped the grip and the empire of media intellectuals, but has now become the public space of these depoliticized intellectuals. It's impossible even to count the number of programmes, especially on weekends, devoted to pompous commentaries on the world of politics, which, despite their claim to lofty analysis, interminably rehash the depoliticized discourse of depoliticization that is the current form of conservative thought.

The combination of autonomy and theoretical-political commitment that defines the genuine intellectual (in relation to both politicians with a certain intellectual capital, and to journalist intellectuals, whose entire life is spent in the world of heteronomy, not to speak of journalists themselves), has its social costs. 'Commitment' is initially a lack of good manners: to intervene in the public space means exposing oneself to disappointment, or worse, shocking those in one's own world who, choosing the virtuous facility of retreat into their ivory tower, see such commitment as a lack of the famous 'axiological neutrality' that they wrongly identify with scientific objectivity, and in the world of politics, all those who see such intervention as a threat to their monopoly, and more generally, all those whose interests are threatened by disinterested intervention.

To intervene in the world of politics is also a derogation; doing politics means exposing oneself to a loss of authority, by transgressing the law of the milieu that imposes a break between 'culture' and politics, the real world of society. To put one's intellectual authority on the line, transgress the borders of sacred academe, which forbids encroachment on the terrain of politics, means putting oneself in a highly vulnerable position. The person who commits themselves to politics in this way immediately becomes *relative*, *relativizable*: anyone can attack his scholarship, using political weapons to do so. This is a constant temptation for all those Zhdanovs of both left and right: today, it is former Stalinists or Maoists who most readily practise Zhdanovism, especially against those who opposed them when they were Stalinists or Maoists.

How can one be faithful to the tradition that Foucault continued, from Voltaire to Zola, from Gide to Sartre? Foucault sought to find a new kind of activism that would enable scholars not to leave their competence and specific values in the cloakroom, in the old style of fellow-traveller or mere signer of petitions. The object was to overcome the opposition, particularly strong in the English-speaking countries, between scholarship and commitment, and restore with full force the French tradition of the intellectual, in other words the person who intervenes in the world of politics but without thereby becoming a politician, with the competence and authority associated with their membership of the world of science or literature, as well as in the name of the values inscribed in the exercise of their profession, as values of truth and disinterest.

What then can one do today, what should we do to continue this tradition? The text that we wrote together in 1981, at the time of the Polish events, remains completely topical in its violent criticism of the 'Socialists' and all their past compromises. And yet many things have changed since then: paradoxically, the CFDT, which seemed quite close to us at that time, so that we could go some of the way together (despite its entourage of apparatus intellectuals), has since become quite distant, particularly by way of its extensions in the intellectual field. We therefore have to redefine strategies, and, faced with a formidable adversary in the form of the neoliberal think-tanks, bring together those whom Foucault referred to as 'specific intellectuals' into a 'collective intellectual', interdisciplinary and international, in association with a social movement that is highly critical of political compromises. The trade unions and other groups in struggle must be supplemented by artists, who are able to give visible and sensible form to consequences of neoliberal policy that are predictable but not yet visible. This collective intellectual must take on the task of producing and distributing instruments of defence against a symbolic domination that most commonly arms itself today with the authority of science. To do this, it will have to invent a way of organizing the collective work of producing realistic utopias and inventing new forms of symbolic action.

I do not want to finish without saying a brief word on the horror of moralism, which I share with Foucault. That would be a way of returning to the point of departure and understanding what is constant and invariant in the 'catastrophic' trajectories I have mentioned in passing. Hegel, in his *Lectures on the Philosophy of Right*, discussed the moralism of pure morality, which on the one hand generates Jacobin terror, the virtuous radicalism of the ethical conscience, and on the other hand Jesuitism and opportunist hypocrisy. How many lives, how many youthful radicalisms ending up in an opportunism of middle age, can be summed up in terms of this conceptual analysis!

Index